Singing the New Nation

How Music Shaped the Confederacy, 1861–1865

E. Lawrence Abel

Foreword by Bobby Horton

STACKPOLE
BOOKS

Published by
STACKPOLE BOOKS
5067 Ritter Road
Mechanicsburg, PA 17055
www.stackpolebooks.com

Printed in the United States of America

10 9 8 7 6 5 4 3 2 1

FIRST EDITION

Library of Congress Cataloging-in-Publication Data
Abel, E. Lawrence.
    Singing the new nation : how music shaped the Confederacy,
    1861-1865 / E. Lawrence Abel ; foreword by Bobby Horton. — 1st ed.
        p. cm.
    Includes bibliographical refrences (p.) and index.
    ISBN 0-8117-0228-6
    1. Music—Confederate States of America—History and criticism.
    2. United States—History—Civil War, 1861-1865—Songs and music—
    History and criticism.   I. Title.
    ML3562.A24   1999
    780'.972'09034—dc21
                                                            99-40645
                                                            CIP

CONTENTS

FOREWORD

The centennial celebration of the Civil War began in 1960, and I, like many other kids around the country, got caught up in it. For five years this country celebrated the valor of nineteenth-century Americans, and people like Lee, Jackson, Grant, Stuart, Forrest, and Lincoln became celebrities again. Places such as Shiloh, Manassas, Antietam, Vicksburg, Gettysburg, and Petersburg were discussed again with passionate "what-ifs?". It became common to hear "The Star Spangled Banner" followed by "Dixie" at ball games and other public functions. From that time to this day, I have been obsessed with the study of battles, strategies, and especially, the people who sacrificed and accomplished so much.

After devouring all the books I could get my hands on, I began to have a general understanding of each theater of operations and the chronology of battles therein. The next step in the process involved biographies of the major players in the deadly drama. And lastly, soldiers' diaries, letters, and reminiscences of common soldiers rounded out what I thought was a thorough picture of America from 1860 to 1865.

In 1984 I was hired to score music for a film set in 1864 America. I knew several "period" tunes such as "The Star Spangled Banner," "The Battle Hymn of the Republic," "Dixie," "The Bonnie Blue Flat," "Goober Peas," and "The Battle Cry of Freedom," and that was all! After only one day of research in the Southern History room of the Birmingham Public Library, I had found more than a hundred tunes. Since that day I have been compiling as many "period" songs as possible, because music was obviously very important to these people, and to get to know them, you must learn their music.

Songwriters of today write music for professional players and singers in hopes that some recording star will record their tunes. Success is measured by the volume of CD and cassette sales, and the composer is compensated accordingly. In the 1860s, songwriters were compensated by the sale of sheet music to common folks. For a tune to sell, the melody had to be "singable," and the lyrics had to relate to the lives and circumstances of the people. Apparently, songwriters did well, for it has been estimated that more than nine hundred Southern tunes were written during the war.

Because music is so prevalent and easily accessible to us in the late twentieth century, we take it for granted and fail to understand its importance to Americans during the War Between the States. For many soldiers and citizens, music was often the most effective and only medium to express their emotions. It provided an escape from boredom, hardships, and those moments of sheer terror that come with total war. It was not "manly" for a soldier to whine, cry, or talk of how badly he wanted to go home—but he could and did sing about it.

As a student gets immersed in the study of the war, he naturally wants to get to know the motivations, concerns, and opinions of the people at various stages of the war. An examination of song lyrics can give such insights. Songwriters wrote of every aspect of life—from the patriotic optimism of the early days, to leaving home, to the horrors of the battlefield, to the bravery and sacrifice of soldiers, to the loss of comrades and loved ones, to victories, to the shortcomings of politicians, officers, and the enemy, to the draft and the draftees, and, most importantly, to the dream of going home.

Music was prevalent in the army. Many volunteers heard sounds they had never heard before—while some regiments had brass bands, others had fifes and drums. Men often brought a variety of instruments from home, such as fiddles, banjos, guitars, concertinas, tin whistles, mandolins, octave mandolins, jaw harps, triangles, and the newly invented harmonica. Martial music led men into battle and helped morale on the march, while folk music could be heard in camp. Soldiers also engaged in the singing of religious as well as secular music with frequency. This presence of music in army life prompted General Robert E. Lee to state, "you cannot have an army without music."

I am fortunate to have the opportunity to do many concert-lectures around the country each year. This amazingly powerful music of the 1860s never fails to move people. The marching songs still cause feet to tap the floor, the songs of battle and sacrifice always bring tears, the satires and comedy tunes always produce laughs—and the tunes have been around for more than 130 years.

Bobby Horton
Birmingham, Alabama

ACKNOWLEDGMENTS

American Antiquarian Society, Worcester, Massachusetts; Eugene C. Barker Texas History Center, The University of Texas at Austin, Austin, Texas; British Museum Library, London, England; Rosine Bucher, Soldiers and Sailors Memorial Hall, Pittsburgh, Pennsylvania; Melissa Bush, Hargrett Rare Book and Manuscript Library, University of Georgia, Athens, Georgia; Chicago Public Library, Special Collections, Chicago, Illinois; Mary Ann Cleveland, Florida Collection, Florida State Library, Tallahassee, Florida; Dr. C. Daniel Crews, Moravian Music Foundation, Winston-Salem, North Carolina; Jeanette Davis, U.S. Department of the Interior, National Park Service, Harpers Ferry, West Virginia; Joan Grattan, Milton S. Eisenhower Library, Johns Hopkins University, Baltimore, Maryland; J. Samuel Hammond, William R. Perkins Library, Duke University, Durham, North Carolina; Harvard Theater Collection, Harvard University, Cambridge, Massachusetts; Nancy A. Heywood, Essex Institute, Salem, Massachusetts; James Kirkwood, Filson Club Historical Society, Louisville, Kentucky; Library of Congress, Music Division, Washington, D.C.; Jan Malcheski, Boston Athenaeum, Boston, Massachusetts; William McClellan, Music Library, University of Illinois, Urbana, Illinois; Sue Lynn McGuire, Special Collections, Western Kentucky University, Bowling Green, Kentucky; Mark A. Palmer, State of Alabama Department of Archives and History, Montgomery, Alabama; Linda Pine, Ottenheimer Library Archives, University of Arkansas at Little Rock; Gunetta R. Rich, W. S. Hoole Special Collections Library, University of Alabama, Tuscaloosa, Alabama; Richard W. Ryan, William L. Clements Library, Southern Historical Collection, University of North Carolina, Chapel Hill, North Carolina; State Archives of Virginia, Richmond, Virginia; State Library of Louisiana, Baton Rouge, Louisiana; State Library of Virginia, Richmond, Virginia; Guy

Swanson, Museum of Confederate History, Richmond, Virginia; Jessica Travis, Historic New Orleans Collection, New Orleans, Louisiana; Tulane University, Manuscripts and University Archives, New Orleans, Louisiana; University of Michigan, Ann Arbor, Michigan; University of Illinois, Carbondale, Illinois; University of Texas, Austin, Texas; Valentine Museum, Richmond, Virginia; Virginia Historical Society, Richmond, Virginia; Steven M. Wilson, Abraham Lincoln Museum, Lincoln Memorial University, Harrogate, Tennessee; Robert W. Woodruff Library, Special Collections, Emory University, Atlanta, Georgia.

INTRODUCTION

For most Americans, the Civil War is this country's romantic war. *The Birth of a Nation, The Red Badge of Courage, Gone With The Wind, The Killer Angels, John Brown's Body, Glory, Gettysburg,* Ken Burns's 1990 documentary on public television, the subsequent 1994 Arts and Entertainment television documentary, and countless other novels, movies, plays, poems, lithographs, paintings, and memorabilia have indelibly impressed the Civil War in our minds.[1]

The Napoleonic clash of vast armies of uniformed men excites us. Historians, professional and amateur alike, debate the fascinating "what-ifs" of the war, as they scrutinize and reevaluate the personalities and abilities of the Civil War's larger-than-life military leaders. Each year thousands of men reenact its battles, and woe to the naïf with inappropriate suspenders or belt buckle.[2]

The battlefield arbitrated the factional dispute, but soldiers relied on their comrades and the home front for moral and emotional support. Among modern historians, Bruce Catton has most emphasized the impossibility of understanding America's greatest bloodbath without first tackling its emotional underpinnings:

> The deeper meaning of the American Civil War, for the people who lived through it and for us today, goes beyond the historian's grasp. Here was an event so complex, so deeply based in human emotions, so far reaching in its final effects, that understanding it is likely to be a matter primarily for the emotions rather than for the cold analysis of facts. It was an experience that was probably felt more deeply than anything else that ever happened to us. We cannot hope to understand it unless we share in that feeling, simply

because the depth and intensity of the feeling are among the war's principal legacies.[3]

Emotionally significant events motivate us. We are more likely to remember the name of a person at a party who touches us emotionally. Similarly, if the person we are speaking to spills a drink on us, we are apt to remember that conversation as eventful.

Poetry tries to emotionalize feelings through words. Music, on the other hand, is nonverbal. It evokes moods and images through powerful sounds intuitively recognized by people from many different cultures.

Music's quintessential emotionality enables us to better remember the words of a song than the words of a speech. Songs are not argumentative; they inspire feelings that bypass the intellect.[4] Songs aim at the heart, not the mind. Their rhythms and rhymes quicken the blood or "soothe the savage breast." Our first sensory experiences are the sounds of our mother's heartbeat and her voice, heard long before we saw her face. The primitive sense of sound secures our first emotional bonds to another person.

The human brain is particularly sensitive to the rhythms of music. By combining musical rhythms with words to form a song, we remember those words much better than if they stand alone.[5] A song can also implant a word, a phrase, or a slogan in our minds. This is why songs are a powerful medium for imparting patriotic messages. Songs have an ineffable power; they can rouse people to confront overwhelming odds.

To appeal to vast numbers of people, both literate and illiterate, songs simplify complex ideas to gain popularity. A songwriter must articulate feelings that reflect a community's interests and vision of itself. This is especially so during the intense nationalism of wartime.

Beyond its political trappings, the nascent sense of Confederate nationalism emotionally bonded people. States provide people with services; nations provide people with identity and community. A nation is therefore "purely emotive," writes Charles Kupchan. Nationalism, he goes on to say, "transforms the administrative state into the sentimental nation."[6] Whereas all nationalistic movements have nation building in common, Kupchan notes that they vary along two basic dimensions. One is content—the symbols, images, and historical experiences that define it. The other is intensity—the level of arousal that these symbols and experiences evoke.[7] Expressive Civil War music, with its potent emotional foundation, rallied national unity in both the North and the South by venerating its symbols, images, and history.

The Civil War's army officers were certainly aware of music's transcendent power and its potential divisiveness. Early in 1862, the crusading Hutchinsons, a well-known New England musical family with outspoken Abolitionist sentiments, gave a concert for Maj. Gen. Phil Kearny's division, which was hunkered down in the mud outside Richmond, near Fairfax Seminary. All went well until the Hutchinsons launched into an Abolitionist hymn. Abolitionists weren't popular with many Northerners. Loud hisses from the back of the room greeted the song. An officer rose abruptly. If he heard any more hissing, he warned, he would toss the rude offender out of the building. A sergeant in the officer's regiment who did not share the Hutchinsons' Abolitionist views bolted from his seat: If the officer were going to toss anyone out, he could start with him. The officer wasn't cowed. If he couldn't throw the sergeant out himself, he said he had a regiment that could. Within seconds, the concert erupted into a melee.

Hoping to prevent another fracas in his ranks, Kearny told the Hutchinsons to go home. The Hutchinsons protested that Simon Cameron, the secretary of war, had personally authorized their concerts. Despite what Kearny thought, they insisted Union soldiers had a right to hear them. Kearny snapped back that he, not the secretary of war, was in charge on the battle line, and he had as little use for Abolitionists as he had for Rebels.

The Hutchinsons weren't easily daunted. First, they took their complaint to Brig. Gen. William Buel Franklin. Franklin looked into the matter and sided with Kearny. He said the Hutchinsons' incediary songs could polarize the army. But the Hutchinsons were nothing if not determined. They appealed to the commander in chief, Maj. Gen. George Brinton McClellan himself. Though opposed to slavery, McClellan refused to countermand Kearny's order. The Hutchinsons had proved that the issue was divisive enough to cripple his army. McClellan sent them packing.

But the Hutchinsons had connections in Washington. The matter was eventually referred to Lincoln, who reversed McClellan's order for political reasons. The Hutchinsons were allowed to resume their concerts. The reports in the Northern press embarrassed the army brass. McClellan couldn't drive out the Rebels, the papers mocked, but he had no trouble driving out the Hutchinsons.[8]

A song also tore apart Fort Crittenden in the far-off frontier department of Utah. Many officers who later rose to prominence in the war, among them Henry Heth, Alfred Pleasonton, Charles F. Smith, Stephen Week, and John Buford, garrisoned the fort. John Gibbon, a captain at the fort, was one of many army officers with divided loyalties. He was a

Pennsylvanian whose slave holding parents lived in North Carolina. When news finally arrived at the post that Fort Sumter had fallen, many officers with Southern loyalties resigned. Gibbon straddled the fence; because he didn't condemn those who did resign, his own loyalties remained suspect. The mistrust erupted in June 1861, when Gibbon's five-year-old daughter left her house during the evening band concert. The girl walked directly to the bandmaster and whispered in his ear; moments later the band started playing "Dixie."

The fort's commanding officers had forbidden the playing of "Dixie," which was closely linked by that time with the Confederacy. But that day part of the force was away from the fort and Gibbon was ranking officer. Gibbon had obviously sent his daughter to the bandmaster. To the rest of the post, his request for "Dixie" meant he was a traitor.

The following day several officers dashed off a letter to Secretary of War Cameron accusing Gibbon of treason. Gibbon's back was to the wall. He swore total loyalty to the federal government. Although he had indeed asked the band to play "Dixie," he insisted he was unaware of its political significance.

A court-martial was held. The one-day trial acquitted Gibbon. The army, not wanting to provoke mixed feelings of loyalty, summarily dropped the matter. Fort Crittenden did not hear "Dixie" again and John Gibbon eventually rose to the rank of brigadier general in the Union army.[9]

Some songs are incendiary because they evoke visceral feelings. Abolitionist songs like those sung by the Hutchinsons are essentially statements of principle. But very few soldiers in the Northern armies were Abolitionists. Most didn't want to interact with black people. Lincoln himself said that although he thought slavery was wrong, his only concern was to contain it.[10] The Hutchinsons' songs foisted their Abolitionist beliefs on Kearny's men and, as Kearny said, created dissension among them.

Songs like "Dixie," as the officers at Fort Crittenden implicitly recognized, are patriotic declarations of nationalism, as much a symbol of a country as its flag. Such songs are especially effective in rallying people to a cause when played and sung in public. Singing or listening to them heightens a people's collective emotions and readies them for sacrifice.

Patriotic songs can be a potent psychological weapon when they bind people together.[11] Union Brig. Gen. Benjamin Franklin "Beast" Butler recognized this insurgent power and did his best to defuse it. Shortly after taking over military command of New Orleans in April 1862, Butler warned the populace that anyone publicly singing "The Bonnie Blue Flag," a popular Secessionist tune of the day, would be charged with treason. To show he meant business, Butler arrested music publisher Armand Blackmar, fined him twenty-five dollars, and whisked him off to prison, even though Blackmar had published "The Bonnie Blue Flag" when New Orleans was still a Confederate city.[12]

John Wilkes Booth was almost sent to the same prison for violating the law against singing "The Bonnie Blue Flag" when he visited New Orleans late in the War.[13] Ironically, had Butler's law been enforced, the course of history might have been altered.

In March of 1863, Lt. Col. William S. Fish, provost chief of the Middle Department, U.S.A., attempted in Baltimore what Butler had done in New Orleans. Each of the city's music dealers and publishers was advised:

> The publication or sale of secession music is considered by the commanding general and the Department at Washington as evil, incendiary, and not for the public good. You are therefore hereby ordered to discontinue such sales until further orders. Also to send this office any such music you may have on hand at present.[14]

The following year, in May 1864, two music dealers, Michael J. Kelly and John B. Piet, were arrested and sent to Fort McHenry for violating Fish's order.[15]

Patriotic songs reflect our emotional attachment to our collective national identities, but there is another class of emotional songs that are thematically more personal. In contrast to exuberant nationalistic music, which appeals to our collective consciousness at group occasions, melancholy songs about our innermost feelings or personal concerns appeal to our individual consciousness. Battle-scarred Johnny Rebs, fresh from the killing fields, preferred tenderhearted songs about home and the "girls they left behind" to musical flag-waving. And in the privacy of the family parlor, their families favored these works as well. Home songs were nevertheless patriotic, since they reminded soldiers and civilians alike whom and for what they were making their sacrifices.

Sentimental songs echoed the perverse, seemingly pleasurable preoccupation with death, of the larger cultural period. Nineteenth-century men, expected to keep their feelings to themselves, were paradoxically free to sing their emotions in public. Those familiar with the standards of Confederate

music, "Dixie," "The Bonnie Blue Flag," the "Yellow Rose of Texas," or a
few other spirited tunes, are often surprised to hear that battle-hardened
soldiers preferred singing, "The years go slowly by, Lorena," or "Somebody's darling, Somebody's pride, Who'll tell his mother where her boy
died" to any other song around the campfire. An appreciation of the peculiar enjoyment that soldiers derived from singing about untimely death
explains the incongruous image of survivors of battlefield horrors sitting
around a campfire singing maudlin tunes without the slightest sense of
self-consciousness.

Before the invention of the radio, American music was always played
before a "live audience." The most popular forum for introducing mass
audiences to opera tunes, art songs, concert music, or any music was the
brass band. In antebellum America, these bands were as commonplace as
dandelions. They sprouted in parks, at picnics, at political rallies, on steamboat excursions, at dances, and at holiday celebrations. Large or small, every
parade had its musical accompaniment, whether it was only a drum and fife,
or a local band. Veterans of the Civil War later fondly remembered the
parades of the war's early days, when columns of men, dressed in uniforms
of varying colors, stepped smartly along the street in gallant array behind an
exuberant brass band. The densely jammed crowds on either side of the
street cheered and waved their handkerchiefs as the cocky volunteers passed
by, their bayonets glistening in the sun, flags streaming in the breeze. Such
parades were among the few romantic experiences in a war that was anything but romantic in its bloodletting. Without a band, a parade lacked
vitality; with a band of any quality, a parade became a pageant. And, oh,
how the South loved pageantry.

A brass band was such an integral part of American culture that soldiers
on each side felt their regiments and brigades were inferior if they did not
have one. A brass band greatly enhanced the prestige of a military unit.
Oftentimes officers paid for bands out of their own pockets. Band music
lightened a march; it surged a soldier's adrenalin before a battle; it rallied
flagging spirits. It was not unusual for a band to play during a battle while
shells exploded all around it.

Military bands extended an army's might and as such they waged musical battles with one another for psychological supremacy. Bands sustained
morale during inactivity or when an army prepared to fight. Some of the
Civil War soldier's most memorable reminiscences were the nightly twilight
concerts when bands played the sentimental songs that reminded men of
their homes and families.

The songs Civil War soldiers sang were not always uplifting. Soldiering was mainly boring routine, "hurry up and wait," and soldiers sang humorous songs to relieve their boredom and alleviate their anxieties about the morrow. Most of the men in the ranks were teenagers or men in their early twenties, and they liked to have fun. They played practical jokes on one another, played cards, read books, wrote letters, sang, arranged impromptu dances, and coped with hitherto unimaginable experiences. Humor has an ineffable way of relieving anxiety, and for almost every homesick or mawkish Civil War ballad, a parody poked fun at its excess sentimentality.

A psychologically important humorous song was the "griping" song. The Civil war soldier, although he never imagined the carnage he would create; knew there would be killing. What surprised him was the loss of personal freedom he experienced as a soldier and the boredom he endured in the army. "Griping" songs were the soldier's safety valve for expressing insubordination. These songs enabled soldiers to vent their anger toward superiors in a way that would otherwise put them in the guardhouse. Superficially humorous, these songs bitterly protested aspects of life in the military that differed from the sanitized images created for the home front. Such songs were rarely recorded except in letters, diaries, regimental histories, and reminiscences. For our generation, however, they are as historically invaluable as any document about the times.

Nearly all "soldier songs" were anonymous. Many of the named composers of sheet music songs during the war have also slipped into anonymity. With the exception of perhaps Stephen Foster, few Civil War enthusiasts, or even historians, know about the men and women who created the patriotic, sentimental, or humorous songs heard by millions of Americans during the war. The two best-known songwriters in the North, apart from Foster, were George F. Root and Henry Clay Work. Root penned rousing military songs like "Battle Cry of Freedom," but he was a versatile composer, and two of his best sentimental songs, "Just Before the Battle, Mother" and "The Vacant Chair," were favored by both sides. Work, who came from an Abolitionist background, did not write sentimental songs, but he was equally versatile in his own way. He wrote humorous songs like "Kingdom Coming," which was as much a favorite in the South as in the North, and martial songs like "Marching through Georgia" (a celebration of Gen. William Sherman's march to the sea), which had little to endear it to the South. Less well known, but far more influential, was another Northerner, Daniel Decatur Emmett, who wrote "Dixie," and was one of the founders of the minstrel show.

Southern songwriters are even less recognized today than their Northern counterparts. The South's renowned music-maker Harry Macarthy, the "Bob Hope" of the Confederacy, entertained troops in the field and wrote many of the Confederacy's cherished rallying songs such as the previously mentioned "The Bonnie Blue Flag," which competed with "Dixie" as the new nation's unofficial anthem. John Hill Hewitt, the "Bard of the Confederacy," composed many of the South's famous volunteering songs, like "The Young Volunteer," as well as poignant sentimental songs like "Somebody's Darling." James Ryder Randall produced one of the Confederacy's most celebrated songs, "Maryland! My Maryland!" along with several others that were sung in homes across the South. Many other, but lesser-known patriotic songs, were written by Southern women. Despite their pervasive influence, almost nothing has been written about them.

If the lives of Confederate song makers are hardly appreciated today, even less valued is the Confederacy's entertainment, especially its music publishing industry; although in historian Drew Gilpin Faust's opinion, the latter was probably the most influential forum for disseminating Confederate nationalism.[16]

While there were fewer theaters in the South than in the North prior to the war, every prominent European entertainer, from Jenny Lind, the "Swedish Nightingale," to Ole Bull included Southern cities in their itineraries. New Orleans was the South's leading entertainment mecca until 1862, when it was captured by the Federals; but Richmond, Charleston, Mobile, and Savannah, as well as smaller cities, hosted all kinds of musical entertainment during the war. The history of the South's musical entertainment industry has also been largely ignored.

When the South went to war, it possessed no national literature of its own. Instead, its favorite reading was Sir Walter Scott's tales of chivalry. Next to the Bible, if a family owned any book it was likely to have been written by Scott. Southern music publishers were less thought of than book publishers. Most of the South's antebellum sheet music came from the North, but the music itself was often written by European, and especially Scottish-Irish composers. Wartime Southern nationalism demanded that the South develop a distinctive literature and music. If it did not do so, the *Southern Literary Messenger* warned its readers that the Confederacy's destiny "will be but a crude and . . . inconsequential projection into time and space, unless along with her political independence she achieves her independence in thought and education, and . . . entertainment."[17]

The greatest cultural triumph in the South was the way its fledgling music publishing industry met the *Southern Literary Messenger*'s challenge. "The South must not only fight her own battles but sing her own Songs and Dance to music composed by her own children," said the publisher of a music series entitled *Southern Flowers*.[18] By 1863 the *Southern Illustrated News* proudly boasted, and it was not an empty boast, that "our publishers are enabled to keep the public constantly supplied with sheet music, which will compare favorably, in all respects, with any published in the land of wooden nutmegs."[19] But like much Southern boasting, the euphoria was short-lived. By 1864, serious paper shortages created havoc for the South's music publishing industry.

***

Scholary volumes have been written about the causes of the war, presenting plausible reasons for the bloodbath of the 1860s.[20] Some cynics have cited the large backlog of unemployed West Point graduates roaming the country as a contributing cause. The arguments are endless and fascinating. Every generation finds new insight into the times.

What has largely been ignored is the role of songs in America's Civil War. This is suprising because, in the words of lyricist Irving Caesar, "popular song is American culture."[21] Likewise, composer Richard Rodgers has observed, "a song is the voice of its times. . . . [songs] log the temper of an entire era."[22]

This book chronicles the war's social history in terms of its seldom discussed musical side, and is told from the perspective of the South. The South was the underdog in that conflict, overmatched in weaponry, manpower, money, machinery, and raw materials, but when it came to singing, the South easily won, and it matched the North when it came to music in general. Outmanned and outgunned during the War, the South was certainly not musically bested.

The connection between songs and the Southern war effort has received little attention by historians despite the fact that songs articulated Southern consciousness and disseminated it to the general population, largely illiterate and therefore unreachable through print.

This book examines the role of songs and music in the Confederacy. The emphasis is on the ideas expressed in song, rather than the technical way they were expressed; it is based almost entirely on the lyrics, titles, and dedications contained in Southern sheet music and songsters (songbooks) published during the war. Part 1 examines how songs created a sense of Southern nationalism. It focuses on the motivations songwriters gave for the South's break with the Union and the symbols of Southern nationalism. Part 2 examines the lives of the soldiers, exploring the way they attempted to deal with the horrors of the battlefield and the insufferable boredom of camp life. These preoccupations are reflected in the songs they sang individually and collectively. Part 3 shifts to the way songs were disseminated through the South's musical entertainment industry, especially through its music publishers, about which little has been previously written.

Although I have attempted to organize these songs thematically, many have their own particular histories apart from the themes under which I have included them. The stories behind songs like "Dixie" or "Lorena," for instance, flesh what otherwise would be a musical skeleton, and therefore I have sometimes interrupted the narrative to discuss these stories at length. In some instances, I have also included a "postscript" to let readers know what happened to a particular song after the war.

Why have I primarily targeted the South's music in this book? Although I find much to admire about Southerners and their war effort, I am not a neo-Confederate. Born in Canada, with no relatives that I know of who lived in either the North or the South during the war, I claim total impartiality with respect to pedigree. I have lived in the North, the South, the West, and now the Midwest. I am particularly interested in the origins of things, and especially in the creative process. Though its origins extend to the beginning of colonial settlement in America, in historical time, the Confederacy emerged overnight. Numerous economic, political, and cultural causes for America's Civil War have been given, but I have been most influenced by Bruce Catton's conclusion in *The Coming Fury*,[23] that there is no rational explanation. Emotional impulses not logic propelled this war. Irreconcilable feelings about themselves and about the other divided the North and the South. The way that songs shaped Southern consciousness invites a closer examination.

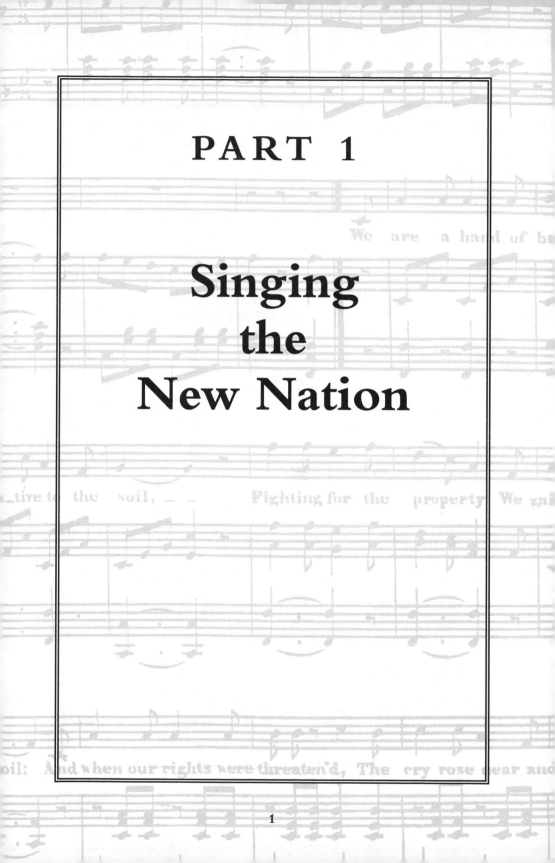

PART 1

Singing
the
New Nation

The news of their military engagement sent Northerners and Southerners from every societal niche streaming to their recruiting centers. They
came by the thousands and tens of thousands. They came from cities, towns,
villages, remote hamlets, and farms—brawny blacksmiths, tightfisted bankers,
frail clerks, sun-tanned outdoorsmen, brawling roughnecks, calloused dirt
farmers, doctors, lawyers, merchants, students, professors, mechanics, tailors,
artists, carpenters, Harvard-educated aristocrats, and illiterate "pecker-
woods"; fathers and sons, hot eager-eyed boys, stooped gray-haired old men,
husbands, bachelors, rich and poor, Protestant, Catholic, and Jew.

These boys and men spoke the same language, shared the same history,
read the same Bible, prayed to the same God, and were led by officers who
were schoolmates at the same military school. Everyone predicted a short
war. Thousands signed up for no better reason than the lure of adventure
and travel. A lifetime of steering a plough on a lonely farm or sorting
clothes on a counter in a dingy store couldn't compete with the excitement
of battle, a change of scenery, the opportunity to meet new friends, or the
chance to shoot a Yankee or a Reb. Others volunteered out of obligation
or because they were swept up in the hot-blooded frenzy. Everyone was
enlisting. Holdouts were socially ostracized, called cowards, and were
snubbed by the local girls or young women. Many were threatened with
physical violence, humiliated, and tossed into nearby ponds. But most of
those who flocked to their colors in the first year of the war enlisted for
deeply held emotional reasons.

For Southerners, the most atavistically emotional reason was to protect
their homes and families from invasion. The alarming news that Abraham
Lincoln was sending seventy-five thousand men to South Carolina to recapture Fort Sumter[1] meant a hostile army would soon be in their midst.

In Henderson, Texas, Douglas Cater had been intently following the
impassioned rhetoric for and against secession, but as a teacher, he said his
duty "was in the schoolroom and I took no part in state affairs."[2] The imminent invasion of the South shook him out of his complacency: "If every man
in the South must be killed, if ash heaps must be made of every home in the
seceded states, and blood must flow in torrents, the president [Lincoln] could
not be changed now. This was our outlook and we must resist invasion."[3]

Twenty-two-year-old William Fletcher, another Texan, was putting the
last course of shingles on a two-story house when a neighbor rode by and
gave him the news about Lincoln's order to invade the South. As soon as
the last shingle was in place, Fletcher set aside his carpenter's tools and

enrolled in Company F, Fifth Texas Regiment.[4] Fletcher's father was personally opposed to the war, but admitted to his son that he was "doing the only honorable thing and that is defending your country."[5]

"Resisting invasion," or its corollary, "defending our country" has been among the most elemental motivations for combat throughout history.[6] Southerners suddenly felt their backs up against the wall. "We are . . . fighting for our homes and those near our hearts" a South Carolinian college student, Richard Simpson, told his sister by way of explaining why he had enlisted.[7] This threat to home and family was a trenchant theme in Confederate songs:

> We fight for our homes, we fight for our wives,
> We fight for our children, their rights and their lives
> We fight for our lov'd ones, our country and its good,
> And we'll fight till we shed the last drop of our blood.[8]

Southerners like Douglas Cater, William Fletcher, Richard Simpson, and thousands of others said good-bye to mothers, fathers, wives, and children not to hold on to a tiny garrison in the faraway harbor of Charleston, South Carolina, or to fight for an abstract principle like "Southern rights" or to protect the slave-owning interests of the planter aristocracy. They said their good-byes to protect their families. As another of their songs said, they were going to war to confront:

> Traitorous Lincoln's bloody band
> (that) Now invades the freeman's land.[9]

There was no other choice but to "Strike for our mothers now / For daughters, sister, wives."[10] Writing to his wife from Tennessee, a twenty-seven-year-old Union soldier from Illinois, Sgt. Onley Andrus, explained why Southerners fought with such determination and were prepared to suffer further privations: "Supposing you were fighting to keep an enemy out of your own neighborhood and protect your property—your own hard earnings. How would you fight? Not that I consider their cause just but, right or wrong, if we thot [sic] or believed we was right it would be the same to us as though god (or any other man) should say it. I tell you you would fight and to the bitter end too and die in your tracks before you would give up."[11]

One common interest transcended all differences between Southern husbands, fathers, sons, or brothers—the primitive instinct of protecting their loved ones from the Yankee vandals threatening their homes.[12] The Federal occupation, and especially "Sherman's March to the Sea," proved their concerns were not imaginary.[13] Faced with imminent invasion and subjugation, their only recourse was to arm and collectively defend themselves.

It was one thing to go to war to protect one's home but another to protect one's homeland. Individuals acting on their own fight to protect their loved ones and their property. But if they are to fight, and perhaps die in defense of someone else's home, they have to feel some kinship with that person.

On the eve of the war, Southerners paid allegiance to their local communities and state, and then to the country as a whole.[14] At a time when most Southerners had not yet begun to think nationalistically of the Confederacy as their "country,"[15] their emotional commitments were much more focused. Southerners, including Robert E. Lee, sided with the Confederacy because they felt their obligations to their state superseded their loyalties to the United States.[16] To sustain a war effort, however, Southerners would have to supplant regionalism with allegiance to a more abstract state. Not only would soldiers in the ranks but also their wives, mothers, and sisters would also be called upon to make sacrifices; their support buttressed the morale of their loved ones in the field. Emotions soared in the first months of the war, but without a sense of political nationalism, the Confederacy's existence would have been short-lived.[17]

Nationalism implies an attachment to the culture and geography of a particular area. Beyond that, nationalism is also a deeply held feeling for the political institutions of that culture to the point that its interests take precedence over regional interests. The aim of every nationalistic movement is political independence. To achieve such independence, its existence as a sovereign nation must be earned, even at the cost of thousands of lives.

Although the South was in many ways like the North,[18] there were many differences between the two sections. The obvious diferences included a sense of place, climate, economic base, and of course the South's support of slavery. But it was not until the 1850s that the South's intellectual elite began to feel theirs was a distinct society. Previously they had evinced a deep loyalty with the Union. John Calhoun's (1782-1850) "doctrine of nullification" held that the polity of the United States was based on a contract between the central government and each sovereign and independent state, and that a state that had entered into such a compact of its own free will had the right to declare any Federal law that violated its compact with the Union, null and void. Although the same compact entitled a state to dissolve the compact if it believed it had been violated, Calhoun offered his nullification argument within the context of allegiance to the Union.[19]

By the 1850s, there was a growing sense among the South's intellectual elite that the Union had been a misguided idea from its outset. The South had emerged as a distinct society. The economies of the two regions, for one thing, were incompatible. Trade policies, especially those involving tariffs, that would benefit one section would have an opposite effect on the other. Southerners also railed against the North's inimical stance against slavery. Not only had it denounced the institution as sinful, it continued to encourage slaves to run away and even supported violent insurrection. The South's political parity with the North kept the North from imposing its will on the South. But the new "black Republican" party opposed the extension of slavery into any new states; this would eventually tip the balance of power in favor of the North. The party's candidate Abraham Lincoln had said that a government could not endure half slave and half free; his election as president clearly signaled the demise of the South as a distinct society. Similar dissatisfactions were fueling nationalistic movements all over Europe.[20] If its special interests and distinct society were to be safeguarded and expanded, the South had to divorce itself entirely from the North's economic and political dominance. To secure its national character, it had to have political independence. That meant secession.

For the most part, these concerns were the province of a small ruling elite. The rest of the population did not think of themselves as uniquely Southern. Virginia, for example, had felt no attachment to a "Southern Cause" when the cotton Confederacy declared its independence. Virginia joined because Lincoln's call to retake Fort Sumter was seen as nothing less than subjugation of all Southern states, itself included; North Carolina and Tennessee had likewise not shown much enthusiasm for the Confederacy until Lincoln's proclamation.[21] As the Confederacy prepared to confront the North, the vast majority of Southerners still had no collective idea of themselves as a political nation.

One is born into a culture; political allegiance is a conscious decision. Southern elites understood that if the Confederacy were to achieve its independence, it had to have the lasting political support of all the Southern classes. To achieve this goal, attributes common to all Southerners had to be articulated—such as their common geographical, historical, and cultural supports. Similarly, easily recognizable symbols needed to reinforce that identity and give it credibility. The South had to see itself as a united people, descended from a common ancestral stock with a distinctive language, committed to the same shared principles of government, with a common economic and psychological outlook. Unless there were complete commitment and unflinching support for that nation, the culture it represented could not be preserved. It was a formidable task, but by the end of the war, a distinctive nationalism had been firmly rooted. Writing about twenty years later, Carlton McCarthy, a private in the Richmond Howitzers, said he still could not "exactly define the cause for which the Confederate soldier fought" save having "assumed for himself a 'nationality,' which he was minded to defend with his life and his property, and thereto pledged his sacred honor."[22] Some historians believe this "nationality" developed as a result of sacrifices and shared defeat. But even if those factors now united the South behind the "lost Cause," the cause itself had to have been articulated culturally, as well as militarily. A consciously constructed wartime effort had to have transformed the South's unarticulated cultural ideas about itself into political nationalism understandable to the hoi polloi.[23]

Initially newspapers spearheaded the effort, but there was a higher percentage of illiterate whites in the South than in the North,[24] and the most effective way of reaching them was still through the spoken word. Southerners, the *Southern Literary Messenger* editorialized, were a "talking people."[25] It could have added they were also a "singing people." The written word was impersonal; the spoken word, intimate. The spoken word could be shared by many people at the same time whereas the written word could only be shared if it were read aloud, and then of course, it was spoken. This was even more so when ideas were communicated in song. Many of the songs later published as sheet music, such as "Maryland! My Maryland!", were first published in newspapers, and then set to music. Because singing was an integral part of the South's oral tradition, songs were a way to disseminate nationalistic sentiments to a largely illiterate rural population.

Historian Drew G. Faust writes that, "the production of songbooks and sheetmusic outstripped every other area of southern publishing during the war, expanding dramatically in response to popular demand."[26] After the words of a song were committed to memory, they could be shared with someone else. Songs, therefore, became the most popular medium for creating and disseminating Confederate nationalism.[27] As such, they provide us with examples of the excitement and optimism of the Southern intellectual elite, and how they attempted to create a national identity. The first chapter in part 1 of this book examines the songs that articulated the themes that became the basis for Southern nationalism: kinship, historical community and destiny, common language, shared ideas of government and economic principles, manners and customs, and racial exclusiveness. The following chapters consider the songs that created emotional commitment and an esprit de corps through a musical celebration of the symbols of Southern nationhood such as its anthem, flag, and leaders.

CHAPTER 1

My Country's Call

When Southerners flocked to their colors, their first loyalties were to their local communities and their state; patriotic feelings rarely extended beyond their own backyards. Few Southerners would have disagreed with a Greenville, South Carolinian's priorities: "I go first for Greenville, then for Greenville District, then the up-country, then for South Carolina, then for the South, then for the United States, and after that I don't go for anything."[1]

Although men enlisted for various reasons, protecting their homes and their communities were foremost. The men in each company and regiment did not go to war with strangers from different parts of the South or even different areas of their state. Instead, they marched off with other members of their family and with boyhood friends. When the time came for them to return, these would be the same people with whom they would live. Every man implicitly pledged to uphold his community's honor and in return, every community pledged to stand behind their men and take care of their families should they need support. Every man knew that when he came home, he would be held accountable for his behavior. The emotional bonds between soldiers and their communities sustained the men, no matter how dire their predicaments, with the knowledge that they had acted in honor.

The sense of localism emerged from the beginning. Every company and regiment elected its own lieutenants and captains who were usually the community's hometown leaders. Rather than having officers imposed on them by the governor or by higher ranking officers, men were led into battle by men from their own hometowns. Discipline was based as much on pride and devotion to the group as on deference to authority.

On the homefront, women sewed the uniforms their menfolk wore and stitched the flags, which they presented to each company. In the public ceremonies, which often preceded a company's or regiment's departure to its training camp, the women of the town, the wives, sisters, daughters, and sweethearts of those going to war, presented captains with silk flags for their company's colors. The captains, in turn, promised those colors would be carried with honor and glory, and on behalf of all the men in the company, pledged to defend them with the last drop of their company's blood.[2]

Ceremonial picnics lionized, feted, and serenaded departing soldiers; prominent citizens effusively pledged community resources to help their families; and parades escorted men to the railway stations or the docks as they left for their training camps.

In some towns and cities, civilians by the thousands gathered to say good-bye. The parade of soldiers departing for Camp Moore (named in honor of Louisiana governor Thomas Moore), about eighty miles north of New Orleans, was the biggest in that city's history. The columns of men, stepping smartly along Canal Street, stretched for almost a mile. When there was no longer any room at the roadside, shopkeepers allowed people to stand on their verandas and in their store windows to watch the spectacle.[3] Large or small, every parade had its musical accompaniment, whether it was only a drum and fife, or a town band.

If the Confederacy were to win its independence, however, national consciousness would have to absorb local allegiances. For their part, Southern songwriters turned to themes of place and climate to emphasize the South's uniqueness. This was hardly surprising. The implicit geographical factors in national consciousness provide the physical bedrock anchoring such feelings.[4] A hill or river is not just a speck on a map; it is an ideological site associated with an important event like a birthplace or a battlefield where an ancestor fought and perhaps died, a martyr to the cause of freedom. Place names honor national heroes and record the history of a region's first settlers or important events that shaped the course of settlement.[5] Hills and rivers may resemble one another, but the "mighty Mississip" is a river that conjures frontier images that no one associates with the "Thames" or the "Danube," which have their own geographical-historical associations.

For Southern songwriters, the South's geographical bedrock was its climate. Whenever the "South" was mentioned as a place in Confederate songs, it was invariably paired with "sunny" ("God save our Sunny South, / For her we live, for her we'll die"; "My home! my home! / My Southern sunny home"; "I'll sing you a song of the South's sunny clime").[6]

The most detailed expression of the South's nationalist splendors occurs in the appositely named "National Hymn,"[7] which celebrates its plant life ("golden fruited orange blooms," "green lemon grove," "tall magnolia," cotton "bursting from their ripened bolls") and its topography ("Cheasapeakes [sic] broad waters," "Florida's white sands," the "Rio Grande's plain"), and contrasts its sunny climate with the "frigid Northern snows," which in turn explains "frigid Northern hearts."

"The South Our Country"[8] contrasts the "the bleak shores of Maine" and the "West with her wide prairies waving in grain," with the South's "bright flowers," its "softest of suns," its "gentlest of showers," and its "sweet balm from the blossoming earth," which "make life a bright vision of pleasure and mirth."

In "Alabama,"[9] the "Northern Lion" lies couched "On his bleak and frozen plain," whereas the Southern eagle soars sunward over "the green Savannahs / Of this sunny land of ours." If the North is not held at bay, "The South"[10] warns its audience, the South's essential beauty will be destroyed:

> Oh, beautiful South! cherish'd home of my birth,
> Thou fairest, thou loveliest land of the earth!
> My heart, like the ivy still clings unto thee,
> Oh, beautiful, beautiful land of the free!
>
> The flowers that bloom in the sun smiling clime,
> And these the base Tyrant would crush to the earth,
> And mangle and bruise on the soil of their birth.

The sunny climate, the flowers, and the special features of the South's arcadian landscape are celebrated not only for their intrinsic beauty, but because they symbolize the South's common heritage and its continuity.[11] Southerners, whether they live in the mountains or on the piedmont, by the shores of a river or on the prairie, share the geographical and ecological features of a legacy worth defending.[12]

DIXIE'S A NATION NOW

Another major nationalistic theme in Confederate songs is the South's status as a new nation. "Southern Dixie"[13] opens with the declaration: "Oh! Dixie's Land's a Nation now." "The Land of King Cotton"[14] hails "Dixie" as "A nation by Freedom begotten." By equating "Dixie" and nation, songwriters consciously tried to shift local loyalties to the newly defined community and transformed "patriotism" (love of one's narrow community) into "nationalism" (aggressive assertion of self-proclaimed national interests over others).[15]

Southern songwriters also raised collective consciousness of that new status through titles like "Our Country's Call" and "The South Our Country," subtitles like "Our National Confederate Anthem," in "God Save the South!"[14] and lyrical references to "our country," "our motto," and "our flag."

Closely related to the "togetherness" theme are songs stressing "kinship," the most powerful force behind group solidarity."[17] Nations are either motherlands or fatherlands. Citizens are either "sons" or more often, "brothers" (rarely "sisters," although states can be "sisters"). Southern songwriters preferred patriarchal devotion. In "Secesh Battle Flag March,"[18] Southerners are called upon to "Strike! for [the] Fatherland!" Kinship is likewise affirmed in "The Bonnie Blue Flag":

> We are a band of brothers
> And native to the soil.[19]

and the "Virginian Marseillaise":

> To arms! Brothers dear;
> Gird on the trenchant band!
> Strike home! Strike home!
> No craven fear!
> For home and native land![20]

Both songs juxtapose brotherhood and country. Nothern songs do not comparably appeal to either a "fatherland," or a "motherland." In fact, the whole idea of a "fatherland" or "motherland," where America is concerned, is a foreign concept outside of the Confederacy. Northern songs refer to "Father Abr'am," and "Uncle Abe,"[21] but except during the Confederacy's brief history, Americans have had no historical notion of a "fatherland."

A RACE OF CAVALIERS

A historical sense fuels nationalistic ideologies. In most instances, the "historic nation" initially includes only a small fraction of a population, usually its privileged elite."[22] In the South, this elite comprised the upper-class

planter aristocracy and the upper-middle class of professionals and businessmen who controlled much of the south's manufacturing and trade. In many
instances, members of this latter class were related through blood or marriage with the landed gentry.

In the decades before the war, these Southern elites began to see themselves as a historical community descended from the Norman conquerors.
As explained by the *Southern Literary Messenger,* the South had been settled
and governed primarily by "persons belonging to the blood and race of the
reigning family [in Great Britain], and belonged to that stock recognized as
Cavaliers." These cavaliers, descendants of the Normans, had conquered the
Britons and the Saxons. They were distinguished by their warlike character
and fearlessness, "r'enowned for their gallantry; chivalry, honor, gentleness,
and intellect. . . ." Northerners, by contrast, were descended from the
Britons and Saxons whom the Normans (that is, the South's ancestors) had
once conquered.[23]

This hereditary difference between the Northern and Southern soldier
is most clearly stated in a Confederate song, "The Southrons' Chaunt of
Defiance:"[24]

> You have no such blood as ours
> For the shedding;
> In the veins of Cavaliers
> Was its heading!
> You have no such stately men
> In your abolition den.

Imbued with the nineteenth century's romantic image of war as a gallant knightly escapade, the Southern elitist saw himself as a peerless horseman, daring, dashing, courageous, ardent, honorable, high-spirited,
youthful, colorful, loyal to friends, devoted to family, and without vice.[25]
Appealing to this chivalric metaphor, Lawrence M Keitt, one of the South's
ardent "fire-eaters," said the South would face its northern foe "with hel-
met on, with visor down, and lance couched."[26] "The Warrior's Farewell"[27]
portrays him as springing "on his jet black steed," his "plume o'er his head
waving," as he "hied with speed" to battle, while tears "like pearly dew"
run down his sweetheart Isabel's cheeks as she sighs farewell.

No musical statement of this cavalier mentality is more clearly celebrated than the rollicking "Chivalrous C.S.A.," sung to the tune of "Vive la
compagnie:"[28]

Chivalrous, chivalrous people are they!
Chivalrous, chivalrous people are they!
In C.S.A.! In C.S.A.!
Aye, in chivalrous C.S.A.!

The fetishism of the cavalier warrior made Southern elites almost contemptuous of the North's obvious advantages in an armed confrontation.
They knew the South had a much smaller population and a limited industrial
capacity compared to the North's highly developed industrial base. The
South's railway system was rudimentary; its navy nonexistent; its few seaboard
ports easily blockaded; its waterways vulnerable to invasion. Despite these dis-
advantages, Southern elites were optimistic.

The South's leaders would hardly have urged a war they believed they
would lose. Looking back at the Confederacy's bid for independence,
Edward A. Pollard, the erstwhile editor of the *Richmond Examiner,* mused
after the war that "something more than numbers makes armies . . . [and]
against the vast superiority of the North in material resources," the South
had "a set-off in certain advantages."[29]

Its cavalier ancestry was widely regarded as one such "advantage." Confederate songs boasted that one Southerner in arms was equal to three of
the enemy.[30] Most Northerners, these songs jeered, had no taste for guns.
"Another Yankee Doodle" dismissed the North as only knowing "how to
steal," whereas the South "knew how to rifle."[31]

The image of the Southerner as a cavalier was largely gleaned from Scottish writer, Sir Walter Scott (1771-1832), whose stories of the defense of Scotland against Saxon invasion through military prowess, personal heroism, and
gallantry toward women entertained Southerners in the monotonous agrarian
antebellum South. Scott's recurrent theme of defense of one's country against
the "incursion of tyrants," opined historian Rollin Osterweis, seemed to
Southern elites to be as true for the Confederacy in the nineteenth century as
the medieval incursions of the Saxons into Scotland that Scott described.[32]
The analogy of Scotland striving to free itself from England's influence did not
seem far-fetched to Southerners pressured by a stifling North.

Osterweis did not exaggerate Scott's influence on the Southern psyche.
Many Confederate soldiers carried copies of Scott's novels with them when
they went to war, and they read them avidly. John Jackman (9th Kentucky
Infantry) wrote in his diary on 23 May 1862 that since it was raining all day,
he was "reading one of Scott's novels."[33] Richard Simpson (Third South
Carolina Volunteers) told his sister he had been "reading some of Walter

Scott's fine tales, and I will tell you they are worth reading and studying." Simpson added that he had left a full set at home and urged his sister to read them as well.[34] Scott's influence is reflected in the previously mentioned "Warrior's Farewell," where the weeping sweetheart is named "Isabel," the leading female character in Scott's Waverly novels. The composer was certain that his audience would grasp the allusion.

Mark Twain and other writers have fingered Scott as the driving force behind the South's ill-fated optimism in going to war. The South would never have confronted the North, said Twain, if Scott "had not run the people mad . . . with his medieval romances." Twain accused Scott of causing "more real and lasting harm than any other individual that ever wrote. . . . Sir Walter had so large a hand in making Southern character, as it existed before the War, that he is in great measure responsible for the War."[35] But Scott only articulated the century's ardent romanticism. His books were also popular in the North. Had there been no hostility toward the North, had there been no threat of invasion, the era's romanticism would not have touched off a war for which no one was prepared.

Ignited by the "Sir Walter disease," as Twain called it, thousands of would-be Southern cavaliers signed up for the chance to shoot invading Yankees. Brimming with self-confidence and boyish enthusiasm, every young soldier saw himself as Bob Roebuck, "The Southern Soldier Boy," who "Miss Sallie" Partington, the "prima donna of the Confederacy," sang to each night at the Richmond Theater:

> Bob Roebuck is my sweetheart's name
> He's off to the wars and gone,
> He's fighting for his Nannie dear,
> His sword is buckled on.
> He's fighting for his own true love,
> His foes he does defy;
> He is the darling of my heart,
> My Southern soldier boy.

The title of the play in which the hit song appeared was, not surprisingly, named "The Virginia Cavalier."[36]

REBEL, 'TIS A GLORIOUS NAME

Southern elites also nourished the idea that the Confederacy was the final epoch in the American War of Independence. The North, they claimed, had distorted the original principles in the Constitution, whereas the Confederacy sought to maintain them. Jefferson Davis and other Southern leaders did not ask the South to abandon its loyalty to the government created by Washington and Jefferson, but rather to continue to uphold the principles of 1776 by supporting the Confederacy as their legitimate heir.[37]

Davis's viewpoint is a persistent theme in Confederate patriotic music. The belief that the roots of America's heritage penetrated more deeply through Southern than Northern soil was expressed in the "Southern War Cry"[38] which first appeared in the *New Orleans Picayune*. Penned to the tune of "Scots, Wha Hae Wi' Wallace Bled," a song commemorating Scotland's rebellion from England, it appealed to the "cavalier" ideology and reminded Southerners of American battles fought and won. "Southrons Attend"[39] linked the South with the Revolution's heroes:

> We will not, cannot e'er forget,
> Our sires for freedom fought and bled,
> When proud Virginia's noble son,
> Our Washington to vict'ry led.

"God Save the South"[40] asserted that Southerners were no less rebels than the country's most illustrious patriots:

> Rebels before,
> Were our father of yore;
> Rebel, the glorious name
> Washington bore.

The same claim was made in a poem by an anonymous writer known only as L. M.:

> Washington a rebel was,
> Jefferson a traitor—
> But their treason won success
> And made their glory greater.[41]

By affirming their identity with the founding fathers, Confederate songwriters provided a way for a large number of Southerners who still felt an affection for the United States to transfer those loyalties to the new government ("Rebels! 'tis our family name").[42] Equally important, by adopting the rebel sobriquet, they included ordinary Southerners in the ranks of America's earlier heroes, thereby giving them a share in the cavalier ethos.

If the South was the Revolution's legitimate heir, Southerners felt they were also entitled to its symbols. Some claimed the "Star-Spangled Banner" for the Confederacy. "Let us never surrender to the North [that] noble song," urged a Charleston correspondent. "It is Southern in its origin, in sentiments, poetry and song; in its associations with chivalrous deeds, it is ours. . . ."[43] Even the "spangled banner" itself was appropriated to a certain extent by the Confederacy's first flag, the "Stars and Bars" which clearly resembled it in many ways.

HONOR

In "Riding a Raid,"[44] a tribute to Maj. Gen. James Ewell Brown "Jeb" Stuart, the quintessential cavalier,[45] "each cavalier that loves Honor and Right" is urged to "follow the feather of Stuart to-night."

For Southern elites, honor was the linchpin of a man's character and hence his social standing.[46] A man who lost his honor was shunned by his friends and even his family. The honor code forbade giving offense to others, but if a man were attacked by another, it was axiomatic that he respond. A state could do no less. Virginia finally cast its lot with the Confederacy to protect its collective honor from the insult of imminent invasion. Had Virginia shared the ideology of the cotton Confederacy, it would not have waited so long to join.

Jefferson Davis succinctly stated the Southern honor code when he told the North, "we desire peace at any sacrifice, save that of honor and independence."[47] On his arrival in Richmond, in May 1861, Davis told a cheering crowd "there beats in the breast of Southern sons, a determination never to surrender—a determination never to go home but to tell a tale of honor," which was greeted with cries of "never" from the crowd and applause.[48] One song epitomized the code by asserting that death was "far better than shame and dishonor."[49] "The Wearing of the Gray," a song written shortly after the war, likewise assured Southerners that "defeat is not dishonor."[50] Following Davis's example, songwriters called upon Southerners to volunteer to preserve the South's collective honor:

> Tis for our honor and our name,
> We raise the battle cry.
> Then weep not, dearest, weep not.

If in her cause I fall.
O, weep not dearest, weep not,
It is my country's call.[51]

"Confederate Land"[52] has the volunteer explain he is joining the ranks, "For honor dear, for hearth stone fire." "God Save the South"[53] urges every Southerner to do the same: "Hark honor's call, / Summoning all." "Cheer, Boys Cheer" (also called "The Southern Boys")[54] combined boyish bravado, defense of family, and commitment to duty:

Cheer, boys, cheer, we'll march away to battle,
Cheer, boys, cheer, for our sweethearts and our wives
Cheer, boys, cheer, we'll nobly do our duty.

"Carolina's Sons"[55] extended the idea to the wives and sweethearts whose "duty" prompts them to stay behind and presumably serve the cause on the home front:

Ye gallant sons of Carolina
Listen to your country's call
She is threatened by the traitors
Who'd rejoice to see her fall
Up! And leave your wives and daughters,
Who would gladly follow on
But their duty promptly tells them
They must stay, you must be gone.

The appeal of these songs to the South's women reflected their pivotal role in the Southern war effort.[56] In many communities, fervent women urged men to enlist. In Arkansas, Henry M. Stanley, the future African explorer, recalled that a warlike frenzy consumed the women in his community. If every man did not set out immediately to meet the enemy, they "vowed they would themselves march out and meet the Yankee vandals." According to Stanley, "In a land where women are worshiped [*sic*] by the men, such language made them [the men] war-mad."[57] Stanley, who had not caught enlistment fever, soon received a package containing a chemise and a petticoat. The next day he enlisted. Another Southern veteran recalled, "There were a great many men in the southern homes that were disposed to be more conservative and to regret the threatened disruption of the Union, but the ladies were all enthusiastically in favor of secession . . . and if the southern men had not been willing to go I reckon they would have been made to go by the women."[58]

SOUTHERN RIGHTS

Northern songs were no less nationalistic than their Confederate counterparts; the main difference lay in the justifications for their war effort. "The Battle Cry of Freedom"[59] places preservation of the Union at the forefront of its cause: "The Union for ever, hurrah, boys, hurrah." In "We'll Fight for Uncle Abe,"[60] the volunteer says, "The Yankee boys are starting out the Union for to save." "The Why and the Wherefore"[61] vows the fight will continue until that unity is restored:

> "When, when, when, and when,
> And when do you mean to come back?"
> "When Rebellion is crushed and the Union restored,
> And Freedom is safe—yes, then please the Lord."

Echoing Abraham Lincoln's comment that "a nation divided against itself cannot stand,"[62] "The Flag of Columbia" says "United we stand, divided we fall."[63]

For the South, the ideological casus belli was "State Rights," or "Southern rights" as it was more familiarly called in song. Citing "Southern rights" as the reason for going to war ennobled the Southern war effort because in declaring undescribed "rights" as their abstract cause, songwriters appealed to a loftier principle than the more ignoble right to take property in the form of slaves into the territories.

Northerners, with the exception of the Abolitionists, were not opposed to slavery where it existed, but they morally opposed its extension into the territories. Lincoln clearly articulated the difference in attitude toward slavery between the two sections. In a letter he wrote in 1860 to Alexander Stephens (who a few months later was elected vice president of the Confederacy), he said, "you think slavery is right, and ought to be extended, while we think it is wrong and ought to be restricted."[64] Southerners believed that such restrictions theoreticaly denied their property rights under the Constitution.

But as historian Bruce Catton recognized, beyond the ideological rhetoric was the realization that restrictions on slavery's expansion would eventually end the "peculiar institution" as it was politely called, and with it the very essence of the Southern way of life.[65]

Defending the right to transport their "property" combined ideological, practical, and emotional reasons for severing ties with the North and is the reason "Southern rights" are so often mentioned as a rallying cry in Confederate songs. "The Bonnie Blue Flag"[66] is one of the few Confederate songs to identify the "property" dispute as the cornerstone of "Southern rights":

> Fighting for the property
> We gained by honest toil . . .
>
> Hurrah! Hurrah! for Southern Rights Hurrah!
> Hurrah! for the Bonnie Blue Flag that bears a Single Star!

Without mentioning slavery directly or indirectly in terms of property, "Southern Rights" became the moral justification for the war in various songs such as "The Volunteer's Farewell":[67]

> Our children's pride shall be
> That their father fought for Freedom
> Southern rights and liberty.

For thousands of Southern women, "I Would Like To Change My Name"[68] clearly affirmed Southern Rights:

> I would like to change my name,
> And settle down in life,
> Here's a chance for some young man,
> That's seeking for a wife;
> But he must be a soldier,
> A vet'ran from the wars,
> One who has fought for "Southern Rights,"
> Beneath the Bars and Stars.

"Southern Song,"[69] by an anonymous L. M., which never appeared in sheet music but was widely reprinted in many of the collections of Southern poetry (often called "war songs"), supports "State rights" as the foundation of any Southern marriage:

If ever I consent to be married,
(And who would refuse a good mate?)
The man whom I give my hand to,
Must believe in the rights of the State.

LIBERTY

Underlying the doctrine of "Southern rights" was the concept of "liberty."
The "Secesh Battle Flag March,"[70] which juxtaposed cavalier and fatherland, exhorted its cavaliers to "Strike For Liberty and Right!" A notice
below the title for "Tillie's Waltz"[71] alerted purchasers that proceeds from
the sale of the tune were "to be appropriated for the benefit of our brave
and gallant volunteers now fighting for our liberty." Songs like John Hill
Hewitt's "Dixie The Land of King Cotton"[72] portrayed the South as liberty's arch defender:

When Liberty sounds her war rattle,
Demanding her right and her due;
The first land that rallies to battle
Is Dixie, the home of the true.

Southern songwriters, however, did not monopolize "liberty." Similar
appeals pepper Northern songs, such as:

Yes, for Liberty and Union
We're spring to the fight,
Shouting the battle cry of freedom.[73]

or:

O, Land of Columbia how glorious the sight,
When millions of freemen rise up in their might,
To battle for Union and Liberty's cause
And aid in defending thy time honor'd laws.[74]

The tree of liberty stemmed from two different roots depending on the
section of the country in which you lived.[75] For both Northerners and
Southerners, liberty meant personal and social freedom. For the Southerner
that freedom would be guaranteed if people were left to pursue their

aspirations free from government interference; for the Northerner, the freedom to pursue one's aspirations was safeguarded by government. The touchstone in the debate, however, always devolved to slavery. As Lincoln noted, "in using the same *word* we do not mean the same *thing*." By "liberty," he said, Northerners mean each person has the right "to do as he pleases with himself, and the products of his labor," whereas for Southerners, "the same word may mean for some men to do as they please with other men, and the product of other men's labor. Here are two, not only different, but incompatible things, called by the same name—liberty."[76]

The overwhelming majority of Southerners didn't own slaves, but the denial of the right to take property in the form of slaves into the new territories seemed to them the antithesis of democracy. This belief stemmed from the triumph of Jacksonian democracy in the 1830s, which made egalitarianism one of democracy's principal attributes.[77] For both Northerners and Southerners, egalitarianism implied equality of opportunity, not only in politics, but in economic circumstances. Because Lincoln opposed expansion of slavery into the territories, Jefferson Davis said Southerners regarded his election as "a distinct declaration of war upon our institutions . . . and property."[78] Seemingly oblivious of an irony that denied the most basic of all liberties to millions of people, Southerners insisted slaves were property and property rights were sacrosanct. A government that interfered with property rights where slavery was concerned could interfere with ownership of any property; freedom itself was threatened. This principle was clearly articulated by an Alabama congressman: "the power to dictate what sort of property the State may allow a citizen to own and work— whether oxen, horses or negroes—on account of its morality, is alike despotic and tyrannical, whether such power is obtained by conquest in battle or by a majority vote."[79] Fighting to maintain slavery therefore was for the majority of Southerners not so much about protecting the property of the wealthy planter aristocracy as it was about ensuring their own economic advancement.

SLAVERY

The abstract principle of "property rights" was one thing, economic realities another. What overly concerned the South's plantation aristocracy about Abraham Lincoln's election was its potential economic impact. In a speech to the Confederate Congress on 29 April 1861, Jefferson Davis clearly expressed such concerns. By prohibiting slavery in the new territories, the Republicans were in effect surrounding the slave states with nonslave states and thereby "rendering the property in slaves so insecure as to be comparatively worthless, and thereby annihilating in effect property worth thousands of millions of dollars."[80]

Although defending the "peculiar institution" was implicit in the South's idea of liberty and "Southern rights," and slavery was inextricably linked to the South's economy and its agricultural culture, there was a more primitive impulse uniting all Southerners in its defense.

"At a time when Americans of the blood prided themselves on their inborn superiority to people who showed even minor differences in accent, in pigmentation, or in cultural background," slavery in Bruce Catton's words, "involved emotions deeper than the pit and blacker than midnight."[81] Southerners might be morally troubled by slavery, but as long as the institution continued to exist, the black man did not have to be treated as an equal.

In the South, the inferiority of the black man enabled the poorest white man to feel he was the equal of any white man anywhere. Years before, John Calhoun had articulated this attitude for the North: "With us, the two great divisions of society are not the rich and poor, but white and black; and all the former, the poor as well as the rich, belong to the upper classes, and are respected and treated as equals."[82] Lincoln himself expressed the view that if he could free all the slaves, his first impulse would be to send them to Liberia. Although morally opposed to slavery, Lincoln readily acknowledged that the "great mass of white people," himself included, would not tolerate making former slaves politically and socially their equals.[83]

For many Southerners, the Northern invasion threatened their ordered society. If the North prevailed, it would "subjugate" the South. The former social order would be completely reversed with whites now existing beneath blacks on the social ladder.[84]

The "Song of the Southern Soldier"[85] by an anonymous P. E. C., which appears only in collections of Southern "war songs," is blunt about the separation of the races:

> The South is my home, where a black man is black
> And a white man there is a white man.

Equally expressive of Southern feelings about equality on the part of Southern women was the anonymous L. M. in "Southern Song"[86]

> To a husband who quietly submits
> To negro-equality sway,
> The true Southern girl will not barter
> Her heart and affections away.
>
> We girls are all for a Union,
> Where a marked distinction is laid
> Between the rights of the mistress,
> And those of the kinky-haired maid.

With the black man enslaved, Southerners did not have to be overly concerned with a change in their social status. But beyond the idea that slavery's end would unleash an inferior being in their midst, Southerners feared that if "subjugation" ended, the black man might express the resentment toward white society that he had been forced to suppress. The slave revolt in San Domingo that resulted in the wholesale massacre of whites, the Nat Turner rebellion, and John Brown's insurrection were vivid reminders of the imminent violence that could follow in the wake of "subjugation."

Despite its centrality to the conflict between the North and South, outside of these few songs, slavery was rarely mentioned directly in Southern songs. This silence may have been due to an unwillingness on the part of Southern songwriters to confront their racial fears. Another reason may have been that making defense of slavery an ideological foundation for the new nation could be self-defeating because nonslaveholding Southerners might then feel they were being called upon to support the interests of the plantation aristocrats. Instead of slavery's defense, songwriters turned to ridiculing the idea of a free black population. In most songs, blacks were called "contraband," a term used by Maj. Gen. Benjamin Butler when slaves first began fleeing to the Northern army.[87] Although it was not Butler's original intention, the term was readily adopted by Southern songwriters because in concept, it did not differ much from the idea of blacks as "property."

"The 'Contraband's Hotel,'" written in 1862, pokes fun at Northerners who now have these newly liberated slaves in their midst:[88]

> I's stoppin' at a tavern de United States Hotel.
> Ole Uncle Sam's de landlord we eat and drink our fill.

A dance tune, "Poor Oppressed, Or The Contraband Schottisch,"[89] features an elegantly dressed black woman carrying a parasol on its cover page, the message apparently being that given their freedom, slave women could soon be acting as if they were well-to-do white women.

"I'm Coming to My Dixie Home, As Sung by Lincoln's Intelligent Contraband,"[90] composed by Charlie L. Ward, a Confederate serving with the 4th Kentucky, assured Southerners that the black man preferred toiling in the field as a slave to living a miserable existence as a free man in the North. Given the choice, he would certainly leave the North for the South:

> And den oh den will dance and sing
> And work de cotton ober
> And make de bones and boys ring
> Way down in Dixie Clober.

Northern songs likewise do not very often raise slavery as an issue. Two noteworthy exceptions are "John Brown's Body":[91]

> "though he lost his life in struggling for the slave,
> His truth is marching on"

and "The Liberty Ball,"[92] sung to the tune of "Rosin the Beau":

> Come all ye true friends of the nation
> Attend to humanity's call;
> Come aid in the slave's liberation,
> And roll on the Liberty ball.

Most Northern songs make it very clear that for them, the issue is restoration of the Union, not emancipation. As a Northern parody to "The Bonnie Blue Flag" says,

> We do not want your cotton,
> we care not for your slaves,
> But rather than divide this land,
> we'll fill your southern graves.[93]

YOU WOULD NOT HAVE YOUR FRIEND REMAIN

Although a majority of Southern men flooded the recruiting centers in 1861, their enthusiasm and the support they received from their families was in large part due to the reassurances Southern elites gave them that the war would not last more than ninety days.[94] The majority of volunteers signed on for only twelve months. Since most Southerners were small farmers, their absence from the family farm prompted a "family crisis" since wives and daughters would now have to take on the work previously done by the males. As the war dragged on, the burdens became overwhelming for many families. "Ask any Confederate officer who commanded troops during [the] latter part of the war," Robert Stiles recalled, and "he will tell you of letters which it would have seared your very eyeballs to read . . . letters in which a wife and mother, crazed by her starving children's cries for bread, required a husband and father to choose between his God-imposed obligations to her and to them and his allegiance to his country, his duty as a soldier; declaring that if . . . he come not at once, he need never come; that she will never see him again nor recognize him as her husband or the father of her children."[95]

Although seemingly upbeat, John Hill Hewitt's "You Are Going to the Wars, Willie Boy"[96] and other Confederate songs urging those who did qualify not to tarry, imply that there were more than a few that did:

> The bugle sounds upon the plain,
> Our men are gath'ring fast;
> You would not have your friend remain,
> And be among the last.

"Our Country's Call"[97] likewise urged Southerners not to "scent the battle from a far."

In the western North Carolina mountain community of Ashe Country, married men living on small farms were least likely to enlist. Only 31 percent of those volunteering in 1861, for instance, were married, whereas in

1862, when conscription was instituted, volunteering among married men increased to just over 52 percent.[98] In 1862 married volunteers were younger and less prosperous than those who had volunteered the previous year. Young married males whose households were struggling to eke out a living from the land were far less likely to volunteer than those who came from families with resources sufficient enough to withstand the enlistment of one or more males from the household.[99]

In Mississippi, men living in river counties were far less likely to enlist than those living elsewhere in the state. The main difference was that there were far more slaves than whites in the river counties; military-aged males living in the river counties stayed home to protect their families and property against real or imagined dangers from slave uprisings in these areas.[100]

Despite the bravado of the many songs heralding honor and duty and the avid support of many Southern women, there were also women who had misgivings about their husbands and sons going off to war.[101] Many of the wartime songs written in both the North and the South urged women to support the volunteering of their men. The South needed all its manpower in arms and songwriters extolled self-sacrifice on behalf of the cause. In some instances, male songwriters empathically adopted a female voice. The narrator of a song like "I Would Like to Change My Name," for example, that declares support for the war in terms of eligible men for marriage, is female, but the composer is male.[102]

Despite the latent anxiety in some of these songs, Southern leaders were optimistic about the Confederacy's prospects, and the wives, mothers, and sweethearts of those who went to war did their best to support the war effort. Songs created a collective sense of national principle and pride. They expressed in clear language the reasons the South was at war, and they appealed to the ideals of duty and honor as the cornerstones of Southern nationalism. The next chapters examine how anthems and musical celebration of the flag created the cohesiveness essential for a successful war effort.

CHAPTER 2

To Live And Die In Dixie

One of the most memorable scenes in the movie, *Casablanca,* occurs when the French musicians and singer at "Rick's" suddenly burst into "La Marseillaise" in response to the German soldiers who are singing their anthem, "Deutschland, Deutschland Über alles." In a film about star-crossed lovers, singing "La Marseillaise" is also an act of love, in this case, patriotic love, which is more moving than the close encounters between the two main actors. Rick's bar is located in Vichy-controlled Casablanca, and the Vichy government is answerable to the Germans. But the French citizenry does not buckle under to the occupation. Armed confrontation would be suicidal, so they express their collective love for country by singing their national anthem. It is a symbolic gesture, but its symbolism is not lost on the Germans. The French city is occupied, but its spirit has not been crushed. We sense these people cannot be conquered.

A comparable symbolic act involving "Dixie" occurred during the Civil War. On 19 July 1864 a contingent of the First New York Cavalry scoured the West Virginia countryside, burning houses belonging to Confederate sympathizers. When word of the rampage reached Shepherdstown, Col. Alexander Boteler's neighbors rushed to his home to help his family. Boteler had served on Thomas Jonathan "Stonewall" Jackson's staff and had been a member of the Confederate Congress. His home was certain to be torched. Panicked, the family, neighbors, and servants frenziedly moved furniture, including the family-parlor piano, onto the lawn. The raiders, they believed, were only interested in torching the home, not its contents.

They were wrong. The servants were ordered to return the furniture to the house and it was set afire. As the flames crackled and smoke billowed out of the house, raiders and townspeople were dumbstruck as sounds of "Dixie" echoed from inside. One of Boteler's daughters, who had slipped back into the house, was showing her defiance. The Federals' paralysis lasted only a moment. They rushed inside, found the girl, and dragged her from the blazing home.[1]

A NATIONAL PLEDGE

Ever since the British adopted "God Save the King" in 1745 as their national anthem, every sovereign nation in the world has had a patriotic anthem. An anthem is a country's musical crest.[2] It has mystical power. A national anthem is a country's flag in sound.

Most anthems are born in national crisis. The words to "God Save the King" were written in support of King George II when his monarchy was threatened by the Stuarts of Scotland in the 1740s, although its melody is much older. France's "La Marseillaise" was written in 1792 during the French Revolution. Francis Scott Key wrote our own "The Star-Spangled Banner" during the War of 1812.

In April 1861 a group of New Yorkers decided the Union needed a patriotic hymn, not a war song. They felt "The Star-Spangled Banner" was too difficult to sing. Its meter was awkward, its high notes beyond most people's ability to reach. It was also completely devoid of sentimentality, an essential feature of many songs and novels in Civil War days. The New Yorkers offered five hundred dollars for a new patriotic morsel, to be dished up in not less than sixteen nor more than forty lines, exclusive of a mandatory chorus.[3]

The competition was ridiculed from the outset. A national hymn simply could not be composed as a contest entry, said *The Musical Review and Musical World*. Such a song could come only from inspiration. In its 25 May 1861 editorial, it mocked the committee by asking if its real intention had been to give unemployed poets and musicians a job.

Twelve hundred composers submitted entries, some from as far away as Germany and Italy. Most of the entries, said committee member George Templeton Strong, were "rubbish." The judges finally decided none was as good as Key's original and called off the contest.[4]

Many Southerners felt the same need for a legitimate national anthem for the Confederacy. "A short while ago, everybody was calling for a national song," Henry Timrod, the South's most eminent poet, wrote in an editorial for the *Columbia Daily South Carolinian*. "The few poets who are to be found in the Confederacy, were importuned to write one, and many attempts to supply the want were made, both by poets and poetasters, without the slightest success."[5] Though he didn't mention it in his editorial, Timrod had also tried and failed to write a memorable anthem, but destroyed his work without showing it to anyone.[6]

Timrod reflected on the futility of writing an anthem under commission. Nations didn't order an anthem or even deliberately choose one, said Timrod. It just happened. A national anthem was the fortunate accidental conjunction of time, mood, and circumstance. Few national anthems had any literary merit, he said. What they did have was glibness, a terse musical sentiment appealing to pride, prejudice, or passion, an effective simple tune, and some unexpected event to give them meaning.[7]

Although he didn't mention it by name, "Dixie," which by that time had become the South's unofficial anthem, fulfilled all of Timrod's criteria. It ran as Timrod said, "glibly on the tongue":

> I wish I was in de land ob cotton,
> Old times dar am not forgotten;
> > Look away! Look away!
> > Look away! Dixie Land.

> In Dixie Land whar I was born in,
> Early on one frosty mornin,
> > Look away! Look away!
> > Look away! Dixie Land.

It also had, as Timrod put it, an "effective, but not complicated air."[8] But most important of all, it had an unalloyed, patriotic chorus that appealed to Southern pride, and gave the South its credo:

> In Dixie's Land, I'll take my stand,
> To live and die in Dixie.[9]

Many songs were sung in parlors and around crackling Southern campfires during the four years of the Civil War. But wherever and whenever Southerners gathered on the home front or the battlefront, they invariably expressed their patriotism through "Dixie." More than just a political symbol, "Dixie" affirmed Southern pride as a national pledge to take a stand, to be counted among the Southerners who cherished their unique way of life and were prepared to die defending it.

The "unexpected event" that gave "Dixie" its special "meaning" occurred in February 1861 during the inauguration ceremonies for Jefferson Davis as provisional president of the new confederacy. Not only was it "unexpected," it was in fact ironic. For one thing, the song was written not by a Southerner but by Daniel Decatur Emmett, a Northerner from Ohio.[10] For another, it was originally a minstrel tune sung in Negro dialect by whites, and finally it debuted not in the South, but in the North in New York City.

In 1859 the Bryant Minstrels who were playing at a theater on Broadway in New York were losing creative energy. After one Saturday night's performance when the audience seemed especially apathetic, Jerry Bryant, the troupe leader, decided the show needed some new songs to stimulate audience enthusiasm. As Dan Emmett, one of his minstrels, was about to leave, Bryant asked him to write a new "walk-around" or "hooray" song.

Minstrel shows of that time usually started off with a number of parlor songs and musical pieces. Then came some distinctly Negro acts and music, usually ending with some operatic burlesque. Scenes and music relating to life on a Southern plantation ended the entertainment. The "walk-around" was the grand finale. Bryant wanted, he explained, a "catchy" tune everyone could easily remember and sing on the streets after the show. And he needed it, he said, in time for rehearsal on Monday morning.

Emmett agreed to do his best even though he hadn't been given much time, but nothing came to him. The next day was rainy and cool. As he sat in the kitchen with his wife, looking out at the rain, an old Negro melody he had heard in the South years before ran through his mind and he recalled the warm, sunny days when he had been a circus musician in the South. Unconsciously, he muttered, "I wish I was in Dixie." As soon as he said it, inspiration struck and the words and music for "Dixie" almost wrote themselves.

The original title of the song was Emmett's lament, "I Wish I Was in Dixie's Land." When it was first performed by the "Bryant's Minstrels" on 4 April 1859, it was listed second to last on the program as a "Plantation Song and Dance," possibly because the Bryants didn't think it good enough to close the show. As a "plantation" piece, it supposedly depicted the gayer side of life for slaves on Southern plantations. The troupe stood in a semicircle in front of a plantation background. When the music started, two or more of the troupe strutted out and alternately sang a stanza while another "walked around" in the inside of the semicircle until the singer got to the center where he began to dance. Then came the musical interlude and the entire troupe joined in the frolic.[11]

The song was an overnight hit. A week after its debut, "I Wish I Was in Dixie's Land" was elevated to the concluding walk-around and was on its way to becoming one of the most popular tunes in America.[12]

DIXIE GOES SOUTH

In 1860, a year after he wrote "Dixie," Emmett sold all rights to the song to Firth, Pond and Co., in New York, for three hundred dollars,[13] a sizable amount of money in those days, especially for a song. Firth and Pond copyrighted it in their own name in June 1860 under the title, "I Wish I Was in Dixie's Land" and subsequently started calling it "Dixie's Land," or simply "Dixie."

By that time, "Dixie" was the feature song in every theater show in America. Writing in December 1860, John Dwight, editor of *Dwight's Journal of Music,* wrote that the orchestra at the St. Louis theater almost ruined the evening's drama by playing it just before the curtain rose. A few moments later, one of the actors stepped on stage in the opening scene, but almost as soon as he did, "a hundred patrons of high old art" started yelling for "Dixie." The audience would not settle down, and the actor furiously strode offstage. The manager then appeared. "Gentlemen, what means this ill mannered confusion, what do you want?" he bellowed with rage. "Dixie," came the deafening answer from the pit boxes and tiers. "Well, you can't have it!" he thundered back. "You've had 'Dixie' once to-night, and you'll have 'Dixie' no more," and off he went, thinking he had settled the matter. When the actor reappeared, however, the crowd roared for "Dixie" louder than before. The only way to appease the audience was to give it what it wanted, and so the curtain came down and the orchestra once again played Dixie's "bewitching strains." After a rousing cheer for the musicians, the audience sat back and waited for the play to begin.[14]

It was much the same everywhere. In March of that year a minstrel troupe in Chicago played to crowded audiences. A tall, sallow-looking attorney named Abe Lincoln was in town arguing a case and decided to take in the show with his junior associate, Henry C. Whitney. Whitney remembered how rowdy the audience became when the minstrels sang "Dixie," and how, like hundreds of others in the crowd, Lincoln shouted for "encore" after "encore." "I never saw him so enthusiastic," recalled Whitney.[15]

The same month Lincoln hooted over "Dixie" in Chicago, the Rumsey and Newcomb Minstrels roused audiences in New Orleans with the song.[16] The show opened on 6 March, but "Dixie" is not mentioned as

part of the act until the nineteenth, and then only in passing in an advertisement in the *New Orleans Daily Picayune* to "a dance in 'Dixie.'" The
"dance" was presumably the hit of the show since by 10 April, advertisements in the *Picayune* were specifically mentioning "Dixie": "Rumsey &
Newcomb's Campbell Minstrels. . . . The whole company in the amusing
plantation scene, Way Down South In Dixie." In the evening edition of the
eleventh, the *Picayune* reported, "Newcomb will distill his inimitable
'Essence of old Virginia,' and all the company will sing and dance 'Dixie.' It
will be worth while to compare the Rumseys and Newcombs with
Powhatan and Pocahontas in this scene."

"Powhatan and Pocahontas" referred to John Brougham's burlesque,
Pocahontas, playing 2 April to 5 May at the New Orleans Variety Theater,
starring Mrs. John Wood, a well-known actress and songstress in America
at the time. Carlo Patti, the orchestra leader at the Variety, had been looking for a rousing musical finale for the Zouave march in the play and had
tried "Dixie." When the Zouaves marched out that first night behind Mrs.
Wood, singing "Dixie," the audience made her sing it over and over again,
seven times in all.[17]

New Orleans music publisher, Philip Werlein, knew a popular hit
when he heard one and his presses were soon grinding out copies of
"Dixie" for sale. Werlein's "I Wish I Was in Dixies [*sic*] Land" listed Newcomb and a W. H. Peters as the lyricists and J. C. Viereck as composer, with
the notice, "Sung by Mrs. John Wood," above the title. The last four verses
were Emmett's, while the second line was from a Northern "Dixie" parody,[18] but the most radical change was that the whole song was anglicized
for the first time:

> I wish I was in the land of cotton,
> Cinnamon seed and sandy bottom
> Look away, away, away in Dixey
> Dixey land where I was born in
> Early on one frosty morning
> Look away, away in Dixey.[19]

By late 1860, "Dixie" had become one of the most popular tunes in
other parts of the South as well. On 20 December 1860, when delegates
meeting in St. Andrew's Hall in Charleston voted to secede, a band played
"Dixie" between speeches. "No words were heard, but the tune took and

caused great enthusiasm, which hardly knew bounds," said one of the participants.[20] In the nation's capital, outgoing president James Buchanan gave the last levee of his administration on 10 December 1860. "Everybody seemed to be merry, the outgoing as well as the incoming," reported the *Augusta Chronicle and Sentinel,* adding, "The band played 'Away Down in Dixey [*sic*]' and closed with 'Yankee Doodle.'"[21]

"DIXIE" BECOMES THE CONFEDERACY'S UNOFFICIAL ANTHEM

Jefferson Davis's inauguration on 18 February 1861 in Montgomery, Alabama, linked "Dixie" inextricably with the South. When Montgomery started making plans for the inaugural celebration, Hermann Arnold, the city's leading bandleader and impresario, was delegated to provide the music. It proved a harder job than he had anticipated since every patriotic song he could think of had a Northern theme. His wife suggested "Dixie."[22] Arnold liked the tune but felt the tempo of "Dixie" wasn't right as a marching tune. He changed it to a military quickstep.[23]

The day of Davis's inauguration was cloudy with occasional showers, not the most propitious day for such an auspicious event. Despite the weather, thousands of Southerners lined the streets and crowded on the steps of houses, on porches, and anywhere else that afforded a view of the history-making pageant about to unfold. For several days, masses of Southerners had made their way to Montgomery by train, steamboat, or private carriage, "loaded to their utmost capacity with wives, daughters, sisters, fathers, sons, and it really appeared," said the reporter for the *Augusta Chronicle and Sentinel,* "that the rest of mankind had been found, and they had appeared here."[24]

Just before noon, Davis emerged from the Exchange Hotel and climbed into a handsome carriage drawn by six gray horses. Vice President Alexander Stephens, along with a clergyman and Davis's personal military escort, joined him. At noon a brass cannon boomed, the signal for the procession to parade up Market street toward Montgomery's white-domed Capitol, where Davis would be sworn in as president. Davis's carriage was positioned right behind Arnold's brass band, and at the sound of the cannon, the band immediately began playing "Dixie" and the parade trekked its way through Montgomery's streets before a cheering crowd, including all the new government's members.

Arnold's arrangement of "Dixie" excited the crowd, Davis noticed. During the inaugural reception that followed, the catchy strains of "Dixie" seemed to be everywhere. Davis sent for Arnold to express his personal appreciation for making the day so memorable and concluded that "Dixie" would make a fine national anthem for the South.[25]

In a letter dated May 1861, Henry Hotze, who had worked as a reporter in Mobile, Alabama, prior to the war, and who was subsequently sent to England as a propagandist for the Confederate cause, expressed his amazement at the "wild-fire rapidity" with which "Dixie" had spread through the South. "Considered as an intolerable nuisance when first the streets re-echoed with it from the repertoire of wandering minstrels, it now bids fair to become the musical symbol of a new nationality, and we shall be fortunate if it does not impose its very name on our country."[26] Six months earlier he would have been prophetic. In May 1861 he stated the obvious— Dixie had become synonymous with the South.

By the end of the year, a song appearing in the *Memphis Appeal*,[27] irrevocably linked Dixie and "the Land of King Cotton":

> Oh! Dixie, dear land of King Cotton,
> The home of the brave and the free;
> A nation by Freedom begotten
> The terror of despots to be.[28]

Although "Dixie" became the Confederacy's unofficial national anthem after Jefferson Davis's inauguration, many Southerners resisted its acceptance because the rest of the song, hardly ever heard today, is pure doggerel:

> Old Missus marry Will de weaber,
> Willium was a gay deceaber,
>   Look away! . . .

> But when he put his arm around er,
> He smiled as fierce as a forty pound'er.
>   Look away! . . .

> Chorus: Den I wish I was in Dixie, . . .

> His face was sharp as a butcher's cleaber,
> But dat did not seem to greab er;
>   Look away! . . .

Old Missus acted de foolish part,
And died for a man dat broke her heart.
     Look away! . . .

Chorus: Den I wish I was in Dixie, . . .[29]

On 30 March 1861, members of South Carolina's secession convention and other prominent secessionists, among them dour Edmund Ruffin from Virginia, were sailing around Charleston's harbor. It was more a picnic outing than a military inspection. At noon there was chicken salad, cake, wine, and a lively band concert. When the band started playing "Dixie," a young officer commented to Ruffin that it seemed "Dixie" was on the way to becoming the South's national air.

"I am afraid so," was Ruffin's response, none too pleased with having what he considered merely drivel as a national anthem.[30]

Though by May 1861, it was clear to Henry Hotze that "Dixie" had become the South's unofficial anthem, Hotze likewise wondered at the "magic potency . . . in those rude, incoherent words, which lend themselves to so many parodies, of which the poorest is an improvement on the original?"[31]

Andrew Bowering, bandleader of the 30th Virginia Infantry in Lee's Army of Northern Virginia, didn't like "Dixie" either. "I never played Dixie unless I was forced to," he admitted long after the war was over, and said there were many in the army who shared his distaste for it.[32]

Other Southerners who were likewise embarrassed by "Dixie's" lack of dignity, attempted to elevate its sentiments. The best known of these, by Arkansas poet-lawyer, Brig. Gen. Albert Pike, appeared within weeks of the outbreak of the war.

Albert Pike (1809–91) was a Northern by birth but had moved to and made the South his home. When the Civil War broke out, Pike, like many Southerns, felt loyal to his adopted home. Robert Toombs, secretary of state for the Confederacy, gave Pike the job of negotiating a treaty with the Southern Indians as Indian Commissioner. Pike succeeded but his agreement with the Indians to be noncombatants was subverted when Maj. Gen. Earl Van Dorn enlisted them in the army. Pike protested to President Davis. When Davis sided with Van Dorn, Pike resigned. During the rest of the war, Pike served as a judge on the Arkansas Supreme Court.[33]

Pike's "The War Song Of Dixie,"[34] which he wrote to the tune of Emmett's "Dixie," was first published on 30 May 1861 by the *Natchez (Mississippi) Courier.* Philip Werlein subsequently published it in New Orleans in sheet music form, crediting the words to Pike and the music not to Emmett but to J. C. Vierick.

Pike's "Dixie" is a war song. Emmett's "Dixie" beckons; Pike's is defiant: Using the archaic "Southrons," it calls upon Southerners to rise to the defense of their country:

> Southrons! hear your country call you!
> Up! lest worse than death befall you! . . .
> Hear the Northern thunders mutter! . . .
> Northern flags in South wind flutter;
> Send them back your fierce defiance!
> Stamp upon the cursed alliance!"

The chorus is especially noteworthy. Whereas Emmett fondly expresses the wish "to live *and* die *in* Dixie," Pike's chorus calls on Southerners "to live *or* die *for* Dixie":

> Advance the flag of Dixie!
>   Hurrah! hurrah!
>
> For Dixie's land we take our stand,
> And live or die for Dixie!
>   To arms!   To arms!
>
> And conquer peace for Dixie!
>   To arms!   To arms!
> And conquer peace for Dixie!

Emmett's "Dixie" captures American zest and exuberance for generations to come; Pike's words were for the moment. For Emmett, Dixie is a part of America; to Pike it is a separate nation with grievances against the North for "faith betrayed and pledges broken, wrong inflicted, insults spoken."

Henry Troop Stanton offered another martial alternative in "Dixie War Song,"[35] which he dedicated "To the Boys in Virginia." Stanton wrote the lyrics in 1861 and sent them to music publisher Armand Blackmar in New

Orleans. Blackmar gave it a musical arrangement under his pseudonym, A. Noir, and published it with no mention of Emmett.

Stanton (1834-99) was the "Poet Laureate of Kentucky." Born in Alexandria, Virginia, he entered West Point in 1849 but left two years later for unknown reasons and took a job in Kentucky. In 1855 he became editor of a newspaper, the *Maysville Express*. In 1860 he moved to Memphis, Tennessee, but when the war broke out, he returned to Kentucky, raised a company, and enlisted under Col. (later, Brig. Gen.) John Stuart Williams. Stanton served as Williams's adjutant until 1864, and subsequently held the same post under Brig. Gens. John Hunt Morgan, John Cabell Breckenridge, and John Echols. After the war he returned to Kentucky where he worked as a lawyer and an editor for several newspapers.

Stanton's "Dixie" repeats the urgency of Pike's "To Arms" and expresses a sense of a besieged nation defending itself. Gone also is the credo of the original:

> Hear ye not the sounds of battle,
> Sabres' clash and muskets' rattle?
> > To Arms! to Arms, to Arms in Dixie!
>
> Hostile footsteps on our border,
> Hostile columns tread in order;
> > To Arms! to Arms! to Arms in Dixie!
>
> Chorus
>
> Oh, fly to arms in Dixie!
> > To Arms! to Arms!
>
> From Dixie's land we'll rout the band,
> That comes to conquer Dixie,
> > To Arms! To Arms! and rout the foe from Dixie!

A few years later, in 1863, a P. W. H. T. created a "Southern Dixie" which bore no resemblance to the original. "Oh! Dixie's Land's a Nation now," it boasts, but then states the obvious, that the Nation is not yet secure: "Battle on for Dixie," it proclaims, and urges its audience to "stand and strike for Dixie."[36] Of the three rivals, Pike's "Dixie" came closest in popularity to (but still never challenged) the original song; Stanton's and P. W. H. T.'s went virtually unnoticed.

Despite the martial and more dignified language of these parodies, Southerners couldn't embrace these uninspiring alternatives. Suggestions for new "Dixies" and arguments over adopting completely different songs filled the newspapers. "An appropriate national song for the Southern Confederacy appears to be one of the mooted questions of the present exciting crisis," said the *Richmond Enquirer.* "Plenty of patriotic poetry can be obtained, but a purely American melody, one that will take with the masses, is hard to be found."[37]

Early in the war, one newspaper at least thought the Confederacy had such an anthem in Earnest Halphin's "God Save The South,"[38] a song that mingled themes of patriotism and selfless devotion to the Southern cause, and contained the obligatory archaism, "chaunting":

> God save the South,
> God save the South,
> Her altars and firesides,
> God save the South!
> Now that the war is nigh,
> Now that we arm to die,
> Chaunting our battle-cry,
> Freedom or Death!

Halphin's words, intoned one Southern newspaper, were "what we have long wished for—a national anthem, breathing a spirit of patriotism and devotion suited to our troublous [*sic*] times. The pure and simple religious feeling which pervaded the poetry of this piece is beautifully interpreted by, and carried home to, the heart, in the deep pathos and majestic tones of the music. The sentiments of the anthem are perfectly in accordance with the religious feeling and faith of our people. . . . As a national anthem, we know nothing to compare with this in sublimity."[39] Philip Werlein, one of several music publishers to issue the song, thought so too and subtitled it, "The Confederate National Hymn."

Two Southern composers had been especially moved by Halphin's words. One was a German American with a pretentious middle name, Charles Wolfgang Amadaeus Ellerbrock, whose version Werlein and Halsey published. The other was C. T. DeCoeniel, a composer-publisher, who published the song in Richmond and credited Halphin with a captain's rank in the Confederate army, although he never served. DeCoeniel's cover for the song featured a kneeling Confederate officer, presumably Halphin, holding a Confederate flag. At the bottom of the page DeCoeniel included an announcement that anyone wanting to buy a copy could do so at his home or at "all the principal book and music stores in the Confederacy."[40]

When some readers failed to share the newspaper's sanguinity about the song's worthiness, the paper attributed the disagreement not to the song, but to having heard it sung by amateurs who didn't have the "depth, compass, flexibility, and tone" to sing it so as to convey its merits. Despite the newspapers's high hopes, "God Save The South" never became even a remote contender as the Confederacy's national anthem.

THE WAR OVER "DIXIE"

One indication of how psychologically potent an anthem "Dixie" was, is the controversies that swirled around it after its adoption by the South.

Northerners fumed over the South's appropriation of a song they considered theirs. The Northern assault to reclaim "Dixie" was waged on two fronts. The first contended "Dixie's" historical and geographical roots were in the North; the second offered a host of "Northern Dixies" as rivals.

In 1861, after the war had broken out, Firth and Pond published "I'm Going Home to Dixie" by Emmett, as a sequel to his original "Dixie." On the caption page of the song, they said they had received "many inquiries . . . in regard to the meaning of 'Dixies Land' and as to its location . . ." Firth and Pond's answer, however, did not hearten those whose pride needed buttressing. "With the southern negroes, Dixie's Land is but another name for Home," it explained. "Hence it is but fair to conclude, that all south of Mason's and Dixon's Line is the true 'Dixie's Land'."[41] In an interview given long after the war, Emmett himself said "Dixie's Land" was merely,

> an old phrase applied to the South States . . . though others have attempted, in vain, to locate it on Staten Island. . . . [Dixie] is nothing but a plain simple melody, with plantation words, the purport of which is that a negro in the north feels himself out of place and, thinking of his old home in the south, is made to exclaim, in the words of the song:—"I wish I was in Dixie's Land!"[42]

The attempt to associate Dixie with Staten Island was one of several far-fetched notions various New Yorkers came up with to legitimize the North's claim to the song. One notion traced the name back to the time of the Dutch settlement on Manhattan, where an alleged planter named Dixye tried raising tobacco in what is now Harlem. When the crop failed or Dutch sentiment turned against slavery, Dixye sold his slaves to a planter in South Carolina who treated them much worse. Soon afterwards, Dixye's former slaves started making up songs expressing a longing to be back with their former master.

A variant of that story centered around a kindly slave owner named Dixie who owned an estate on Manhattan around the time New York state outlawed slavery in 1822. Just before the law went into effect, Dixie sent his slaves South to keep from losing his investment. A variant of that story says he sold them because they were producing children so quickly he ran out of work for all of them to do, and the new owners were not as kind to the slaves who longed to "get back to Mr. Dixie." That longing passed from plantation to plantation, with the Mr. being dropped along the way until "Dixie" eventually came to mean a happier, more content place to live.

> The negroes who were thus sent off . . . naturally looked back to their old homes, where they had lived in clover, with feelings of regret, as they could not imagine any place like Dixey's. Hence it became synonymous with an ideal locality combining ease, comfort, and material happiness of every description. In those days negro singing and minstrelsy were in their infancy and any subject that could be wrought into a ballad was eagerly picked up; this was the case with 'Dixie.' It originated in New York, and assumed the proportions of a song there. In its travels it has been enlarged, and has 'gathered moss;' it has picked up a note here and there; a 'chorus' has been added to it, and from an indistinct 'chant' of two or three notes, it has become an elaborate melody; but the fact that it is not a Southern song 'cannot be rubbed out.' . . .[43]

Journalist William Howard Russell had heard the same story:

> Whether they [the slaves] were ill-treated after he [Dixie] died, and thus had reason to regret his loss, or that they had merely a longing in the abstract after Heaven, no fact known to me can determine; but certain it is that they long much after Dixie, in the land to

which his spirit was supposed by them to have departed, and console themselves in their sorrow by clamorous wishes to follow their master. . . .[44]

The debate about the origins of "Dixie" was all one-sided. For Southerners, "Dixie" was simply a corruption of the "Mason-Dixon line," the imaginary line separating Maryland from Pennsylvania, surveyed between 1763 and 1767 by Charles Mason and Jeremiah Dixon. This boundary, explained Hotze, "both geographically and rhetorically, has expressed the Northern frontier of the South ever since the line was drawn by the surveyors whose names it immortalizes."[45]

No matter how hard some Northerners might argue *Dixie's Land* was originally a plantation on Manhattan, Emmett's song had made "Dixie" synonymous with the South. Southerners never gave these academic arguments a second thought. Dixie was "the land of cotton," and "the land of cotton" was the South.[46]

NORTHERN "DIXIES"

The geographical link between "Dixie" and the South might be impenetrable, but the tune was still up for grabs. Early in 1861, the *New York Commercial Advertiser* urged someone "in this section of the country" to "set words of Union sentiment to its 'ta la, ta la' and 'rum di di di do' etc."[47]

Dan Emmett rose to the challenge with "I'm Going Home to Dixie."[48] Although the cover for the sheet music described it as the "Sequel to the Famous Song Dixie's Land" and said it had been "Sung with Tumultuous Applause By the Popular Bryant's Minstrels of New York," the song flopped. The first verse and chorus, like the rest of the song, simply lacked charm:

> There is a land . . . where cotton grows . . .
> A land where milk . . . and honey flows . . .
> I'm going home to Dixie! Yes! I am going home.

> Chorus

> I've got no time to tarry,
> I've got no time to stay.
> Tis a rocky road to travel,
> to Dixie far away.

"Dixie Unionized" contrasted the "Dixie" of the South with the North:[49]

> O! I'm glad I live in a land of freedom,
> Where we have no slaves nor do we need them.
> Look away, look away, look away to freedom's land.

The uninspiring song failed to capture popular sentiment, but that did not prevent politicians from giving it their unfettered praise, which Firth and Pond unabashedly attached to the last page of the song. A New York congressman, W. C. Parsons, for one, predicted the song would enjoy "unparalleled popularity . . . for the next half century." Fortunately for him, the Congressman was not in the music business.

The first page also carried an endorsement from an L. H. Sigourney, who unctuously commended the composer for his efforts: "You have succeeded admirably in your song for the music of Dixie's Land. It furnishes additional proof of the opinion I have often expressed that no one can adapt words to music so well as musicians," and advised him that Muzzy's anachronism of placing the battle of Bunker Hill prior to Lexington in the second verse "will scarcely be observed, as the euphony of the measure required it." In other words, Sigourney agreed history shouldn't be taken seriously when a lyrical phrase was at stake.

The author of "The New Dixie!" subtitled, "The True 'Dixie' for Northern Singers," took a "sour grapes" approach:

> Den I'm glad I'm not in Dixie
>   Hooray! Hooray!
>
> In Yankee land I'll took my stand,
> Nor lib no die in Dixie
>   Away! away! away down South in Dixie.
>   Away! away! away down South in Dixie.[50]

Most Northerners, however, refused to concede. On 11 January 1862, the *New York Herald* bragged that "Good martial, national music is one of the great advantages we have over the rebels. They have not even one good national theme . . . for 'Dixie' belongs exclusively to our own Dan Bryant."[51] To prove the North meant to hold on to that claim, "Dixie" was incorporated in 1862 into *The Drummer's and Fifer's Guide,* the field musician's manual for U.S. regimental bands; Federal bands continued playing "Dixie" as one of their own marching tunes until 1863.

EMMETT VS. HAYS

One measure of a cultural icon's importance is the passion it continues to engender long after the arguments which spawned it were seemingly settled.

Although the armed confrontation ended in 1865, the war of words and symbols persisted. In 1871 New Yorkers reignited smoldering animosities by reasserting that the term, Dixie, referred to an early section of the city: ". . . no one ever heard of Dixie's land being other than Manhattan Island until recently, when it has been erroneously supposed to refer to the South, from its connection with pathetic negro allegory," the *New York Weekly* editorialized. In 1871 the *Weekly* claimed boys in New York City had been using the term "Dixie's Land" for the last eighty years when playing "tag."[52]

An unlikely defense of the Southern side was made by *The Financial Times* of London in 1911, in which it contended that *Dixie* came from the ten dollar bills issued by the *Citizen's Bank* of Louisiana (which incidentally sided with the Confederate cause and was looted by Union general Benjamin "Beast" Butler, but nevertheless continued to stay in business until 1911). The bank had been chartered in Louisiana in 1833 and prior to the war, had issued several millions in paper money, most commonly in denominations of ten dollars with the French word *dix* (ten) on one side. "Ignorant Americans living along the upper Mississippi river, not knowing how to pronounce the French word, called the bills Dixies.'" These bills became so widely used that Louisiana became known as "Land of the Dixies," or "Dixie Land." Eventually, the expression was broadened to include all the Southern States.[53]

The war over "Dixie" continued to be fought on two more fronts. One was over authorship of the song, the other over revising the lyrics.

"Dixie" was such a phenomenally popular song prior to and during the Civil War that its authorship was claimed by many people. There is some question whether New Orleans publisher Philip Werlein knew Emmett had written the song when he attributed authorship to Newcomb. Werlein may have attributed the song to Newcomb because his minstrel troupe had introduced it to New Orleans. Or Werlein may simply have been trying to avoid paying royalties. When Newcomb told Werlein he wasn't the author, Werlein "corrected" his error and gave another Southerner, W. H. Peters, credit, but he never acknowledged Emmett as the author of "Dixie."

When Firth and Pond learned Werlein was selling pirated versions of "Dixie" they threatened to sue him unless he stopped. Werlein defended himself by disputing Emmett's claim to sole authorship. In fact, he had some grounds for that argument since he had also pirated parts from another "Dixie" entitled, "Dixon's Line!" The argument was settled out of court at a convention of music dealers in New York. An attorney for Firth and Pond presented the evidence for Emmett's authorship. Emmett himself was there and though, in the attorney's words, Emmett "was no speaker," he said the songwriter would be happy to tell how he had come to write the song "in his plain western style," if anyone wanted to hear it.

Everyone did. Emmett told the story "using some mighty plain and powerful language, even unto 'cuss' words, and so completely satisfied all that he and he alone was the author of 'Dixie' that all the publishers agreed to discontinue its publication and send the[ir] plates to Firth, Pond & Co." after selling whatever music they still had in stock. When their inventories were exhausted and it came time for them to print new editions, they agreed to credit Emmett as author and pay Firth and Pond a royalty. But before forwarding their plates as agreed, many of them printed "all the copies that could be sold in five years . . ."[54]

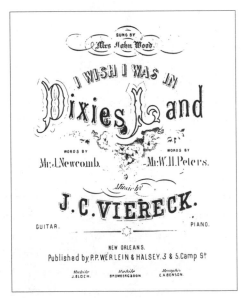

Southern version of "Dixie," crediting Newcomb and Peters as composers instead of Dan Emmett.

For his part, Hermann Arnold, who had introduced the tune at Jefferson Davis's innauguration, came to believe that instead of only coming up with a new arrangement for "Dixie," he'd actually written it. In 1924 the eighty-five-year-old Arnold told a reporter for the *Birmingham News* the melody for "Dixie" was an old German tune that he had transcribed onto a wall at the Montgomery Theater in 1859. Shortly afterward, he said, Emmett was playing at the Montgomery theater. When he saw the tune on the wall, said Arnold, Emmett "was greatly impressed. He at once wanted to write the words to my music and when he went back to his home in Ohio did so."[55]

Arnold may in fact have written the notes on the wall in 1859, but Emmett couldn't have seen them because he hadn't been south of the Mason-Dixon line since 1847 and didn't return until the 1890s.[56] Arnold himself didn't retire from the music business until 1907 and then "not because I was too old, but because I cannot stand 'jazz.' It is terrible!"[57]

After the war, Emmett himself drifted into obscurity except for a brief period when Southern nostalgia raised him to the level of an icon. Despite his success as a minstrel performer and popular songwriter, Emmett couldn't find work in New York after 1865 and he moved to Chicago where he joined one of that city's minstrel shows. But in 1867 he lost his voice because of bronchitis and had to stop singing. For the next few years he eked out a living as a fiddler. In 1888 he returned penniless to Mount Vernon, Ohio, where he lived among his boyhood friends and neighbors in a small two-room cabin. He would probably have lived out the rest of his life in relative obscurity had he not been called out of retirement by a friend from his early minstrel days, A. G. Field. The entrepreneurial Field wanted Emmett for a new minstrel show he was putting together. His gimmick was to have Emmett ride at the head of his parade of minstrels as the founder of minstrelsy and the composer of minstrelsy's best known tune. Sometime during the show, he would introduce Emmett who would say a few words about minstrelsy and his long career. After this brief appearance, Emmett would stay on stage while the orchestra played "Dixie."

Emmett agreed and the show opened in Columbus, Ohio, in 1895. When the time came for Emmett to appear on stage no one was more surprised than Field. Emmett had no intention of just standing like a doddering old man when the musicians played his song. Still a showman, he began singing along and reenacting the old time gestures he had used while performing the song almost fifty years before.

When the show began its tour of the South, neither Emmett nor Field was prepared for the composer's popularity. Instead of a quaint gimmick, Emmett became the show's main attraction. He was cheered on stage wherever he opened and was treated as one of the South's outstanding citizens. In Richmond, the Daughters of the Confederacy showered him with flowers and the best families lined up to be introduced. In Nashville, Gen. John Brown Gordon, a lieutenant general in the Confederate army, introduced him on stage as the author of "Dixie," and he was invited to various parties as the guest of honor.

After the tour, Emmett lived in his native Mount Vernon until his death on 28 June 1904. He would have died in abject poverty except for a five-dollar-a-week pension awarded him by the Actor's Fund of America when some New York members discovered his plight.

Emmett felt he had had a good life and he never complained about his financial circumstances. In his last years he was content merely to tend his garden, raise his chickens, and live with the satisfaction of knowing that he had written one of the best-loved songs in America. Many years later, a wealthy Ohio citizen erected an eight-foot-high monument of "imperial blue" Vermont granite on his grave site, bearing the inscription:

> To the Memory of
> Daniel Decatur Emmett
> 1815-1904
> Whose Song, 'Dixie Land,' inspired the courage
> and Devotion of the Southern People and now
> Thrills the Hearts of a Reunited Nation.

After Emmett's death in 1904, people all over the country began claiming they had written "Dixie." By 1908 there were at least thirty-seven of them. The *St. Louis Post-Dispatch* noted: "One more claimant to the authorship of "Dixie" has been added to the long array of claimers . . ." Only one other popular song has been composed by so many authors— "The Old Folks at Home."[58]

Southerners, bothered by the taunt that "Dixie" had been written by a Northerner, were happy to support such claims by any Southerner. If someone could show that Emmett had plagiarized the song from a Southern songwriter, Southern pride need no longer feel blighted. The most serious claimant was William Shakespeare Hays, best known for his "Drummer Boy of Shiloh."[59]

William Shakespeare Hays (1837–1907) was born and raised in Louisville, Kentucky, and lived most of his life there. When his first poems appeared in 1856 and 1857 in the college paper in Georgetown, Kentucky, where he was a student, he was nicknamed "Shakespeare" and subsequently made it a formal part of his name. Hays moved to Louisville in 1857 and went to work as a clerk in D. P. Fauld's music store, where he also began writing songs.

During his career, Hays is credited with having written more than 350 songs, many of them under pseudonyms such as Syah (Hays spelled backwards), and three small books of poems. As many as twenty million copies of his songs may have been sold, making him one of the most prolific songwriters of the nineteenth century. He was a very versatile songwriter, ranging from sentimentality to minstrel banality to hymns. Some of his songs so resembled those written by Stephen Foster that he was thought to have been the original composer.[60]

Although Hays never claimed Foster's songs, he maintained that he had written the original "Dixie" while working for D. P. Faulds in Louisville in 1858, a year before Emmett.[61]

In May 1907, a feeble Hays, by then seventy years of age, presented his claims to Louisville's Filson Club, a prominent Southern historical organization, and convinced several members he was indeed the author. A subcommittee was subsequently formed to look further into his claim.[62] On 4 June 1907 the chairman of the subcommittee announced he had received a letter from a man in Texas assuring him he had in his possession one of the original editions of the song published by D. P. Faulds. But the song was never produced.[63]

When Hays sickened shortly afterwards, his wife championed her husband's cause. In 1907 she wrote to Oliver Ditson & Co. in Boston, one of the largest music publishing houses in America, asking if it had a copy of the song in its catalog. Ditson responded that there was no trace of "Away Down South in Dixie," with words by Will S. Hays in its files. Hays died soon afterward and his cause remained in limbo. Meanwhile, by 1909, "Dixie" had become the most popular patriotic song in America.[64]

In 1916 Edward Le Roy Rice, a journalist with the *New York Clipper,* contacted Mrs. Hays. He was writing "an exhaustive volume on our immortal song of 'Dixie'" and he wanted to settle the authorship argument. "When I have finished," he assured her, "I will have fixed beyond dispute who the author really was, Dan Emmett or Will S. Hays." There was more support for Emmett than Hays, he confessed, but he assured her he was "absolutely unbiased." If she had any evidence to the contrary, he would give it full consideration. Mrs. Hays had none.[65]

Meanwhile, Thomas J. Firth had taken up Hays's cause. Firth had been a bandmaster in the Confederate army (13th Tennessee Volunteers) during the war and was now working as a music teacher and lecturer in Memphis. In 1908 he interviewed Hays's boss, D. P. Faulds.[66]

Faulds said he had copyrighted Hays's song under the title "Way Down South in Dixie," and had printed fifty thousand copies. He had sent copies to all of his customers in the South and to publishers throughout the country since they all sold each other's music. He couldn't copyright the music, he said, because it was common property, coming from an old English ditty which began: "If I were a soldier wouldn't I go . . ." and had been parodied as a children's song.

Emmett's version, said Faulds, came out a year later using the same tune but different words. "Hays'[s] version," opined Faulds, "was strictly a Southern song; Emmett's was suitable to singing in the North, where he performed."

Faulds had in fact published a song entitled "Away Down in Dixie's Land," with words by "Jerry Blossom" and music by "Dixie Jr.," not in 1857 or 1858 before Emmett's, but in 1860, after Emmett's "Dixie" ("Oh dixie am de paridise / Whar de raise de cotton and de rice"). Faulds claimed to have sold fifty thousand copies of the song and to have copyrighted this version in 1861 under the laws of the Confederate States. He had no extant versions of it, he said, because his shop burned down.

In 1917 Firth wrote to Mrs. Hays asking if she had any copies of the original music.[67] Mrs. Hays had nothing to give him.

After her mother died, Hays's daughter carried on the cause to vindicate her father. In 1937 she wrote to James Coke, editor of *Etude Music Magazine,* assuring him her father was the author of "Dixie" and that he had written the song for the Buckner Guards when they were called south during the Civil War. Coke was open-minded. He had always thought Emmett was the author, he said, but he was prepared to reconsider the matter if she could provide new evidence. There was none.[68]

The challenges to the pedigree of "Dixie" are still not over. In 1993 a new claim for authorship was made on behalf of an African American family, the "Snowdens," from Knox Country, Ohio, where Emmett grew up, visited, and, ultimately, returned in his last years.[69]

The argument here is that Emmett stole (the authors use the more polite "borrowed") the song from the Snowdens. The fanciful evidence is based on "vivid memories of elders in the community," public documents, and family records. The "vivid memories," however, have been handed down over a 150-year period. Many are contained in a newspaper article from Mount Vernon, Ohio, quoting the local librarian who claimed Emmett "probably" got the song from the Snowdens, and a now-deceased pianist from the same community who "imagined" the Snowdens had something to do with it. The oft-quoted historian argued that the Snowdens must have written it because Emmett had no reason to do so and argued, incorrectly as it turns out, that Emmett had never been in the South. The article, strewn with what people "ventured" as likely happened, or "felt" happened, or "suppose" happened, are not "vivid" memories. The "public documents" are advertisements for the Snowdens' minstrel act which do not mention "Dixie" as one of "their" tunes; and the family records consist of letters that indicate the Snowdens wrote some songs, but nowhere is there a hint that one of those songs was "Dixie." Though the book is a very good biography of a musical African American family in nineteenth-century Ohio, it is totally unconvincing in its premise that the Snowdens, and not Daniel Decatur Emmett, wrote the song.

SHALL WE CHANGE THE WORDS OF "DIXIE"?

Southerners may not have liked to admit a Northerner was responsible for their national song, but they couldn't refute it. What still bothered them, was the song's doggerel. "The original words of Emmett's 'Dixie,'" said the United Daughters of the Confederacy (UDC), "were altogether wanting in dignity of thought or exalted sentiment." The UDC urged the South to adopt a new version, either from the many songs sung to the air of "Dixie" or from a new song written expressly for the purpose.[70]

Billboard magazine considered the idea folly: "They will never get Dixie accepted in a rewritten form," the magazine declared. "It is impossible to attain any such purpose with the song ingrained in the hearts of millions as Dixie is."[71]

But *Billboard* hadn't counted on the steady growth of the white pride movement in the South. Southerners admitted Emmett, a Northerner, had written the original "Dixie," but they balked at accepting an anthem with words written in "negro dialect."[72]

Despite their personal feelings, unless the Alabama UDC had the support of Confederate veterans, their plan didn't have a chance. The best way to gain that support, they felt, was to win over veteran leaders. The most prominent of these was General Gordon, who had introduced Emmett

during his tour with Field. As the first commander of the United Confederate Veterans, Gordon thought the idea of a new "Dixie" was worth considering but Gordon cautioned them not to tamper with Emmett's
chorus.[73]

Gen. Stephen D. Lee of Mississippi, one of the two Confederate officers sent to demand the surrender of Fort Sumter in 1861, was also asked
for his endorsement. Lee, who would succeed Gordon as president of the
United Confederate Veterans (UCV), also supported the UDC, although
he too urged that the chorus be kept intact.[74]

S. A. Cunningham, publisher and editor of the *Confederate Veteran,* the
most influential and most widely read of the Confederate veteran news-
magazines, was also asked for his endorsement. Personally, Cunningham did
not favor the idea. Emmett was a friend of his. He had entertained him in
his home in Nashville, and he had visited Emmett at his home in Ohio.[75]
The two still corresponded regularly. Though he agreed Emmett's "Dixie"
was doggerel, loyalty kept him from fully supporting the UDC's project.
Although he refrained from editorializing on behalf of the UDC's venture,
he agreed to publish any "Dixie" poems sent to his magazine along with
any letters written on behalf of the cause.

By the end of 1903, the Alabama UDC had the support of the entire
UDC, the United Sons of Confederate Veterans, and the Confederate
Southern Memorial Association. The only group left to convince was the
veterans—the most important group of all—and they already had Gordon
and Lee's support.

When the Daughters started out for the UCV Convention in Nashville
in June 1904, they had twenty-two different versions of "Dixie" ready for the
delegates to consider.[76] On the eve of the convention they were primed to put
the issue before the delegates for adoption. But events conspired against them.

The main setback was General Gordon's unexpected death. Gordon had
been president of the UCV since its inception in 1889. Choosing a new president was on everyone's mind. The UDC sighed with relief when Stephen
Lee was chosen as Gordon's successor, but only for a moment. When the
results were formally announced, the aging veterans burst into "the words of
the famous and beloved old song, that song which has led many a wild charge
and which has inspired men to die fighting for the cause of the South."[77]
Faced with this spontaneous outburst of voices singing "Dixie," the UDC
decided to postpone raising the issue of a new version.

On the final day of the convention, when the UDC introduced its resolution it was unprepared for the hullabaloo that followed. Many of the vets

were caught off guard and couldn't believe what they heard. Gen. William Lewis Cabell ("old Tige"), United Confederate Veterans' vice president, bent with age, shaking with emotion, hobbled to the podium and denounced the idea as sacrilegious:

> The song furnished us with inspiration through four long years of fighting. It has furnished inspiration ever since, and I do not think that we, standing with one foot in the grave, should permit any changes in those words.[78]

The veterans finally accepted the resolution as a courtesy to the UDC. Given the emotional opposition by Cabell and other veterans, the UDC knew its efforts would come to nothing.[79] The emotional tide turned completely against the UDC's resolution eleven days after the convention when Emmett died.

In the October 1904 issue of *Confederate Veteran,* a writer saddened by Emmett's passing vented her ire at the UDC and its plan to adopt new words "to our loved 'Dixie.'" Another wrote that changing the words of "Dixie" would be sacrilege.[80]

By 1905 the fire to adopt a new "Dixie" had nearly flickered out. When the national UDC convention met in June of that year, the chairwoman of the Alabama UDC spoke apologetically about her chapter's efforts to adopt a "new Dixie."[81] When the United Confederate Veterans met in Louisville the next month, General Lee looked out at the throng of veterans and bellowed: "Shall we change the words of Dixie?" A loud chorus bellowed back, "No, no, never, don't change the old words, let it stay as it is."[82]

Today, the status of "Dixie" as the South's unofficial anthem is still hotly contested, but for different reasons. To many African Americans, "Dixie" smacks of racism. "The playing or singing of 'Dixie' conjures visions of an unrepentant, militantly recalcitrant South, ready to reassert its pernicious theories of white supremacy at any moment," says Sam Dennison, author of *Scandalize My Name, Black Imagery in American Popular Music.* "That is why the playing of 'Dixie' still causes hostile reactions—after more than one hundred and ten years have passed since it was first heard."[83]

There is no doubt that "Dixie," like the Confederate flag, is an inflammatory symbol to many people. But to millions of others, it is a symbol of pride, heritage, and identity. More than a hundred years have passed since the Civil War, but the symbols of that war have not lost any of their atavistic fervor. Shall we change the words of "Dixie"?

CHAPTER 3

The Bonnie Blue Flag

On 9 January 1861, the Mississippi State Convention met in Jackson to decide whether the state would follow South Carolina's lead and sever its ties with the Union. As Chairman William T. S. Barry announced the vote, eighty-three for secession, fifteen against, Mrs. Homer Smythe, wife of the secretary of the convention, rushed to the platform at the head of a pack of cheering women and put a staff bearing a blue flag with a white star in its center into Barry's hands.[1]

A relatively unknown actor named Harry Macarthy was in Jackson at the time and like everyone else, he was at the convention when the vote was counted. As the crowd cheered and Barry waved the flag back and forth, Macarthy was inspired to write down some verses to celebrate the event. When he finished, he showed the pages to a friend who opined that he saw little merit in them.[2]

Macarthy stuck with his instincts and linked the words to an old Irish folk song, "The Irish Jaunting Car," by Valentine Vousden. That night, he sang his new song in the Spengler Music House in Jackson "to an audience drunk with the wine of war."[3] The song, the *Arkansas Gazette* reported, "was greeted with a storm of applause, the singer was forced to repeat it until his voice refused further effort."[4]

A few weeks later Macarthy was in New Orleans. Audiences had responded enthusiastically to his new song in Mississippi so he decided to earn some extra money by publishing it as a broadside in New Orleans. When sales exceeded his expectations, he decided to copyright the song to protect his interests.[5] Then he took the song to music publisher Armand Blackmar. Blackmar recognized a good song when he heard it and bought the rights to it from Macarthy for five hundred dollars and a piano.[6]

Neither Marcarthy nor Blackmar had any idea of how good a song it was. The full extent of its magical power fully dawned on Macarthy in September of that year when he sang it at one of his "personation concerts" and caused a riot.

In the early months of the war, thousands of Confederate soldiers from west of the Mississippi funneled through New Orleans on their way to the Virginia front. It was a place to rest their horses, take on supplies, and relax before heading eastward to have even more fun killing Yankees. The Academy of Music was one of the Crescent City's favorite show palaces in those days, and as soon as the "boys" got settled, they usually headed for St. Charles Street, packing the theater from floor to gallery.

Harry Macarthy, the Academy's star performer, was a short, handsome man, clean shaven, with a straight nose, thin lips, and thick black hair which covered his ears. His specialty was imitating people with various dialects, and he called his acts "Personation Concerts." But Macarthy also had a way with a song. On the day of the riot in September, Terry's Texas Rangers were in the audience.

Macarthy had made "The Bonnie Blue Flag" the centerpiece of his show, but he still experimented with its presentation. On this particular day, he introduced a new staging in which he acted the part of a soldier leaving home for the front. Striding out on the boards in full Confederate dress uniform, he stopped at center stage, gazed at his audience, and without fanfare began to sing the first verses of the song:

> We are a band of brothers,
> And native to the soil,
> Fighting for the property we gained
>   by honest toil;
>
> And when our rights were threaten'd,
> The cry rose near and far,
> "Hurrah for the Bonnie Blue Flag,
> That bears a Single Star!"

As he sang the last two lines, a beautiful girl rushed onto the stage waving a dark blue silk flag with a single star, and she threw her arms around Macarthy's neck. His voice quivering with emotion, Macarthy then took up the chorus of the song:

Hurrah! Hurrah! for Southern Rights hurrah!
Hurrah! for the Bonnie Blue Flag that bears a Single Star.

From every corner of the theater boys and men excitedly jumped to their feet. Every teenager in the audience imagined himself as the departing soldier on stage, the hero of a young beautiful girl back home, and each started cheering and waving his hat. The crescendo was deafening. Macarthy stood silently on stage. When the noise subsided, he sang another verse:

As long as the Union was faithful to her trust,
Like friends and brethren kind were we, and just;
But now, when Northern treachery attempts our rights to mar,
We hoist on high the Bonnie Blue Flag that bears a single star.

When the chorus came around again the audience joined in and sang it over and over. The more they sang, the more worked up they became. Some leapt onto their seats with rousing Texas yells. One of the rangers continued shouting long after everyone else had quieted. A policeman standing in the aisle tapped him on the shoulder to stop, but the boy was too excited. Reflexively, he lunged from the shoulder. The policeman tumbled.

Lawmen from every corner rushed the miscreant. But the Texans weren't about to stand idly by while one of their own was hauled off to some New Orleans calaboose. Fierce hand-to-hand fighting erupted. Punches were thrown, faces were pounded, noses were bloodied. Clenched men rolled and tumbled; noncombatants frantically scattered to stay out of the fracas. More police poured into the theater. There was no stopping the melee. Someone ran for the mayor. Someone else had the good sense to summon Col. Frank Terry. Between the two of them the fight was stopped. The mayor called off his police and Colonel Terry led his defiant rangers off to their camp. Twenty-four hours later the song that had started it all had spread through the Southern army and was soon being sung or hummed in every hamlet, town, and city in the Confederacy. "The Bonnie Blue Flag" had become the rallying song of the South.[7]

BOLD SYMBOL OF DEFIANCE

Although "Dixie" was the song most closely identified with the South and the Confederate cause, "The Bonnie Blue Flag" was an equally powerful musical weapon for arousing patriotic and martial feelings. It was such a bold symbol of defiance that after the Federals captured and occupied New Orleans, Maj. Gen. Benjamin Butler prohibited the singing, whistling, or playing of the tune. Initially the penalty was a twenty-five dollar fine. When that didn't stop it, Butler accused the tuneful lawbreakers of treason and imprisoned them. Armand Blackmar, who had published the song, was arrested and fined five hundred dollars. All the city's music houses and print shops were raided and every copy of "The Bonnie Blue Flag" was burned.[8] Even small boys were arrested for cheering when a band on a British ship, anchored in the gulf, played the song.[9]

Butler's actions succeeded. Some Southerners, like John Wilkes Booth, however, remained defiant. In March 1864, Booth was in town starring in *Richard III, Macbeth,* and other plays. One night, he and some friends were out walking. Booth was known as a devil-may-care sort and someone dared him to sing "The Bonnie Blue Flag," believing there were lines even Booth wouldn't cross. Without hesitation, Booth took up the dare.

"The rest of the party was too scared to think," recalled Ed Curtis, one of the group. "It was treason to sing that song, so they ran away." But not Booth. Booth calmly continued singing the verses as he strolled down the street. The prohibited lyric attracted excited Union soldiers. They surrounded him and drew their weapons menacingly. Booth remained unperturbed. Was there a law against singing the song? He convinced the soldiers he hadn't known of it. He was a newcomer to their city and had only just heard it on the streets. It had a catchy tune and he liked the words. No offense intended.

Such a lame excuse would have landed anyone else in jail. "But Booth could do pretty much as he pleased," Curtis recalled. "He had a way about him which could not be resisted, the way which permits a man to overstep the boundaries of the law, and do things for which other people would be punished."[10] Ironically, had the law been enforced, Booth might have languished in a New Orleans jail on 14 April 1865, instead of sneaking into Abraham Lincoln's box at Ford's Theater in Washington.

Performer that he was, Macarthy kept refining the staging for the song during the next two years. The "bonnie blue flag" grew larger and larger, and as he unfurled it, Macarthy would sing the roll call of seceding states:

> First gallant South Carolina nobly made the stand,
> Then came Alabama and took her by the hand;[11]
> Next, quickly, Mississippi, Georgia, and Florida,
> All raised on high the Bonnie Blue Flag that bears a single star.

Ye men of valor gather round the banner of the right,
Texas and fair Louisiana join us in the fight;
Davis, our loved President, and Stephens, statesmen rare
We'll rally round the Bonnie Blue Flag that bears the single star.

And here's to brave Virginia, the Old Dominion State,
With the young Confederacy at length has linked her faith;
Impelled by her example, now other States prepare
To hoist on high the Bonnie Blue Flag that bears a single star.

Then cheer, boys, cheer, raise a joyous shout
For Arkansas and North Carolina now have both gone out,
And let another rousing cheer for Tennessee be given
The single star of the Bonnie Blue Flag has grown to be eleven.

As each state was called, soldiers from that state would invariably whoop or cheer. The final verses stirred souls and passions:

Then here's to our Confederacy, strong we are and brave,
Like patriots of old we'll fight, our heritage to save;
And rather than submit to shame, to die we would prefer,
So cheer for the Bonnie Blue Flag that bears a single star.

Later Macarthy added a twelfth star when he musically implored Missouri to seal her fate with the other eleven:

And now to Missouri we extend both heart and hand,
And welcome her a sister of our Confederate band;
Tho' surrounded by oppression no tyrant dare deter
Her adding to our Bonnie Blue Flag her bright and twelfth star.

and a thirteenth in anticipation of the day when the South would "Make room upon the Bonnie Blue Flag" for Kentucky.[12]

Macarthy's dramatic staging of "The Bonnie Blue Flag" delighted audiences. There were those in the early months of the war, like Terry's Rangers, who lost their self-control when he performed it. Adolescent soldiers shouted and yelled like madmen, jumped to their feet and ran amok through the theater frantically waving their caps; some would start beating comrades with their fists; others would embrace. Decades later, memories of this bedlam were still fresh in the minds of many Confederate veterans.[13]

FIGHTING FOR THE PROPERTY

Armand Blackmar eventually published nine editions of "The Bonnie Blue Flag." All of the editions carried the inscription, "To Albert G. Pike, Esq., the Poet-Lawyer of Arkansas,"[14] and the note, "sung at his 'personation concerts'" on the cover page. As the popularity of "The Bonnie Blue Flag" grew, Blackmar printed it with an illustrated cover in color, with two red and blue "Stars and Bars." Other publishers issued "variations" and musical improvisations of the song with their own brightly illustrated covers.[15]

Except for the addition of new "stars," most of the editions published by Blackmar had minor variations in text, but early in the song's history there was one substantive conceptual variation. In five of the nine Blackmar editions, the third line of the first verse has "property" as a major issue in the war: "Fighting for the property we gained by honest toil." The other four give "liberty" as the motive.

As noted in chapter 1, when Southerners spoke of "property," they meant slaves. When Macarthy wrote the first verses of "The Bonnie Blue Flag," on 9 January 1861, it was still three months before Abraham Lincoln called for volunteers to regain control of Fort Sumter. It was Lincoln's proclamation, not the threat to slavery, that united Southerners. The Confederacy was born out of the "property" issue; but it was to defend their homes and families against imminent invasion—"liberty"—and to defend their state's honor, that tens of thousands left their farms to go to war. When Macarthy first penned "The Bonnie Blue Flag" he did so with the "property" issue in mind. When invasion became imminent, the South was no longer fighting for "property" but "liberty."

THE ORIGINS OF "THE BONNIE BLUE FLAG"

When Mrs. Homer Smythe paraded to the convention platform in Jackson, Mississippi, waving her blue flag with its lone star, she was carrying on a tradition started fifty years earlier by another woman, Mrs. Melissa Johnson.

Back in 1810, the province of West Florida was part of France's Louisiana territory and included a section of present day Louisiana, east of the Mississippi River, and parts of Mississippi and Alabama. When France turned over New Orleans and all of its territory west of the Mississippi to Spain after the French and Indian War of 1763, the part east of the

Mississippi went to England and became the British territory of West Florida. During the American Revolution, Spain sided with the colonies and wrested West Florida from the British. When France regained the Louisiana territory from Spain, it expected West Florida would also be returned since it had originally been part of Louisiana. Spain refused. When the United States bought the Louisiana territories from France in 1803, it inherited the dispute.

West Floridians preferred Britain's colonial government to Spain's, which was more autocratic. Unable to retain their erstwhile freedoms, they rebelled in 1804, under the leadership of two brothers, Nathan and Sam Kemper. The rebellion was easily quashed but West Floridians continued to press for greater freedom. In 1810 they held a convention and drafted a petition asking the Spanish governor for constitutional guarantees. The governor pretended to be sympathetic. Secretly he called upon the governor of East Florida for armed help to put down what he considered a threat to his position. The delegation discovered the governor's underhandedness, before that support arrived, and left.

On 11 September 1810 armed West Floridians set out for the provincial capital at Fort Baton Rouge under a blue flag with a solitary white, five-pointed star made a few days earlier by Mrs. Melissa Johnson. This time the rebellion succeeded. Baton Rouge was captured without the loss of a single man and the governor was imprisoned. On the twenty-third the blue flag with the single star was raised over the Fort. The president of the West Florida Convention signed a Declaration of Independence on the twenty-sixth and the lone-star flag was adopted as the new republic's emblem.

Now that the Spanish grip over West Florida had been broken, the United States claimed the area; and on 27 October 1810 President Madison declared it was indeed part of the Louisiana purchase and therefore under the governor of Louisiana's jurisdiction. For their part, West Floridians were willing to be included in the United States and on 10 December 1810 the flag of the new republic came down and was replaced by the "Stars and Stripes."

The blue flag with its single star had another brief but memorable moment in history. When Texas followed West Florida and declared itself a republic on 2 March 1836, it too adopted the lone star as its emblem, making the blue flag with a single star a traditional symbolic banner of liberty. When South Carolina put a white crescent moon and a palmetto tree against a blue background on its flag, it was because those symbols had a longer traditional claim on the state's citizens.

Mississippi, the second state to secede, adopted the "bonnie blue flag" with its single star as its first banner. Two weeks later, the state convention adopted a variation of the "bonnie blue flag," which featured a single white star and a magnolia tree on a blue background, with a red trim border. Alabama, Florida, Louisiana, and North Carolina likewise incorporated the revered symbol in their banners.[16]

PARODIES AND RIVAL CLAIMANTS

Like all good songs, "The Bonnie Blue Flag" provoked parodies during the war and rival claims to authorship afterwards. One lackluster Northern parody, called "A Reply to the Bonnie Blue Flag," stated the North's reasons for going to war and ended with the resolve that the "bonnie blue flag" had to be hauled down.[17]

In 1895 a Mrs. Annie Chambers Ketchum of Mississippi claimed that, although Macarthy had written a version of "The Bonnie Blue Flag," it was her rendition that the Confederacy had embraced. Ketchum was a popular minor poet in the South when the war broke out. Her husband was a Confederate officer who had died in 1863 from wounds he received at Shiloh (6 and 7 April 1862).

According to Ketchum, Macarthy's words "reminded me of a lone man trying to dance." She titled her version, "Nec Temere, Nec Timide." Immediately after she wrote it, said Ketchum, Confederate soldiers everywhere began singing it and her husband's own regiment adopted the title as its motto.[18] Several newspapers in the South supported her claim. So did Armand Blackmar's son.[19] All the sheet music versions published by Blackmar's father, however, clearly list Macarthy as author and few gave more than passing notice to Mrs. Ketchum's claim.

THE BOB HOPE OF THE CONFEDERACY

During the war, Harry Macarthy was unquestionably the South's best-known and most popular entertainer, bringing fun and laughter to civilians and soldiers across the Confederacy. But no biography has ever been written about him. Nor has any magazine featured a story about this jolly little man who gave freely and generously to Confederate charities and who entertained troops in the field. He died, destitute in a lonely rooming house in Oakland, California, his passing almost totally unnoticed.

He was born in England of Scotch-Irish parentage in 1834. Nothing is known about his mother or father, where in England they lived, what they did, or why Harry left his home for New York when he was only thirteen years old.[20] By 1858 he was being billed as "the Irish comedian," not because of his origins but because of his "faithful and mirth-provoking" imitations of Irish characters.[21] Dressed in a ruffled shirtfront, with a low set collar and wristbands studded with diamonds, Macarthy had become, in modern terms, a stand-up comedian, specializing in impersonations. Two months later he began touring Arkansas with his "Personation Concerts."[22]

Macarthy was so overwhelmed by the reception the people of Arkansas gave him, he began calling himself the "Arkansas Comedian." During this tour of Arkansas he met Arthur Pike, who was making a reputation for himself as a lawyer and a poet.[23] Macarthy was so impressed with Pike that when he later wrote "The Bonnie Blue Flag," he dedicated every sheet music version of the song to Pike, the "poet-lawyer of Arkansas."

When the war broke out Macarthy could have gone North had he chosen since he was still a British citizen. But his loyalties were with the Confederate cause and he remained in the South for almost the duration of the war, touring and giving concerts in towns, cities, and camps. He was the Bob Hope of his era and his shows did as much for Southern morale during the war as Hope's did during World War II.

When Macarthy arrived in New Orleans from Memphis on 3 August 1861, the city council was discussing plans to open a Free Market for needy families. Macarthy volunteered the profits of his first concert to the cause, just as he had a few weeks earlier in Memphis for the Southern Mothers' Association.[24]

New Orleans's mayor, John T. Monroe, was delighted. "Your patriotic offer to aid the families of our brave volunteers in want, cannot but elicit the approbation of our entire community, and I hope your acting in this matter will meet with the success it deserves."[45] The profits came to $178. Macarthy turned the money over to the city council as promised.[25] In the bargain, Macarthy earned a well-deserved endorsement by the *Daily Crescent,* which included a note that he would sing two of his "new Southern songs . . . The Bonnie Blue Flag and The Volunteer."[26] The following night the *Daily Picayune* raved:[27]

> Harry is a natural genius and has no competition, in his line, indeed we have not listened to more scientific negro minstrels since the days of George Christy. If one wants to enjoy a treat and a hearty laugh, let him go and hear Harry.

The next day the *Picayune* still gushed:

He has a fine voice and understands how to use it. His new National Song of the South, composed by himself and called "The Bonnie Blue Flag With a Single Star" takes his audiences mightily, every one of his many hits it contains telling us with unerring certainty upon their sympathy and their enthusiasm.[28]

The paper also mentioned a "clever actress, singer and danseuse" in the show. Unbeknownst to the newspapers, the "clever" girl was Macarthy's new bride, Lottie Estelle. Lottie was equally a crowd pleaser and was soon getting regular billing under her own name. It was Lottie who strode onto the stage the day the Texas Rangers rampaged during Macarthy's performance of "The Bonnie Blue Flag."

Macarthy gave his last performance of the season in New Orleans on 13 October,[29] then went on tour, bringing his "Personation Concerts" to men in the field. His shows especially inspirited during the winter months when the armies bivouacked and men languished in boredom, doing little for weeks on end besides eating, sleeping, cooking, and policing the camp. Macarthy played for Bragg's army at Pensacola in December 1861[30] and for Hood's Texas Brigade in northern Virginia in 1862.[31]

In December 1864 the Macarthys entertained in Wilmington, North Carolina, and dined with James Ryder Randall, whose "Maryland! My Maryland!" rivaled "The Bonnie Blue Flag" in popularity during the first two years of the war. Randall was serving as a naval officer in Wilmington at the time.[32] Although Randall recognized Macarthy's abilities, Macarthy's "way," he said, was "not exactly mine and it is only proper that we should not be familiar."[33]

LATER YEARS

Shortly afterward, the Macarthys returned to Richmond. By then, the noose was tightening around the Confederacy and all professional actors, with the exception of the manager of the Richmond Theater and a handful of others, were drafted into the army.[34] Macarthy fled North.[35]

When news of Macarthy's desertion reached Augusta, rival composer John Hill Hewitt was infuriated.[36] He denounced Macarthy for claiming to be the 'National poet of the South,' a sobriquet Randall likewise resented ("my brother barred!!!").[37]

Hewitt gave Macarthy his due as "a good vocalist, a protean actor," and an "enthusiastic friend of the Southern cause," but accused him of dodging the conscription act by falsely obtaining papers showing he was a British subject,[38] and he bitterly parodied all of Macarthy's songs.[39] In fairness to Hewitt, however, he rarely had anything good to say about any of his competitors.

After Macarthy fled North he sailed to England via the West Indies. During this next part of his career he kept a scrapbook of his press clippings, which he published in 1870 (by identifying himself as Harry Macarthy, the Arkansas Comedian) under the title, *His Book of Original Songs, Ballads, and Anecdotes, as Presented by the Author in His Well-Known Personation Concerts.*[40]

In 1867 Macarthy returned to the United States for a new round of concerts in the Midwest. The *New Orleans Daily Picayune* described his reception at the Academy of Music where he had once been a featured star as:

> one of the most enthusiastic demonstrations of welcome ever witnessed within the walls of the Academy. Long before the curtain rose, all available space had been occupied by an eager throng, impatient to greet their old favorite. Hundreds were not able to gain admission, and were obliged to seek amusement elsewhere. Although the entertainment which preceded the appearance of Mr. Macarthy was usually amusing, still it was plainly discernible that everybody was in a state of feverish expectancy for the appearance of the popular favorite. When he came before the foot-lights he was received with a storm of applause and a shower of bouquets; and one fervid admirer in the parqueted astonished Mr. Macarthy by discharging at him a new hat.[41]

During the 1870s, Macarthy continued giving concerts across the country traveling as far west as Texas.[42] By the end of the decade, his act had lost much appeal and in the early 1880s Macarthy and Lottie split up. Macarthy went to San Francisco looking for work while Lottie found a job in Helena, Arkansas, but they still wrote to one another. Macarthy was again in poor health and his mind was going. In his last professional appearance in Oakland, California, a dazed Mccarthy missed his cues during a show.

Macarthy died on 8 November 1888, before Lottie could reach him.[43] Lottie informed the editor of the *New Orleans Daily States* of his death and asked if he could raise some money so that she could have him buried in New Orleans where he had been such a popular actor and had so many friends.[44] Macarthy's obituary appeared in the *New Orleans Daily States* on 25 November 1888. In it the eulogist described the performer's long career, praising his uncanny ability for imitation, his acting skills, and his talent as both a songwriter and a singer. Macarthy could do anything, he said, except hold on to a dollar.

None of the other newspapers in the South noticed Macarthy's death until several years later when readers began asking what had happened to the beloved entertainer. Because so little was known of his personal life, some newspapers invented biographical data for him. The *Richmond Dispatch* said he was a member of Terry's Texas Rangers and that he was killed at Chickamauga.[45] His association with the rangers probably came from the melee he created when he entertained them in New Orleans. The Chickamauga reference is uncertain except that he may have been entertaining soldiers in the area at the time of the battle. In 1904 the *Mobile Register* carried a short notice about Macarthy, praising him for the charitable work on behalf of Confederate causes:

> [He] made a great deal of money, but he gave it all to the Confederate cause with the same prodigality that he divided his dollars with any one whom he considered in need.[46]

Although millions of people sang and hummed the songs he wrote, and thousands of men died with those songs echoing in their minds, Harry Macarthy, undoubtedly the best-known and best-loved entertainer of the Civil War, died penniless, alone and forgotten.

THE BARD OF THE CONFEDERACY

And what of James Hill Hewitt, Macarthy's most vehement citic?

If sheet music sales are a key to a country's musical tastes, John Hill Hewitt (1801-90), the first native-born American composer to receive national and international fame, deserves Richard Harwell's accolade, the "Bard of the Confederacy."

Hewitt was one of the most prolific American songwriters of the nineteenth century.[47] His resumé, if he had cared to write it, would have included more than three hundred songs, several operettas and cantatas, and an oratorio. Eighteen of his wartime songs were published as sheet music. His biggest wartime hits were the musical arrangements he wrote for "All Quiet along the Potomac Tonight," which was issued five times by its publishers, and "Rock Me to Sleep Mother," which appeared four times.

In addition to musical works his resumé could have included the many plays, poems, newspaper and magazine articles he wrote, magazines he started, magazines and newspapers he edited, the many concerts he gave on the flute, organ, and piano, his teaching career as professor of music at female seminaries, his stint as a theater manager, and during the latter part of the Civil War, his business venture as a music publisher. In addition to these activities he raised eleven children, watched Samuel Morse send the first telegraph message from Baltimore to Washington, and climbed aboard the first train pulled by a locomotive in America.

Though a Southerner by choice and passion, Hewitt was born in Maiden Lane, New York, in 1801, the eldest son of John Hewitt, a prominent musician, composer, and music publisher. Though Hewitt's father earned his living as a musician, he didn't want his son to follow him in a musical career and apprenticed him in several trades, but Hewitt would not be "'prenticed."

In 1818 Hewitt pursued a military career. With the help of a general who had given him drill lessons he entered the military academy at West Point. Hewitt, however, was not a good student. He didn't like his military classes, but he did look forward to the music classes he took with the leader of the academy band, a virtuoso on the flute and key bugle. His virtuoso father hadn't trained his son; Hewitt received his formal musical training at West Point.

At the end of four years at the academy, Hewitt lacked the grades to graduate. But in his own mind he had graduated,—at least that's what he told General P.G.T. Beauregard in a letter he wrote to him in 1861. He had graduated in 1822 and had been commissioned a brevet second lieutenant, he said, but had resigned his commission to study law.[48] This wasn't the last time he altered significant facts in his life.[49]

The year he failed West Point, he agreed to join his father's theatrical company, which was meeting in Augusta, Georgia. Disaster struck almost immediately. The theater they were playing in burned, destroying all their props and instruments. Defeated, his father headed back to New York. Hewitt stayed in Augusta and opened a music store where he sold instruments and gave lessons on the piano and flute. He soon had enough students to make a living and began to feel very contented because of the respect Southerners, especially prosperous planters and merchants, had for music teachers. But although he was often invited for dinner at the homes of his wealthy pupils, it irked him to play for the wives after dinner as they gossiped alone, while their husbands discussed the weightier political issues of the day. Though he loved his music, and though he was treated with respect, Hewitt realized that the community leaders didn't value the political opinions of musicians.

In 1824 Hewitt moved to Greenville, South Carolina, where he became a music teacher at the Baptist Female Academy and moonlighted by giving private lessons to the children of wealthy planters and merchants. A rival music teacher, whose pupils began leaving him for Hewitt, rumored that Hewitt, who had a dark complexion, was a mulatto. Overnight his pupils shunned him. Hewitt ended the lie by persuading John C. Calhoun to write a letter on his behalf vouching for his racial purity.

The following year, in 1825, Hewitt wrote "The Minstrels Return from the War," a song that made him an international star. Hewitt's brother James had kept up the family music publishing tradition started by their father and was living in Boston. When he visited his brother in 1825, Hewitt brought the song with him and asked him to publish it. Unimpressed, his brother published it anyway. The song went on to become the first international hit by an American songwriter. Since he had published the song as a favor to his brother, James hadn't had the copyrighted it. That mistake cost both brothers thousands of dollars in royalties.[50]

In 1840 the peripatetic Hewitt moved to Washington, D.C., where he founded and edited a newspaper. Five years later he moved to Norfolk. Two years later he moved back to Baltimore. He stayed in Baltimore less than a year, and moved to Hampton, Virginia where he took a job as a music teacher at the Chesapeake Female College. He stayed in Hampton for nine years, moved to Chambersburg, Virginia after John Brown's raid, and then to Richmond.

When the war started Hewitt was a feisty sixty-year-old. Nonetheless, he asked Jefferson Davis to be commissioned in the Confederate army, citing his West Point experience. Davis refused, but because of his military training, offered him a job as drillmaster for new recruits. Hewitt refused. Instead he accepted a job as manager of the Richmond Theater, in November 1861. His autocractic managing style didn't endear him to the actors or owner, and he was replaced in 1863 by R. D'Orsey Ogden when the Richmond Theater was rebuilt after burning down. Jobless again, he moved back to Augusta where he teamed up with Alfred Waldron, who at that time was managing the concert hall in Augusta as well as the careers of his musical family, the "Queen Sisters."

Hewitt wrote skits and songs for the talented family as well as several ballad operas, including his best known "King Linkum the First," and "The Vivandiere." He also kept busy teaching music. Soon after he started teaching, he married one of his new pupils, eighteen-year-old Mary Smith. (His first wife had died while he was teaching music in Hampton.) Well over sixty at the time, Hewitt fathered four more children. His wife must have been an apt pupil since she published two songs of her own during the war.[51]

Between 1863 and 1864, Hewitt traveled through Georgia along with the "Queen Sisters." In March 1863 the "Sisters" debuted one of Hewitt's best-known songs, "All Quiet Along the Potomac Tonight."[52]

Hewitt continued writing patriotic songs, operettas, and melodramas throughout the war. In 1864 he signed a contract with John Schreiner to write songs exclusively for him but secretly also wrote songs for the Blackmars under the name Eugene Raymond, a pseudonym he had begun using in the 1850s. Late in the war he began publishing music with Schreiner, and eventually he bought out the Blackmar music publishing business in Augusta.

Hewitt's business endeavors collapsed after the war and he moved once again, this time to Virginia where he taught music for a time at the Wesleyan Female Institute in Staunton, and the Dunbar Female Institute in Winchester. From Winchester he moved back to Baltimore. In 1872 he headed for Georgia where he lived for a time in Savannah. Still restless, he decided he liked Baltimore better than Savannah and in 1874 he moved back—and lived there until his death in 1890.

A cantankerous curmudgeon, Hewitt resented fame in others. Edgar Allan Poe, whom he had bested years earlier for the poetry prize only because the judges hadn't wanted Poe to win both the prize for poetry and prose, had an undeserved reputation, he said. Poe, he said, was a plagiarist to boot. R. D'Orsey Ogden, the man who had replaced him as manager of the Richmond Theater, was "a fawning sycophant, with just brains enough to know how to fascinate a frail woman and keep himself from the clutches of the conscript officers." He viciously attacked Harry Macarthy, whom he accused of cowardice and plagiarism. He conceded Macarthy was a good vocalist and a protean actor, but he said his songs, including "The Bonnie Blue Flag," were "wishy-washy."

Hailed once as both the "Father of the American Ballad," and the "Bard of the Confederacy," Hewitt, like Macarthy, is now just one of the many forgotten tunesmiths of the war—an unrecognized genius according to his admirers.[53]

CHAPTER 4

A Fever In The Blood

After "Dixie" and "The Bonnie Blue Flag," the third song to vie for status as a Confederate national anthem was "Maryland! My Maryland!" It contended, however, only into the first two years of the war when the South still hoped that Maryland would join the Confederacy. Nevertheless, the song's themes of opposition to the North, pride of country, and singularity of purpose, as well as its message of optimism ("She Breathes, She Burns, She'll Come, She'll Come,"), provided Southerners an assuaging mantra whenever military contests turned against them.

The inspiration for the song, like many other songs written during the first year of the war, is traceable to Abraham Lincoln's proclamation calling for volunteers to crush the insurrection in South Carolina. Southern states like Virginia, that had not yet cast their lot with the Confederacy, refused to comply whereas Northern states eagerly offered to fulfill their quotas; border states with divided loyalties, like Maryland, were in turmoil.

Massachusetts was the first Northern state to respond by sending its 6th Massachusetts Volunteers to Washington. On 19 April, a week after the first shots were fired on Fort Sumter, the train carrying the regiment pulled into Baltimore.

In those days the railway line coming into the city from the North ended at the President Street Depot. Trains for Washington left from another depot on Camden Street. Passengers going on to Washington either walked or took horse-drawn cars between the two stations. As the Massachusetts regiment made its way to the Camden Street Depot along Pratt Street, a pro-Southern mob, waving Confederate flags, surrounded it and shouted insults.

Nine cars passed without incident but the brakes on the tenth car locked and it suddenly lurched to a halt. By that time tempers seethed. The mob pelted the disabled carriage with rocks. Potshots struck the car.

Besieged, the soldiers fired back. When the melee was over, twenty citizens and four soldiers lay dead in the bloodstained street.

Baltimore's mayor, George W. Brown, apologized to the governor of Massachusetts. No one deplored the tragedy more deeply than he, said Brown, but "our people . . . could not be restrained," at the invasion of their city by armed troops.[1]

The *New York Tribune* called the incident unprovoked. The Massachusetts soldiery had merely been passing inoffensively through Baltimore en route to Washington in compliance with the president's orders. They had held their fire even though they had been insulted and pelted with rocks. Only when fired upon did they turn their own guns on the unruly, disloyal mob.[2]

From his tiny room at Poydras College in Pointe Coupee, Louisiana, James Ryder Randall fumed as he read the pro-Southern version of the riot, a version that said the crowd had been provoked. Innocent civilians, the paper said, had been slaughtered in the streets of Randall's former hometown.

Years later, Randall recalled his feelings that night and how he was inspired to write the song that catapulted him to fame. He couldn't calm down, he said. His birthplace had been invaded. Would Maryland invite subjugation? Why did she not declare herself for the Confederacy? What held her back?

His nerves unstrung, he was too distraught to sleep that night. About midnight he rose almost involuntarily from his bed and lit a candle. Zombielike, he made his way to his desk and picked up his pen. A powerful spirit seized his mind. "Karamanian's Exile," a poem by James Clarence Mangan, echoed in his head, its rhythms and meters usurping his thoughts.

Words rushed through his brain in cadence with the rhythm of the poem. Unconsciously, his hand raced over paper capturing the words in his febrile brain. Telling the story years later, he reflected, "No one was more surprised than I was at the widespread and instantaneous popularity of the lyric I had been so strangely stimulated to write."[3]

The following day Randall read his fever-inspired poem, "My Maryland," to his class. The students stirred to its passion. Send it immediately to the *New Orleans Delta,* they urged! Randall responded that he hadn't written it "in cold blood." It wasn't a newspaper poem, he protested. But his students would not be swayed.

The poem was published on 26 April 1861. It appeared during those uncertain frenetic days when every eye was focused on the border states to see which way they would side; virtually every Southern newspaper reprinted it. Letters of praise arrived at the *Delta* daily. Randall became an overnight celebrity.[4]

In "My Maryland" Randall articulated the widespread outrage millions of Southerners felt over Lincoln's invasion of their land and the celebrated pride in their new country. The beginning recalled the violation of Maryland's sovereign territory and called upon Marylanders not to forget the bloody riot of 10 April:

> The despot's heel is on thy shore, Maryland!
> His torch is at thy temple door, Maryland!
>
> Avenge the patriotic gore
> That flecked the streets of Baltimore,
> And be the battle-queen of yore, Maryland! My Maryland!

The next verses invoked his "Mother-state" to defend herself and to recall her past glories and urged her to ally herself with her Southern sister states as Virginia had just done:

> Dear Mother, burst the tyrant's chain, Maryland!
> Virginia should not call in vain, Maryland!
> She meets her sisters on the plain,
> Sic semper![5] Tis the proud refrain.

Further delay, Randall cautioned, courted dishonor. He knew Maryland would suffer the horrors of war if it declared for the South, but better a holocaust, he said, than "crucifixion of the soul." In the final verses Randall urged Maryland not to submit to "the Northern scum,"—the singular vulgarity which undercut the admiration many Northerners felt for it despite its message.

Meanwhile, there was more rioting in Baltimore. In Lincoln's mind, Washington had to be secured. Maryland sat on its doorstep. Its large pro-Southern faction had to be neutralized; it was not enough for Maryland simply to declare its neutrality.

On 27 April 1861, Lincoln suspended the writ of habeas corpus for the corridor between Washington and Philadelphia, which included Baltimore; arrested prominent Southern sympathizers, including members of the state legislature; and sent Federal troops to occupy key positions in the city and other parts of the state. On 29 April the Maryland State Legislature met to vote for or against secession. The vote went fifty-three to thirteen against.

Southern partisans could do little except sneak through the Federal lines to join the Confederate army. About twenty thousand did. Women sympathizers smuggled clothes and messages to the Confederates. On 31 May 1861, "My Maryland" appeared in the *South,* a pro-Southern Baltimore newspaper. Within hours, thousands of broadsides circulated in the city.

A few days later, the Baltimore Glee Club met at the home of Hetty and Jennie Cary. The Carys were one of the most prominent families in America. The first Cary had settled in Virginia in 1640. His progeny were among the most influential political leaders and landowners in the colonies. They were related to Thomas Jefferson and the Randolphs. Wilson Cary, Hetty and Jennie's father, had moved to Baltimore in the 1800s. His daughters were considered two of the most beautiful women in the South. "Invincible beauties," they were called. General Beauregard simply called them the "Cary Invincibles."

The Carys openly sympathized with the Confederate cause. Hetty and Jennie's two brothers, John and Wilson, eventually enlisted in the 1st Maryland Cavalry while the two girls supported the cause.

On the night the glee club was to meet, Jenny was in charge of the musical program and was determined to find a way for the group to express its pro-Southern patriotism.

"What about 'My Maryland'?" Hetty asked. By that time, "My Normandie" had been suggested as a tune for the poem, but the words didn't match the song's meter. Jennie wanted a better fit. What about that song Burton Harrison, their cousin Constance Cary's beau, had been singing? Harrison was a student at Yale and said it was his school song.[6] The tune was "Lauriger Horatius." It was also the tune for the German Christmas carol, "Tannenbaum, O Tannenbaum" ("Christmas Tree, O Christmas Tree").[7] Jennie tried it. It fit the meter of "My Maryland" perfectly . . . almost. The second and fourth stanzas of the poem were short three beats. In another flash of inspiration, Jennie added "My Maryland" to the recurring "Maryland" at the end of some of the verses. Now the match was perfect.

"That night," as the glee club sang Jennie's arrangement, "the enthusiasm communicated itself with such effect to a crowd assembled beneath our open windows as to endanger seriously the liberties of the party."[8]

Everyone in the glee club raved. The song had to be published. But a calmer voice pointed out that Fort McHenry (whose bombardment had inspired Francis Scott Key's "The Star-Spangled Banner") was only a few miles away. The song was treasonous. They could all be imprisoned.

Not to worry, Rebecca Lloyd Nicholson assured the club, she would get it published. Her grandmother had arranged to have "The Star-Spangled Banner" published fifty years before. She was just as intent on doing the same for "Maryland! My Maryland!" Besides, she said, her father was a "Union man in Baltimore and if I am imprisoned he will take me out."

Despite her bravado, the first edition of the song appeared without the name of the author, arranger, or publisher. Subsequently, music publishers Miller and Beacham issued it in Baltimore, attributing it to "A Baltimorean in Louisianna [*sic*]," with musical arrangement by "C. E." (Charles Ellerbrock, a German music teacher who also wrote several pro-Southern songs of his own during the war).[9] Subsequent editions published in New Orleans listed the arranger as "A Lady of Baltimore," and the composer, "A Confederate."

By this time the Cary sisters, especially Hetty, had become more and more open about their Southern sympathies. When Hetty waved a Confederate flag from her window while Federal soldiers were parading by her home, her defiance couldn't be ignored, even if the Carys were the most socially prominent family in the state. Leave Maryland, Hetty was told, or face imprisonment. A few days after the battle of First Manassas (21 July 1861), Hetty, her sister Jennie, and their brother Wilson crossed the Potomac into Virginia.

When he heard the Cary sisters were nearby, Maj. General P. G. T. Beauregard invited them to visit him at his headquarters near Fairfax Courthouse. One night while the sisters were in camp, the New Orleans Washington Artillery band serenaded them. The ladies sent their thanks. Was there anything they could do in return?

"Let's hear a woman's voice!" someone in the unit shouted.

Standing at the door of the tent, Jennie Cary obliged with "Maryland! My Maryland!" The soldiers immediately took the song to heart and soon the whole camp was resonating to the refrain, "Maryland! My Maryland!" As the last notes faded away someone shouted "We will break her chains! She shall be free! She shall be free!" and everyone joined in. That night there wasn't a dry eye in the Cary tent.[10]

Seeing the dramatic effect of the song on his men, Beauregard had copies printed and distributed them to anyone who wanted one.[11] A few weeks later, "Maryland! My Maryland!" joined "Dixie" and "The Bonnie Blue Flag" as the Confederacy's most popular songs.

Years later, Wallace P. Reed, a writer for the *Atlanta Constitution,* described the impact of the song on Southerners:

If ever there was a poet with a Muse of fire that poet was James R. Randall. . . . What Rouget de Lisle was to France, Randall was to the Confederacy. What the Marseillaise was when the entire French nation went mad, "My Maryland" was when the Southern people threw themselves in to the tumultuous horror of our civil war. . . .

What our most eloquent tribunes could not do, it was reserved for the poet to do. Where eloquence failed to move the people, a song set their hearts aflame. It stirred a fever in the blood of age, turned weak women into heroines, and wherever its wild notes were heard, legions of armed men sprang up. It was a bugle-call, a cry to arms, a battle-shout all in one, with a hint of clashing steel and the thunderous rush of charging hosts. . . .

The flaming lyric swept over the land like a conflagration. From the Potomac to the Rio Grande "My Maryland" was everywhere—in the air, on every lip—an inspiration and a prophesy. Millions of Southerners heard it with feelings of divine exultation, intense enthusiasm, or maddened frenzy. On the other side of the border our foemen heard it with mingled anger and admiration. It rolled across the sea, and rolled resurgent back again, to mingle its strange notes with the blazon clamor of war.

In gay salons, in crowded assemblies, on the stage, in the trenches and on the tented field, the song did its perfect work. It sped onward through the day and through the night, ringing out from the mountains awakening the echoes in the valleys, stirring every heart and nerving every arm.

The words alone did not wield this wonderful power, nor the music; it was the spirit back of them that made them immortal.

I had heard it from gentle maidens, and from rough troopers as they rode, booted and spurred, to the fray. I had heard it here in the City of the Siege, at the time when roaring cannon and shrieking shells were its only accompaniement. I had heard it in our celebrations of victory, and again when we were in the throes of a heroic despair.

How it fired the blood and strengthened every arm that wielded a sword! How well it has been called the Marseillaise of the Confederacy![12]

One Southerner remembered hearing Confederate spy Belle Boyd singing it while they were both prisoners in the old Capital Prison in Washington, D.C., "in a way that would make you feel like jumping out of the window and swimming across the Potomac . . ." She sang it "as if her very soul was in every word she uttered. It used to bring a lump up in my throat every time I heard it. It seemed like my heart was ready to jump out—as if I could put my fingers down and touch it. I've seen men, when she was singing, walk off to one side, and pull out their handkerchiefs, and wipe their eyes, for fear someone would see them doing the baby act."[13]

In 1862, heartened that nothing had happened to Miller and Beacham for publishing "Maryland! My Maryland!", two other Baltimore music publishers issued several editions and Miller and Beacham came out with a piano arrangement.[14]

In New Orleans, Werlein and Halsey published several editions in 1862, one so hastily printed it omitted the "My" between the two Marylands, and another with music by P. P. W. (Werlein's initials). James McClure also rushed a version into print in 1861 in Nashville and Memphis as part of his "Southern Collection of Popular Songs for the Piano."[15]

THE BOY-POET OF THE CONFEDERACY

No Southern poet, writer, or composer was more admired or adored than James Ryder Randall. His patriotic poems, many of which were set to music, fired Southern blood with martial spirit and inspired passion and exultation in demure maidens and in rough, coarse men alike. Wherever he went, "crowds rushed to see him, and every city was proud to claim him as its honored guest. Statesmen, warriors and fair women overwhelmed him with their attentions, which he modestly tried to avoid."[16]

Despite his modest efforts to avoid the limelight, politicians and soldiers befriended him. Though he was not a handsome man, women of all ages fawned over him.

Randall was born on New Year's day in 1839 in Baltimore. His father, a prosperous merchant, educated his son well. One of Randall's earliest teachers had also tutored Edgar Allan Poe. When he was ten years old, his father sent him to Georgetown University. At the age of sixteen, Randall graduated and won the University's Medal for Excellence in English. Always in frail health, he suffered two almost fatal attacks of pneumonia during his final year, which delayed his graduation. Failing health plagued him his entire life.

After graduating, Randall clerked in a Baltimore bookstore but soon quit to go on a trip to Rio de Janeiro. When he returned to the United States he taught school in a wilderness outpost in Florida. The frontier was not to his liking and he moved on to New Orleans where he clerked in a shipping-merchant's office. In his spare time he wrote poems, some of which were published in New Orleans's newspapers. His poems did not go unnoticed and at the age of twenty he was offered a job as professor of English and classics at Poydras College, an affluent county college in Pointe Coupee Parish in Louisiana.

Although he continued to write poetry, it was "My Maryland" that made him a celebrity in the South, the North, and abroad. Reprinted in Southern newspapers, the poem was set to music in his native Baltimore, vying with "Dixie" and "The Bonnie Blue Flag" as the unofficial national anthem of the Confederacy. In England, a relative of Lord Byron's read "My Maryland" in an English newspaper, wrote to Randall asking for a manuscript copy of the poem, and invited him to visit his family in London.

Randall had other admirers in England. A woman came up to John R. Thompson, future editor of the *Southern Literary Messenger,* while he was at a party in that country, and asked if he'd like to hear a song from his native land. He would like nothing better he said, whereupon the woman sat down at the parlor piano and sang and played "My Maryland." When she finished she gave Thompson a message: "When you see your friend who wrote that, tell him you heard it sung by a Russian girl, who lives at Archangel, north of Siberia, and learned to sing it there."[17]

Randall enlisted in the New Orleans Crescent Volunteers at the outbreak of the war but was soon discharged because of tuberculosis. Undaunted, he kept trying to enlist. He was finally taken into the Navy in 1863 and transferred to Wilmington, North Carolina. His first appointment was as secretary to the flag officer, with the rank of midshipman. At the time of his appointment he was too poor to buy himself a uniform.[18]

His wife-to-be, whom he met that year while traveling on a train, coaxed him to write for money. He didn't have any compunctions about getting paid for writing poetry, he replied, but hated the idea of selling his poems for trifles to "trashy newspapers." If he did, his "pride of song" would undoubtedly abandon him forever.[19] Many years later, still badly in need of money, he reluctantly accepted an invitation from the Daughters of the Confederacy in Baltimore to give a talk about writing "Maryland! My Maryland!" in return for a hundred dollar honorarium. By then, sentiment no longer matched poverty.[20]

NOT EASILY FORGOTTEN

When Southern forces crossed into Maryland at any time in the early days of the war, they inevitably erupted into "Maryland! My Maryland!"[21]

The best-remembered rendition occurred a few days before the battle of Antietam (14 to 17 September 1862). The Confederate soldiers stripped and carried their guns and clothes above their heads as they waded across the Potomac. Thousands of nude men—their rough voices singing "Maryland! My Maryland!"—etched an unforgettable scene.[22]

Marylanders had several chances to rally behind Confederate forces. Though many towns cheered as the Southerners passed through, few Marylanders allied with them. John Robson, one of "Stonewall" Jackson's "foot cavalry," remembered the disappointment he and others had felt when Maryland failed to join them.

> We had sung ("Maryland! My Maryland!") with a good deal of hope and vim, for this song asserted positively that "She Breathes, She Burns, She'll Come, She'll come," etc., but it didn't take "us generals" of the ranks very long to see that there was a mistake about it somewhere. "Some one had blundered," for she didn't "come" worth a cent; and the people of this portion of Maryland didn't flock to the "bonnie Blue," in defense of southern rights quite as unanimously as we had been led to expect—according to the song.[23]

Marylanders had boasted that given the chance, they would show their mettle. They had not then and they would not later, prompting parodies like this to describe the Marylander's gasconading:

> We can't stay here to meet the foe
> We might get shot and killed, you know.
> But when we're safe, we'll brag and blow,
> Maryland! My Maryland![24]

After Lee's invasion of Maryland was thwarted at Antietam (17 and 18 September 1862) nearly all hope of uniting Maryland with the Confederate cause disappeared and "Maryland! My Maryland!" ceased to be a credible rallying song.

Since Maryland was not part of the Confederacy, exiled Marylanders were not subject to the Confederate draft. In Richmond, where many Marylanders fled not to join the army but to go into business, a Confederate congressman grumbled that they were "always ready to break out into the strains of 'Maryland! My Maryland!' but unwilling to strike a blow for the Confederacy."[25] Another congressman complained that the Marylanders ought to be made "to fight as well as to sing hymns for Maryland."[26]

For their part, Northern songwriters put their own partisan words to Randall's tune. In "Maryland, My Maryland (A Northern Reply),"[27] Septimus Winner called upon the state to ally itself with the North,

> The Rebel horde is on thy shore,
> Maryland! My Maryland!
> Arise and drive him from thy door,
> Maryland! My Maryland!

Once the threat was over, the parodies became more amusing. "Answer to 'My Maryland'"[28] poked fun at the Southern soldier's personal hygiene, or rather the lack thereof. "The Rebel feet are on our shore," the song tells Marylanders, because they can be smelled half a mile or more away. Where Randall saw "the blush upon thy cheek," the song sees only grime and dirt:

> I see no blush upon thy cheek
> Maryland, My Maryland
> It's not been washed for many a week,
> Maryland, My Maryland.

THE LESSER MARSEILLAISES

Likening "Maryland! My Maryland!" to the French "Marseillaise" stemmed not only from its patriotic and martial spirit, but also because Southerners saw many similarities between their own and the French Revolution. The story of the "Marseillaise" also appealed to Southerners.

In 1792 France was about to go to war with Austria. On 24 April of that year, Claude-Joseph Rouget de Lisle (1760–1836) was in Strasbourg. The mayor, who had heard that de Lisle, an engineer by profession, had a talent for writing poetry and music, invited him to dinner. During the evening, the mayor asked the composer if he could write a martial song to send the six hundred volunteers from Strasbourg marching off to join the army the next day. Such a song, he suggested, might also raise the patriotic spirits of those remaining behind.

De Lisle was flattered by the invitation. Already aroused by the crisis, he went home and in an emotional burst of creativity wrote the song that would become the French national anthem. His song so stirred the passions of the crowd gathered in the public square the next day that instead of six hundred, nine hundred men left to join the army.

De Lisle called his song, "The War Song of the Army of the Rhine." The name was changed a few months later when soldiers from Marseille came to Paris singing it, and it quickly was dubbed "the song of the Marseilles [la chanson marseillaise]," and then simply, "Marseillaise."

During the fighting between the French and the Austrians later that year, the French commander saw his right flank was about to be turned and rushed into the melee singing the "Marseillaise." His inspirited men checked the Austrian advance, snatching victory from otherwise certain defeat.

Years later in 1851, George F. Root, who composed many of the best songs of the Civil War, was in Paris on the Fourth of July, along with some countrymen. During their dinner they began singing "The Star-Spangled Banner" and other patriotic American tunes. Someone suggested they should also compliment the French and Root burst out with the "Marseillaise." When they were a few verses into the song, the lady of the house burst into the room and frantically begged them to stop. The song, she assured them, would arouse passersby who would lose their self-control and rush into her house and ruin it. The Americans tried to calm her. Surely she was overreacting. But the woman was right—a large group of people had gathered outside and were about to storm the house. Seeing the danger, an old soldier boarding in the house mollified the crowd by explaining the presence of the Americans. Unknown to Root and his friends, a few years before, the French government had forbade the singing of the "Marseillaise" because of the passions the song invariably aroused among the citizenry.[29]

The "Marseillaise" was especially popular in Louisiana with its large French population. When the war broke out, it was a ready-made rallying tune. Armand Blackmar penned new lyrics to it to make it more appropriate to the Southern cause and jointly published it with H. Siegling in Charleston. The caption title was "The Southern Marseillaise:"[30]

> Sons of the South awake to glory
> A thousand voices bid you rise,
> Your children, wives and grandsires hoary;
> Gaze on you now with trusting eyes
> Gaze on you now with trusting eyes,

> March on! March on!
> All hearts resolved on Victory or Death,
> March on! March on!
> All hearts resolved, on Victory or Death.

By 1862 Blackmar had already put out five editions, the fifth with a cover depicting both the Confederate and French flags. Other Southern publishers issued their own versions, often juxtaposing "Southern" and "Marseillaise" in the titles.[31] Placing "Marseillaise" in the title of a dance tune guaranteed sales, even when the music bore no resemblance to the original. It was merely enough to state that a tune was "Sur le motif de la Marseillaise."

Virginia had its own "Marseillaise." Published jointly by George Dunn in Richmond and Julian Selby in Columbia, South Carolina, it was the most tuneful of the wanna-bes and had a catchy chorus:[32]

> Virginia hears the dreadful summons,
> Sounding hoarsely from afar;
> On her sons she calls, and calmly,
> Bids them now prepare for war.
> Bids them now prepare for war.
> With manly hearts, and hands to aid her,
> She cares not how her foemen swarm,
> She bares her bosom to the storm:
> While she laughs to scorn the proud invader.

Chorus

> To arms! Brothers dear;
> Gird on the trenchant band!
> Strike home! Strike home!
> No craven fear!
> For home and native land!
> Strike home! Strike home!
> No craven fear!
> For home and native land!

POSTSCRIPT

After the war, Randall settled in Augusta, Georgia, where he worked for the next twenty years as a reporter and then editor for the *Augusta*

Chronicle. The Randalls had several daughters, one of whom his wife named "Maryland," so that "should the poem die and our daughter live; or the daughter die and the poem live, in either case you will have 'My Maryland.'"[33]

In 1888 his friends persuaded him to take a job in Washington, D.C., on the staff of two Georgia congressmen. Randall didn't feel comfortable there. He still suffered from ill health, and the city's wintry winds and snow plagued him. He confessed to a friend that he hadn't had a happy week since setting foot in Washington.[34] After a few months, he moved to Baltimore where he worked as an editorial writer.

Although Randall continued to write poetry after the war, all his efforts were overshadowed by "Maryland! My Maryland!" which he felt was not as good as some of his postwar poems. It had "handicapped" him, he said. He had written better poems, but the world still honored him primarily as the author of that wartime lyric.[35]

The best of these postwar poems, he thought, was "At Arlington." Its inspiration came from an incident that occurred at Arlington Cemetery several years after the war. During a ceremonial decoration of the graves of Federal soldiers fallen in the war, a group of women entered the grounds intending to lay flowers on the graves of the thirty Confederate soldiers also interred there. They were stopped at bayonet point and turned back. During the night high winds swept across the burial field. In the morning, the flowers placed upon the Federal plots the day before decorated the thirty Confederate graves. To Randall, it seemed as if God himself had intervened; he commemorated the incident with the poem.

Despite being in the limelight during and after the war, Randall remained a humble man. During the celebration of the Yorktown Centennial, he was one among the tens of thousands of people gathered around the Washington Monument in Baltimore. As part of the festivities, a band played "Maryland! My Maryland!" After the tune ended, people in the crowd jumped to their feet cheering wildly. Someone turned to Randall and asked if he were a Marylander. Yes, he was. Being a Marylander, didn't he feel very proud of that song, the man asked? Not especially, Randall answered. He confessed that he was, in fact, the one who had written it and was willing to bet there wasn't a single person in that whole crowd who would lend him five dollars if he asked for it. "When you are dead we will give you a grand funeral," was the stranger's whimsical response.[36]

In 1907 Randall was the guest of honor at the State's "Maryland Day." A few days after returning to Augusta, he caught cold while attending a

morning mass and died shortly afterwards from complications. In remem-
brance of him as the "poet of the Cause, honored though lost," the state
of Maryland voted his wife and daughter an annuity of six hundred dollars
per year.[37]

"Maryland! My Maryland!" expressed basic human emotions that
broadened its appeal, and it contained a refrain that was easy to remember.
It escaped the historical shackles that inspired it and surfaced anew after the
Confederate States of America became a lost dream. In 1939 the Maryland
legislature adopted the song as its state anthem. Although few people outside the state have heard its lyrics, in the words of Sigmund Spaeth, "it
maintains a reputation far beyond that of any other State song, on a par
with the best of our national songs."[38]

CHAPTER 5

The Stars and Bars

A nation's flag is the visible symbol of its independence. During wartime, one stakes a claim on an enemy's territory with one's flag. A standing flag validates the claim. Its presence at home is reassuring; on an enemy's territory it challenges the adversary's integrity—if it can't remove that flag, it is powerless. Since a nation's flag is so intimately connected with its integrity and pride, it symbolizes a people's will to sacrifice their lives to safeguard or remove it.

The intense emotional attachment Americans have for their flag runs deep. In the repertoire of patriotic songs written in the South during the war, no topic outrivaled the flag and no symbol was more commonly displayed on the song's covers. The flag, an outward expression of atavistic patriotism, galvanized men and women to risk their lives to display it or rip it down. Millions rallied to defend it or keep it off their soil.

When Jefferson Davis took the oath of office as president of the provisional government of the Confederate States of America on 18 February 1861, the Confederacy had yet to adopt a national flag. Individual states within the Confederacy were better prepared. On 17 Novemeber 1860, in anticipation of its secession (which did not occur until 20 December 1860), South Carolina unfurled a white flag with a green palmetto tree on a gigantic pine liberty pole. Thousands of Charleston's citizenry cheered, bells rang throughout the city, a cannon fired a hundred rounds, and a band played the "Marseillaise" and then the "Miserere," from *Il Trovatore,* as a funeral dirge for the erstwhile Union.[1]

Other Southern states adopted new flags when they seceded and adopted even newer ones when they joined the Confederacy.[2] The flag that fluttered over the capitol in Montgomery, Alabama, on Jefferson Davis's inauguration day was that state's new flag—white, with the state arms, its motto on one side, and seven stars surmounting the inscription, "Our Homes, Our Rights, We entrust to Your Keeping, Brave Sons of Alabama," on the other.

Shortly after Davis was sworn in as provisional president, William Porcher Miles, a South Carolinian, and one of Davis's staunchest supporters, was appointed head of the "Committee on Flag, Seal, Coat of Arms, and Motto." Miles's unwritten deadline for adoption of a Southern flag was 4 March 1861 to coincide with Abraham Lincoln's inauguration as president of the United States of America.

Over two hundred flag designs were submitted to Miles's committee, most of them variations of the "Stars and Stripes." The winner had the same three colors of red, white, and blue and the same seven-pointed stars on a blue canton in the upper left-hand corner, one for each state (seven at that time). But instead of thirteen stripes, it had three horizontal stripes ("bars") of equal width. The middle bar was white; the upper and lower, red. The new flag was immediately nicknamed the "Stars and Bars."[3]

Approval of the design came the day of the deadline. Within two hours of its adoption "fair and nimble fingers" stitched it and it was rushed to the capitol in Montgomery where it was raised by Miss Letitia Christian Tyler, granddaughter of former president John Tyler.

"A GREAT INFLUENCE UPON THE POPULAR HEART"

This "is the first time in the history of this country that the Stars and Stripes have been humbled," Francis W. Pickens, South Carolina's haughty governor, boasted to the swarming crowd gathered below his balcony. For two days Charleston's cannons had ripped through Fort Sumter. Now that it had capitulated, Pickens gloated: "That proud flag was never lowered before to any nation on the earth. We have lowered it in humility before the palmetto and Confederate flags. The flag of the United States has triumphed for seventy years; but to-day, the 13th of April it has been humbled, and humbled before the glorious little State of South Carolina."[4]

The "Stars and Stripes" that had flown above the fort was tattered and in shreds. According to the surrender terms, Maj. Robert Anderson, the fort's commanding officer, was allowed to salute the colors a last time. On the day the Federals abandoned the fort, the "Stars and Stripes" was raised once again while fifty of the fort's cannons fired a last salute. During the salvo a spark from the guns ignited ammunition near one of the guns. One soldier was killed outright, another was mortally wounded; several were less critically hurt. As the injured were cared for, the flag was lowered and handed over to Anderson and his men who boarded the steamer for the North.

Pickens was right. The "Stars and Stripes" had been humbled. In the best tradition of entrepreneurial sleaze, a shopkeeper in Charleston sold pieces from the remaining flagstaff as tokens and charms.[5] But by taking the flag with him, Anderson kept it from further insult.

The salvaged banner was stored in a vault at the Metropolitan Bank in New York but was periodically removed by the Sanitary Commission, a social reform group, which relied on its potent symbolism for their fund-raising work. In each town, the commission symbolically auctioned off the flag. Winners demonstrated their patriotism by ceremoniously handing it back to the commission, which then took the flag to the next town. Four years later, on the anniversary of Fort Sumter's surrender, Maj. Gen. Anderson raised that same tattered flag over the fort, restoring it to its former place of honor, while onlookers sang "Rally Round the Flag, Boys" and "The Star-Spangled Banner."[6]

After Fort Sumter's evacuation, the North bloomed with Stars and Stripes. "Every window-shutter is tied with the inevitable red, white, and blue, and dogs, even, are wrapped in the stars-spangled banner," wrote a correspondent to the *Charleston News*.[7] So great was the demand for flags, flag makers couldn't make them fast enough. In New York, the price of bunting rose from $4.75 to $28! Book muslin, the material used to make the stars, rose from 10 cents a yard to $3!

After Fort Sumter's fall, the "Stars and Stripes" became an ineffable symbol to the North. A Massachusetts man named Steele discovered for himself the emotional attachment people felt for that flag. Steele was a Southern sympathizer and flaunted it. In support of his cause, he hoisted a secession flag at his home in East Fairhaven. Steele's neighbors didn't share his feelings. "Take the flag down," they warned him. Steele refused and threatened to shoot anyone who tried to lower it. Incensed, his neighbors converged on his house, overpowered him, and marched him three miles to the town of Mattapoisett where they tarred and feathered him, forced three cheers for the "Stars and Stripes" out of him, and warned him never to raise any other flag.[8]

The first Union officer to die in the war was killed over a flag. Shortly after Virginia seceded, Lincoln sent troops to occupy Alexandria. On 24 May 1861 Col. E. Elmer Ellsworth led the Eleventh New York Fire

Zouaves into the town. Ellsworth, a patent attorney, had trained a militia company in Illinois, and had befriended Abraham Lincoln in Chicago. In New York he helped recruit a regiment of New York volunteer firemen, which he outfitted in the outlandish baggy red uniforms of the French Zouaves. As he led his regiment down Alexandria's streets, Ellsworth spotted a Confederate flag waving from the roof of the Marshall House Hotel. To Ellsworth this symbol was a challenge to the Union that could not be ignored. He rushed into the hotel, his troops behind him, climbed onto the roof, cut the flag down, tucked the trophy under his arm, and headed back for the street. On the way up, he passed the owner, James T. Jackson, a fervent Confederate patriot who had boasted earlier that the flag would never be taken down, except over his dead body. As Ellsworth came down from the roof holding the flag, Jackson shot him. Seconds later he was in turn shot by one of Ellsworth's unit.[9]

Both men became instant martyrs to their respective sides. Ellsworth's body lay in state in the White House. Editorials praised his courage; a broadside titled "Remember Ellsworth" celebrated his heroism. A Southern broadside, "Jackson's Requiem," praised his courage. Another tribute to Jackson, sung to the tune of "Scots wha hae wi," extolled him as a Southern patriot:

> Here's to Jackson brave and true,
> Whom the base invaders slew,
> When their Ellsworth he shot through,
> On old Virginia's soil.

and cited his martyrdom as an example of the Southerner's determination to resist the Northern onslaught:

> There's many a Jackson yet to slay,
> Ere those vandals win the day;
> They may destroy, but ne'er can sway,
> The sons of Southern soil.[10]

In May 1862 displaying any red and white banner, the symbolic colors of the Confederate flag, became a treasonable offense in Maryland. Even a hint of red and white could be considered treasonous.[11]

BARBARA FRITCHIE

The most famous incident of the Civil War involving the flag is now part of American patriotic literature. Barring some poetic license, the event, which may have had some truth to it, occurred as follows.

On 6 September 1862 Maj. Gen. Thomas "Stonewall" Jackson entered Frederick, Virginia. Although the city was divided in its loyalties, no opposition met the Confederates. In fact Frederick looked like a ghost town. The streets were deserted. Every store was closed; every home shut. A few Union flags had once waved over Frederick; on that day, even the halyards were cut.

But as John Greenleaf Whittier describes her, Barbara Fritchie, a ninety-seven-year-old widow, was undaunted by Jackson or his battle-hardened minions. As the Confederates passed her house, she open flung her garret window and defiantly unfurled the "Stars and Stripes."

A Confederate officer barked "Halt! Fire!" Guns roared. The flagstaff splintered, but held.

Resolute, Barbara Fritchie appeared in the window. She broke off the stump, grasped it, and leaned out as far as she could, waving the flag over the Confederates, defying them:

> Fire at this old head, then, boys;
> is it not more venerable than your flag?

Whittier, who immortalized the indomitable Barbara Fritchie in his poem by that name, has Jackson saluting her uncommon valor with the words,

> "Who touches a hair of yon gray head
> Dies like a dog! March on!"

No other shots were fired at the flag. The columns trudged silently past Barbara Fritchie's home and the flag remained outside her window during the entire Confederate occupation of Frederick. Barbara Fritchie died shortly after Frederick was reoccupied by the Union, immortalized by Whittier's poem as one of America's best-loved and heralded defenders of the colors.[12] The South had brave women who were also prepared to give their lives for their flag, but they, unfortunately, did not have a Whittier to chronicle their deeds.

THE SOUTH CHOOSES A FLAG

Although many Southerners, like Governor Pickens, gloated at the humiliation to the "Stars and Stripes," others felt the South had a right to that
same flag. When the Confederate Congress debated the adoption of a new
flag, Mississippi's delegate spoke for many of his fellow congressmen when
he urged the Confederacy to adopt a flag "as similar as possible to that of
the United States, making only such changes as should give them distinction." Pressing his case, he eulogized the associations, which the old flag
represented, in such passionate terms that he was almost accused of treason.
The relation of the new flag finally selected by the Confederate Congress
to the "Stars and Stripes" was obvious.[13]

Many Southerners felt the same nostalgia for the original flag. "Adieu
to The Star Spangled Banner Forever," a song published in New Orleans in
1861, acknowledges "How dear to each heart was the star spangled Banner."[14] Another song, the "Stars and Bars," claimed the South had as much,
if not more, right to at least parts of the flag: "We claim the stars—the
stripes we yield."[15]

An editorial in the *Richmond Dispatch* discussed at length the South's
claim to the old flag: "As the old flag itself was not the author of our
wrongs, we tore off a piece of the dear old rag and set it up as a standard.
We took it for granted a flag was a divisible thing, and proceeded to set off
our proportion. So we took at a rough calculation, our share of the stars
and our fraction of the stripes, and put them together, and called them the
Confederate flag.'. . . We were clearly entitled to from seven to eleven stars,
and three or four of the stripes."[16]

Songs, like Harry Macarthy's "Origin of the Stars and Bars" published
in 1861,[17] eulogized the old flag:

> That flag, with its garland of fame,
> Proudly waved o'er my fathers and me,
> And my grandsires died to proclaim
> It the flag of the brave and the free;

and then explained why it had to be abandoned:

> Her glory, her honor, her fame,
> So we unfurl'd the Stars and the Bars,
> And the Confederate flag is its name.

In the North, Samuel F. B. Morse, inventor of the telegraph, acknowledged the South's legitimate claim to the flag and suggested as a compromise that it be split along the diagonal. The blue union containing the stars, he suggested, could be divided down the middle with the South retaining the number of stars representing the states in the Confederacy. The thirteen stripes could also be divided, with each side getting six and a half stripes.

"If we must be two nations," said Morse, "neither nation can lay exclusive claim to it [the flag] without manifest injustice and offense to the other. Neither will consent to throw it aside altogether for a new and strange device, with no associations of the past to hallow it." By splitting it, both sides would retain some of the "sacred memories of the past." And if in the future both sections found themselves allied against a common enemy, the two flags could be fitted together "and the glorious old flag of the Union, in its entirety, would again be hoisted, once more embracing all the sister States."[18] No one seriously entertained Morse's idea.

ADIEU TO THE STAR-SPANGLED BANNER

Not long after the South adopted its new flag, the citizens of Memphis conducted a public burial for the old flag. Five hundred citizens escorted the eight pallbearers carrying a coffin containing the "Stars and Stripes" to the burial pit in the public square while a band played the "Dead March." As the coffin was lowered into the ground, onlookers intoned "ashes to ashes, dust to dust."[19]

Many Southerners wrote nostalgic musical farewells to the old flag such as the previously mentioned "Adieu to The Star Spangled Banner Forever" and "Origin of the Stars and Bars." Missouri's brigadier general M. Jefferson Thompson's "The New Red, White And Blue" lamented the old flag's demise:[20]

> The Stars still shine bright in the Heavens
> But the Stripes shall be trailed in the dust
> They're no longer the sign of the haven
> Of the brave, of the free or the just.
> The Bars now in triumph shall wave
> O'er the land of the faithful and true
> Or the home of the southern brave
> Shall float the new Red White and Blue.

"Farewell to the Star Spangled Banner," one of the less nostalgic of the numerous "Farewell" songs written after the South's decision to adopt a new flag in 1861.

Other farewell songs were very vitriolic. "The Banner of the South . . . Respectfully dedicated to the Southern Confederacy of States"[21] calls the Union flag a "rag," and praises the constellation of stars in the Southern flag, especially Alabama's.

Northerners volleyed back the epithets in songs like James T. Fields's "The Stars and Stripes":

> Their flag is but a rag—
> Ours is the true one;
> Up with the Stars and Stripes—
> Down with the new one![22]

Once the Confederacy chose its new flag there was no end to the paeans celebrating its adoption as the national emblem. "Our Southern Flag"[23] exulted: "Yes, we've lifted our flag, we've raised it at last!" while "The Confederate Flag!"[24] gushed:

> Bright Banner of Freedom! with pride I unfold thee,
> Fair flag of my country, with love I behold thee.
> Gleaming above us in freshness and youth
> Emblem of Liberty, symbol of truth.

Some songs like "Hurrah for Our Flag" were enthusiastic declarations of patriotism;[25] others, like the "Flag of the Sunny South" were morose even in their dedications: "Dedicated to the Independent Soul That Never Courts a Smile, or Bends beneath a Frown."[26]

"The Stars of Our Banner" was self-conscious and maudlin, but sold so well the publisher issued four editions.[27] Since pretentious metaphor was marketable, the same songwriter subsequently composed "The Flag of the Free Eleven," and gave his audience pure bathos:[28]

> Over land and seas let it kiss the breeze,
> For the smile of approving Heaven
> Shall gleam in love from the realms above
> On the flag of the free Eleven.

Among the other tributes to the flag issued in sheet music was the "Southern Constellation," featuring a colorful cover with a woman holding the "Stars and Bars" in one hand and a sword pointed to the ground in the other.[29]

Many of these early tributes to the flag in sheet music are historically inter-esting because the covers reflect the anticipation that the Confederacy would eventually include many of the border states. When first issued, the cover for the "Confederate Flag," for instance, featured the "Stars and Bars" with fifteen stars, in anticipation of Delaware, Maryland, Missouri, and Kentucky joining the Confederacy; when reissued, there were only thirteen stars since Delaware and Maryland opted to stay in the Union.[30] "The Palmetto Song,"[31] with a lithographed cover by a pro-Southern Louisville, Kentucky, firm, Hart and Maphother, anticipated the eventual entry of the border states by depicting a palmetto tree between two "Stars and Bars," each with fifteen stars.

As each border state voted to remain in the Union, the number of stars on the covers was slowly reduced. The "Secession Quickstep" was pub-lished with a lavishly printed cover containing the Confederate flag with fourteen stars in three rows.[32] The cover for the first edition of the "Con-federates' Grand March"[33] featured an engraving of a soldier holding the "Stars and Bars" with fourteen stars. When it reached fifty thousand copies, the number of stars was reduced to thirteen.[34] In 1862 the "Stars and Bars" on the cover was replaced with the "Stainless Banner,"[35] the Confederacy's next flag (see below).

Despite reality, the publisher of "The Song of the South"[36] was opti-mistic that the recalcitrant border states would eventually come over to the Confederacy and printed the cover for the song with two "Stars and Bars." One of the flags had eleven stars and the caption below it, "The Flag As It Is"; the other had fifteen stars below which the caption was "The Flag As It Will Be."

THE CONFEDERATE BATTLE FLAG

The similarity between the "Stars and Bars" and the "Stars and Stripes" sometimes made it impossible to tell them apart from a distance, especially if the air were clogged with dust as it was during the Battle of First Manas-sas on 21 July 1861. Toward the end of the battle Confederate major gen-eral Jubal Early made a flanking movement, which turned the tide in favor of the South. During the maneuver, Maj. Gen. Beauregard, among others, had some trouble distinguishing whether soldiers on the field belonged to his army or the enemy's. In fact, after the battle, many on both sides believed each had used the other's flags as a stratagem.

Should the South continue to use its banner on the field, Southerners might fire on their own men. One alternative was to have troops fight under their own state flags. Beauregard was given the job of getting this approved. He wrote to William Porcher Miles, chairman of the House Military Committee, asking official approval for the change. But none of the Southern states, except Virginia, had furnished their troops with state flags, so the plan couldn't be implemented. Miles suggested the army adopt a unique flag of its own, and recommended a red flag with a blue Latin cross and stars. He himself had submitted this design to the Confederate Congress when it was considering a national flag but it had been rejected.

Beauregard liked the basic design but preferred a St. Andrew's instead of a Latin cross. The Cary sisters, Hetty and Jennie, and their cousin, Constance, were visiting Beauregard at his headquarters at Centreville, Virginia, at the time. A few days earlier they had introduced the new song "Maryland! My Maryland!" to the Southern army[37] and Beauregard asked what they thought of his idea.

The sisters offered to make several prototypes. The one Beauregard chose was a red flag, with a blue St. Andrew's cross running from corner to corner, the arms of which were bordered by a white stripe. Between the borders, the cross was spangled with twelve white stars representing the current Confederate states (and Kentucky). Each branch of the service was assigned a different-sized version of the flag. The infantry's flag was to be four-by-four feet; the artillery's was three-by-three; and the cavalry's two-and-a-half by two-and-a-half.

The new flag was ceremoniously presented to Brig. Gen. James Longstreet on 28 August. The sun posed brightly in the sky as Longstreet's ten-thousand-strong division marched to a high plain near Centreville, where they were then drawn up in battle array. Nine flags were planted in the ground in three groups of three. Standing next to the flags were Maj. Generals Beauregard, Johnston, Longstreet, Van Dorn, and others, all brilliantly outfitted in their uniforms of gray and gold. A command sounded and the various regimental bands began to play as the army took square formation.

Once the divisions were in place, a colonel rode forward and read the orders concerning the new banner. A chaplain then blessed the flag and the bands struck up the "Marseillaise" to the shouts of a thousand "huzzahs." After the band finished, thousands of voices called out for Beauregard to appear. The general dutifully mounted his black charger and rode along the lines as men cheered and regimental bands played "Dixie." Cheers came for Johnston, then Longstreet. Each high ranking general, in turn, rode through the lines amid thousands of cheers. After the ceremony, the rank and file were dismissed while all the officers gathered at Longstreet's quarters where they drank and caroused for the rest of the day.[38]

Although the army had adopted the new flag, it still had to be approved by the War Department, which officially did so on 1 October 1861. On 28 November the Cary sisters presented three battle flags, made from the silk of their own dresses, to Generals Johnston, Beauregard, and Van Dorn. Owing to its feminine origins, the color of the first battle flags under which the Confederate army fought was more pink than red. Years later, the flag made by Jennie Cary for General Beauregard draped his coffin as it had earlier that of Jefferson Davis. This same flag now hangs in the Washington Artillery Museum in New Orleans.

Additional flags were also made from dress material but silk did not hold up very well on the battlefield and had to be replaced. By 1862 all new battle flags were made of first-quality English wool bunting. Whereas the first silk flags had twelve stars (the extra for Kentucky), the wool flags had thirteen to accommodate Missouri, and instead of a yellow border on the outer edges, an orange one. The only other change to the battle flag occurred after the Battle of Chancellorsville (1 to 4 May 1863) when the orange border was changed to white. There were, however, actually two battle flags. Although both had the same design, the one carried by the Army of Virginia was square; that carried by the Army of Tennessee was rectangular.

Like the "Stars and Bars," the battle flag inspired a spate of new songs such as the "Confederate Battle Flag March,"[39] the "Battle Flag Grand March,"[40] and the "Battle-Flag Polka."[41] "Our Battle Flag!"[42] by James Pierpont (1822–93) explained the origins of the flag:

> 'Twas born a-midst the battle glare,
> 'Twas born a-midst the battle glare,
> Amidst th' Artillery's roar:
> 'Twas born while Southern steel repell'd
> The invader from our door;

James Pierpont is not a household name, but one of his songs, "Jingle Bells," is more popular today than when he wrote it in 1857. The original title was "The One-Horse Open Sleigh." When the Boston firm of Oliver Ditson reissued it in 1859, it renamed it "Jingle Bells."

Though he was an ardent Southerner and lived in the South during the war, Pierpont was born and educated in the North. While "Jingle Bells" is his best-known song today, during the war he was better known as the composer of "Gentle Nettie Moore." (Coincidentally, Pierpont was an uncle to financier J. P. Morgan; the P. stands for Pierpont).

Although "The Cross of the South"[43] seems like it was also inspired by the battle flag, it actually predated the new flag by several months. Published in Baltimore, around March 1861, it was written to the tune of "The Star-Spangled Banner."

Likewise, another song, "The Southern Cross," by Richmond lawyer St. George Tucker, with music by C. L. Peticolas, an equally prominent Richmond composer of that time, was also written in March 1861 before hostilities began.[44]

ADIEU TO THE STARS AND BARS

In addition to approving adoption of a battle flag, the Confederate Congress was also pressured into scuttling the "Stars and Bars" because Confederate soldiers were still mistaking it for the "Star-Spangled Banner" and were firing on their own side.

On 7 December 1861 the *Richmond Dispatch* called adoption of the similar flag "a natural, but most pernicious blunder." Beauty and good taste were desirable attributes, but the essential feature of a flag was distinctiveness—a country's flag had to look unmistakably different from any other's. This was basic, fundamental, elemental, and in this, the Confederate flag was "a lamentable and total failure, absolute and irredeemable." The paper explained the necessity of having a distinctive flag:

> Our enemies are of the same race with ourselves, of the same color, and even shade of complexion; they speak the same language, wear like clothing, and are of like form and stature.
>
> Our general appearance being the same, we must rely solely upon symbols for distinction. The danger of mistake is great, after all possible precautions have been taken; sufficient attention has never been paid to this important matter, involving life or death, victory or defeat. Our badges, uniforms, flags, should be perfectly distinguishable from those of the enemy. Our first and distant information is dependent solely on the flag.[45]

THE STAINLESS BANNER

Bowing to pressure and circumstance, the Confederate Congress adopted a new flag on 1 May 1863. By that time there was much less fervor attached to "sharing" the "Stars and Stripes," and the idea was abandoned. To avoid any possible similarity to the Federal flag, the new Southern flag had no bars and no stripes, just a white field, which was twice as long as it was wide.

Although the battle flag was immensely popular, the Confederate Congress never adopted it as the nation's emblem. Instead it incorporated it in the union located in the upper left-hand corner of the new flag.

A white standard was appropriate, wrote the editor of the *Savannah Daily Morning News,* because "as a people, we are fighting to maintain the Heaven-ordained supremacy of the white man over the inferior or colored race; a white flag would thus be emblematical of our cause."[46]

The only song to celebrate the new flag was "The Star Spangled Cross and the Pure Field of White." Published in 1864, the cover featured a lithograph of the new flag and a defeatist chorus that reflected the South's fortunes at the time:[47]

> We'll stand by the Cross and the pure field of white,
> While a shred's left to float on the air:
> Our trust is in God, who can help us in fight,
> And defend those who ask Him in prayer.

Five other pieces of sheet music celebrating the new flag on their covers are "Confederates' Grand March," "Never Surrender," "I Dream of Thee," "The Southern Marseillaise," and "Battery Wagner." The outpost honored in the latter almost fell to a black Massachusetts regiment in 1864, and the battle was commemorated in the movie "Glory."[48]

Front page for "Battery Wagner" depicting "Stainless Banner." The assault on Battery Wagner was the focus of the movie "Glory."

From the start, the new flag, nicknamed the "Stainless Banner" because of its large field of white, emblemized fallen hopes. It was used to drape "Stonewall" Jackson's coffin on its passage to Hollywood Cemetery in Richmond. Owing to its association with Jackson's funeral, the flag was sometimes called the "Jackson flag," an association strengthened by the juxtaposition of Jackson's portrait and the flag on bonds and money issued by the Confederate government in 1864 and 1865.

To many Southerners, the "Stainless Banner" was a white elephant. Against a cloudy background, it was hard to distinguish from a distance and it soiled easily. Oversized, it didn't flare gracefully in the breeze and when it rested limply on the flagstaff it looked like a flag of truce—a use to which it was put shortly after its adoption.

On 7 May 1863 the Rebel ironclad, *Atlanta,* sailed out of Savannah harbor, the new banner proudly waving in the breeze. The ship was to go to sea via Warsaw Sound, proceed to Port Royal, and damage Federal shipping as much as possible. But the ship's progress was delayed, and on 17 June the *Atlanta* was confronted by two Union ironclads. After a fifteen-minute battle, the captain of the *Atlanta* hauled down the new rebel flag, tore off a large patch from its white banner, and hoisted it in surrender.[49]

The Confederate Congress soon admitted its blunder and, about a month before Lee surrendered at Appomattox (9 April 1865), adopted a modification of the "Stainless Banner," which was less ungainly. The new flag retained the union with the battle flag and added a red bar at the edge of the white field to keep it from being mistaken for a flag of truce.

Like the "Stainless Banner," it too went unheralded.

FURL THAT BANNER

Perhaps there is no better insight into the hearts and minds of those millions of Southerners who still cling to the Confederate flag with such devotion than "The Conquered Banner,"[50] a poem written at the close of the Civil War by Father Abram J. Ryan, a former chaplain in the Confederate army.

Abram Joseph Ryan (1838-86) was born in Norfolk, Virginia, the son of Irish immigrants. He took his vows in 1856 and when the war broke out, he enlisted as a chaplain in the Confederate army and was stationed for a while in Clarkesville and Nashville, Tennessee. During the smallpox epidemic in New Orleans from 1862 to 1863, he tended the sick.

After the war, he was sent to Augusta, Georgia, where he lived for five years and founded a Catholic paper, *The Banner of the South*. In 1870 he was transferred to Mobile, Alabama, and shortly afterward, began giving lectures throughout the North and West for the benefit of charities looking after Southern victims of the war. Ill health forced him to leave the priesthood and he retired to Louisville where he spent the remainder of his life.

Various events and tragedies during the war inspired him to write many poems, several of which were set to music such as "In Memorium" and "The Sword of Robert E. Lee." These tributes endeared him to the South but it was his poem "The Conquered Banner," more than any other of his works, that earned him the title of "Poet of the Lost Cause."

Ryan wrote "The Conquered Banner" in Knoxville, Tennessee, shortly after Lee's surrender. Like many of the memorable poems of the war, it was written in less than an hour. Ryan expressed the feelings of the entire South. Overnight, it became the requiem for the "Lost Cause":

> Furl that Banner, for 'tis weary,
> Round its staff 'tis drooping dreary:
>   Furl it, fold it,—it is best;
> For there's not a man to wave it,
> And there's not a sword to save it,
> And there's not one left to lave it,
> In the blood which heroes gave it,
> And its foes now scorn and brave it:
>   Furl it, hide it,—let it rest!
> Furl that Banner, softly, slowly;
> Treat it gently—it is holy,
>   For it droops above the dead;
> Touch it not—unfold it never,
> Let it droop there, furled forever,—
>   For its peoples hopes are fled.[50]

POSTSCRIPT

Few Americans, North or South would have argued with the *Huntsville Democrat* on 6 February 1861, when it said flags may seem like a "trifling consequence to some," but to many others they exercise "a great influence upon the popular heart."[52]

Deeply held emotions are attached to flags because they represent not only a political entity but a particular culture. Under a siege mentality, regions, communities, cultures, and nations close ranks and cherish the symbols of their identity. This is the reason songs about the flag were so common during the Civil War, especially in the South. It is not surprising that the Confederate battle flag is undoubtedly the most identifiable icon of the Civil War and the symbol most closely associated with the Confederacy.

In the last two decades many cultural battles have been fought over that symbol. In 1997 the Maryland State Motor Vehicle Administration recalled a number of license plates containing the Confederate battle flag's image, which it had issued to members of the Sons of Confederate Veterans. The reason for the unprecedented decision, it said, was the volume of complaints it had received from thousands of African Americans who identified the symbol with slavery, cross burnings, and lynchings.

South Carolina equally wars with itself over the removal of the flag from its capitol dome. The flag was removed after Gov. David Beasley said he changed his mind after a prayer and Bible study session, which made him see that the emblem had become a symbol of strife. His invocation of the Bible immediately led a number of Christian pastors to nail a notice to his door entitled, "A Moral Defense of the Confederate Flag," which asserted the flag was a "Christian symbol" based on the cross of St. Andrew. It was also a Christian symbol, they said, because the X-shaped cross was the Greek letter, "Chi," which has long been a Christian abbreviation for "Christ." Although the pastors did not dispute that white supremacy groups used the flag as their symbol, they contended that this did not make the flag itself a symbol of hate.[53]

For the Sons of Confederate Veterans and for thousands if not millions of Southerners, the Confederate battle flag is a symbol of a proud heritage for which their grandfathers and great-grandfathers died. As an icon the flag recalls duty fulfilled, not a mushy idea about a "Lost Cause." Men gave their lives to prevent their flag from falling into enemy hands; the first casualties of the war were over a flag. The raising of the Confederate battle flag is no less a potent symbol for many Southerners than is the indelible image of the raising of the American flag on Iwo Jima for all Americans.

For millions of African Americans the banner symbolizes a time in their collective history when they were "property," human chattel. It reminds them of an era when they could be trafficked like pigs or cows. It represents the various hate groups that have adopted it as their emblem because of the flag's association with slavery.

The conflicting passions attached to this flag cannot be amicably settled. The "house" is still divided against itself. For millions the Confederate battle emblem is a symbol of racism; for millions of others it is a symbol of Southern pride. When it comes to the flag, the Civil War is not yet over.

CHAPTER 6

Jefferson Davis
and His Generals

The sense of national consciousness that followed the creation of the Confederacy needed not only to focus on material symbols but also on "eidolons." Eidolons are "ideal figures," public personages endowed with almost mythical stature who personify the core values and aspirations of a large population.[1]

Eidolons are the larger-than-life individuals who become abstractions who symbolize hope and purpose for large numbers of people. Public eidolons are especially important for creating emotional bonds between a nation's leaders and its populace. The absence of eidolons leaves a void in national collective emotional psyches. Nation-builders need eidolons to personify their nationhood and its ideals.

Although Robert E. Lee is unquestionably the South's most beloved exemplar, Lee's status as a national icon did not emerge until after the war. Lee is hardly mentioned in Confederate songs. Jefferson Davis, on the other hand, never achieved Lee's eidolonic stature, but as the Confederacy's first president, he was the natural candidate for the Confederacy's model-seeking songwriters.

The earliest musical accolades to celebrate Davis as the South's ideal symbol came from outside the Confederacy when Baltimore music publishers, George Willig and Henry Mcaffery, each published sheet music for dance tunes dedicated "To President Jefferson Davis." The cover for Willig's tune, the "Confederacy March," is especially noteworthy for featuring Davis's portrait and a copy of his autograph. Willig followed up this tribute with another tune with Davis's name specifically in the title.[2]

Musical recognition of Davis within the Confederacy appeared almost as quickly. In New Orleans, Werlein and Halsey published several pieces of music with Davis's name in the title or dedicated to him, among them, "Jefferson Davis, First President of the Confederate States of America," which like "Confederacy March," featured an engraving of Davis on the cover.[3]

New Orleans publisher, Armand Blackmar, had a major hit in "Our First President's Quickstep."[4] The title reflects both the composer's confidence in the Confederacy's prospects and his intent to place Davis on an equal footing with America's other iconic figure, Washington. The sheet music, which featured Davis's lithographic image on its cover, was reissued nine times during the first two years of the war. The Federal occupation of New Orleans, forced Blackmar to close his presses but his brother set up shop in Augusta, Georgia, where he reprinted the "ninth edition" of the tune. Undoubtedly among the reasons for its popularity was its optimistic title and Davis's lithographed image. Displaying sheet music in their homes, which had Davis's portrait and the words "First President of the Confederate States," afforded Confederate families from all walks of life a relatively inexpensive way of sharing in the ethos of their emergent nationalism.

Besides these tunes, there were eight additional musical tributes published in Davis's honor in 1861. One of these is particularly noteworthy because of its regal dedication: "To His Excellency President Jefferson Davis."[5] Another piece of sheet music had an ornate colored cover featuring the "Stars and Bars" and contained the presumptuous dedication to

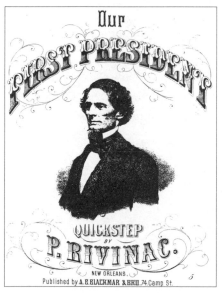

One of several musical tributes to Jefferson Davis in the early days of his presidency, featuring Davis' lithographic image on front page.

"His Excellency Jefferson Davis, President of the Confederate States of North America."[6]

Apart from the tributes to him in the titles or dedications of these dances and songs, Davis received much less attention in the lyrics of Confederate songs, especially those published as sheet music. Harry Macarthy's "The Bonnie Blue Flag"[7] mentions him in its first verse ("Davis, our loved President") and he is also mentioned in "The Southern Wagon" ("Jeff Davis is our president"), but apart from those songs, his name does not appear in any other sheet music.

There are, however, several tributes to him in other songs that were never turned into sheet music. "The Song of the Exile,"[8] a broadside written to the tune of "Dixie" in 1861 in Martinsburg, Virginia, features Davis as the champion of the Southern cause, and lamely rhymes "navies" with "Davis":

> We have no ships, we have no navies,
> But mighty faith in the great Jeff. Davis;
> Fight away, fight away, fight away
>   for Dixie's land.
>
> Abe's proclamation in a twinkle,
> Stirred up the blood of Rip Van Winkle;
>   Fight away, [etc.]
> Jeff Davis's answer was short and curt;
> "Fort Sumter's taken, and 'nobody's hurt'!"
>   Fight away, [etc.]

"Yankee Vandals,"[9] a parody of "Gay and Happy," has Davis in the vanguard, along with Generals Beauregard and Johnson, ready to turn away any invasion, just as they had at Manassas:

> Brave Jeff and glorious Beauregard,
> With dashing Johnson, noble, true
> Will meet their hireling host again,
> And scatter them like morning dew.

At the same time that Southern songwriters and composers were turning Davis into an eidolon who embodied their ideals and aspirations, they were articulating Lincoln's negative persona. As Davis's natural foil, these songs provided Southerners with an "inverted image of virtue" to bolster their self-esteem.[10] A popular Confederate ditty compared Davis's and Lincoln's mounts as metaphors for their respective personae:

> Jeff Davis rode a dapple gray,
> Lincoln rode a mule
> Jeff Davis is a gentleman,
> Abe Lincoln is a fool.[11]

One of the interesting aspects of Southern war songs is that they devote more attention to examining Lincoln's behavior and appearance than they do to praising Davis. One of the earliest and lengthiest of these derisive songs centered around Lincoln's surreptitious passage through Baltimore on his way to his inauguration. Warned of a rumored assassination plot, a disguised Lincoln decided on discretion rather than valor and passed through the city in the dead of night. The flight was lampooned in "The Abeiad,"[12] the cover of which shows a cartoon of Lincoln who flees a cannon just fired by a Confederate soldier. The soldier stands beneath the "Stars and Bars" flag of the Confederacy (with 7 stars). Lincoln wears a military cape and a Scottish cap, his alleged disguise during his clandestine passage through Baltimore.

> Away went Abram, meek or naught,
>   all in the midnight dark!
> Away went Abram, fast he flew!
>   no Judge that time could mark!
> And dreading still, Grimalkin's corpse,
>   or brickbat's envious blow,
> At dead of night, he slyly pass'd
>   thro' dreadful Baltimo'!
> So Abe stole into Washington,
>   (alas! the woeful day,)
> And fondly thought, poor foolish Abe!
>   "Well, four years here I'll stay!
> I'll stay, I'll stay,
>   Well, four years here I'll stay!"

Lincoln's dash through Baltimore, and his preinaugural assurances that "nobody's hurt,"[13] were also ridiculed in "The Song of the Exile":[14]

> Abe Lincoln tore through Baltimore
> In a baggage-car with fastened door;
> >   Fight away, fight away.
> And left his wife alas! alack!
> To perish on the railroad track!
> >   Fight away, fight away

"The Hobbie"[15] aimed at Lincoln's plight:

> Abe Lincoln's great hobby was playing the clown,
> With cloak and scotch cap, he put his foot down,
> Through Baltimore sneaked like a cunning expert;
> I'm safe, cried Old Abe, and there's nobody hurt!

"Jeff in Petticoats"[16] was the North's long awaited answer to Lincoln's humiliating midnight dash through Baltimore. Davis was taken prisoner on 10 March 1865 in Georgia, as he attempted to elude his captors. Newspapers claimed that prior to his capture he had donned his wife's dress as a disguise (this claim has never been substantiated).

Most of the songs and satires in the South featuring Lincoln were generally, if not good-natured, at least somewhat witty. Although highly partisan, John Hill Hewitt still humorously described Lincoln in "King Linkum the First," a musical burlesque he staged in 1863, as "the last of his die-nasty, a long drawn tyrant, uneasy in conscience, and addicted to rail-splitting."[17]

The Southern elite had little use for Lincoln, but they drew the line at personal insult. William Russell Smith's poem, "The Royal Ape" (1863), for example, was denounced by Southern newspapers for being abusive: " . . . we confess that such spiciness is not what we desire to see in Southern literature," said the *(Richmond) Magnolia Weekly.*[18] The *Index,* a vehicle for Confederate propaganda published in England, was equally reproachful. The poem, it told its readers, dealt with the Federal defeat at the first battle of Manassas and the subsequent confusion and consternation in Washington. "It is to be regretted that even in an avowed fiction a Southern writer should attempt to cast the slightest slur upon the domestic life of Mr. Lincoln. . . . If Mr. Lincoln were personally immoral—which he is not—it would still be indecorous to drag his private life into a public controversy."[19] Northern songs and literature were equally reticent where Davis's personal life was concerned.

Contemporary songs also reveal some interesting takes on how each side saw their respective leaders. Southern songwriters never alluded to

Davis's patrician past, whereas Northern songwriters praised Lincoln's humble origins, as in "Old Abe Lincoln Came Out of the Wilderness,"[20] sung to the tune of "The Old Gray Mare":[21]

> Old Abe Lincoln came out of the wilderness,
> Out of the wilderness, out of the wilderness
> Old Abe Lincoln came out of the wilderness
> Many long years ago.

"Lincoln and Liberty,"[22] sung to the tune of "Rosin the Beau," likewise celebrates his persona as a man of the people: "the son of Kentucky, The hero of Hoosierdom, The pride of the 'suckers' so lucky," and takes satisfaction in his lowly origins:

> They' find what by felling and mauling,
> Our railmaker statesman can do;
> For the people are everywhere calling
> For Lincoln and Liberty too.

Northern songwriters also felt a much greater personal warmth for Lincoln than Southern songwriters felt for Davis. Northern songs, for instance, refer to Lincoln as either father ("We Are Coming, Father Abr'am" and "Abraham's Daughter") or uncle ("We'll Fight for Uncle Abe").[23] Southern songwriters completely avoided such familiarity.

ALEXANDER STEPHENS

In contrast to Jefferson Davis, Alexander Stephens, Davis's vice president, is rarely mentioned in Confederate songs. "The Bonnie Blue Flag" acknowledges Stephens after first mentioning Davis, as "Stephens, Statesman rare,"[24] while "The Southern Wagon" refers to him only in passing ("Jeff Davis is our President, With Stephens by our side").[25] With the exception of another of Macarthy's songs, "The Volunteer," and two issues of "The Beauregard or Fort Sumter Polka,"[26] one of them with a portrait of Stephens, and the other quoting a statement by him in praise of General Beauregard, there are no other allusions to him in Confederate sheet music.

Stephens, who weighed less than a hundred pounds, was a spunky politician. He once started a fight with a man who weighed three hundred pounds and would have been killed if his adversary hadn't been restrained.

Despite Macarthy's tribute to both, Stephens and Davis didn't get along and Stephens often undermined Davis's presidency.

Other than Davis and Stephens, few Southern politicians are named in Confederate sheet music. One noteworthy exception is "fire-eater" William Lowndes Yancey, who received a brief mention in an 1861 song heralding "The Minute Men"[27] of South Carolina:

> With Calhoun for model and Yancey for guide
> Palmetto's brave cohorts are first in the field.

James Murray Mason and John Slidell are the only other Southern politicians to be cited in Confederate sheet music. These two Confederate ministers to England, whose illegal removal from the British ship, *Trent,* prompted a diplomatic row between England and the Federals, were jointly honored with a quickstep.[28] The "*Trent* Affair" also inspired a song, "The Gallant Girl That Smote the Dastard Tory Oh,"[29] about an incident that occurred during the removal of Slidell and his family from the *Trent.* In escorting the women off the ship, a Union officer placed his hand on the shoulder of one of Slidell's daughters. In anger, the girl retaliated by slapping the officer on the cheek.

Northern politicians are also rarely referred to in Confederate sheet music. William Henry Seward, who served as Lincoln's secretary of state, is the only Federal politician mentioned in this format. In "The Minute Men,"[30] Seward, rather than Lincoln, is held responsible for secession and the war:

> But where is that phantom your ancestors nursed?
> The Union!—base Seward has settled its doom,
> That demon of discord, for ever accursed!
> Its fate has consigned to a merciless tomb.

Politicians, with few exceptions, don't make good subjects for nationalistic songs. There was no shortage of parodies poking fun at them, but such songs had no place in the family parlor, and so weren't turned into sheet music.

Jefferson Davis's wife Varina Howell Davis, nicknamed "Queen" by some of her admirers, also received a brief musical tribute in "Our Queen Varine." Interestingly, the song was written and published by a Southerner living in England:[31]

President, The gallant and the brave;
Revered by all who own his sway,
By freedom and by slave,
Here's to the fair and brilliant one,
Who by his side is seen. . . .
Long may she be,
Long may we see
Varine our Queen,
Our Queen Varine.

All of the songs and marches dedicated to Davis in sheet music, with the exception of a single tune published by John Burke in Macon, Georgia, were issued in New Orleans or Mobile in 1861 or 1862. By 1863 people across the Confederacy were disenchanted with Davis's leadership. He was too private, humorless, and inflexible; not a man to invite closeness. He was also a micromanager. Trained at West Point and seasoned in the Mexican War, he second-guessed his field commanders and conflicted with high ranking generals such as Pierre Beauregard and Joe Johnston. His impetuosity, personal dislikes, political inflexibility, and poor judgment of people tarnished any personal appeal he might have enjoyed as president. Instead of praising their uninspiring president, Southerners reserved their affections for their military leaders, beginning with General P. G. T. Beauregard.

BEAUREGARD

The Louisiana Creole, Pierre Gustave Toutant Beauregard ("Old Bory"), was the Confederacy's first eidolon. Fort Sumter's surrender, brought about by his bombardment, catapulted him into the limelight and inspired musical tributes like "The Beauregard, or Fort Sumter Polka March."[32]

As with many of the first patriotic songs about the South, some of the earliest musical homages to Beauregard were published in Baltimore, among them "Beauregard's March" and "Salut a Beauregard."[33] The latter carries a publication date of 1862 but the text shows it was written much earlier:

Sumpter's [*sic*] fought, the victory won,
Abe's flag hauled down by Anderson.
Now the Border States no more will retard,
But wheel into line under Beauregard.

As with cannon, mortar, and petard,
We march to the rescue with Beauregard.

New Orleans composer and music publisher, Armand Blackmar, liked the way the author of "Salut a Beauregard" rhymed "petard" (a demolition charge) with Beauregard, and reprinted it with a slight variation on the cover of "Gen. Beauregard's Grand March: With Mortar, Paixhan and Petard, We send Old Abe our Beau-Regard."[34]

Sumter's fall also inspired a thirty-three-verse poem, "Sumter: A Ballad of 1861," by E. O. M., which first appeared in the *Columbia Banner;* and later, condensed in sheet music, was dedicated to and prominently featured Beauregard as the Confederacy's first national hero.[35]

The Southern victory at Manassas, where Beauregard also distinguished himself, inspired several other musical tributes to him, especially in Louisiana, his native state.[36] Significantly, Harry Macarthy's "The Volunteer; or, It Is My Country's Call,"[37] which mentions both Beauregard and Jefferson Davis, puts Beauregard first as the South's deliverer:

With Beauregard and Davis,
We'll gain our cause or die,
Win battles like Manassas.
And raise our battle-cry.

Confederate sheet music published during the first two years of the war regularly featured lithographic portraits of Beauregard on their covers. "The Beauregard Manassas Quick-Step,"[38] by A. Noir (Armand Blackmar's pseudonym), had a half-body portrait of Beauregard on the cover. After Blackmar opened his new shop in Augusta, Georgia, he reissued the piece with a new cover, featuring a small round portrait of Beauregard in the center flanked by two Roman-like figures.[39] Werlein and Halsey, Blackmar's New Orleans competitor, issued the same tune with a full cover lithograph of Beauregard astride his horse.[40]

Shortly after New Orleans was captured, Armand Blackmar published "Beauregard."[41] To protect the composers who probably lived in the city, he only listed their initials—"F. E. D." and "H. D." The song calls upon Beauregard to rescue the South from the Federals:

Freedom calls in time of need, Beauregard!
    Beauregard!
Freedom ne'er in doubt will plead, Beauregard!
    Beauregard!
Our soil's now tramp'd by hostile foe,
From afar, with steady hands strike blow for blow,
    With our Beauregard!
Beauregard! Beauregard! Beauregard!

By late 1862 Beauregard's star began to fade. James Ryder Randall's "There's Life in the Old Land Yet,"[42] however, still pinned Southern hopes on his prowess:

Minions! we sleep, but we are not dead,
We are crushed, we are scourget [*sic*], we are scarred;
We crouch 'tis to welcome the triumph tread
Of the peerless Beauregard.

Beauregard's confidence in himself was not shared by his superiors, especially Jefferson Davis. Beauregard, absorbed in his own persona, was often vain and arrogant. He quarreled with fellow officers and was resented

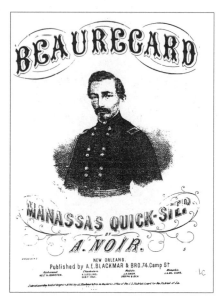

Dual musical celebration of the Confederacy's favorite eidolon, General P.G.T. Beauregard, and its first important military victory.

by many. He was brave, courageous, and an inspiring leader, but a mediocre general. His short temper and soaring ambition undermined his effectiveness. Though celebrated in more sheet music than any other Confederate military figure,[43] when he publicly embarrassed the president, Davis sent him west and Beauregard disappeared from the limelight.

In 1863 Beauregard's only musical tribute appeared in Herman Schreiner's "Beauregard's Charleston Quickstep, To the Hero of Shiloh & Charleston,"[44] which his father John Schreiner published in Macon and Savannah. In 1864 Beauregard's wife died in New Orleans and two pieces of sheet music were issued in her honor,[45] the only such tributes to a wife published during the war.

ROBERT E. LEE
Oddly, the stately and saintly Robert E. Lee was rarely mentioned in the lyrics of any Confederate sheet music, although his name appeared in the titles of a number of dance tunes such as "Gen. Lee's Grand March," which went through at least four editions.[46] After the war, a growing number of musical tributes celebrated Lee's musical apotheosis, including several tributes with the same title, "The Sword of Gen. Lee."[47]

"STONEWALL" JACKSON
Next to Beauregard, the Confederacy's most prominent musical eidolon was Maj. Gen. Thomas "Stonewall" Jackson. Prior to the war, Jackson had been a teacher at the Virginia Military Institute, where he instructed his students in the fine points of artillery as well as physics and chemistry.

Jackson was harder on his men than any general, yet no general was better loved by his men except perhaps Lee. Jackson was committed to the war effort. A deeply religious Presbyterian, he credited his God for every victory. His men called him "Old Blue Eyes" because of his luminous blue eyes. His trademarks were a faded blue coat and a hat he wore slouched over his head.

Jackson's first musical tribute came in 1862 with "The Stonewall Jackson Grand March."[48] His best-known musical tribute, however, was "Stonewall Jackson's Way,"[49] which describes Jackson's appearance and the dedicated men who follow him despite the hardships he causes them and their families to endure:

We see him now—the old slouched hat
Cocked o'er his eye askew;
The shrew'd, dry smile; the speech so pat,
So calm, so blunt, so true;
The 'Blue-light Elder' knows em well—
Says he, "that's Banks,[50] he's fond of shell,
Lord save his soul! we'll give him—well,
That's Stonewall Jackson's' way."

What matter if our shoes are worn?
What matter if our feet are torn?
Quick step! "We're with him before dawn!"
That's Stonewall Jackson's' way.

The song was published anonymously in Richmond by J. W. Randolph, with the fictional notice that it had been "Found on a Confederate Sergeant of the old Stonewall Brigade taken at Winchester, Va." The reason for the anonymity and the falsification was to keep its author, John W. Palmer, from being arrested as a Southern sympathizer.

Born in Baltimore, John Williamson Palmer (1825-1906) was the son of a physician who followed in his father's footsteps into medical school. Instead of going into practice in Baltimore, however, he became a "forty-niner" and trekked to San Francisco, where for a time he was the city's only doctor. Later he began writing professionally.

In 1861 he accepted a job as war correspondent for the *New York Times.* Fired because of his overtly pro-Southern bias, he quickly found a job at Horace Greeley's *New York Tribune.* Years after the war, Palmer described how he had come to write his best known poem.

In September 1862 he was staying at a hotel in a part of Maryland near the Virginia border. Early on the morning of the sixteenth he heard the loud roar of guns in the air. It was the signal for a great battle.

I knew that Stonewall was in it, whatever it might be; it was his way—'Stonewall Jackson's way.' I had twice put that phrase into my war letters, and other correspondents, finding it handy, had quoted it in theirs. I paced the piazza and whistled a song of Oregon lumbermen and loggers that I had learned from a California adventurer in Honolulu. The two thoughts were coupled and welded into one to make a song; and as the words gathered to the call of the tune I wrote the ballad of 'Stonewall Jackson's Way' with the roar of those guns in my ears. On the morrow I added the last stanza.

After the battle Palmer made his way to Baltimore where he showed the song to his father. He in turn showed it to certain members of the Maryland Club. They took it to a trusted printer who struck off a dozen copies, principally for private distribution. "That first printed copy of the song," says Palmer, "was headed 'Found on a Rebel Sergeant of the Old Stonewall Brigade, Taken at Winchester'," to mislead the Federal provost marshall, as were the address and date: Martinsburg, 13 September 1862, should it be found by the Federals.[51] After the war, Palmer wrote several other poems that were set to music, a number of travel books, and a novel; and translated two books from French to English.

In 1863 the publication of several other musical tributes as sheet music honored Jackson, among them "Stonewall Jackson's Grand March," a piano piece "Illustrative of 'Stonewall Jackson's Way'."[52] Other musical tributes included "'Stonewall' Jackson's Grand March," which went through two editions and is especially noteworthy for its dedication to "Lt. Gen. Thomas J. Jackson: The Southern Hero."[53] Two pillars and a list of Jackson's battles on each base illustrated the cover. Shortly thereafter, the "Stonewall Jackson's Midnight Review Grand March"[54] was published, with a notice on the caption page that it "was played the same night when he received his mortal wound."

Dead, Jackson inspired more musical tributes than when he was alive. Thomas DeLeon said he had in his collection no less than forty-seven melodies and dirges on Jackson.[55] The best of these was "The Stonewall Brigade, Dedicated to the Memory of Stonewall Jackson, The Immortal Southern Hero, and his brave Veterans":[56]

> A gallant Christian hero of untarnished fame,
> General Stonewall Jackson was his famous name;
> He led us oft in brilliant charge and fearful fight,
> And where we went the foe was always put to flight.

Although a Confederate, Jackson was also highly esteemed in the North, and he received a very unusual homage in 1864 from a New York music publisher in "'Stonewall' Jackson's Prayer,"[57] the only Confederate general to be so honored.

"JEB" STUART

James Ewell Brown "Jeb" Stuart was one of the most adored of the Confederacy's generals. He was both a "man's man," admired widely for his courage, and a "lady's man," the heartthrob of the Confederacy.

Stuart was undoubtedly the most flamboyant figure in the Confederacy, resplendent in his brilliant gold-braided uniform and his black-plumed hat. He was also the most musically inclined and frequently led his men into battle singing, while his banjo player Sam Sweeney strummed a tune behind him.[58]

Brave, handsome (his classmates at West Point called him "Beauty"), resourceful, colorful, never despondent, laughing, singing, and dancing late into the night at "The Bower," his headquarters near Charleston, Virginia, or whistling as he went into battle, "Jeb" Stuart was the kind of "cavalier" about whom romances were written. It is somewhat surprising, therefore, that Stuart was the subject of so few songs. "Riding a Raid," the song that is always associated with him, was issued with two distinct covers. One has a lithograph of Stuart on horseback, sporting a wide sash, high boots, and his trademark plumed hat;[59] the other has a picture of Jackson, under whom Stuart served.[60] Written to the tune of the Scottish folk song "Bonnie Dundee," which goes back to the 1620s, it gives Jackson top billing, but the real hero of the song is Stuart:

> 'Tis old Stonewall the Rebel that leans on his sword,
> And while we are mounting prays low to the Lord
> "Now each cavalier that loves Honor and Right,
> Let him follow the feather of Stuart to-night. . . .

Also surprising is the almost total absence of any mention in sheet music of Stuart's hundred-mile ride around George G. McClellan's one hundred thousand strong army on 12 to 16 June 1862 in which Stuart lost only one man.[61] Though the exploit gained the South very little by way of a military victory, it lifted Southern morale tremendously and made

Stuart a dashing hero. Stuart's own men celebrated their exploit in "Jine the Cavalry":[62]

> We're the boys who rode around McClellian [sic]
> Rode around McClellian [sic].

The only reference to the extraordinary feat in sheet music was Earnest Halphin's "Coming at Last!"[63] which was published not in the Confederacy but in Baltimore. The song describes the exploit's bravado and intimates worse things to come:

> Circling Mac's army, Three days at work,
> Under that smile of theirs, Famine may lurk
> Our with the best you have, Fill the bowl fast,
> For Jeff's Ragged Riders, are Coming at last!
> Jeff's Ragged Riders, are Coming at last!

There were also a few other songs and dances dedicated to Stuart. The "Southern Troopers,"[64] by Charles C. Nordendorf, has the most ludicrous chorus of any Civil War song:

> Hurrah hurrah hurrah
> Go on my charger in gallop
> hop, hop hop hop hop, hop hop hop hop hop
> Go on my charger in gallop
> hop hop hop, hop, hop, hop in gallop.

Another song, "A Confederate Raid,"[65] dedicated to and in praise of Stuart, is interesting mainly because it was written and published in England by a Confederate sympathizer carried away by his or her romantic image of the cavalier at war:

> Who are they who ride so rapidly, merrily,
> Splashing and dashing o'er broad Potomac?
> There they go, on the go valiantly, gallantly,
> Daring and scaring the foe on their track.
> 'Tis Stuart! 'tis Stuart! hurrah!
> With his bold Cavaliers of the West:

'Tis his twentieth raid, hurrah!
No rest for brave Stuart, no rest!
Now see them returning so cheery, tho' weary,
And laden with spoil of every kind,
With boots and with blankets,
With all sorts of toggery
Each is adorning himself to his mind.

A song written by William W. Blackford, an officer on Stuart's staff, to the tune of "The Cavalier's Glee,"[66] echoes the esprit de corps among Stuart's own men.

Spur on! spur on! we love the bounding
Of barbs that bear us to the fray;
"The charge" our bugles now are sounding,
And our bold Stuart leads the way

Spur on! spur on! we love the rushing
Of steeds that spurn the turf they tread;
We'll through the Northern ranks go crushing,
With our proud battle-flag o'erhead.

"Stuart," a song published in 1864 and published as part of Blackmar's *Southern Songs of the War*,[67] was probably written shortly after Stuart's death at the Battle of Yellow Tavern (11 May 1864) and eulogizes the fallen cavalier who "At the feet of our country's God, in Heaven,/Thou has laid another sword."

JOHN HUNT MORGAN

Although less celebrated in history, partisan ranger John Hunt Morgan was a genuine folk hero, rhapsodized in many more pieces of music than the more flamboyant Stuart. Six feet tall, weighing about 185 pounds, he was lean, handsome, and gifted with a winsome smile. In the minds of thousands of Southerners, he was the epitome of the chivalrous swashbuckler of old.

A native Kentuckian, Morgan joined the Confederate army as a scout and then became leader of a guerrilla band of about four thousand men, with the rank of brigadier general. He was arrested and imprisoned in 1863 in Columbus, Ohio, but managed to escape by tunneling out of his cell and scaling a twenty-five-foot high wall. The first verses of "How Are You? John Morgan" describe his capture, imprisonment, and the attempt to humiliate him. Hunt's escape by digging a tunnel with a knife climaxes the song and the description of his return to "Dixie" riding a mule is intended to hearten the South to fight on and eventually triumph:[68]

> And thus the Rebel chieftain's pride,
> They sought to humble low,
> But Southern valor dont [sic] subside
> No less in prisons grow.
>
> Upon his Mule, He's gone they say
> To Dixie's promised Land,
> And at no very distant day
> To lead a new command.

"Three Cheers for Our Jack Morgan!"[69] also mentions Morgan's escape. The song was written by John Hill Hewitt under the pseudonym of Eugene Raymond and was set to a tune ("Old K.Y, Kentucky") originally composed by Daniel Decatur Emmett:

> Jack Morgan is his name,
> The fearless and the lucky;
> No dastard foe can tame
> The son of old Kentucky.
> His heart is with his State,
> He fights for Southern freedom;
> His men their General's word await,
> They'll go where he will lead em

Other tributes included "John Morgan March," "John Morgan Polka," "John Morgan's Bride Polka," C. D. Benson's "Capt. John Morgan Schottisch," subtitled, "Now you'v [sic] got him. Now you haven't," and "Gen'l Morgan's Grand March."[70] In September 1864 Morgan was shot through the head and killed during a cavalry skirmish at Greeneville, Tennessee.

MUSICAL TRIBUTES TO OTHER GENERALS

Other generals won their share of musical recognition, although in many cases those tributes were as short-lived as their military successes. In 1861 former Texas Ranger Ben McCulloch was the hero of "Gen. Ben McCullough's [sic] Grand March" and the "Oak Hill Polka."[71] The latter referred to a battle, also known as "Wilson's Creek," fought on 10 August 1861, near Springfield, Missouri, which neither side won.

The widely unpopular Braxton Bragg was one of the least likely military leaders to be celebrated in music. He often looked angry and, in fact, was usually in a bad mood. He was impatient and sarcastic to his men, and when his plans failed, he blamed his subordinates. The only one who thought good of him was his friend, Jefferson Davis, who refused to relieve him of his duties. The public needed to see generals as heroes so, despite his shortcomings, Bragg received his due in "Gen. Bragg's Grand March" and "The Song of the Exile."[72]

Nathan Bedford Forrest, the "Wizard of the saddle," was hailed in "Forrest Polka" and in "The Forrest Scottisch."[73] He is now considered one of the best strategists and leaders of the war. A broadside written in 1864 in his honor to the tune of "Columbia: the Home of the Brave" lists all the battles in which he fought.[74]

Gen. Albert Sidney Johnston, whom President Davis considered the best general in the Confederate army, had a march named after him in 1861.[75] On 6 April 1862, however, he was mortally wounded at Shiloh.

After his victory at Manassas, Joseph "Joe" Eggleston Johnston was saluted in the "Gen. Joseph E. Johnston Manassas Quick March."[76] George Pickett's ill-fated assault at Gettysburg was recognized in "Pickets [sic] Charge March."[77] Gens. James Longstreet, Hugh Mercer, and Persifor F. Smith each had "grand marches" named in their honor,[78] although Smith's march was a reissue of a march written in his honor during the Mexican War. Kentuckian John C. Breckinridge, who had once been vice president of the United States, was also paid homage with a "grand waltz,"[79] while South Carolina's Wade Hampton received his due with a "quickstep" and John Winder with a "galop."[80]

A number of other officers had marches or dance numbers dedicated to them in sheet music, among them Sterling ("Old Pap") Price, William "Extra Billy" Smith, Felix Zollicoffer, Nathan George Evans, and Richard Stoddert Ewell.[81] Leonidas Polk, who was also an Episcopalian bishop, Benjamin Franklin Cheatham, and Gideon Johnson Pillow, a one-time candidate for vice president of the United States, were collectively recognized in the dedication to "Belmont Quick Step."[82]

Some generals not recognized in Confederate sheet music were honored by publishers in Maryland or in broadsides. Portly major general

"Prince" John Bankhead Magruder, better known for his hospitality and leadership with a knife and fork than as a military strategist, was recognized in "Magruder's March."[83] Magruder and Generals Beauregard, Johnston, Price, and Bragg are mentioned in a broadside entitled "We'll Be Free In Maryland."[84] Written in January 1862, its opening verses await the day when "The boys down South in Dixie's land, / Will Come and rescue Maryland." Magruder also received recognition in "My Texas Land,"[85] a broadside parody of "Maryland! My Maryland!" written in 1863 after his transfer to the Trans–Mississippi theater:

> With brave Magruder at his post,
> Texas land, my Texas land!
> We can whip Abe Lincoln's host,
> Texas land, my Texas land.

Most of the broadsides extolling Magruder come from Texas and include the rollicking "Johnny B. Magruder:"[86]

> Come, listen to my lay, of a man who came this way,
> You may never see a bolder or a ruder;
> For many bloody pranks has he play'd upon the Yanks,
> And this man is Johnny, Johnny B. Magruder!

Other tributes to Magruder include "Bombardment and Battles of Galveston," "The Recapture of Galveston," "The Horse Marines at Galveston," and many more.[87]

Another cavalry officer singled out for special honor was the rugged Turner Ashby, who was killed early in the war.[88] John Singleton Mosby and his two hundred partisan rangers, whose raids through the Shenandoah Valley caused it to be called "Mosby's Confederacy," were mentioned in the dedication of J. W. Davies and Sons' edition of "You Can Never Win Us Back."[89] Gen. Simon Bolivar Buckner received his due in "The Kentucky Battle Song," Maj. Gen. Richard Anderson was recognized in "Soldier's Greeting," and Brig. Gen. Harry T. Hays was heralded in "Southern Shout."[90]

A few lesser ranking officers were also honored with marches or other musical works published as sheet music. Colonel J. J. Thornton of the 6th Mississippi Infantry had a march named after him,[91] as did G. A. Dreux.[92]

Little is known of Thornton. Dreux was a native of Louisiana and the first Southern officer to die in the war (Yorktown, Virginia, 5 July 1861). Five musical tributes to him were published in New Orleans, beginning with a dedication to him as Captain Dreux in the "Louisiana Guard March" and ending with "Elegy on the Death of Lt. Col. Dreux," the cover of which explained that Dreux had been "killed in defending his Country on the 5th of July 1861. In the Vicinity of Yorktown Va."

The only naval officer to be honored in sheet music was Adm. Raphael Semmes, captain of the Confederate raider, *Alabama*.[93] The *Alabama* captured or sank almost seventy ships before it was bested by the *Kearsarge,* off Cherbourg. Semmes was rescued and returned to the Confederacy, where he was promoted to rear admiral, and then brigadier general, the only officer on either side to hold rank in both the navy and the infantry.

CHAPTER 7

We Conquer or Die

The arbiter of which side was right or wrong was the battlefield. Battlefield victory was tangible evidence not only of military, but moral superiority, since it was assumed that divine approval and assistance guided success. "God sides with the right," proclaimed the words of "Trust to Luck Alabama."[1] Other Confederate songs contain similar sentiments of divine intervention such as:

> God, the God of war,
> Who defends the just,
> Give thine arm the power,
> To defend thy trust.[2]

and

> May the God of Battles guide you
> And kind angels hover o'er,
> Till you drive the black fanatics,
> From our dear loved Southern shore.[3]

From the songwriters' perspective, confrontation on the battlefield was a holy war. If God did not approve of the South, it could not prevail. His approbation validated the moral justice of the Southern cause, and if so, the South must be the victor. Piety is also reflected in the description of the nationalistic crusade as "righteous" ("the God of the righteous and free"),[4] "sacred" ("when our sacred cause is won"),[5] and "holy":

Give them thy Holy Spirit
To bear our cross on high,
That through its sacred merit
They win the victory.[6]

Each battle in this crusade reflected divine support. With His aid the new nation would survive, without it, it would perish. As one song succinctly affirmed, "this be our watchword, 'we conquer or die'."[7]

The South's early battlefield successes appeared to vindicate the conviction of the "Southrons" that God was on their side. Each battle in the early months of the war was confidently celebrated in broadsides and sheet music, no matter how insignificant the outcome.[8]

The battle of First Manassas proved to Southerners that God was on their side and that independence would soon be theirs. Fought on 21 July 21 1861, near a stream called "Bull Run," close to the northern Virginia town of Manassas, First Manassas was the biggest military engagement fought in North America up to that time.

Federal politicians, goaded by an impatient public and a haranguing press led by the *New York Tribune*'s Horace Greeley, urged Lincoln to end the rebellion quickly, before the Confederate Congress reconvened on 20 July. A short time earlier, the Confederate government relocated its political capital to Richmond, rather than remaining in Montgomery, Alabama. The Confederate capital was now only fifty miles from Washington. Northern politicians believed its capture would demoralize the Confederacy into immediate capitulation. Impatient politicians ranted "on to Richmond." A pressured Lincoln ordered Brig. Gen. Irvin McDowell, who had been put in command of the newly formed Army of the Potomac in May 1861, to lead the assault.

McDowell's army was unprepared but he had no choice. His green volunteers, inexperienced support staff, and overly complex plans fell short. The defeated Union army retreated in utter disarray to Washington. Northern politicians and their families, like New York congressman Alfred Ely, who had come to watch as if they were at an afternoon picnic, were taken prisoner and were ignominiously escorted to the Rebel capital.

Innumerable Southern broadsides immediately extolled the Confederate triumph. "Flight of Doodles," a song written by an anonymous Southerner to the minstrel tune, "Root, Hog, or Die," gleefully describes the disorganized flight of the "Yankee doodles" back to Washington and extols the exploits of various Confederate units: South Carolina shook "the dirty Yankees till she broke all their jaws"; Virginia whipped "the dirty crew"; Georgia "cut down the Yankees almost to a man"; Alabama stood "like a giant in the contest so warm"; Texas "made the Yankees bile"; North Carolinia "knocked down the Yankees and made their bones rattle"; and Florida "came in with a terrible shout" and "frightened all the Yankees till their eyes stuck out. . . ."[9] "Another Yankee Doodle" equally rhapsodized:

> Yankee Doodle soon found out
> That Bull Run was no trifle;
> For if the North knew how to steal,
> The South knew how to rifle.
>
> Yankee Doodle wheeled about,
> And scampered off at full run
> And such a race was never seen
> As that he made at Bull Run.
> No tyrant hand shall ever dare
> Our sacred Southern homes despoil,
> No tyrant foot shall e'er invade
> Our free Virginia soil.[10]

Sheet music saluted the Southern victory with the "Battle of Manassas," the "Manassas Polka," "Evening at Manassas," the "Victory of Manassas Grand March," "Our Triumph at Manassas: Fantaisie Mazurka," and the "Manassas Quickstep."[11]

The Confederate victory, due more to chance than military finesse, reinforced the widely held Southern beliefs that any Southern soldier equaled three Yankee soldiers, that the South had prepared for the war effort, and that moral superiority more than matched material advantage. Sheet music likewise heralded Southern victories at Oak Hill,[12] and Belmont, Missouri.[13] These early songs and sheet music publications reflect a Confederacy overreacting to its early victories. They reinforced the the idea that the war would be over by Christmas and undermined the more prudent need to prepare for a protracted conflict.

The following year, Southern songwriters and composers faced reality. Songs continued to herald martial deeds but now they began to eulogize sacrifice. The standoff at Shiloh (6 and 7 April 1862) in Southern Tennessee near the Alabama border was hailed in the "Shiloh Victory Polka"[14] as a Southern victory, but the battle's terrible losses shook both sides out of their complacency. It was the first of many bloody encounters to come; the shocking death of thousands of young boys and men was poignantly driven home by "The Drummer Boy of Shiloh,"[15] whose death on battlefield musically signaled the loss of innocence.

Graphic battles were too demoralizing to turn into sheet music. Instead, civilian songwriters and composers focused on encounters in Virginia where the South gained the edge in the early years of the war. Dan Emmett's "Jordan Is a Hard Road to Travel," parodied by John R. Thompson, editor of the *Southern Literary Messenger* into "Richmond Is a Hard Road to Travel,"[16] is a virtual history of the early "on to Richmond" campaigns:

> Would you like to hear my song,
> I'm afraid it's rather long,
> Of the famous "on to Richmond" double trouble;
> Of the half a dozen trips, and half a dozen slips,
> And the very latest bursting of the bubble?
> Then pull off your coat and roll up your sleeve,
> For Richmond is a hard road to travel;
> Then pull off your coat and roll up your sleeve,
> For Richmond is a hard road to travel I believe!

The song, written in 1863, credits "Stonewall" Jackson with turning back the Northern invasion and does not mention Lee. In boisterous meter, it relates how "McDowell, bold and gay, set forth the shortest way" by way of Manassas, but ran up against a "Stonewall." Likewise, "Commissary [Maj. Gen. Nathaniel] Banks, with his motley foreign ranks . . . Lost the whole of his supplies," when he too encountered "the Stonewall." "[Maj. Gen. George Brinton] McClellan followed soon, both with spade and balloon, To try the Peninsular approaches," but "his best rate of speed, Was no faster than the slowest of 'slow coaches.'" Maj. Gen. John Pope is similarly thwarted by Jackson, and "Last of all the brave [Maj. Gen. Ambrose Everett] Burnside, with his pontoon bridges tried/A road no one had thought of before him "[fording the Rappahannock], but when it was over, "the river ran with more blood than water."

Speaking as the Northern narrator, the final verse asks who will be next to lead the ill-fated "Richmond expedition":

> Yet the contraband was right when he told us they would fight,
> "Oh! yes, massa, they fight like the devil!"

There were few victories to celebrate after Burnside's defeat at the Battle of Fredericksburg (12 to 15 December 1862). The title of a dance tune like "Never Surrender Quick Step"[17] was written in the shadow of the siege of Vicksburg and heartens Southerners that "Mississippians know not and refuse to be taught how to surrender." The implicit message is that, like the Mississippians, all Southerners should fight to the last. To emphasize the message, Edward Eaton, the composer, also wrote "We'll Die, but Never Surrender."[18]

BOYS, KEEP YOUR POWDER DRY

When there was little to celebrate militarily, Confederate songwriters dwelled on the bravery of the South's soldiers. As long as the South held its own, songs were upbeat, extolling the pride and the steadfastness of Southern cavaliers. By 1863 when the tide had begun to turn, songs such as "Boys, Keep Your Powder Dry"[19] encouraged soldiers to remain resolute, and reminded and simultaneously worried them that they were fighting to protect their loved ones at home:

> Does a love'd one home await you,
> Who wept to see you go,
> Whom with a kiss imprinted
> You left with sacred vow
> You'd come again, when warfare
> And arms are all laid by,
> To take her to your bosom?
> "Boys, keep your powder dry."
>
> Does a father home await you?
> A sister whom you love?
> A mother who hast reared you,
> And prayed to Him above:
> "Protect my boy, preserve him,
> And when the battle's done,

> Send to his weeping mother,
> Bereft, her darling son!"

By 1864 the former ebullience was dissipated. Now songs tried to bolster spirits by celebrating the sacrifices being endured by men in the field as symbolized by their tattered uniforms:[20]

> Tho' torn and faded be each coat, their buttons tarnished too,
> I know beneath each soldier's dress a Southern heart beats true;
> We honor every gallant son who fights for us to-day,
> And Heaven protect the noble boys who wear a suit of grey!

These tattered uniforms are symbolic of the Confederacy's imminent demise. The coats, an unintentional metaphor for the Confederacy's protective shield, have fallen apart. Its "buttons," the pride of its military prowess, are tarnished. No longer is the deity being summoned to give the South its deserved victories; now the exhortation is to protect—to let the South somehow survive.

Despite their underlying defeatism, Southern songs in the latter part of the war frequently stressed the common bond of sacrifice between men in the field and women at home. Songs described the sacrifices women made and the hardships they endured to support the war effort, and emphasized the need for manufacturing independence in support of Southern nationalism.

Prior to the war when a Southern woman of means wanted a new dress or some other clothing she sent North for it. As their clothes became threadbare, Southern women had to find new ways to clothe themselves. In place of pins, they used neatly trimmed thorns. For buttons they used dried persimmon seeds or pieces of gourds, pierced with holes for needle and thread. The loss of a sewing needle became a household calamity. Hats and bonnets were made out of corn shucks, palmetto, and various kinds of grasses. Every girl and woman learned how to card and knit, if she had never mastered those skills before.

Songs like Carrie Bell Sinclair's "The Homespun Dress,"[21] written to the tune of "The Bonnie Blue Flag," extolled Southern women for doing their best to cope with their privations:

> Oh, yes, I am a Southern girl,
> And Glory in the name,
> And boast it with far greater pride

Than glittering wealth or fame.
We envy not the Northern girl,
Her robes of beauty rare,
Though diamonds grace her snowy neck,
And pearls bedeck her hair.

The homespun dress is plain, I know,
My hat's palmetto, too;
But then it shows what Southern girls
For Southern rights will do.
We send the bravest of our land,
To battle with the foe
And we will lend a helping hand—
We love the South, you know.

A similar song, "My Girl with the Home-Spun Dress," carried the notation, "A song for the times."[22]

The "Homespun Dress" tried to bolster flagging spirits on the home-front by saluting the indomitable spirit of the Southern woman and emphasizing her contribution to the war effort. Despite the hardships, there is no hint of despair. Noteworthy for its collective consciousness, the song's heroine boasts of being "a Southern girl," who "glories in the name"; instead of I, it is "we" who "love the South." The implication is that women from every walk of life are behind the South's war effort.[23]

Despite the grimness of the Southern soldier's life in 1864, Southern songwriters still put the best face they could on camp life for those at home:

When the battle is o'er, and the sounds of fight,
Have closed with the closing day,
How happy around the watch fire's light,
To chat the long hours away.
To chat the long hours away my boy
And talk of the days to come,
Or a better still, and a purer joy,
To think of our far off home.

Homesickness, however, could not be denied:

> How many a cheek will then grow pale,
> That never felt a tear,
> And many a stalwart heart will quail,
> That never quailed in fear.[24]

To keep up their morale, soldiers were reassured they had not been forgotten in "Yes We Think of Thee at Home,"[25] whereas steadfastness was preached in "Keep Me Awake! Mother,"[26] written as a companion piece to the popular antebellum song, "Rock Me to Sleep Mother." However, there is a pervasive sense of overriding war weariness in the song:

> Dreams of my childhood have faded or flown,
> Objects I cherished, repulsive have grown,
> All things seem fleeting, no pleasure endures
> But mother, dear mother, the same lot was yours;
> Such dreaming, such mourning, hoping and trust,
> Such crumbling of air-built castles to dust,
> Bravely as thou didst, my part let me take,
> Keep me awake, mother, keep me awake.

"The Southron's Watchword!", subtitled "The Grave of a Hero or Victory!"[27], written in 1862, continued to eulogize the fallen hero, "shedding his blood for his Southern home." Such songs appealed to the emotional ideal of the fallen soldier as martyr. But this was before the impact of the thousands of men, whose blood had been shed, began to be felt. The theme of "The March of the Southern Men,"[28] published the following year in 1863, superficially was a paean to sacrifice and comradeship, but it fatalistically described men marching to their deaths:

> How bravely they move under fire, tho' they know
> Their kindred they ne'er may see more,
> And cheerfully follow their chief to the field,
> Where the've[sic] gathered their laurels before.

> I hear their war-cry sounding, sounding,
> Deep over mountain and glen,
> Behold, their battalions are charging again;
> 'Tis the march of the Southern men.
> 'Tis the march, 'tis the march,
> 'Tis the march of the Southern men.

"No Surrender,"[29] written in 1864 and dedicated "To the Southern Cause," attempted to bolster flagging spirits but it echoed with overwhelming despair, especially in the lines:

> And tho' fortunes smiles be few,
> Hope is always springing new,
> Still inspiring me and you
> With a magic, No Surrender!

POSTSCRIPT

Like many of the well-known songs written during the war, authorship of "The Homespun Dress" was claimed by or attributed to many other writers. According to an article in the *Cincinnati Enquirer*, John Hunt Morgan's cavalry sang the song as they rode through Stringtown (Florence), Kentucky in 1862 on their way to Cincinnati. A short time earlier, the article said, Bragg's army had beaten Buell's army to Lexington and an impromptu ball was given in their honor, in which the women appeared in dresses made of homespun. Seeing them in this homespun finery inspired a Lieutenant Harrington from Alabama, who was subsequently killed at Perryville, to immediately write the poem. A Miss Earle, "an accomplished musician present [at the ball], improvised the air and sang it with piano accompaniment." After the battle, part of the Southern army advanced toward Covington to threaten Cincinnati. It was while Morgan's men rode by on their way to Covington that a Dr. Lloyd heard them singing "The Homespun Dress." After the war Lloyd was writing a book about Confederate war songs and wanted to include "The Homespun Dress," but all he could remember was the first verse. He offered fifty dollars for a copy of the entire song, which someone located for him in a book written by one of Morgan's men, George Dallas Musgrove.

Lloyd's version was immediately attacked by Gen. N. Saussy, who had been a lieutenant colonel in the Confederate army. Saussy said Sinclair had written the song in Savannah in 1862 and he had heard it sung there at the theater by the Queen Sisters while he was home on furlough from a wound he had received at Sharpsburg.

The article also caught the attention of an ardent feminist, Mary C. Wright, living in Greensburg, Indiana. Wright fumed at the idea that a man wrote the song. "I wish to enter the lists [of people claiming authorship] as champion of the rights of authoress for my sex. A woman wrote the song in question, and I object to any male claimant for a song that has been in publication 35 years with as authentic a history as the "Homespun Dress." Wright referred to Musgrove's book, "an old volume in my father's library," and reproduced the anecdote Musgrove had included with the song.

Professor Lloyd himself was inundated with about five hundred letters from various readers, many of them claiming the fifty dollars as authors of the poem. The controversy, he said, had become a "perplexing" and personally "painful" national issue.

The debate also found its way into the *Confederate Veteran*,[30] which rehashed most of the original article from the *Enquirer* and added that the amount of the award offered by Lloyd was one hundred dollars not fifty dollars, and that a second offer of fifty dollars had now been offered for the true author, the final decision to be made by a committee of judges from the Cincinnati court.

The court awarded the one hundred dollars to a Cincinnati man, Mr. W. J. Bryan, as the first to deliver a copy of the complete ballad and the correct name of the author, and the fifty dollar prize to Mr. Charles W. Hubmer of the Carnegie Library in Atlanta for producing "uncontrovertible proof" that the author was indeed Miss Carrie Bell Sinclair.

PART 2

"When We, Through Peace, Shall Be Set Free from Tattoo, Taps and Reveille"

Although the Northern and Southern armies were mustered to fight, soldiers spent most of their time in dull camp routine. Late fall, winter, and early spring meant total inactivity as far as warfare was concerned. Garrison life was repetitious, boring, and vegetative: "Whilst we are on the march or fighting," a soldier wrote home, "I get along pretty well, as I have something to excite and occupy my mind, but this dull and monotonous camp life, is almost intolerable."[1]

The monotonous camp life was organized around a recurrent schedule of drum and bugle tunes that regulated a soldier's every waking moment. These tunes were so incessant and insistent that horses in the artillery and cavalry responded to them without waiting for their riders. Shot three times during the Battle of First Manassas (21 July 1861), a little sorrel in the Union army was stripped of his bridle and saddle and left to wander off and die. But the horse was so conditioned to respond to the bugle blast that when he heard the call to retreat, instead of wandering off, he "found his true position with the battery, which is more than most of the human mass engaged on the field could boast of doing." The horse was taken back to Washington, recovered from his wounds, and was "ready for another fight."[2]

Musical anodynes that soldiers relied on to cope with military life became amusing "work songs." Composed to the tune of drum or bugle calls, these songs expressed resentment against the military system and ridiculed their own existence, especially their food and living conditions.

Humor has long been a safety valve for dealing with anger and frustration.[3] Even without psychological reasons, the Southern soldier, said Maj. Gen. John Brown Gordon, had an "irrepressible spirit for fun making, for jests and good natural gibes."[4] Their bitter undercurrent aside, quips were usually amiable.[5]

Most Confederate soldiers were either teenagers or young adults, and practical jokes abounded. Congregational singers were just as likely to be the butt of these jokes as unrepentant sinners. Sometimes the spiritual singers seemingly invited tomfoolery. Like the night pranksters poured water down the chimney of the tent just as members of the Surrey Light Artillery's religious choir turned to this refrain from a hymn they sang regularly at night:

> Scotland's burning! Scotland's burning!
> Cast on water! Cast on water![6]

Officers were also not above playing tricks. During the winter of 1864 several officers in the 21st Louisiana Volunteers put together an "orchestra" containing a fractured drum, a wheezy clarinet, a trumpet, and a banjo, and headed for Col. J. B. G. Kennedy's tent, rousing him from his sleep with their racket. Kennedy pretended to be amused and passed around a bottle of whiskey after the serenade was over. Only it wasn't whiskey. It was ipecac. The "musicians" polished off the bottle before they realized what was in it and spent the rest of the night vomiting. The next morning they all reported for duty, pale faced and swearing revenge.[7]

Psychologically, laughter lessened despair. "If there ever was a condition of things that existed in our army, however straitened it might have been, when there was not some soldiers ready with a humorous remark, my memory is at fault," recalled Lt. Albert Goodloe, who served with the 35th Alabama Infantry. "In the dreariest of bivouacs, under the sorest of privations, on the hardest of marches, and even in the lulls of battle, the ludicrous would pop out of some one, not necessarily a wag, and often to the unspeakable relief of his comrades who were enduring next to intolerable tension."[8]

In the aftermath of Chickamauga (19 and 20 September 1863), John Jackman, a soldier in the "Orphan Brigade," described the peculiar juxtaposition of death and mirth common in the ranks: "The dead of both sides were lying thick over the ground. I saw where six Federal soldiers had been killed from behind one small tree, and where eight horses were lying dead, harnessed to a Napoleon gun. Men and horses were lying so thick over the field, one could hardly walk for them. I even saw a large black dog lying mangled by a grape. . . . The boys were lying in line of battle, and cracking jokes as usual. Many of them I noticed to be in the finest spirits were in a few minutes afterwards numbered with the slain."[9]

Of all the ways of relieving camp boredom, none was as popular as music. When the first volunteers went to war they packed everything they thought they would need for soldiering. Many sported brass-buttoned, double-breasted jackets, over which they wore long, heavy overcoats and capes. A small, stiff cap perched insouciantly atop a soldier's head completed his military dress. Necessities were carried in a knapsack strapped around the shoulders and included a change of underwear, soap, comb, hairbrush, toothbrush, mirror, string, bandages, buttons, needles, thread, eating utensils, pencil, pen, ink, photographs, smoking and chewing tobacco, and pipes. With a blanket and oilcloth carried on the outside of the knapsack, this kit weighed about twenty-five pounds, a sizable weight for a man to carry—even for a short distance. Many wore thick, heavy-soled boots in the belief they would make marching easier. Besides these artifacts, a soldier toted a canteen, one or more revolvers, a bowie knife for hand-to-hand combat, a musket, a bayonet, and if he owned one, a fiddle.

It didn't take long to rid themselves of nearly all of it. The long, heavy boots gave way to broad-bottomed brogues with flat heels; short-waisted jackets replaced long-tailed coats. An overcoat was simply too heavy; even if it kept a man warm in winter, the burden of carrying a coat outweighed the comfort it gave. Caps were tossed away in favor of soft felt hats. Almost every other "necessity" was abandoned. Revolvers and bowie knives were useless and were sent back home; bayonets were discarded. The one thing a soldier never discarded was his fiddle.

The fiddle was the quintessential folk instrument in the South from the time John Utie, America's first fiddler, landed in Virginia in 1620.[10] Thomas Jefferson played it; so did Patrick Henry, neither of them tolerably well.[11] Parson Mason Locke Weems, clergyman, itinerant book peddler, and sometime biographer, who created the fable of George Washington and the cherry tree, used to attract book buyers to his wagon with his fiddling.[12] Even the dour "Stonewall" Jackson tried to master it when he was a boy, although he had no gift for music.[13]

The pioneers who settled the Southern frontier on foot or on horseback, in wagons or by boat, often toted fiddles with them, even when they couldn't carry much else. If they didn't have fiddles when they set out, they made them out of boxes or buckets, with hair from a mule's tail for string and pine tree sap for rosin. Homemade fiddles helped many a Southern soldier pass a lonely evening in camp.

The Southerner's passion for fiddling is amusingly reflected in the life of James Gamble, one of the best antebellum fiddlers in middle Tennessee. When the Great Revival of 1801 swept across the South, some Southern Protestants frowned on fiddling. Fiddlers, they said, were lazy; laziness led to sin. Many fiddlers felt pressured to give up their instruments. Not James Gamble. Gamble loved to fiddle. It was his life. No other pastime interested him. But when the Great Revival marched on Tennessee, Gamble devoted time to religious devotion. Instead of fiddling constantly, he read his Bible, then fiddled; he prayed, then he fiddled; he asked a silent blessing on his meals, gave thanks, then fiddled; he went to meetings, sang the songs of

Zion, joined in all the devotional services, went home, then fiddled. He sometimes fiddled in bed and always fiddled when he got up.[14]

Whereas the fiddle was the favorite musical instrument in rural areas, in towns and cities across America, men began taking lessons or teaching themselves how to play brass instruments. In the previous century only "gentlemen" amateurs owned and played (wooden) musical instruments; by the 1840s any male who could make a noise on an instrument seemed to be tooting away, from the banker to the blacksmith. Local brass bands mushroomed across the country, appearing at the welcoming of the first white woman to arrive in Columbia, California, in 1851 to the opening of the suspension bridge between Minneapolis and St. Paul in 1853.[15] In 1838 The *New Orleans Daily Picayune* complained of a "mania in this city for horn and trumpet playing." Brass "blowers," it moaned, were on every corner.[16]

In large part, the passion for "brass blowing" followed dramatic improvements in the design of these instruments. Early brass instruments were very much like the bugle—capable of producing a limited number of harmonic tones and that done only by changing the tension of the blower's lips at the mouthpiece. In 1815 the key bugle came to America. Conical in shape, rather than cylindrical like the trumpet or trombone, with side holes and large wart-like keys attached to long levers scattered over its surface, the key bugle allowed a musician to play the chromatic notes that lie between harmonic tones by moving levers which slid a key off its opening and then back. "Keys" eventually gave way to a whole new class of valved brass instruments in the 1840s called saxhorns, after their French inventor, Antoine-Joseph "Adolphe" Sax. These forerunners of the modern saxophone had long winding brass tubes and a flared bell at their ends which gave them a soft mellow sound. Saxhorns came in three basic styles: one had the bell (the part of the instrument from which the sound is emitted) pointing forward, another pointed upwards, and a third pointed over the shoulder, projecting the music backward. These new valved instruments, made from relatively commonplace materials, were fairly easy to manufacture, and enabled amateurs to play songs previously within the ability of only skilled musicians. The combination of low cost and easy mastery touched off a "Golden Age" for brass bands in America that lasted well into the next century. It was also a "golden age" for instrument makers and sellers because there was no common pitch standard. If a band wanted to add new instruments to an already existing repertoire, it had to either contend with some discordance or buy an entirely new set.

Traditionally associated with the military, bands were symbolic of military authority, and many early bands attached themselves to local or state militias. Besides playing marches and quicksteps and various patriotic tunes reflecting America's sense of growth, expansion, and nationalism, civilian and militia bands included light-hearted waltzes and quicksteps, popular sentimental and romantic ballads, and concert and opera tunes in their repertoires. Many of these bands were honored by having the designation, "as played by," on sheet music versions of the music they played or by having tunes named after them. The better these bands became, the more public concert invitations they received. This encouraged them to extend their repertoires even more.

Since brass bands were associated with local militias, playing in a brass band was widely regarded as a manly activity.[17] Playing itself was believed to build strong lungs, broaden shoulders, and increase muscular strength, vigor and endurance. It was virile and patriotic. During the Civil War, bands even became symbolic military weapons. A wedding, a funeral, the opening of a canal, a picnic, a balloon ascension, a meeting, a race, an election, or an execution—whatever the occasion, there was bound to be a brass band. People regarded them as culturally "elevating" and democratizing. The brass band movement evidenced the Victorian emphasis on social cohesiveness.

In the antebellum years itinerant bandmasters were as common as itinerant singing and dancing masters. Meredith Willson's *Music Man,* set in early twentieth-century America, could just as easily have been set in nineteenth-century America before the Civil War. Most Americans shared the opinion that "no town or village . . . [could] pretend to have attained much progress or social esthetics which is not blessed with a grand brass band."[18]

The most common and popular musical entertainment in camp during off-hour duties, however, was singing. Singing was almost a daily occurrence in camp. Pvt. James Huffman (10th Virginia Infantry) said that soldiers kept songbooks with them wherever they went "and passed much of [their] leisure time singing. I carried my book even through prison and brought it home with me."[19] "The South," quipped one historian, "was magnificently equipped if the war could have been won by singing."[20]

Despite the bravado usually associated with the military, soldiers who fought in the American Civil War, and soldiers who have fought in the great wars that have since occurred have little interest in any songs expressing nationalism or fighting mettle. "Soldier songs" are not the patriotic songs usually associated with war. They are not bombastic; few would consider them "military songs." Most "soldier songs" are not concerned with patriotism at all, although they nevertheless reflect the turmoil of wartime. Instead of singing about their country or flag, soldiers sang about two things: home and the injustices of army life.

Sentimental songs about home, the most popular of soldier songs, were a psychic anodyne, an escape mechanism from battlefield horrors. The Civil War soldier had an undeniable fondness for the most sentimental, lugubrious, and maudlin of songs about home and family. A universal preoccupation with going home was followed closely by themes about family and sweethearts. Although some officers banned singing "home" songs in camp because they seriously undermined morale and allegedly caused desertion,[21] it was these home ties that strengthened combat morale not weakened it. As noted earlier, songs reminding soldiers about their homes and loved ones inspired greater devotion than patriotic songs urging them to fight for their country, because they are personal. Songs about home and loved ones are one of the most powerfully subtle psychological ways of sustaining military morale.[22] At the same time, home songs were as important a safety valve for assuaging bitter feelings about the military brass as "griping" songs.[23]

Many of the sentimental songs that bands played during twilight concerts and that soldiers sang to themselves—with their yearnings for home and preoccupations with the death of young maidens—were not a product of the war, but were instead an expression of the cultural ethos called "romanticism," which was pervasive in America and Europe in the early nineteenth century.[24]

The eighteenth-century Enlightenment had emphasized limitations on spiritual freedom; nineteenth-century romanticism reacted to such limitations by reasserting the human spirit, especially its immortality. Romanticism was intensely emotional and heroic. The Enlightenment appealed to the head; romanticism's appeal was to the heart. The world of romanticism was spiritual; it saw endless potential in every individual, one's irrational as well as one's rational side, and so strongly believed in immortality that it gave rise to what seems to us in the twentieth century a bizarre, brooding preoccupation with death.[25] Books and magazines were filled with stories about dead and dying spouses, sweethearts, and children, and joyful reunions in the hereafter. People treasured mementos of their dead loved ones. Keepsakes were prominently displayed in their homes. Baby shoes were pasted on pictures of weeping willows. Locks of hair from dear, departed loved ones were woven into jewelry. All of these images found their way into popular song.

By the 1850s, popular songs became more haunting and mawkish, the forerunner of the modern "hurtin'" songs. Songs about lonely wanderers far from home were commonplace, conjuring up on the one hand warm, domestic scenes of days gone by, and on the other, a feeling of identity. Many such songs recalled a particular locale—a river, a field, or any area for which there was a special attachment, or they lamented leaving a sweetheart or mother. During the war, when hundreds of thousands of families experienced these separations firsthand, such songs had special poignancy.

Being a "romantic" antebellum American did not connote being hopelessly in love as it does today, although sentimentality was a hallmark of romanticism. Artists, writers, and composers were obsessed with an individual's place in society, including his or her duties and responsibilities to home and family. Spontaneity, sincerity, emotionality, imagination, and personal self-expression were important, but the overriding concern was where and how an individual fit into society.

A major theme in parlor songs, and one that is repeated over and over in Civil War songs, is separation, the civilian or soldier isolated from his loved ones by circumstances beyond his control and yearning to be reunited. An Irish songwriter, Thomas Moore (1779-1852), one of the best-known songwriters of the time, specialized in highly emotive songs about the sadness of separation as families and lovers (always men) emigrated to far-off America to find work or seek their fortunes in the frontier gold fields. One of the favorite metaphors for symbolizing the separation theme was the flower, representing a lonely girl who has been left behind, as depicted in Moore's "The Last Rose of Summer":

> Tis the last rose of summer
> Left blooming alone,
> All her lovely companions
> Are faded and gone!

Published in 1813 the song sold a half-million copies in America. During the war sheet music editions were reissued by several Confederate music publishers, and its lyrics were reprinted in several Confederate songsters.[26]

The most popular of these sentimental songs was "Home, Sweet Home," which tearfully lamented the narrator's exile from his native land.

A variation on this theme has a soldier away from home, worrying about what will happen to his mother in his absence, or a mother tearfully worrying about her son, and both dreading the possibility that either one may die alone, away from friends and family.

The ultimate estrangement, in this context, was death. Although Victorian America idealized this world's beauties, it ecstatically imagined the glories beyond the grave. Edgar Allan Poe, who articulated the thoughts of millions of nineteenth-century Americans, said beauty was a transcendental "elevation of soul—best expressed in sadness and tears. Melancholy is thus the most legitimate of all the poetical tones. What could be more melancholy and, therefore, more poetic," said Poe, "than the death of a beautiful woman?" The voice best suited for expressing this feeling was the bereaved lover's, its sincerest affirmation—tears. Tears enabled those on earth to experience the rapturous joys to come.[27] The macabre celebration of death was the solemnization of everlasting beauty.

In romanticism, the more melancholy a song, the more erotic. Overt eroticism, by contrast, was not tolerated. Its only outlet was the kiss. Occasionally that kiss led to matrimony; more often than not, heartbreak. Over and over again, the basic songwriting formula called for boy to meet girl, boy to fall in love at first sight, boy and girl to marry, girl to die unexpectedly, boy to mourn forever. The death of a young child, especially one dying for his country, was a common theme in song before it received its pathetic apotheosis in "The Drummer Boy of Shiloh" (see Chapter 12).

Potential song buyers were attracted by song covers, elaborately lithographed in color, featuring tombstones and weeping willows. These popular death and misery songs inspired musical euphoria and lugubrious nirvana. Every middle-class American household wallowed in it. That was why Stephen Foster's sentimental songs about dead or sleeping maidens were as popular in the South as in the North, whereas his plantation songs flopped south of the Mason-Dixon line. "I See Her Still in My Dreams," "Lula Is Gone," "Parthenia to Ingomar," "Why No One to Love," "Come Where My Love Lies Dreaming," and "Fairy-Belle"[28] were all reissued in the South during the war while "Old Black Joe" and "Old Folks at Home" were not. Songs about a fair maiden dying in the midst of youth struck a responsive chord wherever they were heard.

These "parlor" songs, as they came to be known, took their designation from the room in which they were typically sung or played in. By the time of the Civil War the family parlor was the central room in every

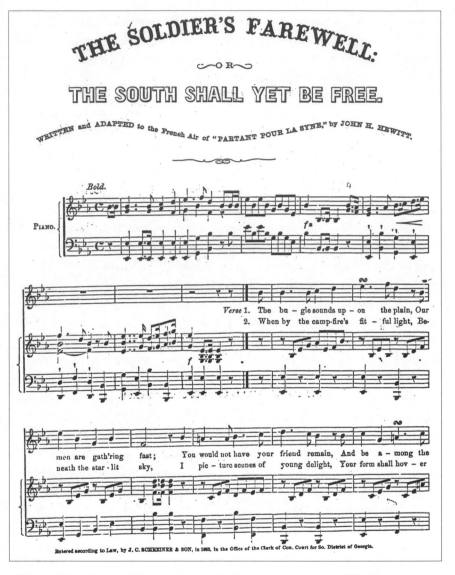

"The Soldier's Farewell," a sentimental ballad written by John Hill Hewitt, shown here in an 1863 J.C. Schreiner & Son edition.

middle-class and upper-class urban home and had become, as Russell Lynes put it in *The Domesticated Americans,*[29] "the bottomless pit of the family budget." The family parlor in antebellum America was the one room in a house especially for show, the modern day "living room," lavishly furnished for the sole purpose of impressing visitors, for proving to them and to the household itself that the family who owned that parlor had achieved the American dream. In the restless, ambitious, materialistic society of antebellum America, the parlor was a tranquil island, the place for formal entertaining and best behavior. It was a special place ruled over by the lady of the house, who safeguarded its dignity. It could be a corner of a two-room log cabin on the frontier or a room all to itself in a city mansion. What went on in that space made it a parlor. Books on parlor etiquette guided the lady of the house from averting every imaginable parlor room gaffe. That sense of gentility dictated the kind of music that was socially acceptable in the parlor—the sentimental tunes soldiers mention so often in their diaries and memoirs.

The biggest expense contributing to the "bottomless pit" was the obligatory piano. By the 1840s, pianos had become "democratized"; every family that could afford a piano had one; it was the symbol of American domesticity.

By 1860 annual sales for pianos in America reached twenty-one thousand. This amounted to the sale every working day of seventy pianos! On the eve of war one out of every fifteen hundred American families had a piano.[30] Despite their popularity, pianos were not cheap. An inexpensive instrument in New Orleans during the early months of the war sold for $225 to $250,[31] still beyond the reach of many families. To lure prospective buyers, piano sellers came up with gimmicks that are still seen today: "PIANOS GIVEN AWAY" is the attention grabbing headline Jules Faivre used in his advertisements in the *New Orleans Picayune* in 1861. Here's how Faivre gave them away:

> You rent a Piano for a certain sum, per month, which will be reasonable, and when the said rental amounts to the price of the piano, the instrument becomes your own.[32]

In other words, time payments at no interest. A family that could not afford to part with that much money even on time could satisfy its musical hunger with a melodeon, a reed organ that came close to a piano's musical output—at about a third the cost. If this were beyond the family's pocket-book, there was still the guitar.

The best known pianos in America were the Chickering and the Stein-way. Chickering pianos were made in Boston while Steinways were manu-factured in New York. The latter was named after the German family who opened a piano-making firm in New York in 1843. The Steinway was especially sought after because of its deep melodic sound, but the Chicker-ing had a stronger and more durable frame. No matter how good a piano sounded in the shop, if it wasn't sturdy enough to survive an overland trip, it wouldn't be worth more than kindling when it finally arrived in the fam-ily parlor.

By 1850 a girl in America was not considered "accomplished" unless she had had singing lessons or could play the piano. But piano mania was not just a female affliction. Men took just as much pleasure at playing. "Jeb" Stuart certainly knew his way around the keyboard, and both men and women packed the theaters to hear and see the piano virtuosos that barn-stormed America in the 1840s and 1850s, all of whom were men.

The parlor piano was such a dominant entertainment item in America before and during the Civil War that no song could be profitably published if it didn't have a piano arrangement. Arrangers became even more popular than composers. Today, Stephen Foster is America's best-known nine-teenth-century music figure. But in his day he was overshadowed by Charles Grobe. When Foster died in 1863, he had written several hundred songs. Pianist-composer Charles Grobe's published works numbered almost one thousand! Totally unknown today, in the 1850s and 1860s Grobe's name was as well known to middle-class girls as the names of the young men courting them.

Being adept at the piano or guitar not only reflected a family's social status, it was also a way for young women in middle-class homes to impress suitors. Mollie McDowall, who grew up in her aunt's house in Bastrop, Texas, near San Antonio, used to spend three hours practicing in the morn-ing before she went to school, a period at noon, and another after school. She then had an early supper, studied her lessons until nine o'clock, and then put in another hour of practice.[33]

Mollie's piano was made of mahogany and had six carved legs with two drawers for music. She was the only child taught by her music teacher, a Miss Holmes from North Carolina; all Miss Holmes's other students were adults. Miss Holmes was a good musician, but she had little patience with children. Mollie's next teacher was a Dr. Ploeger, a German musician who had brought a piano with him when he came to Texas. Mollie's aunt bought the piano from him but looked for yet another teacher when it was obvious that he too did not teach well. Professor Stadtler, another German musician, next tutored Mollie "by pencil." Although Mollie's hands were too small to play some of the pieces Stadtler assigned her, he was unsympathetic, and when she missed a note he whacked her knuckles with his pencil. Eventually she mastered the pieces.[34]

The fact that her aunt was able to hire three different piano teachers in far off Bastrop indicates, at the very least, the extent to which the piano dominated American musical life by the 1850s. By the 1860s, a piece of sheet music had no chance of large sales unless it had a piano arrangement. Covers for how-to books on playing the piano, and sheet music often showed a young woman sitting at the piano, faced by an adoring man.

By the 1860s the favorite evening pastime for families and friends centered around the parlor piano. When Jefferson Davis was a senator in Washington, his wife Varina used to entertain friends in their home with her piano skills. After she moved into the Confederate "White House," she entertained distinguished visitors to the city with a variety of "matinee musicales" featuring the city's best amateur musicians and singers. Inevitably, the guests would join in, accompanying themselves on the Davis's parlor piano.[35]

Well-to-do parents throughout the North and South also sent their daughters to private girls' schools to learn how to pound melodically on piano keys. Private girls' schools, or "female seminaries," "academies," or "institutes," as they were often called, were among the most pervasive influences on parlor music and middle-class and upper-class musical tastes in America during the nineteenth century. Many of the best-known composers, arrangers, and songwriters of the civil war years taught at these schools before the war: George Root at the Abbot's Institute for Young Ladies,[36] Charles Grobe at the Wesleyan Female Seminary in Wilmington, Delaware,[37] Augustus J. Turner at the similarly named Female Institute in Staunton, Virginia. Armand Blackmar was professor of music at Centenary College in Jackson, Louisiana;[38] Philip Werlein headed the music department at the Clinton, Mississippi, Female Seminary;[39] John Hill Hewitt was professor of music at the Chesapeake Female College in Hampton, Virginia, in the 1850s,[40] and gave private lessons in Augusta during the war;[41] Charles Chakyde Nordendorf taught at the Danville Female College;[42] S. Schlesinger was professor of music at the Summerville Female Seminary in Mississippi;[43] William Hartwell, at the Sharon Institute near Jackson, Mississippi.[44]

These teachers had a lasting influence on the musical tastes of their pupils, and it was often through their classes that girls became familiar with the works of European composers.[45] Other well-to-do families hired private instructors, "music masters" or "professors" as they sometimes called themselves, to teach their daughters. Many of these music teachers were impoverished aristocratic émigrés from Europe and enjoyed fairly high social status in antebellum America. On remote plantations they were social peers and dined with the family in the evening. After the evening meal they accompanied the family to the parlor where their protégés entertained by playing and singing. When they weren't teaching young ladies how to play the piano, these same "professors" taught them to play the guitar or how to sing and dance. In cities like Charleston, they sold sheet music and instruments, conducted the local orchestra, played the church organ, and arranged the music for balls. During the war, many music teachers sympathetic to the Southern cause fled south. In 1862 Maurice Bodle, formerly of Maryland, informed any of his former pupils now living in Augusta, along with everyone else in the city, that he was available to "teach the various branches of music, viz., piano, singing, thorough-bass, and organ." He was only going to take a limited number of pupils, however, and terms would be low, "to suit the times."[46]

Private schools taught young girls to play musical instruments, sing, and draw. During the early war years, the Lucy Cobb Institute, which opened in 1859 in Athens, Georgia, announced that

> exercises will be resumed on Wednesday, Jan. 15 [1862] under the charge of the undersigned [W. Muller] a native of South Carolina, once connected with the Richmond Academy of this city, and for upwards of twenty years employed in the instruction of young ladies in Columbia and Charleston, S.C. The ablest teachers are secured. Among them there will be resident in the family, a French lady educated in Paris and Germany, whose special office will be not only to impart a thorough grammatical knowledge, but also to encourage and cultivate a colloquial use of the French and German languages. Arrangements are made to impart a thorough and complete system of education, embracing all the branches both useful and ornamental usually taught in Female High Schools.[47]

Tuition and sundry fees for the 100 to 125 students for the ten-month scholastic term were listed directly beneath the announcement:

Boarding, with Washing, Fuel, Lights	$210
Tuition in English, Classics, and Scientific Depart's	50
Tuition in Primary Department	30
Music on Piano	60
Use of Piano in practice	30
Music on Harp	80
Use of Harp	10
Music on Guitar	50
Use of Guitar	5
Modern Languages, each	20
Pencil and Crayon Drawing	30
Water color and Grecian Painting, each	30
Oil Painting	50
Ornamental Needlework	30
Wax, Fruit, Flowers, etc, per lesson	1
Incidentals to each pupil	2
Vocal Music, free of charge	

Fees were only slightly less expensive at the Female Collegiate Institute in far-off Little Rock, Arkansas, where five months of instruction on the piano, guitar, or harp, was $25.[48]

The parlor songs taught at these institutes and subsequently played and sung at home were the last vestiges of the "romantic" era in musical taste. They catered to amateur singers and musicians, rather than skilled performers, and resembled English, Scottish, and Irish ballads. Stylistically, they were highly sentimental. Written for expressive rather than powerful voices, they were meant to be sung against a background of soft-stringed instruments like the parlor piano or guitar, which were to be played unobtrusively. Musically, the tunes were simple; most were written in the easier major keys in 4/4 rhythm, and tunes predictably rose and fell. More difficult songs were simply arranged, usually for the piano, to keep them within the modest abilities of the great majority of Americans, who were their own accompanists. All stanzas in a song were set to the same tune, which made it easier for a singer to learn them. Songwriters repeatedly used the same notes. This had the twin virtue of keeping songs simple and heightened the emotional content of the lyrics. Few songs contained expressive notations. This left vocalists free to sing softer or louder where they felt such dynamics best fit the mood of the lyrics.[49]

To us, viewing the Civil War from the end of the twentieth century, the pleasure that civilians and soldiers derived from singing and playing songs about orphaned or dying children, widowed or frail mothers, and dead or dying sweethearts seems bizarre. But in the parlors of nineteenth-century America and around the campfire, parlor songs about death did not seem out of place. Only by appreciating the ethos of the time can we understand how battle-hardened soldiers, fresh from the killing fields, could seem so blasé about enjoying these tear-drenched songs.

CHAPTER 8

Calls To Duty

The heady anticipation of battlefield glory did not last long after military life became a reality. Most soldiers were unprepared for the monotonous boredom of camp life. Richard Simpson (3rd South Carolina Volunteers) told his sister, "The dull routine of camp life continues daily, and I am becoming entirely disgusted with anything that pertains to this form of life. . . . [a soldier] sees but little pleasure in the things transacted in camp."[1] Writing in his diary, Capt. John Dooley (1st Virginia Infantry), also felt that "the quiet and monotony and most tedious irksomeness of camp life goes very much against the private soldiers. . . . these trials are not altogether so sweet as patriotism's first glow in the breast would have us imagine."[2]

Nothing epitomized "the tedious irksomeness of camp life" more than the incessant tap-tap of the military drum or blare of the army bugle. When the Confederate soldier first marched off to war he thrilled to drum music. Entry into military service quickly soured his enthusiasm for that instrument. The drum tap became his master's call, and he thought himself no less a slave to its constant beat than were the slaves on the plantation. Although several books have been written about the brass bands that escorted men to war and serenaded them on the killing field, for the ordinary soldier, the music of the Civil War was foremost the music of the drum and bugle: "You are bugled to breakfast, bugled to guard-mounting, bugled to dinner, bugled to battle, buggled to bed. . . . These 'calls' are pleasant little devices for translating curt English orders into music."[3] The twenty-five "General Calls" that regulated camp life in both the Union and Confederate armies were identical and were contained in William Joseph Hardee's *Rifle and Light Infantry Tactics: For the Exercise and Manoeuvres of Troops When Acting as Light Infantry or Riflemen,* a two-volume manual first published in 1855.[4] Hardee's manual continued to be used in the North until replaced by one written by a Federal officer, Brig. Gen. Silas Casey. Casey's manual described fifteen different "general calls," apart from "police calls," and twenty additional calls for skirmishers. Cavalry buglers had even more calls to master. Julius Leinbach, a musician attached to the 26th North Carolina Infantry, did his best to memorize the calls, but there were so many he couldn't remember them all. "I was much in the condition of the small boy going to school without knowing his lessons," he recalled. But he consoled himself that if he didn't know them all, neither did anyone else, "so if I gave the wrong one, no one would be the wiser."[5] Even Gen. Ulysses S. Grant was at a loss when it came to recognizing all the infantry tunes.[6] The three tunes no one ever confused, however, were "reveille," "taps," and the "long roll."

REVEILLE

"Reveille" was wake-up call. In garrison, it sounded at daybreak—around 5:00 A.M. in summer; 6:00 A.M. in winter.[7] In the field, reveille might sound at anytime if a battle were imminent. Cool summer dawn with the sun breaking in the east or frigid winter morning with snow swirling about—it made no difference—reveille had to be obeyed.

At the sound of reveille, the first sergeants in each company strode among the sleeping bodies, bellowing the command to "turn out for roll call." In the Confederate Army, men traveled very light. If they slept in tents, they slept two together in pup tents. In their tents or out in the open, men in each company slept near each other but not in formal camping "streets." When the first sergeant strode through the company, if he were not alert he would trip over his men.

As the last notes of reveille faded, men sprang to life, many of them hopping on one foot as they tried to put the other into a boot; others ran with one arm in a shirt trying to insert the other into a flapping sleeve. Some men appeared fully dressed, not because they were fastidious, but because they cared little for personal cleanliness and slept in their uniforms to gain another minute's rest.

When the field musicians stopped sounding reveille, the first sergeant barked, "roll call." As his men stood before him, he took attendance in the presence of the company captain or lieutenant, read out general orders, and assigned each man his duties for the day. He then dismissed his company and searched for absentees. The only enlisted men who did not have to appear at roll call were the guards, the sick, and those who had been excused.

Years after the war, when they no longer had to rise before dawn, nostalgic memories conjured up transcendent images of reveille. The irksome wake-up call was transmuted into an "electrifying" experience orchestrated by virtuoso drummers and buglers. As the bright tinge of morning suddenly appeared in the eastern sky, a single bugle sounded the cockcrow and drummer boys stationed at each regimental headquarters beat their "rat-ta-ta-plans." The sound echoed throughout the camp, giving a man a sense he was not merely a soldier but a warrior, bonded to thousands and thousands of other warriors; a force so vast as to be invincible.

Those writing about reveille in their daily diaries did not record the same fondness for the hated wake-up tune, which simply heralded another monotonous day of mindless drills. The listless "rap-tap-taps" by half-awake drummer boys evoked a low chorus of grumbling and cursing, not a mystical experience.

Both sides had their own version of Irving Berlin's "Oh, How I Hate to Get Up in the Morning." In the Confederate army, cadets at the Virginia Military Institute, who would later fight with distinction at New Market (15 May 1864), sang:

> Wake-up-rats-and come to Reveille
> If you want to get-your-corp-orality,
> Wake up rats! Come to Reveille
> If you want to get your corporalite-e-e-e![8]

TAPS

The last call of the day was "taps." At 8:30 P.M. the drums sounded "attention" followed five minutes later by "assembly." This ended socializing and the men, once again, moved into formation for the final roll call to the notes of "tattoo."

As the final notes of tattoo disappeared into the night, the sergeant read out the names in his platoon and the men responded accordingly. One veteran romanticized that roll call somewhat resembled an acappella concert:

> I believe it to be among the abilities of a man of close observation to write out quite at length prominent characteristics of an entire Company, by noting carefully the manner in which the men answer 'Here!' at roll call. Every degree of pitch in the gamut was represented. Every degree of force had its exponent. Some answered in a low voice, only to tease the sergeant, and roar out a

second answer when called again. There were upward slides and downward slides, guttural tones and nasal tones.[9]

After the tattoo roll call, the company was dismissed; after that no one could leave camp without special permission from the officer of the guard. At 9:30 P.M. came taps. This was the signal for "lights-out," plunging the camp into darkness. Except for officers. Rank had its privileges here as elsewhere. Whereas a private could expect some punishment for even talking in his tent after "lights-out," officers often caroused well into the night. The only others who spent much of the night awake were those on picket duty.

The only new field music to appear during the Civil War was a version of taps composed by Union general Dan Butterfield in 1862 after the "Seven Days'" battles (25 June to 1 July 1862). Butterfield gave it to the headquarters bugler to play in place of the official version and it was soon picked up by buglers in other regiments.[10]

THE LONG ROLL

The most energizing music in camp was the rapid paired strokes of the "long roll," the call summoning men to arms. When that tune reverberated through camp no one tarried. Hearts raced. Blood rushed. Where only seconds before men merely played at soldiering, now the game was real. No more drill. No more practice. Sprawled out beside a campfire, a man could bluster about the men he would kill or joke about how other men had skedaddled in battle. When the long roll beckoned, the bravado and humor vanished.

ROGUE'S MARCH

A coward could never be counted on and was literally "drummed out of camp." He was stripped of his uniform and equipment and his head was shaved. A humiliating placard, hung on his back and chest, proclaimed his cowardice. Thoroughly disgraced, he was marched out of camp under guard while a drummer and fifer played the "Rogue's March."[11] If he were found back in camp, he could expect to be shot. During the Civil War being "drummed out of camp" was as great a disgrace as could befall a soldier.

Being "drummed out of camp" to the tune of the "Rogue's March" was also the punishment for stealing. The ceremony was almost identical, the only difference being that the sign around the guilty man's neck said "thief."

When wagon master Thomas Harmon stole some mules and deserted from Camp Jackson in Arkansas, he was pursued, brought back to camp, tried, convicted, and marched out of camp in front of the whole brigade. Instead of playing the customary "Rogue's March," the drummers alternatively beat a tune which conveyed disgrace in the Confederate army—"Yankee Doodle."[12] Harmon was warned not to come within a mile of the camp at the risk of death. Word of his disgrace preceded him home. Upon his arrival he was told he wasn't wanted in those parts either. Harmon ignored the warning and was summarily hanged by his neighbors. "The way of the transgressor (at least in Arkansas) is hard," commented W. L. Gammage, who chronicled the event.[13]

Confederate drummers began substituting "Yankee Doodle" for the "Rogue's March" early in the war. When Brig. Gen. Simon Bolivar Buckner and his staff were being escorted from Fort Donelson after they had surrendered to Grant (16 February 1862), a Federal band derisively struck up "Yankee Doodle." One of Grant's officers, walking beside Buckner, sarcastically asked him if the tune revived recent, more pleasant memories. Buckner opined that it did. It reminded him of an incident, he said, a few days before in camp. A soldier was being drummed out to the tune of the "Rogue's March" when the miscreant, retaining some dignity in his shame, called, "Stop." They were playing the wrong tune, he insisted. "Play `Yankee Doodle,'" he suggested, "a half million of rogues march to that every day." The reactions of the Union officer and of General Grant, who was also walking with the Confederate general when he turned the tables on his taunter, went unrecorded.

The "Rogue's March" was also played at military executions, which officers staged for maximum shock as a deterrent.[14] The ceremony was basically the same in both the Confederate and Federal armies. Soldiers were formed into three sides of a rectangle in two double ranks, each rank facing inward. The condemned man had to walk through the file. First in the procession came the provost marshal astride a horse, followed by the musicians playing the "Rogue's March." Next came a squad of twelve executioners, two from each company of the regiment to which the deserter belonged. The guns of six were loaded with blanks, the other six carried live ammunition. In this way none would know if his shot killed the prisoner. Besides playing during executions, musicians were sometimes assigned the grisly job of loading the guns for these firing squads.[15] Next came the coffin carried by four men followed by the prisoner who was surrounded by four guards.

A chaplain, flanked by a guard on either side, followed. Last came another armed squad to fire a second round if the first round did not kill.

The file was long and deep. When the procession finally came to the open side of the rectangle, the prisoner was either pinioned to a stake or bound with his hands behind him and either placed on his knees on the ground or on the end of his coffin. The box was positioned in front of the grave so it wouldn't have to be carried. The firing squad formed into two ranks twenty to thirty feet from the condemned man. The chaplain prayed both silently and then with the doomed man. A drum or bugle then sounded. The provost marshall approached the prisoner, bound his eyes with a handkerchief, and read the order for the execution. After the sentence was read the drum or bugle sounded again. The officer stepped aside. Next came the command, loud but calm, as if it were only a drill: "Ready! Aim! Fire!"

After the execution, the entire brigade filed past the dead man to absorb the full measure of his crime.[16] Once again, the musicians led the procession; instead of the "Rogue's March," they played a lively, insensitive quickstep, like "The Girl I Left behind Me," to move the procession along quickly. Some men pretended to take little notice of the dead man; others hid their feelings behind caps pulled furtively over moist eyes; still others brushed away tears dripping down their weather-beaten faces. Those refusing to be part of the firing squad were themselves court-martialed and sentenced to at least four days on bread and water in the guardhouse.[17]

WHEN BUGLERS SHALL NO LONGER PLAY

A Union soldier spoke for soldiers on both sides when he mused how "irksome [it was] for freeborn American citizens to be called to church, to visit the surgeon, to get ready for fatigue, guard, or dress parade, to go to bed, in short to perform all the varied duties of the camp, to the everlasting tap-tap of the drum."[18] Like other frustrations of army life, rank-and-file soldiers lightened their boredom by turning many of these tunes into humorous ditties. In the Confederate army, griping about the "irksome" music of the camp was turned into a humorous paean to the omnipresent bugler. Entitled, "Upi-dee,"[19] it began making the rounds in Confederate camps during the winter of 1862 to 1863.

The bugler, says the song, spends his day patrolling the camp deliberately looking for ways to make a soldier's life miserable: "No matter, be there rain or snow, that bugler still is bound to blow, / U-pi de-I de-I da! / U-pi de! U-p da!"

Spying a soldier in his bunk just before daybreak, the bugler muses, "There's too much comfort there . . . and so I'll blow the 'Reveille'." Since "Cabin fires, warm and bright," personally afford him no heat, the bugler unhesitatingly sounds "Retreat." Seeing a fire with a pot in which the "choicest viands [are] smoking hot," the miffed bugler says "you shan't enjoy the stew," and "'Boots and Saddles' loudly blew." Or scarcely does a soldier's half-cooked meal begin, ere he hears the order to "Fall in!" Even after starving all day and marching all night, "Perchance if you get bread and meat / That bugler will not let you eat."

"Oh, hasten then, that glorious day," the forlorn soldier-narrator pleads:

> When buglers shall no longer play;
> When we, through Peace, shall be set free,
> From "Tattoo," "Taps" and "Reveille."

FIELD MUSICIANS

The men or boys who beat the "rat-ta-ta-plans" on the drum or played those war tunes on the fife or bugle were called "field musicians" or simply musicians, in contrast to the "musicians of the band." The job of the "musicians of the band" was to instill patriotism, raise flagging spirits, and inspire courage and esprit de corps. The field musician's job was to regulate and coordinate camp life. He was an army's timepiece. An army could get by without "musicians of the band," but not without field musicians. Their rudimentary tunes told soldiers when to wake up, when to sleep, when to eat, and when to rest. They dispatched him to the marching field, signaled him to fix bayonet, unfix bayonet, lie down, get up, march quick time or double quick time. They summoned him to battle and sent him crashing into death's very maw.[20]

Field musicians were so essential to warfare during the Civil War that each infantry company in the Union and Confederate armies was assigned two of them. If one were killed or wounded, the company had a backup to sound the calls while a replacement was trained. Whereas a few companies in the Confederate army were fortunate to have three field musicians (two drummers and a fifer), many companies had no field musicians. In those cases, officers did the next best thing—they coordinated their daily activities with nearby Federal tunes.[21]

In the infantry and the marines, field calls were played on the drum alone or along with a fife.[22] In most cases, bugles regulated daily activities in the cavalry and artillery, although occasionally an infantry unit had a bugler, and some artillery units had drummers as their field musicians.

The Confederate army was not only often in need of drummers, it was also often in need of drums upon which to play. In some regiments drummers and tanners were even given a few days leave to go home, on condition they bring back dog-skins for drumheads. Drums were in such short supply in some companies that drummers risked their lives to protect them. Often drums were taken from dead or wounded Union drummers or picked up after they were thrown away by frightened enemy drummers during a "skedaddle." Units in the Southern army technically could requisition drums and other instruments from the quartermaster department, which was obliged to honor those requests. But the quartermaster general had no national manufacturers to call upon, and companies often acquired drums on their own from private manufacturers. One of these manufacturers was the New Orleans firm of Werlein and Halsey, which assured potential buyers that its drums were made "using the best materials" and warned against "purchasing instruments of this kind from persons who get them up on a cheap plan, as they cannot be relied on for use." Business was business, even in wartime. The competitor Werlein and Halsey accused of getting military drums "up on a cheap plan" was Louis Grunewald, who invited "the attention of military companies to his stock of home-made drums and fifes which he offers at the lowest prices."[23]

Besides playing the camp tunes, field musicians performed menial chores around camp, including fetching water, carrying messages, barbering, and sharpening surgeons' knives. Although buglers accompanied their companies into battle, drummers and fifers tapped and blew signals from immediately behind the advancing line. After a battle, field musicians were expected to help carry wounded soldiers to hospitals, haul amputated limbs for burial, and dig graves.

Contrary to the romantic image of the drummer boy "beating the rally" to give scattered soldiers a gathering point from which to re-form, "no drummer in my regiment ever played a drum on the battlefield or could see any sense in doing it," said Charles Bardeen, a field musician with the 1st Massachusetts Volunteers.[24] During a battle, drums could scarcely be heard over musketry, cannon, and screaming men, and drummers were told to keep out of the way. "Amid the confusion and noise of battle, there is little chance of martial music being either heard or heeded," erstwhile drummer boy Harry Kieffer wrote in his memoirs. "Our colonel had long ago given us orders . . . You drummer-boys, in time of an engagement, are to lay aside your drums and take stretchers and help off the wounded! And so we sit down there on our drums and watch the line going in with cheers."[25]

Sometimes, however, an excited drummer boy, instead of sitting on his drum and watching, scooped up an abandoned rifle and began firing alongside the combatants.[26]

Although any company could have a bugler, in practice buglers were usually assigned to cavalry and artillery units, whereas drummers and fifers were assigned to the infantry and marines. The obvious reason was that balancing and beating a drum with one hand, while holding a horse's reins in the other, wasn't practical.

Blowing a bugle also required much more skill and talent than beating a drum. Unlike other brass instruments of the day, the army bugle had no valves. Without valves, a bugler could only sound a limited number of notes. Few musicians had the skill to vary the rhythm of those notes so as to produce recognizable calls. By the end of 1862 Confederate officers were privately offering as much as sixty dollars a month, along with a clothing allowance, for a "good bugler."[27] But there weren't enough buglers to go round and units had to settle for drums to signal their commands.

Since bugles and trumpets[28] were much harder to master than drums and fifes, buglers and trumpeters were paid more than drummers. Monthly pay for infantry and artillery field musicians, regardless of age or training, was eleven dollars; cavalry buglers earned twelve dollars a month.[29] The extra dollar reflected the increased hazard of the bugler's job since he rode with his company into battle. Principal musicians were likewise paid more if they served with the cavalry compared with the infantry. A principal musician's pay in the cavalry, for instance, was thirty-four dollars a month, the same as a cavalry sergeant's, plus an additional seventeen dollars a month hazardous pay, whereas principal musicians in the infantry were only paid twenty-one dollars a month.

ALL SENTIMENT WILL DIE OUT

Officers coveted good field musicians for the prestige they added to their units. When Douglas Cater (3rd Texas Cavalry) turned down being an officer in his cavalry company, Captain Cumby, the commanding officer, was relieved. His company needed a good bugler, he said, more than a good junior officer.[30]

Although most drummers were adults, many drummers in both armies were mere waifs who had run away from home in search of adventure. The tradition of recruiting young boys into the army as drummers followed a centuried custom. Writing in 1768, one authority recommended enlisting boys younger than fourteen because they had the flexibility and time to undergo long training as drummers and, "being bred in the Regiment from their infancy, they [would] have a natural affection and attachment to it, and [would be] seldom induced to desert, having no other place to take shelter at."[31] Those enlisting in the Confederate or Union army who were underage needed a letter or other document proving parental consent before their acceptance. Many enlisted under false names to frustrate disapproving parents. Although most officers overlooked the obvious, on occasion, boys were discharged for being underage. One such boy, discharged as a drummer from the 46th Georgia Infantry in 1862, was appointed chief musician of the same regiment a year later![32]

Drummers in both armies were supposedly taught by the regiment's "principal musician," drum major, or another drummer in their regiment.[33] Since there were very few professional field musicians in the Confederate army, the training was typically bad. All musical instruction in the Confederate army was by rote and all tunes were played from memory—drummers and fifers didn't read music. Drummer boy Delevan Miller felt their only purpose in beating calls like reveille "was to make noise enough to wake even the heaviest sleepers." John Jackman ("Orphan brigade") wrote in his diary that his field band acquired about a dozen drums, which they began thumping through the "streets" in camp during Reveille making a "noise . . . sufficient to wake the Seven Sleepers."[34] A dismayed Thomas Caffey, an artillery officer trained in the English army, groused that Confederate fifers "seem to be in an intense screeching agony, whenever called upon, and know no tune except 'Dixie,' or the doleful and eternal 'My Maryland'."[35]

James Tolle, chief musician of the Confederate 6th Kentucky Infantry, became so exasperated at the discordant thumping of Company F's drummer that he says he almost throttled him.[36] A North Carolinian, worrying what the dismal abilities of his field musicians might do to morale, reflected: "If we do not soon have an improvement upon our fife and drum, all sentiment will die out of the Regiment."[37]

Since there was no formal training for field musicians, there was no uniformity of "calls" in the Confederate army. "What one regiment beats for 'tattoo' its next neighbor will furiously drum for 'reveille,'" complained Thomas Caffey. "All the men know is that drums are beating for 'something'," and he warned of a repetition of the debacle at Oak Hill (Wilson's Creek), Missouri, if the calls were not standardized. On 10 August 1861 the

Confederates, under Maj. Gen. Sterling Price and Brig. Gen. Ben McCulloch, were camped some distance apart, but could hear each other's drum calls. Since the two Confederate regiments used different calls, soldiers only answered to those in their own camp. As a result, when Price was suddenly attacked by Brig. Gen. Franz Sigel's Federals and the drummers sounded the call to arms, McCulloch took no notice, "until Sigel opened fire upon his pickets, [and] he ascertained that for once the Missouri drummers meant something by their thumping."[38]

There was less criticism of buglers since the difficulty in playing a bugle meant that buglers often had previous musical training. "Good" buglers were especially praised. Confederate major John Esten Cooke, Maj. Gen. "Jeb" Stuart's staff officer, wrote that a bugle played by a trained musician was "eloquent with poetry and battle!"[39] The habitually critical Thomas Caffey commented on the "splendid effect" of the bugle in the cavalry and artillery corps and wondered "Why cannot our infantry be commanded with the bugle?"[40]

The most famous bugler in the Confederate army, although nothing is known about his bugling ability, was Frederick Nicholls Crouch of the Richmond Howitzers. When he wasn't calling signals, Crouch led the Howitzer Glee Club and composed songs. Prior to the conflict, he had composed the music for "Kathleen Mavourneen," one of the most popular tunes of the war in both the North and South.[41]

A Union veteran recalled a bugler in the 2nd New York Infantry who was particularly inspiring: "There was music in every sound he made, and I have seen officers of other commands stop and listen when the little Swiss was trumpeting the calls. Because his bugle could be heard clearer and farther than others, he was chosen to sound the charge that sent 20,000 Federal soldiers into action against Lee's Confederates at Cold Harbor, Virginia [3 June 1864]. A few moments later, when he saw the ghastly procession of mangled and bleeding comrades coming back, the bugler "sat down and wept like a child."[42]

CHAPTER 9

A Song For All Hardships
and Troubles

Along with the mind-numbing monotony of camp life and the incessantly irksome drum taps and bugle calls, soldiers complained bitterly about the indignity of being told when to get up, when to go to bed, and when to stop talking. For men who prided themselves on their independence, the humiliations and inequities associated with rank particularly chafed. "A soldier is worse than any negro on Chattahoochee river," Thomas Lightfoot (6th Alabama volunteer Infantry) complained to his cousin. "He has no privileges whatever. He is under worse task-masters than any negro. He is not treated with any respect whatever. His officers may insult him and he has no right to open his mouth and dare not do it."[1]

The humorous psychological defense was just as important when someone became overly morbid. "It was a favorite pastime to break into the sublime with the ridiculous," a veteran recalled, "as when . . . 'And Oh! You'll Not Forget Me, Mother, / if I'm numbered with the slain,' is followed by, 'Little brown jug I love thee / Ha, ha, ha, for you and me',"[2] while the words of a favorite marching song consoled tired and weary soldiers by assuring them they were "gay and happy":

> We're the boys so gay and happy,
> Wheresoever we chance to be—
> If at home, or on Camp duty,
> Tis the same—we're always free!

Chorus

> Then let the Yanks say what they will
> We'll be gay and happy still;

156

Gay and happy, gay and happy,
We'll be gay and happy still.[3]

Many, however, were not gay and happy about military life, especially in the latter years of the war when the future looked bleak. Since they were anything but "free" on "camp duty," to equate it with "at home" was ironic.

The first realization that his freedom had ended came during "basic training." Men unused to taking orders now had to obey without question or suffer punishments. Although many officers tried to father the soldiers serving under them, there were others whose rank inflated their sense of self-importance, turning them into petty tyrants. Gen. Daniel Ruggles forced Robert Patrick (4th Louisiana Infantry), his secretary, to sleep at the table where he wrote so he would be available to write orders at any time of the night. Patrick also had to remove his hat and ready a chair for the general whenever he entered the room.[4]

Especially galling were the privileges versus the inequities in the freedom accorded officers and privates. Pvt. Edwin Fay (Minden Louisiana Rangers) echoed thousands of low-ranking soldiers when he wrote to his wife that, "There is too much difference between officers and privates in the army as regards conveniences."[5]

Humor was a defense mechanism, one of the few ways soldiers could alleviate their sense of common resentment without fear of punishment.[6] The forthright Confederate solder quickly learned that in any dispute with the "eagle buttons," he would come out second, landing in the stockade or worse. Poking fun at their situation was much less likely to get him into trouble with authority than direct confrontation. A popular musical safety valve was "The Brass-Mounted Army,"[7] sung to the same tune as "The Southern Wagon," which runs through a litany of inequities, including the importance of withholding "chosen words and phrases" when dealing with officers:

Of late I've been thinking of this great Army school,
With iron regulations, and rather rigid rule;
But chosen words and phrases I need not further speak,
The facts as soldiers know them a stronger language speak.

Oh how do you like the army
The brass-mounted army,

The high falutin' army,
Where eagle buttons rule?

The song targets the difference between the private's food rations and the bountiful feasts that the officers enjoyed:

Our Generals eat the poultry, and buy it very cheap,
Our Colonels and our Majors devour the hog and sheep;
The Privates are contented (except when they can steal,)
With beef and corn bread plenty to make a hearty meal.

At every big plantation, or negro-holder's yard,
Just to save the property the General puts a guard;
The sentry's then instructed to let no Private pass—
The rich man's house and table are fix'd to suit the brass.

Another verse dwells on the officer's alluring uniform, which gave him a distinctive edge over the foot soldiers when it came to the ladies:

And when we meet the ladies we're bound to go it sly—
Head-quarters are the pudding, and the Privates are the pie!
They issue Standing Orders to keep us all in line,
For if we had a showing the brass would fail to shine.

A Southern woman of the day could not resist "a Confederate soldier with brass bars and stars on his coat collar," recalled one miffed soldier in the 1st Alabama Volunteers.[8]

Further resentment of "the brass button gentry's" unfair advantage when it came to the ladies is expressed in "The Officers of Dixie," written by the appropriately named A. Growler, to the tune of "Dixie."[9]

Swelling 'round with gold lace aplenty,
See the gay "brass button" gentry,
The ladies! bless the darling creatures!
Quite distort their pretty features—
And say (I know you've seen it done, sir),
"They'll have an officer or none," sir.

The "gold lace fever" in the song refers to the yellow lace decorations that officers wore on their sleeve cuffs as another insignia of rank.

Despite their humor, these songs bristle with resentment, as another verse from the "Brass-Mounted Army" readily admits:

> If I tell no falsehood there can be nothing wrong;
> If any be offended at what I have to sing,
> Then surely his own conscience applies the bitter sting.

Despite the biting criticisms, however, there is no ring of defeatism in these songs:

> These things, and many others, are truly hard to me,
> But still I'll be contented, and fight for Liberty!

When the war is finally over, says the song,

> O what a jolly time!
> We'll be our own Commanders, and sing much sweeter rhymes.

> We'll see our loving sweethearts, and sometimes kiss them too,
> We'll eat the finest rations, and bid old Buck adieu;
> There'll be no Generals with orders to compel,
> Long boots and eagle buttons, for every fare ye well!

> And thus we'll leave the army, the Brass-mounted Army,
> This highfalutin army where eagle buttons rule.

TOBACCO IS A NOXIOUS WEED

An army's purpose was the annihilation of as many of the enemy as possible, but the annihilators were human beings, who succumbed to the immediacy of death. In battle a soldier focused on killing and avoiding being killed. Afterwards, his nerves remained on edge and the tension inside him needed to be released. It was very difficult to pretend indifference over the loss of a friend or relative, or the sight of "brains, fractured skulls, broken arms and legs, or the human form mangled in every conceivable and inconceivable manner."[10] To assuage the recurrent images and

fears tobacco and alcohol (two of history's most popular chemical anodynes) beckoned.

The Confederate soldier may have lacked enough food, but what he
most sorely missed was his tobacco. Most Johnny Rebs chewed and smoked
tobacco constantly, whether in camp or on the march. One of them even
created a bit of doggerel about the habit:

> Tobacco is a noxious weed.
> Davy Crockett sowed the seed.
> It robs your pocket and soils your clothes,
> And makes a chimney of your nose.[11]

Soldiers constantly complained to the folks at home about the exorbi-
tant prices they were paying for their scarce "chews." When Confederate
money lost almost all its value, tobacco became currency. Square bits of
tobacco were cut into 'chaws' for high-stakes card games. While on picket
duty, Johnny Reb knew he could often trade tobacco for coffee, newspapers, or other items with his Union counterparts. Writing to his sister and
brother in Richmond, Milton Barrett explained how this was done: "We
stood close together and could talk to each other, then when the officers
were not present we exchanged papers and barter[ed] tobacco for coffee.
The way we managed this is with a small boat. With sail set it will go over
by itself then they send back in return the same way. Some of our boys
went over and stayed awhile. The Yankees would let us know when to
come back. This correspondence," he cautioned, "has to be kept secret
from the officers."[12]

WHISKEY LASTS BUT A SHORT TIME IN CAMP

Drinking was another habit Southern boys learned very early in life when
the "'red-eye' was passed around in an old tin coffee-pot, and every man
helped himself by word of mouth'."[13]

Southerners celebrated even trivial events with all-day drinking ses-
sions. They drank "on all occasions, whether from sociability or self-indul-
gence, and at all times from rosy morn to dewy eve, and long after. . . ."[14]
A Southern congressman confessed "no person who is temperate and lives
cleanly and like a gentleman, and who will not therefore condescend to
drink and hurrah with Tom, Dick and Harry, need ever hope for political
preferment." He himself was no hypocrite on that score.[15]

Drinking was against the rules in both armies but commonplace. "The average soldier can smell pot-liquor a mile off, and he will go for it every time, unless he is tied," fretted one teetotaler.[16] Whiskey, said private Robert Moore, "lasts but a short time in camp."[17] Soldiers staggered back from ostensibly going to a spring to fill their canteens with water, "leaving upon the minds of the beholder the impression that the stream ran brandy."[18]

Men of all ranks frequently drank to the point of drunkenness, including officers in charge of disciplining other soldiers for drunkenness.[19] Maj. Gen. Thomas "Stonewall" Jackson said he feared liquor more than the Pope's army.[20] Those in the lower ranks, however, resented the fact that they alone were punished for breaking the rules:

> Whisky is a monster, and ruins great and small,
> But in our noble Army, Head-quarters get it all;
> They drink it when there's danger, altho' it seems too hard,
> But if a Private touches it they put him "under guard."[21]

An integral part of male culture, drinking also enabled soldiers to steel themselves or to blot the horrors of war from their minds. It offered an escape from the anxieties about dying or fears of cowardice in the face of the enemy. Soldiers drank virtually anything made with alcohol to experience any euphoria—although they didn't admit it in their letters.

Bringing alcohol into camp was against the rules, but some sutlers sold it on the sly, not just in small containers, but in five-gallon kegs. Messmates pooled their money to buy one and buried their keg in their tent. If the mess were ordered out on assignment, each man filled his canteen with whiskey before setting out. Some men carried their liquor with them in their musket barrels, using a cork drummed tightly into the muzzle and a cap on the nipple to keep it from spilling out.[22]

A comic song around Confederate campfires described the escapades of Tom Jennings, a drunk who promised his wife he'd stay sober at a party to which he'd been invited.

> Tom Jennings who never could drinking avoid
> Thou' vows he was always a making.
> But at each bout he was ever annoyed
> With a nervousness and a head aching.

> Going out to a party one evening last week
> His wife said to him as a warning,
> "Be careful dear Thomas and mind what you take.
> And think of your head in the morning."

Despite his good intentions, Tom succumbs, and pays the price the next morning:

> At last he reached home with his hat without brim,
> And he spoke to his wife rather fawning,
> "I've been (hic) struck by a brute (hic) because I said to him:
> To think of my head (hic) in the morning."
> Too tipsy for bed as he lay on the floor,
> How he caught it for scorning her warning.

Charles L. Ward, who wrote the song while serving with the 4th Kentucky Regiment, dedicated it "to all the commissaries, quartermasters and surgeons in the Confederate army." The song was published with an engraved cover depicting Jennings leaving home with his wife holding up a warning finger in one frame, and Jennings entering his home in a drunken stupor, with his wife throwing up her hands, in the other.[23]

MISTER, HERE'S YOUR MULE

A practical joke, occurring early in the war, led to a favorite expression in the Confederate army—one eventually turned into a rollicking song and sold as sheet music.[24]

A sutler known as "Pies," because he specialized in pies and other edibles, did business from a small, dilapidated wagon, drawn by a little, black shaggy mule, at the Camp of Instruction in Jackson, Tennessee. Some of the soldiers decided to play a practical joke on him—they stole his mule while he was off on a chore and hid it in a tent. They then loafed around his wagon pretending nothing had happened.

When Pies realized his mule was missing, he anxiously searched for him. The miscreants, meanwhile, taunted the sutler about the mule's disappearance. Pies was too upset for repartee. Encouraged by his anxiety, his tormenters passed the word around camp that old "Pies" had lost his mule.

One of the mischief makers finally ambled over to a tent far from the sutler's wagon and shouted, "Mister, here's your mule!" The sutler trotted in the direction of the shout but could find neither his mule nor who had shouted. A few minutes later, a voice from another corner of the camp called, "Mister, here's your mule!" and Pies sped off; again, no mule.

When "Mister, here's your mule" started echoing from every section of the camp, the old man realized he'd been had. Totally frustrated, he raised his hands in despair and begged for the return of his mule. When the mule, which was hidden in a nearby tent, heard the sutler's voice, it brayed loudly. The mule's braying was instantly followed by a spontaneous yell by all the pranksters of "Here's your mule!" The sutler took the joke good-naturedly. With his mule back, he eventually sold all his pies and left, and "Here's your mule" went into the soldier's lexicon.

Although the expression surfaced in Jackson, Tennessee, it spread rapidly through the Confederate army. Though most Johnny Rebs did not know its origin, they realized that the expression exemplified the frustration they felt about army life. The soldier was no less a "fool" than the sutler who lost his mule, and he yelled out the expression whenever he made fun of someone or something.[25] The only thing more "enchantinger" was "eating goober peas":[26]

A Farmer came to camp one day,
With milk and eggs to sell,
Upon a "Mule" who oft would stray,
To where no one could tell,
The Farmer tired of his tramp,
For hours was made the fool,
By ev'ry one he met in camp,
With "Mister, here's your Mule."

Chorus

Come on, come on, Come on, old man,
And don't be made a fool,
By ev'ry one, You meet in camp,
With "Mister here's your mule."

"Mister, Here's Your Mule" was such a big hit in the Southern army, Confederate regimental bands began playing it as part of their repertoires and songwriters wrote parodies to it. The song also inspired a dance number, "Here's Your Mule Schottisch," with a music cover featuring a mule and the caption, "Found at last."[27]

THE VALIANT CONSCRIPT

On 16 April 1862 the Confederate Congress adopted conscription. The act not only drafted all men between eighteen and forty-five years of age, it also extended the service for another two years of the soldiers who had voluntarily flocked to the colors just a year before. Again the soldiers groused. Most of the conscripts who were now forced to enter the army were nonslaveholding small farmers, usually married and the fathers of small children. Many volunteers deeply resented having to serve with them because they considered conscripts less committed to the Southern cause and less reliable in a fight.

Songs written during or after the war did not reflect the attitudes of these conscripts toward their impressment or their reception in the ranks. Instead, songs about conscripts were largely negative, and often focused on their draft evasion and desertion.[28]

There were certain exemptions to conscription. A white man who owned a plantation with at least twenty slaves was exempt from the draft. A man could also purchase a substitute. These exceptions led to the bitter recrimination that the ordinary soldier was fighting someone else's war: "It's a rich man's war and a poor man's fight."

During the war, the conscript's unreliability under fire and his penchant for trying to persuade surgeons to excuse him from activity inspired "A Conscript's Troubles," "The Conscript's Lament," "The Fancy Conscript," and "The Valiant Conscript."[29] The latter was a popular musical gibe at the conscript's false bravado, sung to the tune of "Yankee Doodle":

> How are you, boys? I'm just from camp,
> And feel as brave as Caesar;
> The sound of bugle, drum, and fife
> Has raised my Ebenezer.
>
> What's that? oh dear! A boiler's burst,
> A gaspipe has exploded,
> Maybe the Yankees are hard by
> With muskets ready loaded.
> Oh, gallant soldiers, beat em back,

I'll join you in the frolic,
But I've a chill from head to foot,
And symptoms of the colic.

SHORT RATIONS

As setback upon setback inexorably took their toll on the South, the irreverently humorous songs the Confederate soldier sang while grudgingly going about his duties were one of the few remaining outlets left to him in dealing with his bleak existence. "As to the songs in camp'," a Confederate artilleryman reminisced, "they were an ever-recurring attendant of the daily life of the men."[30] During the siege of Vicksburg (1 April to 4 July 1863), starving Confederates had to burrow into the ground or find shelter in caves to keep alive, yet they kept their spirits up by singing.[31]

Not surprisingly, many songs groused about miserable food rations. In the Northern army, soldiers sang paeans to "the Army Bean," and moaned, "Hard tack come again no more" (hardtack was a flour, salt, and water biscuit), but they staved off their hunger. The Southern soldier subsisted on a diet of corn, wheat, rice, tubers, and when he was lucky, some meat. The main staples were "cush," a moldy corn bread baked from coarsely ground cornmeal mixed with pork grease; corn "dodgers," crude biscuits made by boiling doughballs in a pot (the boiling water gave them a dodginglike motion); and "blue beef," badly preserved meat. Often the food was maggot ridden. Those finding insects in their food were kidded about cheating the commissary out of fresh meat. The diet contained very little vitamin A, resulting in widespread night blindness.[32]

Writing from Port Hudson, Louisiana, about twenty-five miles north of Baton Rouge, in June 1862, John Jackman of the "Orphan Brigade" (1st Kentucky Brigade) complained about the meager rations, the poor quality of camp food, and the inflated prices farmers were charging for their wares. He said bitterly that these farmers were not above charging fifty cents for peeping over their fences to look at their vegetables.[33]

John Casler, around the same time, recalled that when rations diminished for the Stonewall Brigade, the Confederates started "conscripting" everything in the way of food: "We would not allow any man's chickens to run out into the road and bite us as we marched along."[34] Although better fed, Union soldiers tired of hardtack and quickly dispatched Secesh chickens that "would not take the oath."[35]

By February 1863 the Confederates at Port Hudson were starving. Instead of cornmeal, soldiers were simply given raw corn on the ear. "If better food is not provided for the troops we will certainly lose a great many men from this cause alone," one of them bitterly complained.[36] Lamented John Casler of his hunger, "I have cut the blood off from [hard] crackers [taken from the bodies of dead Federals] and eaten them."[37]

During Grant's siege of Vicksburg the Confederates survived on mule meat[38] and pea bread,[39] a diet celebrated in A. Dalsheimer's (3rd Louisiana Volunteers) "A Life on the Vicksburg Bluff,"[40] which he wrote to the popular antebellum tune, "A Life on The Ocean Wave":

> A life on the Vicksburg bluff,
> A home in the trenches deep
> Where we dodge "Yank" shells enough,
> And our old "pea-bread" won't keep.
>
> Texas steers are no longer in view,
> Mule steaks are now "done up brown,"
> While pea-bread, mule roast and mule stew,
> Are our fare in Vicksburg town.

"Goober Peas,"[41] a comic song written in the last years of the war by A. Pindar with music by the appropriately named P. Nutt, trivialized the starving rations that forced soldiers to resort to eating peanuts (goober peas) to stay alive:

> Sitting by the road side on a summer day,
> Chatting with my messmates, passing time away,
> Lying in the shadow underneath the trees,
> Goodness how delicious, eating goober peas!
>
> Just before the battle,
> The Gen'ral hears a row,
> He says, "The Yanks are coming.
> I hear their rifles now."
> He turns around in wonder,
> And what do you think he sees?
> The Georgia Militia,
> Eating goober peas!

Chorus

> Peas! Peas! Peas! Peas! eating goober peas!
> Goodness, how delicious, eating goober peas!

The final verse of the song anticipates the freedom from rags and fleas at the end of the war:

> I wish the war was over
> When free from rags and fleas,
> We'd kiss our wives and sweethearts
> And gobble goober peas![42]

With humor the Confederate soldiers made the best deal of their plight. In 1864 the already meager food ration allotted to the Southern foot soldier was trimmed, inspiring "Short Rations," a song "Concocted by Ye Tragic," with "Music Gotten Up by Ye Comic," dedicated "To the Corn-Fed Army of Tennessee."[43] The optimism of the early war years has faded:

> The heavens look'd dismal and dirty,
> And the earth look'd unpleasant and damp,
> As a beau on the wrong side of thirty. . . .

The Confederate soldier, "taking these troubles with quiet," became concerned, the song says, when it was rumored that the army was about to be "put on a diet." Whereas previously, "We had one meal a day," which "was small," the song asks, "Are we now, oh! ye gods! to have none?"

The song's closing comments that no matter how adverse the conditions, the resilient Confederate soldier would stoically take whatever came his way, relying on his innate humor. The Confederate soldier, the songs says, "Has a joke for all hardships and troubles," and he "will conquer in spite of starvation."

By this time, the Blackmars, who had set up shop in Augusta, were also rationing their paper, like music publishers throughout the South.[44] Instead of a cover page for "Short Rations," the Blackmars placed their illustration for the song on the top half of the first page and the first bars of the song below it. The cartoon features the head of a mule, which stands by an empty trough whose wooden sides it has eaten away. Coming out of the mule's mouth is a balloon inscribed with the words "Not enough."

Front page for "Short Rations." Although the song describes food shortages, the title is as apposite for paper shortage in Confederacy in 1864, as reflected in placement of illustration and music on same page.

That sex is totally missing from these songs has perpetuated a mythology that the Civil War soldier was chaste and modest. Carlton McCarthy, a Confederate veteran, for example, claimed never to have heard a vulgar or obscene song in the army.[45] Illicit sex, however, was frequently common in the Southern army; prostitutes and venereal disease were no strangers to soldiers in camp.[46]

McCarthy's statement in his memoirs, which were written long after the war, that "vulgar" or "obscene" songs were scarcely heard is hardly credible. Although such songs were rarely recorded in memoirs, they were recorded in diaries. Until recently, many of these entries were expunged when the diaries were published. Some entries have recently been published[47] and undoubtedly more will come now that publishing's self-imposed prudery has been lifted.

CHAPTER 10

Fiddling And Singing

Southerners were passionately fond of music. "There was music in plenty," recalled Alexander Hunter of his early barracks days in Alexandria, Virginia, while his company awaited their orders. "What if the neighbors did complain of the uproar, especially one irate old fellow, who said in his wrath, 'I will sue the barracks as a nuisance!' He had no soul for music, the said barracks had, and so melody floated in the poisoned air about one-half the time."[1] Many soldiers were so attached to their fiddles that they marched with them even though they threw away most of their other belongings. There were few times when a fiddle or banjo wasn't heard at a mustering center[2] or aboard the trains and steamers that carried men to camp.[3] "Often there would be a hundred or more men present to listen to the music. . . ."[4]

If they didn't initially bring their fiddles with them, soldiers eventually sent home for them. One Confederate desperately missed his instrument, but had held back from sending for it because he was afraid it might get lost, "and I would not lose it for any consideration as my father gave it to me."[5] He finally took a chance, because when the lights were dim, he couldn't read or write, but he could play the fiddle to "amuse myself during the long evenings."[6]

A soldier in the 30th Georgia Infantry was devoted to his fiddle. Just before the regiment was to go into its first battle he strapped the instrument to his back. "If I die," he said, "I want to die to the sound of Betsy," a nickname many soldiers gave to their fiddles. After the battle he was found resting at the foot of a tree, badly wounded in the leg, quietly sawing away on Betsy.[7]

If they didn't have fiddles of their own, they made them with horsehair, or they stole them. Returning from their raid into Ohio, the musicians

"white and colored," riding with Maj. Gen. John Hunt Morgan, 'confis-
cated' some violins and a guitar and a banjo and started a good-natured
competition. "The sentimental guitarist" started playing and singing
"Juanita," but was promptly interrupted by one of the fiddlers playing a rollicking version of "The Hills of Tennessee." Another fiddler sawed "The
Arkansas Traveler" so vigorously he broke one of the strings on the violin
and threw it away. One of the homesick black musicians picked up the
banjo and started singing "Old Folks at Home." The impromptu concert
ended when a bugle blast sent everyone scrambling to their horses to avoid
being overtaken by their pursuers.[8]

Confederate ships also had fiddlers aboard. The *Alabama* had an Irish
fiddler who was "the life of the forecastle." During off duty hours he would
play while fellow seamen danced to his lighter strains. Sometimes he
orchestrated mock battles, dividing the crew into Northerners or Southerners and set them fighting "to the spirit-stirring strains of a march, in
which the Northerners [were] invariably beaten."[9]

Not everyone who played the fiddle was good at it. The Texas Brigade
had a fiddler named Blank who "had no music in him, and he was the only
man in the regiment who did not know it." His messmates abused him;
pleaded with him; offered him bribes to quit. They tried to buy his fiddle.
Failing in their efforts, they threatened to smash it. Blank remained unfazed,
singing and sawing day after day, night after night.

Finally everyone "in range of that old fiddle" became so paralyzed by
Blank's screeching that they petitioned the company captain to suppress
him. The captain, also distracted by Blank's incessant noise, believed firmly
in "individual rights, free speech, and free music." He declined to get
involved. "Like an evil shadow" the fiddle followed the regiment.

When it seemed the company was doomed to suffer Blank's screechings
for the rest of the war, a miracle intervened. A sutler who had agreed to carry
Blank's fiddle in his wagon fell miles behind the brigade and missed the ford
across the Rapidan. When he tried to get across, his wagon and all its contents were all swept away, including Blank's fiddle. The sutler escaped from
drowning but, happily for the company, the fiddle sank to a watery grave.[10]

DANCING CONFEDERATES
When he wasn't fiddling or singing, Johnny Reb liked nothing better than to
dance. There were almost as many dances in the South during the war as
before. Sam Watkins remembered going to a dance every night when he was

stationed in Perryville, Kentucky, even with Maj. Gen. Don Carlos Buell and his Federals on their doorstep.[11] It wasn't unusual for a prayer meeting to occur in one part of the camp while a dance occurred in another.[12] And wherever there was a dance, there was always at least one fiddler.

Dancing was a popular amusement in the South almost from the time it was first settled. In colonial days, Southern males were not considered gentlemen unless they knew how to move gracefully on the dance floor, although not too gracefully—that was considered effeminate. By 1823 dancing had become so integral a part of a gentleman's education it was incorporated into the curriculum as a required course at West Point, because dancing was not only a social grace but a form of exercise.[13] Even the small frontier town of Alto, Texas, had a dancing master, a Professor Tannin, who gave lessons at the local hotel. Douglas Cater was a music teacher staying at the hotel and though he wasn't one of Tannin's pupils, Tannin asked him to "exercise" with his class anyway. Among the "exercises" Cater learned were cotillions, reels, the schottische, polkas, and the waltz.[14]

Although it was a popular Confederate comic song about beard-wearing officers and female coquetry, "The Captain with His Whiskers"[15] glimpses the dance etiquette of the day:

> When we met at the ball,
> I of course thought 'twas right
> To pretend that we never had met before that night,
> But he knew me at once, I perceived by his glance,
> And I hung down my head when he asked me to dance.
> Oh! he sat by my side at the end of the set,
> And the sweet words he spoke I shall never forget;
> For my heart was enlisted and could not get free,
> As the Captain with his whiskers took a sly glance at me.

In the antebellum years, plantation owners hired "professors of music and dancing"[16] to teach their children the latest steps and "calisthenics" etiquette. In towns, affluent Southerners learned the various fashionable dances of the day from several different "professors" who advertised in the daily newspapers. Cities like New Orleans were "one vast waltzing and galloping Hall."[17] In 1824 six balls were held in the city on successive Fridays at the Orleans Hall, while balls were given every Tuesday and Friday at the French theater.[18] Elegant balls featured a full orchestra where couples

danced the waltz, polka, and schottische. Nightly cotillions, with music provided by one or more fiddlers, graced hotel ballrooms. A guest staying at
New Orleans's fashionable St. Charles Hotel complained of not being able
to sleep because of the "stirring and animated sounds occasioned by a 'car-
pet dance,' with its accompanying giggling, fiddling, and floor shaking."[19]

Less affluent Southerners held their dances in the fields around their
homes and cavorted with less-dignified clog dances like the "Highland
fling," the "fisher's hornpipe," and the "pigeonwing." Some dances, like
"Chicken in the Breadtray," required the dancer to move his feet, hands,
and head like a chicken pecking at crumbs in a bread tray and were learned
by watching slaves dancing.

The essential requisite for a dance, wherever it was held, was a music
maker, preferably a fiddler. Dances often lasted from sundown to broad daylight the next day. Mothers wrapped their babies in shawls, tenderly laid
them underneath wooden benches, and cavorted the night away with reels
and cotillions, with only the light from flickering tallow candles to keep
them from crashing into one another.[20]

Southerners continued to dance the night away even in the midst of
war. In June 1864 Elijah Petty, serving with Walker's Texas Division, wrote
to his wife Ella about a party he had just attended where country belles and
their rustic beaux danced from "dewy eve to easy morn" to "the scraping
of a miserable 'fiddle'."[21]

Although a fiddler's skill was widely admired, what impressed dancers
most about a particular fiddler was not the number of different tunes he
could play but his stamina. James Huffman, an infantryman in the 17th Virginia Volunteers, remembered a night in the fall of 1861 when he went to a
wedding near Fairfax County Courthouse in Virginia. The guests danced to
the music of a fiddle, played by an old Negro named Dan, until about two
o'clock in the morning. By that time Dan's arms had weakened and his fingers had cramped; he said he couldn't play anymore. But the revelers would
have none of it. They plied the old fiddler with liquor and promised him
double his fee if he would continue. At three o'clock in the morning, two
lines formed across the floor and Dan struck up the "Old Virginia Reel."
"The dancers went at it with a will," recalled Huffman; the faster the music,
"the quicker answering feet kept time, until the old house shook and quiv-
ered again." The enraptured dancers eventually realized that Dan wasn't
keeping up and the tune he was playing hadn't changed for quite some time.

The dancers demanded variety, but Dan didn't hear them—he was fast asleep, "his head had sunk on his shoulder, his breathing was regular, while from his nose was issuing an orthodox, unmistakable snore." "It was," said Huffman, "a remarkable opportunity for noting the automatic power of the muscles while the senses were locked in deepest sleep." Dan still held his fiddle in the usual way, except that instead of resting it under his chin it was on his chest. His bow still managed to saw out a recognizable tune, although occasionally it scratched on the wrong side of the bridge. Everyone suddenly stopped and huddled around the old fiddler as he unconsciously sawed away. What they were seeing was nothing unusual, explained the host of the party, for old Dan often combined "the power of Orpheus with that of Morpheus . . . the later held him, the former used him."[22]

In camp Johnny Reb danced with his messmates—the "ladies" tied a handkerchief around their left arms. These dances usually started spontaneously; out came an old battered fiddle and someone bowed away. "We would trip the light fantastic toe on the greensward with as much zest as at home in the dance hall with the girls, but not with the same pleasure, affection and love defined by one of the boys as 'an inward impressibility and an outward all-over-ishness'."[23] Officers sometimes participated in the revelry.[24] Many of these dances, like "Chicken in the Breadtray," were popular in camp, but "the execution by our boys, like all imitations," said a soldier in the North Carolina Anson Guard, "was inferior to the darkies, who are expert dancers."[25] These impromptu dances occurred anywhere, even during an irksome delay on a march when a column had to halt because it couldn't cross a bridge.[26]

When possible, dance-loving Rebs arranged informal dances at the houses of people around the countryside.[27] During the winter of 1861 to 1862, the Richmond Howitzers were encamped at Goose Creek, near Leesburg. To relieve the boredom, they reconnoitered the neighborhood for diversions. Rumors of a "fiddler's green" nearby sent imaginations soaring. The "fiddler's green," however, turned out to be nothing more than a small shanty inhabited by a widow and her three daughters, each of whom played the fiddle. They sold groceries and moonshine to boot; what better place for a grand ball?

A lavish affair ensued. A buffet loaded the table; the moonshine flowed freely. The reels, jigs, quadrilles, waltzes, lancers, and polkas continued nonstop until dawn when the revelers staggered back to camp. Years later, a Howitzer fondly recollected that night as "the embodiment of fairyland."[28]

Sometimes the Rebs invited their enemies to these dances. On one such occasion during the winter of 1862 to 1863, a Confederate picket officer called to his Union counterpart across the Rappahannock asking if he'd like to come over after dark and accompany him to a dance at a farmhouse near the lines. The Union officer was hesitant but agreed after the Confederate promised, on his honor as a soldier, that he would see him back safely. At the dance, the Union soldier, dressed in civilian clothing, was introduced to the local girls as a new recruit who had just arrived in camp. After a festive evening the Union officer was back behind his own lines before daylight.[29]

One of the biggest balls of the Civil War occurred on 8 September 1862, just after the Confederate army invaded Maryland. Flamboyant Maj. Gen. "Jeb" Stuart wanted to win the Marylanders over to the Southern side. At a ball, Marylanders would see his men as friends instead of invaders.

Urbana was the site. All the families in and around the town were invited, "rabid Northerners as well as friends of the Southern cause." The large hall where the dance was to be held was aired, swept clean, and festooned with roses. Everything was in place at the appointed time. As Stuart hoped, people turned out from miles around.

Despite the elaborate preparations, disaster struck. Not aware of the dance etiquette followed at formal balls, Stuart's Prussian-born chief of staff, Maj. Heros Von Borcke, had instructed the orchestra to start with a polka. When the music began and he placed his hands on his partner, she immediately balked at being asked to indulge in a round dance with a gentleman to whom she was not related. Von Borcke quickly realized his faux pas and switched from a polka to a quadrille. Gay and happy cavalrymen whirled about in the candlelight with their debonair partners.[30] Dancing with Von Borcke was a "breathtaking" experience, Constance Cary remembered. Von Borcke led his partner in swift, circling dance steps, never reversing his direction. If he encountered an obstacle on the ballroom floor, he simply lifted his partner off her feet, without altering a step, and deposited her safely beyond.[31]

SOCIAL JAMBALAYAS

Jefferson Davis's wife, Varina, was especially fond of music and dancing and used to host fortnightly "receptions" in Richmond, in imitation of the custom at the Lincoln White House. "Social jambalayas" Thomas De Leon called them, "appetizing enough to tickle the dieted palate of Richmond's exclusiveness."[32] The "exclusive" guests included cabinet ministers, congress-men, heads of departments, generals, admirals, diplomats, dainty debutantes and belles, along with sturdy artisans, their hands scrubbed to whiteness so that they would be clean enough to shake the president's hand, and specula-tors, looking for a chance to make valuable political contacts. In the early days, a military band played popular and sometimes classic music to add to the festive spirit. The high point of these soirees was the evening dance in which Varina and the other leading ladies would swirl around the floor with "Jeb" Stuart and other young officers temporarily on leave from the front.[33]

The first winter of the war, said De Leon, "was one [to] be written in red letters, for old Richmond rang with a chime of merry laughter that for the time drowned the echo of the summer's fights and the groans of the wayside hospitals." Even during the desperate latter part of the war, people in Richmond continued to host dances in their homes, "the young ladies appearing in the old, resurrected costumes of the Revolutionary period of ancient Virginia belles and grandmothers, and right glad to get them of that or any other period."[34]

When the "jambalayas" gave out, Richmonders hosted "starvation par-ties" where high ranking officers and junior officers from "gentlemanly" units like the New Orleans Washington Artillery could relax or whirl for hours with their belles.[35] When they weren't dancing with their belles, they slaked their thirst on *eau de James River,* vintage 1864. The only expense at these soirees was the musicians.

Hosted by some of the leading social families in Richmond,[36] these dances and parties were attended by many of the Confederacy's intellectual elite. Richmond's socially prominent families also hosted more informal gatherings where they served homemade dinners, and guests entertained one another with songs and poems. Although informal, these get-togethers occurred so often they became known as meetings of the "Mosaic Club." John R. Thompson, editor of the *Southern Literary Messenger,* was a mem-ber, and many of his poems, which appeared in the paper, were discussed while the hypersensitive Thompson nervously listened to the comments. John Esten Cooke, the "Walter Scott of the South," also dropped by when his duties on Gen. "Jeb" Stuart's staff permitted a "flying visit to Rich-mond." Innes Randolph, who also served under Stuart and is best known for writing the unrepentant "Oh, I'm a Good Ole Rebel" after the war, was another attendee. Gen. John Pegram also liked to drop in. Though he didn't play any musical instruments very well, he was an "artistic whistler."

Sometimes Stuart himself attended, singing "Jine the Cavalry" as he rode back to camp or wherever he was going to sleep.[37]

WHILING AWAY WINTER NIGHTS

Amateur theatricals were another favorite pastime and drew enthusiastic audiences in camp and on the home front.[38] In addition to glee clubs, soldiers in various Southern units formed amateur musical troupes and minstrel groups such as the Confederate Minstrels (Pickett's Division) and the Washington Light Infantry Minstrels (from Charleston, South Carolina).[39] The best-known of these groups was Hood's Minstrels from Hood's Texas brigade. One reason they were so highly regarded is that many of the group's performers had worked as professional and amateur musicians before the war.

At first Hood's Minstrels played in the open air, but as the winter of 1862 approached, they built a log house theater with the help of comrades happy to have something to do to relieve the boredom of winter camp.

The men cut logs, dragged them through the snow, split and hewed them, and drove them into the ground. They tore old planks from deserted frame houses and carried them to camp on their backs to make a stage, and they used tents to make a drop curtain. One of the camp artists painted the curtain with a scene inspired by Dante's *Inferno,* showing demons engaged in mortal combat with green-eyed sea monsters flaring long red tongues. The theater was packed six nights a week; on the seventh, it served as the camp church.

Music for the amateur theatricals was supplied by the 4th Texas brass band. Sometimes General Stuart's banjo player Sam Sweeney was a guest star. Other guest stars included Harry Macarthy, author of "The Bonnie Blue Flag," who came from Richmond to entertain the troops.[40] The show was such a big hit that the brigade put it on every winter after that. In the winter of 1864 it was joined by a group of professionals and amateurs who called their act the "Varieties." The professionals were Mollie Bailey, the wife of Gus Bailey, the leader of Hood's Minstrels, and her sister. Generals Hood, Lee, Longstreet, (Louis) Wigfalls, and Beverly Robertson were in the audience one time or another.[41]

For one of these shows in February 1863, a special railway train was run so that scores of ladies from around Fredericksburg could attend. General Longstreet and his staff turned out as did officers from all the divisions of the army. Some of "Stonewall" Jackson's men walked twenty miles to see the show.[42] General Lee sent a note expressing his regrets at not being able to be there and wished them every success.[43]

John Casler (Stonewall Brigade) recalled that "the theatre became a great place of resort to while away the dull winter nights."[44] They also merged large numbers of officers and ordinary soldiers in a friendly atmosphere of high spirits and provided an informal place for them to reaffirm the comunity bonds of prewar days. Minstrel shows poked fun at authority, and in the army, these humorous barbs released pent-up tensions against officers. Of all the ways soldiers in camp devised for amusing themselves, none were enjoyed more than these amateur theatricals, opined surgeon LeGrand Wilson.[45]

THE SINGING MAN

Southern soldiers, including some of their best-known officers, also loved to sing themselves. On one night early in the war, Generals Beauregard, Johnston, Longstreet, (G. W.) Smith, and Van Dorn were sitting around a banquet table discussing the merits of various alternatives to "Dixie" for a national anthem. Some championed "Maryland! My Maryland!" Others, especially Van Dorn, argued on behalf of the liberty duet from Bellini's opera, *I Puritani,* and began singing it.

"Up on the table and show yourself; we can't see you," bellowed Longstreet.

"Not unless you stand by me," Van Dorn bellowed back.

Longstreet and Smith rose to the challenge. They climbed on the table with Van Dorn, put their arms around one another, and began lustily singing from *I Puritani* while Generals "Johnston and Beauregard stood near with twinkling eyes of amusement and enjoyment." Despite their avowed fondness for the liberty duet from *I Puritani,* the generals decided to stick with "Dixie."[46]

Maj. Gen. "Jeb" Stuart was the best-known singing general of the Civil War. Stuart "sang as he fought," said Gen. John Gordon.[47] Capt. Fitzgerald Ross, an English officer who visited Stuart's camp, recalled how Stuart and his officers would sit around the campfire singing while Sam Sweeney strummed along on the banjo.[48] A night rarely passed at "The Bower," Stuart's camp at the Dandridge plantation near Charlestown, Virginia, without a dance or a concert under Sweeney's direction.[49] Stuart himself, said Borcke, was "always the gayest and noisiest of the party," and usually closed the festivities with "Jine the cavalry," the song most closely associated with his exploits. As soon as Stuart started, "the whole of the excited Company, young and old, joined in and kept singing, the last notes sounding far through the still air of the night as we walked back to our tents."[50]

Val Giles, one of Hood's Texans, recalled the first time he saw Stuart. It was in April 1862, when his brigade was camped near Williamsburg on its way to Yorktown. "About ten o'clock we heard the jingling of spurs, the clanking of sabers, the tinkling of a banjo, and somebody singing. . . . General Stuart was riding in front and old Sweeney, rode by his side, picking his banjo and singing 'Bonnie Jean,' with Stuart and his men joining in on the chorus."[51]

Just before he died at the battle of Yellow Tavern in May 1864, Stuart again headed his column, his long black plume waving in the gentle breeze, singing "Lorena." His dying request was for someone to sing "Rock of Ages" to him.[52]

Gen. Fitzhugh Lee, who served under Stuart, enjoyed a good time and a good song as much as his superior. Unlike Stuart in appearance, Lee was short and stout, with a short neck and broad shoulders. His resemblance to Stuart lay in his ruddy beard, his animal spirit, and his joyous voice. Lee was also an extrovert who unabashedly performed song and dance routines at the Richmond salons and sang "corn-shucking tunes." Like Stuart, he also sang "Jine the Cavalry" when he rode off from these evening entertainments.[53]

Capt. Arthur Fremantle, an English officer passing through Texas on his way to Lee's army in 1863, recalled the night Gen. "Prince" John Magruder and his nephew entertained him with numerous songs accompanied by a Captain Dwyer on the fiddle.[54]

Even the dour, laconic Jefferson Davis liked to sing. His wife Varina claimed he had a high baritone singing voice. Although Davis did not possess "musical culture," she maintained he had a good ear and could sing any song "very sweetly" after hearing it rendered accurately. Among his favorites were "The Harp That Once in Tara's Halls," and "The Minstrel Boy."[55]

Some officers were remembered for their bravery under fire; some for their singing. Benjamin Jones, who served with the Surrey Light Artillery (3rd Virginia Volunteers), reminisced about an especially melodious officer in his regiment:

> I think Lieutenant Foreman is listened to more than the rest. . . . When he strikes in on sweet "Annie Laurie" or the "Bonnie Blue Flag," all the rest stop to listen. But it is when he is threading his way with a loving heart through his own "My Maryland," that his soul seems to melt in tenderness, till his song vibrates and recedes,

almost like harp notes borne away by the evening breeze. He is tenderest then, for his heart is touched. And then there are "Dixie," and "Sweet Evelena," and "Stonewall Jackson's Way," and half a score more songs that are favorites with our boys.[56]

Benjamin Jones fondly remembered the evening songfests as he and his messmates sat around a campfire. "There are quite a number here who have good voices, and the twilight hour, and early darkness before taps, is generally enlivened with song."[57] The "singing man," as Carlton McCarthy of the Richmond Howitzers called him,

was generally a diminutive man, with a sweet voice and a sweetheart at home. His songs had in them rosy lips, blue eyes, golden hair, pearly teeth, and all that sort of thing. Of course he would sing some good rollicking songs in order to give all a chance. . . . There were patriotic songs, romantic and love songs, sarcastic comic and war songs, pirates' glees, plantation melodies, lullabies, good old hymn tunes, anthems, Sunday school songs, and everything but vulgar and obscene songs—these were scarcely every heard, and were nowhere in the army well received or encouraged.[58]

Many of these "singing men" had taken lessons in prewar days from singing teachers who set up schools for that purpose in every city and town across the South. In some towns, doctors made more money giving singing lessons than practicing medicine.[59]

The inspiration for taking singing lessons in many communities was partly congregational singing, which owed its inspiration to the religious revivals that swept over the South in the early nineteenth century.[60] In much of the South, which was more rural than the North, singing in church was where most of the community singing took place. Sunday was the official day for congregational singing in camp, but there were many men who joined informally to sing hymns at night throughout the week.[61]

"Stonewall" Jackson, who didn't have an ear or voice for singing, began each Sunday service at the Presbyterian Sabbath School for Slaves that he oversaw with "Amazing Grace," the only tune he could recognizably render.[62]

Whereas nightly hymns were commonplace in many regiments, the First Virginia Infantry preferred listening to Sgt. Bill Dean's Company G glee club. The First Virginia, said Capt. John Dooley, was "a very irreligious body of young men," compared with the other regiments in his brigade (Kemper's).

Dooley surmised this was because most of its members were from the city while most of the men in the other regiments were from the country.[63]

Southern soldiers formed glee clubs not only for the enjoyment of singing together, but because it was a communal activity. These leisure activities re-created feelings of home and family. Singing in a glee club was a way of spending leisure time in others' company. As cordial games evoked a sense of home in lieu of actual family, glee clubs brought men of different social backgrounds together in a kind of controlled intimacy.[65]

Glee clubs were also an inestimable source of troop morale. Listening to men collectively singing provided a theater-like diversion from the war's turmoil; at the least it lessened the boredom of camp life. Every soldier who wrote about his company's or regiment's glee club said his was the best. "The sweetness and beauty of it all may never be duplicated in song or scene" June Kimble said of the 14th Tennessee Infantry's Glee Club.[66] "I have heard good music in my day," Captain J. H. Jones (38th Mississippi Infantry) said of the 3rd Louisiana glee club, "but I do not think I ever listened to singing that impressed me as that did."[67] Other glee clubs mentioned in Confederate diaries or memoirs include the Orphan Brigade's, Parker's Virginia Battery, 3rd Alabama Infantry, the Richmond Howitzer, and the First Tennessee.[68] The latter's musical talents were mentioned on the cover of "Kingdom's Coming: As Sung by the First Tennessee Opera Troupe," which was published in Augusta by the Blackmars.[69]

IT IS BETTER TO BE MERRY THAN SAD

In the winter of 1864, while the South was beginning to disintegrate, Richmond was unusually blithe. The *Richmond Whig* noted the incongruity between all the festivities going on in Richmond's homes and the desperation outside:

> There has never been a gayer winter in Richmond. Balls and parties every night! One night last week there were seven parties. . . . Go on, good people. It is better to be merry than sad. The wolf is far away from your doors, and it signifieth nothing to you that thousands of our heroic soldiers are shoeless and comfortless; or that a multitude of mothers, wives, and children of the gallant defenders of our country's rights are sorely pinched by hunger and want—aye, starving, or dying from broken hearts.[70]

In addition to the other public and private parties, private theatricals, and tableaux going on in the winter of 1864, in January the President and his wife also began hosting weekly soirees on Tuesdays. Although Richmond was slowly starving, the guests were feted with champagne and cake.[71] Mary Chesnut rationalized the gaiety of those somber days by saying she couldn't see how sadness and despondency would help anyone. "If it would do any good, we could be sad enough."[72]

William Owen, a lieutenant in the elite New Orleans Washington Artillery, recalled "some demure, long-faced people," saying "it was a shame to be dancing while our soldiers were suffering in the field." But soldiers like Owen welcomed a chance to dance, "for who could tell how soon any of us might fill a ditch, or a soldier's grave?" Besides, General Lee himself had given his approval: "Let the young fellows enjoy themselves, they'll fight all the better for it."[73]

Even in the bleakest moments of the war, with Federal troops perched outside the city, dances were a nightly occurrence.[74] Not the bright soirees of earlier years, but carefree dances with hundreds of young men and women, including officers on leave from or leaving for Petersburg. Henry Kyd Douglas, assistant adjutant general on the Stonewall Brigade, recalled that even in the dying moments of the war:

> Social pleasures were abundant and, while the tenure of life was so uncertain, entertainments, dances, marriages were plentiful. The sound of parlor music and of "Dancers dancing in tune" might be heard within cannon shot of the enemy. To go into a parlor for a call or for a waltz with sword and spurs, while orderlies outside held horses ready to mount at the first alarm was no unusual thing. To spend half the night in the saddle that the other half might be spent in social revelry was not strange enough to cause comment.[75]

Looking back on those times, however, Thomas DeLeon saw these "spasms of gayety" as superficial and symptomatic of the last feverish gasps of a dying country. Mrs. Roger Pryor agreed: "All who remember the dark days of the winter of 1864–1865 will bear witness to the unwritten law enforcing cheerfulness. It was tacitly understood that we must make no moan, yield to no outward expression of despondency or despair."[76]

CHAPTER 11

Ensembles for Rhapsodizing Warriors: Confederate Brass Bands

Virtually every military activity during the Civil War had its musical accompaniment. Not only was there a brass band to provide the music for spirited parades for civilians, military dress parades, brigade reviews, solemn funerals, daytime marches, and twilight concerts. Every major battle of the war had some musical accompaniment. In some instances regimental bands played during the battle itself.

When regiments marched through towns and cities, their brass bands proudly led the way. In partisan towns, people cheered and waved at the troops. Alexander Hunter, an artilleryman in the 17th Virginia Volunteers, recalled the parade as he and thousands of other men in Robert E. Lee's Army of Northern Virginia marched through Richmond on their way to Yorktown in March 1862. "It was a scene never to be forgotten by any old Johnny who had cleaned his musket, washed his shirt and mended his rags to show off before les grandes dames of that city." The side-walks were crammed with cheering crowds of old men, boys and girls, and here and there a hobbling wounded veteran of the War with Mexico. Every window, balcony, and portico on Main Street was packed with "the beauty and fashion of Richmond, and Richmond had the loveliest women in the world then. As [it] marched in solid column down the roadway, a full brass band to each brigade, and a drum and fife to each regiment," Hunter was intoxicated by the pageantry:

> On they came, Longstreet's corps in advance, stepping jauntily to the air of "The girl I left behind me." . . . The steady tramp of marching thousands to the measured beat of soul-stirring music, scintillating sun-gleams on burnished guns and glittering bayonets, the bloating of banners, the waving of hats to the shouts of the

multitude wrought into irrepressible ardor by the splendid pageantry, was a spectacle that photographed itself upon the memory of every bystander and all soldiers who witnessed it or were in the ranks that day.[1]

Throughout the war military bands were prominent at brigade reviews where they embellished the spectacle. In 1861 civilians took picnic lunches and traveled many miles on horseback and in carriages to watch the magnificent pageantry of these military extravaganzas. When a French dignitary, Napoléon-Joseph-Charles-Paul Bonaparte (son of Jérôme Bonaparte), reviewed Beauregard's Confederates at Centreville, Virginia, in August 1861, the First Virginia regiment "went through all the evolutions of infantry for the Prince's inspection; and while the movements were going on, the band of the regiment . . . played the 'Mocking Bird,' and all the well known tunes, impressing itself upon the memory of everybody present, as an inseparable 'feature' of the occasion!"[2] It was, in the words of Giles of Hood's Texas Brigade, a "big show," with generals riding at the head of the procession and smartly dressed staff officers, colonels and majors prancing close behind, and behind them, thousands of men stepping proudly, "each fellow looking as if the success or failure of the Confederacy depended on him alone."[3]

Once the troops were drawn up in formation, each captain barked the order "Parade rest!" to his command. This was the signal for the bands to "beat off." Each band marched down its regiment playing a slow tempo and marched back to a quick step. Officers then moved four paces to the front, majors and lieutenant colonels at the head. Sergeants stepped to the center of the column and reported to the adjutant. The adjutant then reported to the colonel and stepped behind him. Next came a brisk exercise in arms, after which "Parade rest!" was repeated. Officers then proceeded to the center, faced the colonel, and led by the adjutant, marched up to him touching their hats. They then encircled him and waited for his remarks and orders. After the colonel spoke, the officers returned to their posts and the regiment broke into companies. The company sergeant then led his company back to its quarters and dismissed it.

On some occasions more than thirty regimental bands occupied the field. Batteries fired salutes, battle flags and state flags flashed and waved in the sunlight, and the air reverberated with patriotic airs as regiment after regiment passed in review. A band elevated a dress parade from a routine inspection to a pageant.

CLOSE UP!

It was not all pageantry and cheering crowds, of course. Those were the exceptions—recalled with such vividness because they contrasted so sharply with the drudgery of camp life and the hardship of long grueling marches.

In summer these marches filled a soldier's ears, nostrils, and throat with dust. In his dry mouth he could feel the grit between his teeth. Dust in his eyes nearly blinded him. It filled his shoes, penetrated his clothes, lay against his entire body. When it mixed with his sweat the grime rubbed his skin raw. Once the sweltering heat of summer passed, he anticipated sleet, snow, and cold. "This takes the poetry out of war, don't it," muttered a weary Reb.[4]

Rain was a soldier's greatest torment, more dispiriting than the bitterest cold. Rain meant waterlogged shirts, pants, shoes, and blankets; mud to slog through and sleep in; sodden wood to burn, or more likely, not burn; soggy rations, wet arms and ammunition; swollen creeks to ford and murky springs from which to drink. And all the while, echoing in his ear, the constant command to "Close up!"[5]

Regimental band playing in the vanguard of their columns kept exhausted soldiers from registering their misery. Music was an army's anodyne; it kept footsore and weary bodies from thinking about the grueling miles already tramped and the many still ahead.[6] "Soldiers rarely ever get too tired to catch the step when a brass band strikes up a lively air like 'Dixie'," mused Val Giles.[7] Another soldier reflected on "how inspiring it is to hear a good band strike up a cheerful tune on a long march, how stragglers jump to their places, how quickly the file is dressed, and how easy the step becomes, no matter how weary or how long the march may be!"[8] Without a tune to mark time, he said, his regiment looked like "geese marching through town."[9]

During the Confederate march to Gettysburg in June 1863, Maj. Gen. Robert Emmett Rodes's division was so exhausted that his men could hardly lift their feet. Gen. Robert E. Lee noticed their bedraggled condition and ordered Brig. Gen. George Pierce Doles's 4th Georgia Infantry Band to play. The music lifted everyone's spirits and Rodes's men stepped briskly once again, inspired by Lee's presence and by the strains of "Tom, March On." "I never saw anything so magical in its effect," recalled a veteran of that campaign.[10] When they reached Chambersburg (Pennsylvania), the band was playing so boisterously, "some thought it might be the music of the circus that was supposed to come to town."[11]

POLKAS, WALTZES, AND THE HISSING OF SHELLS

That band music energized men was so widely recognized it was joked about. Five days after being crushed in the Battle of Mill Springs, Kentucky (19 January 1862), routed Confederate troops were back at Camp Buckner at Cumberland Gap in Tennessee. Asked why it had taken them so much longer to march to Wildcat than return, one of the soldiers joked "they had marched there to the tune of 'Dixie' and came back to the tune of 'Fire in the Mountain, Run Boys Run'."[12]

Band music inspired men to heroics. Stimulated by their bands, fearless soldiers charged behind barely visible tattered flags at row upon row of long hot muzzles spitting wave after wave of fiery death. Waiting to go into action in 1861, a South Carolina private listening to "Pop Goes the Weasel" wrote that he "could whip a whole brigade of the enemy myself, but after due reflection I concluded that I couldn't."[13] Washington Ives (4th Florida Infantry) wrote to his sister that the 32nd Alabama infantry band's rendition of "Down in Alabama . . . makes anyones [sic] blood rise to the point necessary for charging bayonets."[14]

Listening to Confederate and Federal bands just before the Battle of Dinwiddie Courthouse in Virginia (31 March 1865), a soldier in the First Maine Cavalry became so aroused he wanted to charge the enemy right then and there, because "that [music] puts the fight right into me!"[15]

On one occasion, music actually turned the tide of battle. At Williamsburg, Virginia (4 to 5 May 1862), Federal troops in Maj. Gen. Joe Hooker's division were frustrated at their inability to break through the Confederate lines. The Confederates then counterattacked. Hooker's corps commander, Maj. Gen. Samuel Peter Heintzelman, decided he'd better find some way to raise the morale of his wilting men or they'd be overrun.

"Beat the drums!" he bellowed. But the drums were all soaked "and did not give forth cheerful sounds." He then noticed a few bandsmen. "Play something!" he shouted furiously. But there were too few of them to be heard over the battle's din. One of his staff officers scoured the area for more musicians. The music did the trick. "The strains wafted through the old forest, and were heard by our weary troops above the roar of the battle, and inspired them with fresh vigor to perform new deeds of valor," wrote Heintzelman in his official report.[16]

Men also fought and died to music at Gettysburg. From his perch atop a tree at Lee's headquarters on Seminary Ridge, Col. Arthur Fremantle, an

English officer observing Confederate army tactics, was amazed by a Confederate band playing polkas and waltzes, "accompanied by the hissing and bursting of the shells."[17]

THE DEAD MARCH

Before wholesale slaughtering prohibited it, men killed in action or dying in the hospital were laid to rest in a funeral procession. These processions were headed by a drummer and fifer when the deceased was a soldier in the ranks or a junior officer, or by a regimental band if he were a high ranking officer. The prescribed funeral tune in either event was George Frideric Handel's 1730 interlude from *Saul,* better known as the "Dead March." As the coffin passed to its grave, the drummer tapped the dolorous beat on a drum muffled by a piece of cloth placed under loosened snare cords, while the fifer trilled a dirge. The escort following the coffin marched with a slow, measured tread in time to the somber music, then fired a salute at the grave site as the body was laid to rest.[18]

The largest funeral in the South during the war honored Thomas "Stonewall" Jackson, who died shortly after being accidentally wounded by his own pickets after the Battle of Chancellorsville (4 May 1863). Jackson's body was brought by train to Richmond where it laid in state. The mournful cortege accompanying the body to the Lexington cemetery moved through the streets in a silence broken only by the solemn strains of the "Dead March," an artillery blast every half hour, and the sobs of thousands of people weeping "as though mourning a brother."[19]

Andrew Bowering, leader of the 31st Virginia Infantry Band, which led the funeral procession, was in tears. "I have played to men standing against the walls awaiting the cannon that would send them to eternity, in the hospitals I have done my best to soothe the dying hours of men of Virginia, but never was I so much impressed. . . . we played as we had never played before. . . ."[20]

A year later, almost as many tears were shed as the body of "gallant [Major John] Pelham" passed down the same streets, just seven days after his marriage in the same city. "Far down the street . . . we heard the tramp, tramp, of many feet and the unearthly, mournful sound of the dead march," wrote a mourner. "We knew what it was. They were bearing to his last resting place the 'gallant Pelham.' We watched the sad procession file past the door and the music floated to our ears like the wail of a human voice. . . . Such scenes were now frequent and we were soon called upon to bear the heaviest grief yet laid upon the people, who were to be overwhelmed in sorrow before the end should come."[20a] "Now it seems we are never out of the sound of the 'Dead March' in Saul," grieved Mary Chesnut. "It comes and it comes until I feel inclined to close my ears and scream."[21]

AS WAS OUR DUTY

Band musicians in the Federal and Confederate armies normally raised morale and entertained the troops, but they could be called upon to bear arms. In the Federal army, especially in Gen. Phil Sheridan's command, playing music was usually their only job. Not so in the Confederate army. Since the Confederate soldier was often outnumbered in the field by as much as three or four to one, every Confederate band musician was also a combatant. He received the same training as ordinary infantry soldiers,[22] and could be put into the line whenever a unit was seriously undermined.[23] In early 1862 the bandsmen of the 5th Virginia Volunteers ("Stonewall Brigade" Band) were delegated as couriers, with the job of delivering messages and orders regardless of weather or ground conditions. As losses, sickness, and desertions took their toll, more and more musicians carried a rifle as well as their instrument. By December of 1862 the 5th Virginia bandsmen were serving on the line. The only military duty they were exempted from was guard detail.[24]

Man for man, however, musicians were much more effective as morale builders than fighters. "The Ridley Family Band," opined LeGrand Wilson, a doctor in the Confederate army, "was worth more to its brigade as a health promoter than two surgeons . . . with well-filled chests of medicine." Whenever it rendered "Old Folks at Home," or "I'm Going Back to Dixie," or "Sweet Evelina," said Wilson, it would invariably elicit "a cheer that would cause your hair to straighten out."[25]

Although they were sometimes called into the ranks when they weren't tooting, bandsmen on both sides were more often used as stretcher bearers and nursing aides. Cornetist Julius Leinbach and his fellow musicians in the 26th North Carolina Regimental Band[26] "dressed wounds and assisted surgeons in performing gruesome amputations . . . as was our duty to do."[27] By the time of the Petersburg campaign (June 1864 to May 1865) Leinbach "could amputate a man's leg as well as some of the doctors; having so often helped in the several processes of applying tourniquet, cutting and slipping back the skin for a flap to cover the ending of the stump, then cutting the flesh, tieing [sic] the arteries, sawing and trimming the bone and closing the wound. . . ."[28] Other musicians were equally adept."[29]

Despite being ordered to remain in the rear during battles, bandsmen frequently disobeyed and gravitated toward the fighting, tending the wounded and carrying them to ambulances. Years later Confederate brigadier general Xavier Blanchard Debray paid homage to their selflessness. "That self-imposed duty of devotion," he said, endeared them to their regiments.[30]

"I DON'T BELIEVE WE CAN HAVE AN ARMY WITHOUT MUSIC"

Some Confederate bands were renowned for their musical abilities; others were simply noisy. Good or bad, every man was proud of his regiment's band; a regiment's esprit de corps was always higher if it had a band of its own. A Confederate in the Stonewall brigade wrote of how "proud a sight it was marching in gallant array down a street behind a brass band. Many of the companies were made up of mere boys, but their earnest and joyous faces were as reassuring as the martial music was inspiriting."[31] Whenever a crowd gathered to welcome them, "the band played merrier and livelier tunes [as] the citizens cheered and the ladies waved their handkerchiefs and threw us bouquets."[32]

During military occupation, singing or playing one's patriotic songs shows defiance. By the same token, an invading force sings or plays its patriotic tunes in foreign territory to assert control by snubbing the enemy. This is why the armies of the North and South played patriotic tunes when they marched through the captured towns and cities of their enemies. To hear an enemy band playing their patriotic tunes was humiliating. It symbolized defeat.

Greencastle was the first town the Confederates entered in their invasion of Pennsylvania in June 1863. It was a small, clean town of about three thousand inhabitants, with straight wide streets bordered by brick houses and lined with rosy-cheeked girls. The high-spirited Confederates stepped lightly to "The Bonnie Blue Flag," "My Maryland," and other Southern songs. The girls' looks were as sour as crab apples. The uncomprehending soldiers felt blameless; the Confederates hadn't come to harm or molest the girls; they were only passing through.[33]

When one of the bands began playing "Dixie," a young girl rushed onto her porch defiantly waving a Union flag and shouted, "Traitors—traitors—traitors, come and take this flag, the man of you who dares!" Gen. George Pickett defused the situation by doffing his hat, bowing to the courageous girl, and even saluting her flag. He then turned to his men. Though he said nothing, each man clearly understood his unspoken order. These men, he later wrote his wife, "were all Virginians and didn't forget it . . . almost every man lifted his cap and cheered the little maiden who, though she kept on waving her flag, ceased calling us traitors. . . ." Moved to tears by their unexpected chivalry, the girl lowered her flag and cried out: "Oh, I wish—I wish I had a rebel flag—I'd wave that, too!"[34]

Chambersburg was home to about twice as many people as Greencastle. As the Confederates tramped their way along its roads on 27 June, "the inhabitants watched them from the streets or through their windows, with scowls or bewildered faces as the Confederate troops marched gaily by to the tune of 'Dixie'." One woman stood defiantly at her door, a contemptuous expression on her face, a large Yankee flag on her "ample bosom." Several oblivious companies marched by, but finally, a Texan gravely remarked, "Take care, madam, for Hood's boys are great at storming breastworks when the Yankee colors is on them." Sterner words and she might not have yielded; these caused her to beat a precipitant retreat.[35]

The poignant twilight concerts that lifted the spirits of demoralized armies, may have been music's most noble contribution to the war effort. These evening concerts highlighted the soldier's camp life and the best vantage point was about a half mile from the band.[36] "Soldiers as a class are passionately fond of music," said a Confederate in the 3rd Louisiana Infantry, who fondly recalled these tranquil diversions from the drudgery of army life and the brutality of battle.[37] Patriotic tunes were de rigueur for marching in front of civilians, but for these nighttime rhapsodies soldiers preferred nostalgic parlor songs and sacred hymns on the Sabbath like "Jesus, Savior of My Soul," "How Tedious and Tasteless the Hours," "Nearer, my God, to Thee," "Savior, Breathe an Evening's Blessing," and "America."[38]

On 15 July 1863 General Lee summoned Julius Leinbach and his fellow bandsmen to his headquarters. The anxious musicians believed Lee was going to insert them into the ranks because his army had been crippled at Gettysburg.

But Lee amazed them. Not only did he tell them that in his opinion they were one of the best bands in his army, he asked them to use their musical talents to raise the morale of the dispirited troops.[39] Some time later, before the Battle of the Wilderness (5 to 7 May 1864), the band serenaded Lee and his officers as they planned to engage Grant. While the band played outside his tent, Lee mused, "I don't believe we can have an army without music."[40]

BATTLE OF THE BANDS

Confederate and Federal bandsmen not only provided the music that sent thousands of men into battle, they waged psychological warfare against the enemy and fought musical duels with their counterparts. "There was the same rivalry among the musicians as among the sharpshooters," recalled a veteran of the 20th Massachusetts Volunteers.[41]

Early in the war, a Federal army under Maj. Gen. Nathaniel Prentiss Banks was encamped around Leesburg, Virginia. Confederate forces were bivouacked so close they could hear the Federal bands. After listening to "Yankee Doodle," and "Hail, Columbia," over and over for several weeks, John Esten Cooke, an officer on Maj. Gen. "Jeb" Stuart's staff, "grew desperate, and was filled with unchristian desire to slay the musicians, and so end their performances.

"So, something like joy filled the heart of this writer when the order came to march to a point lower down the river. The column moved; the point was reached; the tents were pitched—then suddenly came the 'unkindest cut of all.' The very same band struck up across the river, playing 'Hail Columbia' with energy, in apparent honor of our presence opposite. When we had moved, it had moved; when we halted, it halted—there was the wretched invention of Satan playing away as before with enormous ardour, and evidently rejoicing in its power over us."[42]

After the Battle of Fredericksburg, the Union and Confederate armies were encamped on either side of the Rappahannock. The hot war was over for a time, but the battle of the bands never ceased. If a Federal band came down to the river bank and began playing some popular Northern airs, a Confederate band would hunker down on its side of the bank and let loose its patriotic tunes.[43]

To not respond to an opposing side's band invited a stinging humiliation.[44] If the affronted side did not have a band of its own to counterattack musically, it met the challenge with the music of artillery fire.[45] In anticipation of being fired upon, musicians sometimes dug pits for themselves and scrambled into them when the shells began to rain down.[46]

A soldier in the 13th New Hampshire Volunteers recalled one night during the battle at Cold Harbor (1 June 1864) when his regimental band engaged the Rebel band opposite it in a "competition concert." The Rebels played their favorites and the Federals replied with theirs. The Rebels then started shelling the Federal band but the Federal band kept playing through the entire bombardment.[47]

Even in the closing moments of the war, the battle of the bands waged on. On 31 March 1865 a Union band made its way to the skirmish line at Dinwiddie Courthouse and faced off with "Yankee Doodle." The Confederates answered with "Dixie." When the Federals struck up "Red, White, and Blue" the Confederates retaliated with "The Bonnie Blue Flag," and "all the time the men on both sides were shooting at one another at every opportunity."[48] The war carried on and every song thrust and bullet had to be parried.

THE COST OF BAND MUSIC

At its peak, there were about 120 bands in the Confederate army and about 1,200 bandsmen,[49] far fewer than most soldiers would have liked: A North Carolinian training at Fort Caswell wrote to his sister early in the war complaining that "banjos and fiddles could be heard at any hour but good brass bands were hardly to be found."[50] Another stoically admitted to himself that "although uniforms, fine bands, pipe clay, and all the rest are desirable things enough, we must, for the present, be content to do without them."[51]

Confederate army regulations allowed up to sixteen band musicians in addition to a bandmaster, officially known as a chief musician, to every regiment and battalion. Cavalry regiments were also allowed sixteen musicians.[52] Brigade bands were allowed up to twenty-four musicians.

Few regiments in the Confederate Army approached their quotas, although some actually exceeded them. The 66th North Carolina had the largest regimental band in the Confederacy with twenty-eight musicians; the 25th Georgia Volunteers came next with twenty-five musicians at its peak. Then came the 8th Georgia Volunteers with twenty-three, and the 31st Georgia Volunteers with twenty.[53] Confederate brigadier general Lucius Eugene Polk's brigade band had one of the most unique ensembles with one brass horn, two violins, two flutes, and a guitar.[54]

At the start of the war, the Confederate army did not distinguish in pay among bandsmen, field musicians, and privates; each was paid eleven dollars a month.[55] In 1863 bandsmen were given a slight raise and were paid more than field musicians and privates.

Band musicians in the Federal army earned much more than their counterparts in the Confederate army: a fourth of the musicians in each band in the Federal army received the same pay as sergeants in the engineers (thirty-four dollars a month); another fourth were paid the same as a corporal in the engineers (seventeen dollars a month); the remaining half were entitled to the pay of a private first class in the engineers (twelve dollars a month). Monthly pay for a drum major or bandleader was the same as for a second lieutenant in the infantry.

Benjamin Larned, paymaster general of the Federal government, was flabbergasted when he discovered the Federal bands were costing the government a staggering $5 million a year![56] In October 1861, he forbade new volunteer regiments to muster bands and let vacancies for musicians go unfilled.[57] A year later, on 17 July 1862, Congress repealed its previous act authorizing the formation of volunteer regimental bands, and on 9 August 1862, Maj. Gen. George Brinton McClellan was ordered to muster out all the volunteer regimental bands under his command.[58] In their place, Congress provided for the establishment of bands at the brigade level, each of which was to consist of no more than sixteen musicians.[59] Many of the musicians previously serving in the regimental bands promptly reenlisted in the brigade bands. Others reenlisted as combatants and played for their regiments when there was no fighting.

Since a band automatically added prestige to any regiment or brigade, many officers tried to lure musicians into joining their units by offering bonuses or supplements to their army wages. In the North, some local bands were lucky enough to be involved in a bidding war like the one between Col. William Watts Hart Davis and Col. Horatio Gates Sickel of the 3rd Pennsylvania. Both officers wanted the Ringgold Cornet Band of Reading, Pennsylvania, in their ranks. Davis offered them thirty dollars a month if they'd join his regiment. Sickel outbid him with an offer of forty dollars.[60]

Col. Alfred Holt Colquitt, commander of the 46th Georgia Volunteers, offered five hundred dollars to one thousand dollars for a "fine band of music."[61] This was much better than the eleven dollars a month bandsmen normally received in the Confederate army and two weeks later Colquitt had ten musicians for his band.

There were often no musicians to attract. In such cases, some regimental companies raised money to buy instruments and to pay a salary for a civilian who would teach willing soldiers how to play them in a band.[62] One such band debuted at a dress parade just three months after being formed.[63] Another bandleader, given the job of forming men who had never had music lessons into a regimental band, led his newly created ensemble at guard duty and dress parade just three weeks after giving them their first lesson, an astonishing accomplishment that he attributed to "the goodwill of the boys, backed up by the military system."[64]

Free black musicians did not regularly enlist in the Confederate army, but if they did, they received the same pay as regularly enlisted musicians (if the brigade commander did not object to having them in his ranks). White soldiers did not complain if a band or drum corps was made up exclusively of blacks, but a band with both white and black musicians was not so easily accepted by white musicians.[65]

Carlton McCarthy, a private in the Richmond Howitzers, felt the Army of Northern Virginia had quite a few bands early in the war and thought them relatively good, but toward the later years "bands became very rare and their music very poor. . . ."[66] The Washington Light Infantry Band (25th South Carolina Infantry) made up mainly of German-born musicians led by a man named Muller was considered rather good. One appreciative veteran wrote of them: "The performers on the brass horns, belonging to the band under his [Muller's] direction made music surpassing the finest organ. . . . the sweet music which they discoursed beguiled camp life of much of its tediousness."[67] E. Y. McMorries boasted that for proficiency, his First Alabama Volunteer Infantry band had "certainly no superior if no equal in the Confederate service. Their instruments, too, were first class. They played for us on drill and at night after taps took their position at the colonel's tent and played us to sleep."[68]

Although James J. Kirkpatrick described his band, the 16th Mississippi (led by William Henry Harwell), as "never the sweetest or most harmonious,"[69] musicians in the 26th North Carolina regimental band thought the Mississippi band's rendition of "Dearest I Think of Thee" at a military review "the finest thing we ever heard."[70] Heady praise from musicians whose own band was considered one of the best in the Confederacy.

Few of the other bands in the Confederate army were as talented at the 26th North Carolina or 16th Mississippi. Since many Confederate soldiers had never heard professional musicians they were not very critical. A band that made a familiar tuneful noise was considered to be a good band. How closely a band's playing resembled the drum and fife tunes heard earlier at musters was the basis for judging its quality.[71]

Many, if not most, of the Confederate bands mustered with militia units had been amateur town bands before the war. Some of the Confederate bands were formed by men with no previous musical training. Within weeks or months, men who had been chair makers, mechanics, box makers, coopers, or carpenters, prior to the war, found themselves "tooters." Several English military men, who traveled through the South during the war or actually served in the Confederate army, wrote about the Confederate bands from their own experience with European bands. Lt. Fitzgerald Ross, generally sympathetic to the Confederacy, couldn't find much to praise when it came to its musical efforts. "Many of the regiments had little bands of three or four musicians, who played rather discordantly," he said. Although Southerners had a reputation for liking music, Ross found "they seldom take the trouble to learn to play themselves, and seem not very particular as to whether the instruments they hear are in tune or not."[72]

When Lt. Col. James Fremantle of the Coldstream Guards was in Texas on his way to Virginia, he was entertained by musicians from Pyron's regiment. The band, Fremantle said, was composed of "eight or ten instruments braying discordantly."[73] Another Englishman, Thomas Caffey, serving as an artilleryman in the Army of Northern Virginia, was also critical:

> [in] those regiments which have succeeded in getting up bands, the performance is so wretched for a few months that their dismal noises are an intolerable nuisance.[74]

Thomas DeLeon, who toured extensively through the South during the war, agreed: "The bands of the southern army—so long as they remained existent as separate organizations—were indisputably mediocre, and when not atrociously bad."[75]

Benjamin Fleet, an officer in the 26th Virginia infantry, reckoned Federal bands were better because most of them were formed before the war "and their instruments are much better than we can procure."[76] DeLeon rationalized Confederate musicians weren't as good as Northern musicians because "the better class of men—who usually make the best musicians—always preferred the musket to the bugle."[77]

THE BRAVE INVARIABLY RESPECT THE BRAVE

Regardless of their musical talents, proud bandsmen were as brave and devoted to the Confederate cause as any man in the Southern army. That dignity especially showed itself just after the Battle of Saylers Creek (6 April 1865) on the eve of Appomattox. As Confederate prisoners were being led off to the rear, one of the Confederate bands, which had also been captured during the fighting, took up their usual position in the front of the column and struck up "Dixie" one last time. A Federal drummer recalled the effect of the music on the exhausted Confederates: "They were prisoners of war, bleeding from wounds, faint and famished, ragged and nearly barefoot and their last hope gone, but as the familiar strains of the music floated back over the line their faces brightened, their steps quickened and they marched as they had marched many a time behind their beloved leader, General Lee.

"Our men had too much respect for these brave men to jeer at them. The brave invariably respect the brave, and as the soldiers of the 'Lost Cause' passed the veterans of the second corps all were silent and respect-ful, except for an occasional burst of applause which manifested itself by the clapping of hands."[78]

CHAPTER 12

Home, Sweet Home

Although soldiers on both sides sang about the trials of army life, the most popular songs in the Northern and Southern armies were often sentimental, lugubrious tunes about tender mothers and faithful wives and sweethearts; the metaphor, representing all for which they yearned was the home. Since the average age of the Southern fighter was an insecure eighteen, feelings about mother and family intensified during the war. Concern for loved-ones is universal among men in battle. Such songs crossed sectional boundaries with only a few substitutions in wording. Even a hundred and fifty years after they were written, many of these songs, with their unabashed emotionalism, still excite the heart.

JUST BEFORE THE BATTLE, MOTHER

An entire genre of songs were devoted to "mother." Among the most popular of these in both the Union and Confederate armies was George F. Root's, "Just before the Battle, Mother," written in 1862. Although the song was as much a favorite in the South as it was in the North, it wasn't printed in the South until 1865.[1] Other than omitting Root's name as composer, the publisher, J. W. Davies & Sons of Richmond, adhered to the original with very minor changes, the most noticeable being the substitution of "if" for "all" in the second stanza, fifth line, possibly reflecting local criticism of the war effort:

> Just before the battle, Mother,
> I am thinking most of you.
> While on the field we're watching,
> With the enemy in view.
> Comrades brave are round me lying,

Filled with thoughts of home and God;
For well they know that on the morrow,
Some will sleep beneath the sod.

Chorus

Farewell Mother, you may never
Press me to your heart again;
But O, you'll not forget me, Mother,
If I'm numbered with the slain.

Oh, I long to see you, mother,
And the loving ones at home;
But I'll never leave our banner
'Till in honor I can come.
Tell the traitors, *if* around you,
That their cruel words, we know,
In every battle kill our soldiers
By the help they give the foe.

"Just before the Battle, Mother" combines the nineteenth century's emphasis on love for one's mother with the angst of dying alone.[2] Although the song's ending verse reflects the soldiers' duty to remain steadfast ("I'll never leave our banner") and the pervasive sense of honor that kept them in the ranks ("Till in honor I can come [home]"), they still brooded about dying alone. In a letter to his sister, eighteen-year-old Ted Barclay (4th Virginia Infantry) confided that "I would like to die amidst my friends," and consoled himself that if he were "to lie upon the field with nothing to mark the spot" at least God would know where his remains were located.[3]

Songs featuring soldiers saying good-bye to their mothers underscored the dying-away-from-home theme and resonated on the home front and in camp. Among the more enduring were "Kiss Me before I Die, Mother!," "Mother, Oh! Sing Me to Rest," "Keep Me Awake Mother!" Rock me to Sleep, Mother," "Mother! Can This the Glory Be?," and "Mother Is the Battle Over?"[4]

In "Dear Mother I've Come Home to Die,"[5] the soldier survives long enough to say his last good-bye directly to his mother and family:

Call Sister Brother to my side
And take your Soldier's last good bye.
Oh Mother dear, draw near to me;
Dear Mother, I've come home to die.

In "Who Will Care for Mother Now?"[6] self-sacrifice and lonely death yield to the uneasiness that a dying soldier feels as he asks how his mother will cope now that he will not be back home to take care of her:

Tell me, comrades, is this death?
Ah! how well I know your answer;
To my fate I meek-ly bow,
If you'll only tell me truly,
Who will care for mother now?

With thousands of husbands and sons dead and dying, this question tormented many minds.

Composer-publisher Charles Carroll Sawyer was popular on both sides of the Potomac because of the universal themes of his lyrics. The Connecticut-born Sawyer took deliberate pains not to inject any partisanship in his songs. They contained no insults, no rancor, no celebration of military battle. Every soldier could appreciate the emotions and situations Sawyer described. Sawyer also published music, and he was not above inventing dramas to personalize and heighten the tragedy of his songs. For "Who Will Care for Mother Now?" he added a note on the caption page describing the event that had allegedly inspired the song: "The affecting incident recorded in this beautiful Song occurred after one of our great victories. The fallen Hero, in the arms of his comrades, had no anxiety about himself or his condition, but fixed his last thoughts on earth on His Mother." The incident was invented; the sentiment behind it was real.

Sawyer created another scenario for "Mother Would Comfort Me."[7] This time, the narrator is a dying soldier wounded at Gettysburg. Told that his wounds will kill him, he stoically resigns himself to his fate, wishing only that his mother were with him in his dying moments: "Mother would comfort me if she were here. . . ."

Sawyer's best songs were maudlin. His masterpiece, "When This Cruel War is Over"[8] (also called, "Weeping Sad and Lonely" from the first line of the chorus), sold millions of copies and inspired numerous "answers" and "parodies."[9] The narrator of the song's Southern version is a soldier's sweetheart who reminds him of the last time they were together:

> Dearest love, do you remember,
> When we last did meet,
> How you told me that you loved me,
> Kneeling at my feet?
> Oh! how proud you stood before me
> In your suit of grey,
> When you vow'd to me and country
> Ever to be true.
>
> Weeping, sad and lonely,
> Hopes and fears how vain!
> Yet praying,
> When this cruel war is over,
> Praying that we meet again.

Other verses of the song echo apprehension that the soldier will lie on the battlefield, "Lonely, wounded, even dying, Calling, but in vain," with no one to "whisper words of comfort." The melancholy image evokes a definite moral, since it exalts his death as in "Just before the Battle, Mother" by describing it as the honorable fulfillment of duty ("But your country called you, darling").

Shortly after the war, the *Milledgeville (Georgia) Federal Union* lauded Sawyer as "one of the north's most gifted sons":

> His sentiments are fraught with the greatest tenderness, and never one word has he written about the south or the war that could wound the sore cords of the southern heart. He is a gentleman, moreover, of wonderful versatility of genius. He can not only write songs in the language of rapture, but he can compose as sweet strains of music as ever mingled melody with harmony.[10]

Present-day critics are divided over the reasons for the song's success. One called it "a technical masterpiece, guaranteed never to fail in inducing the ready tear." Another critic failed to understand its impact:

There is nothing in this sentimental song that enables one to read the riddle of its remarkable popularity during the Civil War. It has no poetic merit; its rhythm is commonplace, and the tune to which it was sung was of the flimsiest musical structure, without even a trick of melody to commend it. The thing was heard in every camp every day many times every day. Men changed it on the march, and women sang it to piano accompaniment in all houses. A song which so strongly appealed to two great armies and to an entire people is worthy of a place in all collections of war poetry, even though criticism is baffled in an attempt to discover the reason of its popularity.[11]

THE DRUMMER BOY OF SHILOH

The image of a young soldier giving his life for his country epitomized the noble attributes of duty, honor, and courage, heralded in song. The impact was further enhanced by lowering the age of the soldier to that of the younger drummer boy and several tunes were written about them, the most popular of which was "The Drummer Boy of Shiloh."[12]

Shiloh (6 to 7 April 1862) was the bloodiest mauling on the North American continent up to that time. The Confederates, under Gen. Albert Sidney Johnston, were encamped around the railway junction at Corinth, Mississippi, near the southwest Tennessee border. The Federal army, under Maj. Gen. Ulysses S. Grant, was encamped near Pittsburg Landing on the Tennessee River, about twenty miles away. Johnston launched a surprise attack on Grant's numerically equal force of forty thousand before he could be reinforced by Maj. Gen. Don Carlos Buell, whose Army of the Ohio was moving west to link with Grant's. Together, the two armies would far outnumber the Confederates.

The Confederates left Corinth on Thursday, 3 April, but didn't get into position until Saturday, the fifth. When the Confederates attacked, the stunned Federals fell back but the Confederate attack stalled near a small Methodist meetinghouse called Shiloh Church. This gave Buell time to introduce his forces into the battle. Johnston was mortally wounded in the ensuing fight and the Confederates were subsequently driven from the field.

In the short space of this three-day battle, the North suffered thirteen thousand killed or wounded, the South over ten thousand. Proportionately, there were more casualties in this one battle (twenty-four percent) than in any other battle of the war. The toll of dead and injured exceeded the combined casualties in the American Revolution, the War of 1812, and the Mexican War. After Shiloh, Americans grasped the horror of war.[13]

The song about the last words of a dying drummer boy vivified for Americans the dreadful personal carnage of that battle—in which mere boys were wounded and killed:

> On Shiloh's dark and bloody ground
> The dead and wounded lay;
> Amongst them was a drummer boy,
> That beat the drum that day.
> A wounded soldier held him up.
> His drum was by his side;
> He clasped his hands, then raised his eyes,
> And prayed before he died.
> He clasped his hands, then raised his eyes,
> And prayed before he died.

The song's cover page was as evocative as the song. The scene is the aftermath of the battle. The dying drummer boy is on his knees, hands clasped together in prayer, supported by a kneeling soldier. To his left, a distraught soldier has covered his face with his right hand. Three other soldiers

Northern edition of "The Drummer Boy of Shiloh."

are to his right. One is dead. Another, wounded, is looking mournfully at
the dying boy. A third has his head buried in his hand in grief:

> For gather'd round a little group,
> Each brave man knelt and cried;
> They listened to the drummer boy,
> Who prayed before he died.
> They listened to the drummer boy,
> Who prayed before he died.

The pathos of the "Drummer Boy of Shiloh" was irresistible. Who
could not feel moved by the image of a young boy dying on the battlefield
like a man, yet still very much the innocent child, whose last words speak
of his sacrifice on behalf of his country and his God:

> "Oh, mother," said the dying boy,
> "Look down from Heav'n on me,
> Receive me to thy fond embrace,
> Oh take me home to thee.
> I've loved my country as my God,
> To serve them both I've tried,—
> He smiled, shook hands—death seized the boy
> Who prayed before he died.
> He smiled, shook hands—death seized the boy
> Who prayed before he died.

Soon after the song became a popular hit in the North, Armand Blackmar republished it in Augusta, Georgia, with a cover specially designed for
Southerners. Again the scene is the aftermath of battle. A kneeling Confederate soldier, his head bandaged, supports a dying Confederate drummer
boy whose hands are clasped in prayer. A dead soldier lies to his right and
slightly behind him. Two others approach from his left.[14]

The "Drummer Boy of Shiloh" was a commercial success largely
because it reflected America's preoccupation with innocent death. The song
was published first in the North, primarily because its author, William
Shakespeare Hays, was living in Louisville, Kentucky, which was under
Union control. A Southerner by upbringing, Hays generally reflected
Southern attitudes in his songs.

In comparing letters written by Northern and Southern soldiers during the war, historian Michael Barton[15] discovered that the most common element in Southern letters of condolence, also clearly seen in the "The Drummer Boy of Shiloh," is a highly stylized, dramatically posed description of the soldier's death. When the soldier does not die instantly, he is pictured calmly awaiting death in the company of friends, his mind bent on prayer and his loved ones. In the "Drummer Boy of Shiloh," the wounded boy is surrounded by friends who tearfully watch and listen as he prays before he dies:

> Ye angels round the Throne of Grace,
> Look down upon the braves,
> Who fought and died on Shiloh's plain,
> Now slumb'ring in their graves!
> How many homes made desolate—
> How many hearts have sighed—
> How many, like that drummer boy,
> Who prayed before they died!
> How many, like that drummer boy,
> Who prayed before they died!

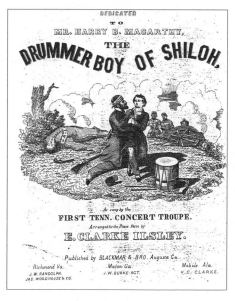

Southern edition of "The Drummer Boy of Shiloh." Note absence of composer's name, and dedication to Harry Macarthy.

Southern letters to the families of the slain often emphasize the self-control of the dying soldier: "He smiled, shook hands—death seized the boy / Who prayed before he died." As in song, Southern condolence letters rarely mention the soldier's suffering before death. In letters, like "Drummer Boy'," the soldier dies in the company of his comrades, who cannot restrain their tears when he finally dies: "Each soldier wept then like a child." Another theme common to both sympathy letters and the song is a reference to heaven: "'Oh, mother,' said the dying boy, / 'Look down from Heav'n on me, / Receive me to thy fond embrace, / Oh take me home to thee'."

Southern condolence letters also typically say something about the disposition of the body, usually that the dead man has been decently buried and that the grave has been marked if the family later wants to transport home the body: "The flag his winding sheet, God's Book / The key unto his grave. / They wrote upon a simple board. . . ." These songs and letters are also noteworthy for what they don't say. Unlike their Northern counterparts, they express little bitterness and rarely mention the political conflict.

Northern songwriters quickly turn pathos into bathos, creating scenes in which drummer boys gasp dying words to music at Antietam, at Vicksburg, and at Nashville, where they are "cut off in their bloom," their manhood "crushed." They poignantly give the drummer boys names like "Little Harry" or "Little Eddy," both of whom meet early deaths.

These songs totally differ from "The Drummer Boy of Shiloh" in their political subtext. One of the best-known of the other drummer boy songs, Henry C. Work's "Little Major,"[16] for example, propagandizes, portraying Southern soldiers as hard-hearted and uncaring, refusing to give water to a dying drummer boy:

> Oh! for love of Jesus,
> Grant me but this little boon!
> Can you friend, refuse me water,
> Can you when I die so soon?

Like "The Drummer Boy of Shiloh," "Little Major" dies with a prayer on his lips, but his prayer is for water not for forgiveness. He appeals to Jesus, for help, not salvation. Heavenly peace is not mentioned. Nor are his last thoughts on his home and family. "Little Major" is not self-controlled; unlike the peaceful "Drummer Boy of Shiloh," he spends his last moments in agony. His greatest anguish, however, is being abandoned by his friends:

There are none to hear or help him
All his friends were early fled.

. . . to die, by friends forsaken,
With his last request denied
This he felt his keenest anguish,
When at morn, he gasp'd and died.

Even "Little Major's" own comrades ignore him when they discover his dying body. Though he pleads for water,

They refuse his dying prayer.
"Nothing but a wounded drummer,"
So they say, and leave him there.

SOMEBODY'S DARLING

The numbing news of a dead husband or son sometimes came by telegram. Mary Chesnut described its stunning psychological impact:

You leave it on your lap. You are pale with fright. You handle it, or dread to touch it, as you would a rattlesnake—worse worse. A snake would only strike you. How many, many, this scrap of paper may tell you, have gone to their death.

When you meet people, sad and sorrowful is the greeting; they press your hand, tears stand in their eyes or roll down their cheeks, as they happen to have more or less self-control. They have brothers, fathers, or sons—as the case may be—in the battle. And this thing now seems never to stop.[17]

Mothers kept hoping that perhaps there was a mistake. Mary Chesnut goes on to describe an insensible scene of mistaken identity:

A woman . . . heard her son was killed—had hardly taken in the horror of it, when they came to say it was all a mistake—mistake of name. She fell on her knees with a shout of joy. 'Praise the Lord, oh, my soul!' she cried in her wild delight. In the midst of this jubilation, the hearse drove up with the poor boy in his metallic coffin.[18]

The disheartening burden of informing a mother that her son had died was poignantly captured in Marie Revenel De La Coste's "Somebody's Darling":[19]

> Into the ward of the clean whitewash'd halls
> Where the dead slept and the dying lay;
> Wounded by bayonets, sabres and balls,
> Somebody's darling was borne one day.
> Somebody's darling, so young and so brave,
> Wearing still on his sweet, yet pale face,—
> Soon to be hid in the dust of the grave,
> The lingering light of his boyhood's grace.

Chorus

> Somebody's darling, Somebody's pride
> Who'll tell his mother where her boy died.

"Somebody's Darling" was a subgenre of "mother" songs that focused on distraught mothers grappling with the tragic news of their dead sons, a subgenre which also included "My Warrior Boy," "La Jeune Mére Louisianaise," and "The Mother Of The Soldier Boy."[20] In "The Mother of the Soldier Boy," the recurrent theme of dying away from family or friends underlies the anguished mother's search for some trace of her fallen son as she wanders the battlefield:

> Her only son had fallen there,
> To some . . . time brings relief,
> Unmark'd she passes with despair,
> Still recent seems her grief;
> Since then, though many suns have shone,
> The matron dreams of joy,
> And daily wanders forth alone
> To seek her soldier boy.
> To seek her soldier boy.

"Let Me Kiss Him for His Mother," a song written in Boston in 1859, was reprinted by Southern publishers during the war, even though the tragic victim was a Yankee, possibly because it appealed to the underlying anxiety all Americans had about death far from home. To heighten the pathos, its maudlin introduction described the circumstances which had supposedly inspired the song:[21]

> During the ravages of the Yellow Fever in New Orleans, a young man from the State of Maine was attacked with that dreadful disease, and soon died, with no relative to watch by his bedside, or soothe him with that sympathy which none but those of our own 'dead kindred blood' can feel or manifest. He died among strangers, and was buried by them. When the funeral service was over, and the strange friends who had ministered to him were about to close the coffin, an old lady who stood by stopped them and said, "Let me kiss him for his mother."

Her words became the song's title and refrain:

> Let me kiss him for his Mother,
> What though left a lone stranger here;
> She has loved him as none other,
> I feel her blessing near.
> Though cold that form lies sleeping.
> Sweet angels watch around;
> Dear friends are near thee weeping,
> O lay him gently down.

THE VACANT CHAIR

No sentimental niche was left unprobed in Civil War songs. In "Mother Is the Battle Over?"[22] the songwriter shifts the focus from a dying or dead son to a husband, and multiplies the emotional pain by picturing a mother telling her child that his father has been killed ("your noble father is one numbered with the slain"). A related theme common to this genre concerns a son's distress at coming back to a home with no mother ("What Is Home without a Mother?").[23] This tearfully popular antebellum song was turned into a tune for music boxes across the country.[24]

The impact of a son's death was poignantly described in "The Vacant Chair,"[25] which despondently relates how a family kept the memory of a fallen loved one alive by placing his empty chair in their midst during their evening prayers. John Davies and Sons, who published the song in Richmond, printed it with a cover showing a mother standing behind a vacant chair and looking at her dead son's portrait. Walter Montgomery, a second lieutenant in the 12th North Carolina Infantry, remembered how the song brought instant tears to a woman whose family had invited some of the men in his company to their house for supper. The men were used to singing for their suppers and asked if the family would like to hear some songs. When they started singing "The Vacant Chair," a young woman in the family broke down. They immediately realized their error. The woman had recently lost her husband in the war:[26]

> We shall meet but we shall miss him,
> There will be one vacant chair;
> We shall linger to caress him,
> While we breathe our ev'ning pray'r;
> When one year ago we gathered,
> Joy was in his mild blue eye,
> Now the golden cord is severed,
> And our hopes in ruin lie.

Henry Washburn, the composer, ostensibly wrote the song after coming home from a Thanksgiving Day dinner in 1861 at the Grout family house in Worcester, Massachusetts. Eighteen-year-old John William Grout, expecting his first furlough around Thanksgiving and planning to spend it with his family, was killed on 21 October 1861, at the battle of Ball's Bluff. The family still observed the holiday, the boy's chair in its usual place, vacant.[27] There would be many more vacant chairs before the war was over.

THE GIRLS THEY LEFT BEHIND

Nearly every "somebody's darling" left behind a sweetheart, or imagined he did, when he went to war.[28] When he reminisced about his girl, he surely recalled a host of antebellum sweetheart songs, reprinted during the war, like "I Am Fondly Dreaming of Thee," "Ever of Thee," "I Am Dreaming Still of Thee," "I See Her Still in My Dreams," "Her Bright Smile Haunts Me Still," and "The Brightest Eyes."[29]

The "sad and lonely" theme of British composer George Linley's "Ever of Thee" (written in 1859, with music by Foley Hall), created a superseller for the Confederate music industry:

> Ever of thee, when sad and lonely,
> Wandering afar my soul joy'd to dwell,

Morn, noon, and night,
Where'er I may be,
Fondly I'm dreaming ever of thee,
Fondly I'm dreaming ever of thee!

Maj. Gen. "Jeb" Stuart hummed the tune in the midst of battle,[30] and rank-and-file soldiers throughout the Confederacy favored it.[31]

The Confederate army's most popular musical heartthrobs, in alphabetical order, were "Sweet Alice," "Annie Laurie," "Annie of the Vale," "Aura Lea, the Maid with Golden Hair," "Belle Brandon," "Blanche Alpen," "Darling Little Blue-Eyed Nell," "Bonny Eloise, "Belle of the Mohawk Valley," "Carrie Bell," "Carrie Vaughan," "Claribel," "Ellen Bayne," "Gentle Nettie Moore," "Hally," "Kathleen Mavourneen," "Katy Wells," "Lillie Terrell," "Lily Dale," the incomparable "Lorena," "Lula," "Mary of Argyle," "Minnie Lee," "Nelly Asleep in the Hazel Dell," "Nelly Gray," and "Sweet Evelina."[33] Johnny Reb didn't feel unpatriotic singing his heart out to these beauties, even if many of them were Northern girls who were equally adored by Billy Yank. Some of these songs merit attention because of their content or the stories behind them.

"Kathleen Mavourneen" was musically courted by Johnny Reb and Billy Yank alike.[33] Confederate bugler Frederick Nicholls Crouch composed the music for the popular song in 1840 before he emigrated from England.

"Kathleen Mavourneen" was one of the many wandering songs of the early nineteenth century. The pathos of estrangement fills the song, which combines thematic separation with the iconic dying female lover. No matter how much they regretted having to leave their sweethearts behind, there was no alternative for either the thousands of Irish emigrants, or later on, the thousands of soldiers who left their homes. "Kathleen Mavourneen" is too distraught to say goodbye:

Mavourneen, Mavourneen, my sad tears are falling,
To think that from Erin and thee I must part,
It may be for Years, and it may be forever,
Then why art thou silent thou voice of my heart.

Nine years after he wrote the music for "Kathleen Mavourneen" and many other songs, Crouch settled in Richmond. When the war broke out he enlisted in the First Virginia Infantry, "Richmond Greys," and served as a bugler, giving up a $4,000 a year job for one paying $144, the money for which he said "he never got."[34]

"Ben Bolt" is a ballad about a girl named Alice who is buried in the corner of a churchyard, "obscure and alone," the most dreaded conditions in Victorian America. Alice "lives" under "a slab of granite so gray." (This idea of "living" instead of being dead and buried calls to mind several of Edgar Allan Poe's morbid stories of living burials.) The brooding theme in "Ben Bolt" then shifts to the surroundings. In the distance is a mill where Alice and her lover once frolicked. The decayed mill and the dry brook, which once fed it, symbolize death.

Ironically, "Ben Bolt" was originally a sea poem. Its author, Thomas Dunn English (1819-1902), was born in Philadelphia but lived most of his life in Fort Lee, New Jersey. At various times he worked as a doctor, lawyer, politician, newsman, playwright, and poet. He once accused Edgar Allan Poe of forgery. Poe didn't sue him for slander; he just beat him up.

English wrote "Ben Bolt" in 1848 at the invitation of the *New York Mirror,* which was struggling financially. The paper wanted a poem about the sea, but English drifted back to his early years. Instead of a sea poem he wrote "Ben Bolt." Realizing he had strayed from his assigned task, English covered himself by adding the line, "Ben Bolt, of the salt sea gale!" to the last verse.[35]

A few years later a theater manager in Pittsburgh asked minstrel Nelson Kneass to write a song for *The Battle of Buena Vista,* a play he was about to produce. Kneass couldn't think of anything suitable until a newspaper friend suggested "Ben Bolt." The newsman couldn't remember the whole poem. He wrote down as much of it as he could recall, about three stanzas, and some of that he made up himself. Kneass liked it anyway and adapted a German melody to the verses. Kneass's version of "Ben Bolt" was the big hit of the show. It was rushed into print, ultimately becoming one of the most endearing songs of the nineteenth century. In the 1890s it still transfixed audiences who watched a mephistophelian Svengali hypnotize innocent Trilby into singing it in the melodrama of the same name.

Hally was the very popular dead heroine of Septimus Winner's "Listen to the Mocking Bird,"[36] the signature tune of the regimental band of the First Virginia Infantry.[37] Though Winner was a Northern songwriter (writing under the pseudonym of Alice Hawthorne), the song's setting is the South. Many Southern families named their daughters Hally, after the girl in the song. Hally is dead, a feature of similar songs that were popular both before and during the war:

I'm dreaming now of Hally! sweet Hally,
   sweet Hally,
I'm dreaming now of Hally,
For the thought of her is one that never dies;
She's sleeping in the valley, the valley,
   the valley,
She's sleeping in the valley,
And the mocking bird is singing where she lies.

Listen to the mocking bird,
Listen to the mocking bird,
The mocking bird is singing o'er her grave;
Listen to the mocking bird,
Listen to the mocking bird,
Still shining where the weeping willows wave.[38]

"Juanita"[39] was no less a favorite, although her admirers were more likely to think of her while sitting around a campfire than riding off to battle. The song was written by Mrs. Caroline Norton (1808-77), an English composer whom Southerners had esteemed prior to the war.

Born in London, England, the granddaughter of Richard Brinsley Sheridan, Mrs. Norton led an unhappy life. A marriage to George Norton failed and she was forced to give him custody of her three children. Denied visitation, except under humiliating circumstances, she spent much of her life trying to persuade Parliament to change the restrictive laws concerning the rights of married women. She managed to write fifty-five songs while waging this battle. Mournful "Juanita," her best-known song, was written while she was in Portugal nursing her convalescent son. The melody was a Spanish tune her son played on his guitar. Today, the song is mainly remembered for its chorus:

Nita! Juanita! Ask thy soul if we should part!
Nita! Juanita! Lean thou on my heart.

"Juanita" was issued by nearly every music publisher in the Confederacy including John Schreiner in Macon, Georgia; Blanton Duncan in Columbia, South Carolina; C. D. Benson and Jason McClure, both in Nashville; the Blackmars in Augusta; and by Philip Werlein and Louis

Grunewald in New Orleans. It also appeared in five different Confederate songsters.[40]

Not all the songs about girls were morbid. "The Yellow Rose of Texas," for example, was a high-spirited marching tune sung by Gen. John B. Hood's "Texas Brigade."[41] Originally a minstrel tune published in New York in 1858, the song praised an African American girl as its "yellow rose":

> There's a yellow rose in Texas that I am going to see,
> No other darkey knows her, no darkey only me;
> She cried so when I left her, it like to broke my heart,
> And if I ever find her, we never more will part.

Chorus

> She's the sweetest rose of color this soldier ever knew,
> Her eyes are bright as diamonds, they sparkle like the dew;
> You may talk about your Dearest May and sing of Rosalee,
> But the Yellow Rose of Texas beats the belles of Tennessee.

In 1864, Hood replaced Gen. Joseph E. ("Uncle Joe") Johnston in a last-ditch effort to keep Atlanta from falling to Sherman. When Atlanta was finally overrun, Hood marched northward to Tennessee to break Sherman's line of communications. Hood was defeated at Nashville and Johnston was once again put in command. During the retreat, the army sang a parody of the song:

> And now I'm going southward,
> For my heart is full of woe;
> I'm going back to Georgia,
> To find my Uncle Joe.
> You may talk about your dearest maid,
> And sing of Rosalie,
> But the gallant Hood of Texas
> Played hell in Tennessee.[42]

The real "yellow rose of Texas" is believed to be a young mulatto woman from Texas who deliberately seduced Mexican general Santa Anna, keeping him too preoccupied to prepare for a fight with Sam Houston and his Texans.[43]

The most popular musical sweetheart in the Confederate army was "Lorena." By 1861 "there [was] a girl in large hoops and a calico frock at every piano between this place [Charleston] and the Mississippi, banging [out 'Lorena'] on the out-of-tune thing—and looking up into a man's face who wears [the] Confederate uniform," scoffed Mary Chesnut.[44]

"In the latter days of the war," mused Brig. Gen. Basil Duke,[45] Lorena's "melodious but intensely melancholy strains" saddened and soothed. Duke probably embellished an anecdote that he recorded about an argument between Maj. Gen. Benjamin Franklin Cheatham and Brig. Gen. John Stuart Williams while they were riding home together from North Carolina to reclaim their ravaged homes, Cheatham's in Tennessee, Williams's in Kentucky. At first they pondered the "what-ifs" of the war. Cheatham claimed that had Kentucky joined the Confederate side, the South would have won. Williams said Kentucky would have aided the Confederacy if Tennessee had entered earlier than it had. But there were more serious objections to Kentucky's allying itself with its neighbor, said Williams, one of which was "Lorena."

"If I had nothing else against your people, Cheatham," Williams said, "I'd avoid them because they're always singing that infernal heartbreaking song, 'Lorena'."

Cheatham denied it. He adamantly swore that no Tennessean had ever sung it or would ever sing it. The argument continued for several miles until Williams bet Cheatham two silver dollars that the next Tennessean they encountered would be either singing 'Lorena' or singing it before he left their hearing. Cheatham accepted the bet.

Many Confederate soldiers were trudging home. Soon they came upon one sitting on a log, resting.

"Where are you from?" Williams asked him.

"That's hard to say," the soldier answered, explaining that for the past four years he had been in the Confederate army and now he felt he no longer hailed from anywhere. He was originally from Tennessee, so he could say he hailed from there, he posited, and at this point a verse popped into his mouth—"It matters little now Lo-ree-na."

Williams instantly turned to his companion and demanded his money.[46]

First published in Chicago in 1857, "Lorena"[47] is a sentimental ballad about a frustrated love affair, but its fixation on love beyond the grave ('Tis dust to dust beneath the sod; But there, up there, 'tis heart to heart) contains all the trappings of the popular elegiac songs of the era.

The author, Reverend Henry D. L. Webster, was born in New York and moved to Ohio in 1824. At eighteen he injured his right arm. Unable to perform manual labor, he became a preacher in the Universalist Church. While ministering to a small parish in Zanesville, Ohio, he met Eleanor Blockson, who sang in the choir. The two fell in love. They became engaged. But Eleanor's wealthy married sister, with whom she lived, opposed the marriage. Webster was relatively poor; if Eleanor married him she would live in poverty. In Webster's words, the sister "raised 'old ned' about it." Eleanor wanted to run away with Webster, but the pastor feared that the scandal would ruin his career and that the aunt would disown her niece if Eleanor married him.

The lovers could do nothing. They met the last time atop a hill where they spoke of undying love and broke their engagement. Webster left Zanesville for a pulpit in Warren, Massachusetts, trying to forget Eleanor. Eleanor eventually married a lawyer who later became the chief justice of the Ohio Supreme Court.

The memory of Webster's lost love haunted him. Unable to contain his feelings, in 1853 he wrote about his love affair in a poem he called "Bertha." Webster subsequently changed the title to "Lorena," so as not to embarrass Eleanor. In 1857, while preaching in Racine, Wisconsin, he met musician/composer Joseph Philbrick Webster (no relation) who set the poem to music:

> The years creep slowly by Lorena,
> The snow is on the grass again;
> The sun's low down the sky, Lorena,
> The frost gleams where the flow'rs have been;
> But the heart throbs on as warmly now,
> As when the summer days were night;
> Oh! the sun can never dip so low,
> As down affection's cloudless sky.
> The sun can never slip so low,
> As down affection's cloudless sky.
>
> A hundred months have passed, Lorena,
> Since last I held that hand in mine,
> And felt the pulse beat fast, Lorena,
> Though mine beat faster far than thine.
> A hundred months, 'twas flowery May,
> When up the hilly slope we climbed,

To watch the dying of the day,
And hear the distant church bells chime.
To watch the dying of the day,
And hear the distant church bells chime.

It matters little now, Lorena,
The past is in the eternal past,
Our heads will soon lie low, Lorena,
Life's tide is ebbing out so fast.
There is a Future! O, thank God!
Of life this is so small a part!
'Tis dust to dust beneath the sod!
But there, up there, tis heart to heart.
'Tis dust to dust beneath the sod!
But there, up there, tis heart to heart.

Years later, when he looked back on the affair, Webster mused, "I can honestly say that the girl did infinitely better—after I got over it."[48] "Lorena"'s tremendous popularity helped him to write "Paul Vane; or, Lorena's Reply"[49] a short time later, in which Lorena confesses she has not forgotten him though many years have passed:

I've kept you ever in my heart, dear Paul,
Thro' years of good and ill;
Our souls could not be torn apart, dear Paul,
They're bound together still.
I never knew how dear you were to me
Till I was left alone;
I thought my poor, poor heart would break, the day
They told me you was gone.

Joseph Webster continued to write songs during and after the war. His other major triumph was "In the Sweeet By and By," a hymn he wrote in 1867 with Sanford F. Bennett, a pharmacist. He died in 1875.

"Dear Evelina, Sweet Evelina," was everyone's sweetheart, including "Jeb" Stuart's. Val Giles recalled hearing him pledging his undying love to "Sweet Evelina, dear Evelina" as he and his men mounted their horses and rode off from camp one day in April 1862.[50] Evelina is the unspoiled

"dove" who lives "down in the valley . . . where the wind from the mountains ne'er ruffles the rose." She is "fair like a rose" and "meek like a lamb,"
uses no "paint on her cheek," has "raven black hair," and smells so sweet
"she never requires perfumery." It is three years since he has last seen her.
Evelina still lives in the valley, but for some reason, the singer is "fated to
marry her never." Despite his fate, he sings:

> Dear Evelina, sweet Evelina,
> My love for thee shall never, never die,
> Dear Evelina, sweet Evelina,
> My love for thee shall never, never die.

"Bonny Jean"[51] was another of Stuart's favorites. Bob Sweeney sang it
while accompanying himself on the banjo; Stuart and his entourage joined
in at the chorus:

> Bonny Jean, your smiles are always with me,
> When absent, love from thee,
> Making joy and sunshine round my path-way,
> Where ever I may be.

"That old 'Bonnie Jean' song sounded so sweetly in the still piney
woods," mused one of Hood's Texans as he listened to Stuart and his men,
"it carried many a soldier back to his old home in far away Texas, where he
had heard his mother, sister, or sweetheart sing it when all was peace and
happiness in our Southland."[52]

THE DEAREST SPOT OF EARTH

Given their age and the fact that almost none of them had every been away
from home, the title and words of "Home, Sweet Home" spoke to the
longing thousands of soldiers felt for their homes and families. By all
accounts, this was the most popular song among soldiers in both the North
and South. Every nighttime band concert or songfest usually ended with its
immortal sentiment, "There's no place like home":

> 'Mid pleasures and palaces though we may roam,
> Be it ever so humble there's no place like home!
> A charm from the skies seems to hallow us there,
> Which, seek through the world, is ne'er met with elsewhere:

How sweet 'tis to sit 'neath a fond father's smile,
And the cares of a mother to soothe and beguile.
Let others delight 'mid new pleasures to roam,
But give me, oh! give me the pleasures of home.
To thee I'll return, over-burdened with care.
The heart's dearest solace will smile on me there;
No more from that cottage again will I roam,
Be it ever so humble, there's no place like home.
Home! home! sweet, sweet home!
There's no place like home; there's no place like home.

The music for "Home, Sweet Home" was written by English composer Henry Bishop (1786-1855); the words by an expatriate American,
John Howard Payne (1791-1852), who earned his living adapting European
plays for the English stage. Bishop set Payne's adaptation of *Clari; or The
Maid of Milan* to music and on 8 May 1823 the musical opened at Covent
Garden. "Home, Sweet Home," Payne's opening song, sold over one hundred thousand copies in its first year and was subsequently reprinted in
more editions with more variations than any other song of its time.[53]

Neither Bishop nor Payne made much money from "Home, Sweet
Home." Bishop was paid twenty pounds and his name was prominently displayed on the cover. He was later knighted by Queen Victoria, his reputation enhanced as the song's composer, but he died penniless. Payne was
promised twenty-five pounds if the play ran for twenty consecutive nights.
Since the play was staged during the last part of the theater season, it closed
before its twentieth performance. Although it opened the next season, the
performances were no longer consecutive. Payne not only was cheated out
of his royalty, but the publishers failed to send him a copy of the song and
left his name off the original song sheet. On 9 June 1883 Payne's body was
brought back from Tunis, where he died, and was reburied in Oak Hill
Cemetery, just outside of Washington, D.C. The body was accompanied by
a mile-long procession which included Pres. Chester Arthur and his cabinet. In 1928 the village of East Hampton, Payne's boyhood home, raised
sixty thousand dollars and bought the then two-hundred-year-old house
where he had grown up, and turned it into a public museum honoring his
memory.

Bishop fared better during his life. A music conductor and composer of
over 125 operas, operettas, ballets, and other pieces of music, he was the
first composer to be knighted.

Homesickness demoralized Johnny Reb and Billy Yank, both of whom were away from home for the first time.[54] Some Federal officers forbade their bands to play "Home, Sweet Home," believing that the song undermined morale,[55] but the song cohered the listeners because it reminded every soldier of whom and for what he was fighting.[56] The separation theme became the icon for patriotic devotion to duty. Attempts to ban its playing or singing were fruitless, because it gripped the hearts of too many soldiers.

In October 1863 Val Giles was on picket duty on the Tennessee River at the foot of Lookout Mountain. It was Indian summer. A soft mellow haze bathed the Tennessee valley. Battle was imminent, but the weather's gossamer spell tranquilized pickets. Both sides agreed on a brief armistice. "If these soldiers could have had their say then, an honorable peace could have been made. A few notes from 'Home, Sweet Home,' from a first-class band on the summit of Lookout Mountain would have ended the war," Giles mused.[57]

The same sentiment was shared by thousands of soldiers, North and South, when a Federal band struck up "Home, Sweet Home" after the Battle of Fredericksburg (13 December 1862). As usual, it was the night's last piece and men on both sides of the Rappahannock silently communed with their souls. Each man wondered if he would see his home again when the notes of "Home, Sweet Home" floated into his revery. Almost at once a Confederate band repeated the strain. Then one after another every regimental band in both armies joined in. Had there not been a river between them, reflected Frank Mixson, a private in the First South Carolina Volunteers, the two armies would have settled the war on the spot.[58] Col. (later Maj. Gen.) Gilbert Moxley Sorrel, Lt. Gen. James Longstreet's chief of staff, agreed. There weren't many dry eyes after the singing ended that night and he mused that the power of "one touch of nature" could "make the whole world kin."[59] Another Confederate wondered if such a wartime display of emotion could happen anywhere else on the planet. Only Americans could understand how "men who had faced each other but a few weeks ago in one of the bloodiest battles of the world," could then unite "on a mere suggestion."[60]

Regardless of their allegiance, men and boys sitting around their campfires invariably visualized their own homes whenever someone sang, "Be it ever so humble, there's no place like home!" Those few words were, and still are, basic to the human psyche—universal and elemental. During the

Civil War, Federal and Confederate soldiers never tired of hearing or singing them, and soldiers were still singing its timeless sentiments in later years as well.[61]

"Home, Sweet Home" inspired other antebellum nostalgic songs about home that enjoyed a new popularity in the South during the war years. Many of these songs, with their themes of home and mother, like "Who Will Care for Mother Now," "Mother Kissed Me in My Dream," and 'Mother Would Comfort Me If She Were Here,"[62] were continuations of a theme put into song in England during the Crimean War between England, France and Turkey on one side against Russia, which was fought mainly around the Black Sea, 1853–1856. Whereas the underlying motif reflected the mid-Victorian angst of the wanderer far from home, the real-life anxiety of wartime separation added poignancy. One of these songs, "The Dearest Spot of Earth to Me Is Home,"[63] repeated "home, sweet home" over and over again, ostensibly on the premise that if something is worth saying, it's worth saying *ad nauseam.* Southerners agreed. They bought so many copies of the song, Confederate publishers issued it no fewer than seven times:

> The dearest spot of earth to me,
> Is Home, . . . sweet Home!
> The fairy land I've longed to see,
> Is Home, . . . sweet Home!
> There how charm'd the sense of hearing!
> There, where hearts are so endearing!
> All the world is not so cheering,
> As Home! . . . sweet Home!
> The dearest spot of earth to me,
> Is Home! . . . sweet Home!
> The airy land I long to see
> Is Home! . . . sweet Home!

Other antebellum songs celebrating the "sweet home" theme that were republished as sheet music in the South during the war included "Take Me Home," "My Natal Home," "Dear Mother, I've Come Home to Die," "The Old Cabin Home," "The Dear Ones at Home," "My Sunny Southern Home," "Home to Our Mountains," "The Old House by the Bay," "When the Swallows Homeward Fly,"[64] and countless others.

The subgenre of antebellum "home" songs reflected the fear that the separation from home might be permanent. "Do They Miss Me at Home?"[65]—reissued during the war—was less nostalgic and was preoccupied with being forgotten:

> Do they miss me at home, do they miss me?
> 'Twould be an assurance most dear,
> To know that this moment some love one
> Were saying, "I wish he were here."

"Do They Think of Me at Home?" prompted the reassuring wartime answer:

> Yes, we think of thee at home,
> Oh, we often think of thee,
> In the fullness of our grief,
> In the moments of our glee,

> For bless'd will be the day,
> That shall see thee safe at home.[66]

"Home" songs, pervasive in the Civil War, stemmed from social changes that began to occur in America during the 1830s. Europeans came to America; native-born Americans left their farms and their extended families and moved to the city. By the 1820s the pioneer spirit had disappeared from the eastern seaboard and the frontier was moving far beyond the Mississippi. Industrialization had transformed large sections of the country and rural stability had yielded to urban dislocation and a deeply rooted feeling of alienation. Old, familiar craftsmanship gave way to efficient mass production. Urban society admired the consumption of goods rather than their creation. Rootlessness fostered insecurity, which was expressed in literature, art, and music. Humble cottages were eulogized; lazy, meandering rivers were iconized; bygone days of childhood were idolized. Songs like "Home, Sweet Home" struck such a responsive chord because remembering home countered the pervasive sense of separation and alienation.

Rootlessness was especially common in the North where changes were occurring much faster than in the South. With very few exceptions, the antebellum writers of "home" songs were Northerners who inevitably put home in a South that they had never visited. No matter how homesick a songwriter felt, he never yearned to be back in blustery Maine, bustling New York, backwoods Illinois, or any snow-covered Northern state. Instead, he wished he was back "in the land of cotton," or in his "Old Kentucky home," where he would once again be with "The Old Folks at Home."

To uprooted Northerners, the image of the South, with its balmy climate, slow pace, picturesque countryside, and winding rivers, was idyllic. The fast-paced life in the industrialized North was bewildering. Southerners didn't have to be reminded of the simple joys of country life, but they too were migrating to towns and cities, and a nostalgic longing for loved ones in England, Scotland, Wales, and Ireland still tugged at their hearts.

The seemingly unchanging life in the agricultural South appeared happier to Northerners because the pace was slower. More than any other writer, painter, or songwriter, Stephen Foster stamped the image of a happy, sunny, nostalgic South into the American psyche. Yet Foster himself had virtually no personal contact with the South. The nearest he came to seeing it was in 1825 when he took a steamboat down the Mississippi to New Orleans. He saw little or anything besides some mansions from the rail of that vessel. The Suwannee River, which he immortalized in "Old Folks at Home," is a mud stream in Florida a thousand miles from the Mississippi.

No matter. The millions of Northerners who sang, whistled, and hummed his plantation songs were smitten by an image of an immutable South where people could wake up the next day and the next and the next and not feel bewildered or displaced. In "Old Folks at Home," "Old Black Joe," and "Massa's in de Cold Ground," three of Foster's most popular plantation tunes, the sunny South brims with serenity, happiness, and friendship. It is a place free from care. Slaves don't complain of hardships in the fields or on the docks; masters are avuncular. Southerners, at least those who bought sheet music, cherished the idyllic images of their homeland all the more during the emotional turmoil that threatened its continuance.

TENTING ON THE OLD CAMP GROUND

One of the most impassioned "home" songs on both sides of the war was "Tenting on the Old Camp Ground."[67] The third and fourth verses are especially poignant for their expression of the widespread sense of war weariness. Instead of the "tenting tonight" refrain, after the last verse, the repetitive chorus of "dying tonight, dying tonight, dying on the old camp

ground" reflects the widespread despondency of soldiers as the war continued to take its toll:

> We're tenting tonight on the old camp ground,
> Give us a song to cheer
> Our weary hearts, a song of home,
> And friends we love so dear.

Chorus

> Many are the hearts that are weary tonight,
> Wishing for the war to cease;
> Many are the hearts looking for the right,
> To see the dawn of peace.
> Tenting tonight, tenting tonight,
> Tenting on the old camp ground.
> (Dying tonight, dying tonight,
> Dying on the old camp ground.)
>
> We've been tenting tonight on the old camp ground
> Thinking of days gone by,
> Of the lov'd ones at home that gave us the hand,
> And the tear that said "Good bye!"
>
> We are tired of war on the old camp ground,
> Many are dead and gone,
> Of the brave and true who've left their homes,
> Others been wounded long.
>
> We've been fighting today on the old camp ground,
> Many are lying near;
> Some are dead, some are dying,
> Many are in tear.

"Tenting" is far removed from the ebullient volunteering songs of the
early war. Instead of bravado, it expresses a deep longing for "the dawn of
peace" so that the soldier can return to his quiet home and his former civilian life. "Hearts," says the song, are "weary" and "many are in tear."

Other songs like "Brave Boys Are They"[68] looked forward to the day when the soldier would come home: "God bless you, boys! We'll welcome you home"; but made that welcoming contingent upon "when tyrants are in the dust," in other words, when soldiers could come home with honor.

Such songs motivated soldiers in the field. Instead of eroding morale, these songs raised it by reaffirming the necessity of combat and sacrifice. The songs also underscored the obligation of those at home to not forget the individual soldier even though thousands had gone to war. In essence, these sentimental "soldier songs" about home were collective letters exchanged between soldiers and civilians.

PART 3

Triumphs and Woes of the Confederate Music Industry

On the eve of the Civil War, America was bursting with song. Immigration, urbanization, domestication, education, westward expansion, and trade created soaring American prosperity. Unskilled laborers didn't fare well; but America's middle class—its shopkeepers, businessmen, and skilled laborers did. The country had been transformed from a backwoods colony into a bustling nation. If, like Walt Whitman, you stopped to listen, you heard the carols of that nation:

> Those of mechanics—each one singing his, as it should be, blithe and strong;
> The carpenter singing his, as he measures his plank or beam,
> The mason singing his, as he makes ready for work, or leaves off work;
> The boatman singing what belongs to him in his boat—the deckhand singing on the steamboat deck;
> The shoemaker singing as he sits on his bench—the hatter singing as he stands;
> The wood-cutter's song—the ploughboy's, on his way in the morning, or at the noon intermission, or at sundown;
> The delicious singing of the mother—or of the young wife at work—or of the girl sewing or washing—Each singing what belongs to her and to none else;
> The day what belongs to the day—At night, the party of young fellows robust, friendly,
> Singing, with open mouths, their strong melodious songs.[1]

These "strong melodious songs" included Irish ballads, Scottish folk tunes, English parlor songs, and German art songs, as well as Italian opera, "Italia's peerless compositions," Walt Whitman called them.[2] In fact, what vexed the *Charleston Daily Courier* most on 23 November was not the nation's demise, but that so few people had shown up for the previous evening's performance of *The Barber of Seville!* Lincoln's recent election frenzied the South. Yet the *Daily Courier* lamented "that the political excitement should interfere with the aesthetical tastes of our numerous Opera-lovers."[3]

Opera's popularity in both the North and the South during the nineteenth century largely stemmed from its combination of eye-popping spectacle, epic story line, stagecraft, flamboyant acting, singing virtuosity, instrumental music, and special effects. "Opera," writes music historian, N. Lee Orr, "proved just the vehicle to express the forceful, emotional, and volatile American character."[4] In an age of emotional restraint, opera vicariously released the inner feelings that Americans were required to repress. Romanticism's great themes imbued operas, enjoyed by "nob and snob," and popular songs from favorite operas became part of America's musical repertory.

Another reason for opera's popularity in nineteenth-century America was that most of the favorite foreign operas were "Englishized" so that the lyrics could be understood by everyone.[5] Arias from these and other adaptations became leading pop tunes in America, were published for the sheet music market, were played and sung in public and singing schools and in family parlors across the country, and were reprinted with words only, in many Confederate songsters.[6]

Italian composers dominated opera; German composers ruled art songs. The popularity of German music in America coincided with the waves of immigrants that came to America in the 1830s and swelled to millions in the aftermath of the political crises in Europe during the 1840s. Unable to find work in their homeland, German journeymen musicians and singers sailed to America where they joined already existing musical societies or started new ones on the frontier.

A universal market awaited this music. Floridians were singing German art songs when their concert was interrupted by the news of Lee's surrender.[7] George F. Root, destined to become one of the most brilliant American composers during the Civil War era, was keenly aware of the German influence on American music, so much so, that when he first began writing songs, he published them under the name Wurzel, the German word for Root.[8]

The Civil War did not change America's passion for music or musical tastes, it itensified them.[9] Widespread public familiarity with every kind of music throughout what was still primarily a rural country prompted pubishers to print songs and instrumental tunes in confident expectation of sales. A "golden age" for music reigned in antebellum America.

In the days before record players and radios, Americans from every class often heard the newest songs and musical numbers at concerts, operas, minstrel shows, and even during intermissions at plays. Every theater in every large city had a musical director, an orchestra, and singing actors and actresses and specialty acts. In antebellum days, when people went to the theater, they went for the night, and nothing changed during the war. Five-hour shows were common. Some theater managers interpolated as many as thirty songs into a play like Shakespeare's *The Tempest*.[10] Critics complained dramas were simply fillers among the songs and musical numbers and that audiences often came just as much for the music as the plays.[11] And they were right. Basically, the format for a play called for an instrumental over-ture, usually from a familiar opera, to precede the play; song and dance acts were interpolated into the show or were interspersed during intermissions; and one-act operas, little comedies, farces, pantomimes, or novelty acts were presented as "after pieces." As much as 50 percent of American the-ater programming during the nineteenth century was musical in nature.[12]

In addition to the manager's programming, entertainers also inter-spersed songs that had nothing to do with the script whenever they thought they were losing the audience's attention. During "The Barber of Seville," which was being performed in Italian, the lead actress–singer sensed the audience's frustration at not being able to understand the language and incorporated a "favorite Scotch song" into the act. The appreciative audi-ence shouted "encore" from every part of the house. The singer complied with "Home, Sweet Home," delivered "with more science and effect than we ever heard it before."[13]

The most popular songs from these programs would then be sung by other performers at their shows, and often would appear for sale almost overnight so that people could sing them at home or in social gatherings. Hit songs from a show often appeared with the caption "as sung by . . . at her concert at the . . . ."

Most Americans did not question interspersing folk songs with opera, or with art songs, parlor songs, or what was to become the most popular song type, minstrel tunes. Entertainment was entertainment.

Americans were familiar with operatic arias and German "art" songs, because every city and town in America, including those in remote areas, was on a theater circuit. Port cities in the South like New Orleans and Charleston, which were easily accessible by boat, were entertainment hubs from which well-known entertainers toured inland by train. Lesser-known entertainers contented themselves with bringing their shows to more remote inland towns by rickety stagecoachs, wagons, and mule-drawn barges. There were fewer theaters in the South than in the North, but even semifrontier towns had a makeshift theater. By 1850 even remote Dal-las, Austin, and San Antonio were on the itineraries of traveling opera companies.[14] The South may have had fewer towns, remote or otherwise, than the North, but relatively speaking, they enjoyed the same entertainment as the more populous North.

The "star system" that dominated the antebellum American stage carried over from England. "Stars" made their own arrangements with local theater managers and were able to charge whatever the market would bear; in America, the insatiable appetite for entertainment seemed bottomonless. To European entertainers, America was the "El Dorado of the musical world."[15] America was inundated with visiting opera companies, orchestras, and virtuosos offering their own unique brand of showmanship. Lesser-known entertainers reshaped the arias and art ballads, originally written for people with literary backgrounds, for less refined audiences in every out-of-the-way town and frontier settlement. Although the words might slightly differ, Americans were generally singing the same songs across the country.

Brilliant singers and musicians catered to the insatiable lust for individual expression in the nineteenth century. In addition to singer-performers like Henry Russell, there were musicians with entertaining gimmicks, like pianist Leopold de Meyer, "Imperial and Royal Pianist to the Emperors of Austria and Russia," who played on his fists and elbows, and Norwegian violinist, Ole Bull, whose gimmick was a diamond-studded bow and an unparalleled virtuosity.[16] In 1853, ten thousand people turned out for one of his concerts—not in New York or New Orleans—but in Memphis, Tennessee, where he undoubtedly inspired many a country fiddler in the audience.

Here was the professional side of romanticism's "cult of the individual." Audiences packed theaters to listen and watch; just as they do today, they mobbed the performers after the show. Superstars started their tours in Europe and then brought their acts to America, not to nurture American musical tastes or to raise America's musical standards, but to make money. And make money they did.

In Memphis the minimum price of a ticket to hear the "Swedish Nightingale," Jenny Lind, was five dollars, twenty to fifty times higher than for most shows. Nonetheless, demand was so great, seats had to be auctioned.[17] As her concert tour neared its end in New Orleans, the *Daily Picayune* declared that "Not to have heard Jenny Lind, is to have heard nothing."[18] In the course of earning fortunes the virtuosos nonetheless nurtured and raised American musical standards.

Henri Herz, "Pianist to the King of France," played in Richmond, Memphis, New Orleans, and other cities throughout the North and South

in the 1840s. After he returned to Europe, he wrote a book about his concert tour, *My Travels in America,* which amusingly described antebellum
American audiences.

His manager, Herz said, always looked for ways to capitalize on America's penchant for spectacle. For one of the performances he advertised that
the concert hall where Herz was to perform would be lighted with 1,000
candles. Herz's virtuosity never failed to please his audiences, but at one of
those candlelit extravaganzas a theatergoer counted only 996 and demanded
her money back.[19]

For another concert, Herz's manager positioned eight female pianists,
two each at four pianos, on stage with him. When that proved to be a
crowd pleaser, he doubled the number. In New Orleans, the manager was
one pianist short but decided to go ahead anyway. Herz's artistic sense,
however, was bothered by the lack of symmetry on stage created by an odd
number of pianists. When the first theatergoers appeared, Herz approached
a young woman in the audience—a nonmusician—and asked her to fill in.
The rest of the audience had no idea she was merely window dressing until
there was a momentary pause in the music. The woman's hands continued
to skim the keys with soundless virtuosity. At the end of the concert she
was applauded as loudly as the other pianists.

Today, we applaud performers and give them standing ovations if they
have pleased us. In the 1840s and 1850s, if someone in the audience
enjoyed the show, he (never a she) would climb onto a chair and wave his
arms to get the rest of the audience's attention. While the performer
remained on stage, the fan would praise her or him. When he sat down,
another would give a speech, and so on and so on; the performer stood
through it all.

At one of Herz's concerts, one of these orators used the occasion to
drum up a little business. Instead of staying in the audience, he rushed on
stage, grabbed Herz's hand, and turned to the audience:

> Ladies and gentlemen, it is not because I am a lawyer and wish to
> profit cunningly from every means which offers itself of showing to
> the public the easiness with which words come to me, the force of
> my argumentation and the charm of my diction that I speak today
> before a numerous and well disposed audience. No, gentlemen, I
> have, God be thanked, more clients than I could hope for; I have,
> in fact, only the embarrassment of choosing among the many cases

offered to me, both criminal and civil. My office is always crowded with deceived husbands who demand divorces, with deceiving wives who wish to appeal, and with dupes and rascals; it is a pretty scene. If then I speak to you at this time it is solely to obey a sentiment which animates me and to share with you the enthusiasm which is excited in me by this great composer whose hand I hold.

And then he went on to say how much the musician's concert had pleased him.

Custom required the musician thus honored to respond. Fortunately, Herz was mentally nimble. "What can I say to you, gentlemen," he answered somewhat tentatively, and then proved that one did not have to be a lawyer to beat one at his own game. "I love lawyers," he assured the audience, "and after the piano, the clarinet, the cornet and the bugle, the instrument most gentle to my ear as well as my heart is the voice of an appreciative lawyer blended with the approval of the public."[20] No one marveled at the exchange.

Other solo performers barnstormed the country playing "financial music," as these concerts became known because of all the money they earned. Even complete orchestras sailed the Atlantic to entertain America. A twenty-four piece symphony orchestra from Germany came to America in 1848 and played at Zachary Taylor's inauguration. By the time it disbanded in 1854, more than a million Americans had heard it.[21]

These artists, however, were only stage performers compared with Thomas Green Wiggins (1849-1908), known throughout the South as "Blind Tom." "Blind Tom," was a musical wonder, perhaps the most talented musician to tour the South prior to and during the war.[22]

Tom was born into slavery in Georgia. Blind at birth, he was "thrown-in" when Col. James Neil Bethune, a lawyer and newspaper editor from Columbus, bought his parents and two of his brothers at a slave auction in 1850. The slaves in Bethune's home were house servants, not field hands. When Tom was about four years old, he slipped into the family parlor to pick out tunes he had heard Bethune's daughters playing on the piano.

As Tom's natural abilities manifested themselves, Bethune's daughters' amusement turned to appreciation. The eldest daughter, who had studied music with an eminent New York teacher-composer, gave Tom lessons. When Tom was only eight, the Bethunes took him to Atlanta, Macon, and

Athens, Georgia, where he gave several public concerts, featuring works by Beethoven, Mozart, and other European composers.

At first curious, audiences were soon astonished at Tom's virtuosity. Shortly afterwards, Perry Oliver, a tobacco planter, paid James Bethune fifteen thousand dollars for the rights to exhibit Tom around the country for the next three years. By 1860 Tom was composing his own songs, two of which were transcribed and subsequently published in Boston by Oliver Ditson—with Tom's picture on the cover to prove that the composer was only eleven years old. By 1861 he had become so well-known he played in a private concert at Willard Hall in Washington, D.C., in honor of the first Japanese delegation to visit America.

When the war broke out, Oliver canceled Tom's Northern engagements to concentrate on raising money for Confederate causes. In January 1862 Oliver brought Tom to Richmond, where he was advertised as "The Negro Boy Pianist—the Wonder of the World, A Musician, Composer, Singer, and Orator." Later that year Tom reunited with the Bethunes, who used his talents for the same end.

"Blind Tom" played works by European masters as flawlessly as any of the virtuosos who had toured America before the war. Truly astounding of the man, actually still a boy during the war years, was that he could simultaneously play a different tune with each hand and sing yet another at the same time. To cap it, he could also play the piano with his back to the instrument!

The insatiable antebellum market for music and spectacle sparked the creation of a type of mass entertainment that shunted American musical tastes on an entirely different tangent.[23] Satirically called African or Ethiopian Opera, the minstrel show was singularly American. It featured blackfaced entertainers who strummed banjos, shook tambourines, and rattled bones—all instruments invented by blacks. Speaking in Negro dialect, they joked with their audiences, bantered with one another, poked fun at politicians, parodied grand opera and concert music, danced, and sang popular songs of the day, often introducing big hits. The minstrels entertained mainly urban white audiences, but people from all social strata eventually came to see and hear the foot-stomping exuberance, vitality, and fast-paced, nonstop action—the fun was too infectious to be confined to any one class. The minstrel show was quintessentially mass entertainment dished up at a price people could afford, and Americans loved it.

The humor was crude. (By modern standards the delineations of blacks are offensive.[24]) During the 1840s and 1850s the shows were simply entertainment, and they became the main means of exposing the populace to pop songs before the Civil War. *The Republican and Nashville Whig* recognized their influence in a comment on how minstrel shows had become the major medium for popularizing parlor songs:

> The burden of the song is generally about some maiden, who lives near some river, (Sewanee for example), who did nor didn't do something, who died somehow, and is supposed to be loved by the singer to the last pitch of distraction. . . . [T]he appearance of a new piece of this kind is hailed with great joy by all the young ladies of the Hum-Drum Africanus school, and their name is legion. They steal a couple of hours from their morning slumbers to practice it secretly. They get it first by note, then by ear, then by heart.[25]

While demure girls were practicing those songs in secret, said the paper, children and wagoners were singing them on the streets; tailors, drug clerks, gardeners and draymen were singing on the job; brass bands were "bleating" and "braying" them on the thoroughfares; and young suitors were serenading their ladyloves with them at night, until the tunes either died a natural death or went on to become classics like many of Stephen Foster's hits.

Although minstrel shows catered primarily to working-class white Americans, some shows tried to dignify their performances so that middle-class audiences, and even the elite, would want to come. Some theaters reserved their front seats for ladies and families and provided security guards so they wouldn't be disturbed. Advertisements described minstrel shows as "fashionable concerts" and bragged they were patronized by the better class. A notice in the *Charleston Daily Courier* in 1861 for the Christy Minstrels told readers "the large proportion of ladies attending these entertainments evening after evening" was "sufficient proof that nothing is offered to offend the purest hearer."[26]

The forerunner of the minstrel show was the lone blackfaced performer singing and dancing on stage as a filler between the acts of a play. Stage impersonations of Negroes were not new; they occurred before the Revolution. Basically, the routine called for "Ethiopian delineations"—stereotypical portrayals of white America's image of the plantation slave—happy-go-lucky, lazy, wide grinned, and unable to pronounce long words without twisting them so that they were barely recognizable. The great showman, P. T. Barnum, worked a brief stint as a minstrel. Barnum was so convincing, he was believed to be a black man and was almost shot as such for taking the side of a white man in an argument.[27]

The minstrel show as feature entertainment was born in 1843. America was economically depressed; entertainers needed a gimmick to work. Daniel Decatur Emmett, who would later write "Dixie," came up with one. Instead of using the "Ethiopian delineation" only during the intermission, Emmett created an act in which minstrels were the show. His "Virginia Minstrels" began as a four-man troupe and opened at the Branch Hotel on the Bowery in New York. Setting a pattern for later minstrel shows, the troupe sat in a semicircle partly facing the audience and partly facing each other so that they could coordinate their rhythm. Emmett played fiddle and sat in the center while each of the other three strummed a banjo, shook a tambourine, or clacked a set of bones. The four wore distinctive, gaudy pants and shirts, tall, funny hats, and black makeup. Typically, one began a song as a soloist and then the other three joined in during the second part of the song, the words of which were spoken in imitation of Negro dialect. Emmett wrote many of the songs or adapted them from standard music of the day. When they weren't playing or singing, the minstrels danced, acted out small skits, and engaged in humorous repartee with "Mr. Bones" and "Mr. Tambo" at either end baiting one of the middle men who was called "Mr. Interlocutor."

The "Virginia Minstrels" played to sellout crowds throughout the eastern United States and Emmett decided to tour the show in England in 1843. Although the show flopped overseas and the group disbanded, Emmett returned to New York in 1844 to find that minstrelsy had won over the country. Unable to form a lasting troupe of his own, Emmett joined the Bryant minstrels. It was while he was a Bryant minstrel that he wrote "Dixie."[28]

Although Emmett created the concept of the minstrel show, it was Edwin Pearce Christy and his Christy Minstrels who established the format subsequently used by most minstrel troupes. Christy divided his show into three parts. The first opened with a musical number in which the minstrels, dressed in black frock coats, striped trousers, and white gloves, strutted around the stage singing and dancing and banging their tambourines, until one of them, the "interlocutor," barked "Gentlemen, Be Seated!" That signaled the minstrels to dash to chairs arranged in a semicircle on stage. Emmett's "Virginia Minstrels" was a four-man act; Christy's Minstrels had eight or nine main performers. The "interlocutor" was the emcee. As the straight man he sat in the middle; the two main comics, "Brudder Tambo" and "Brudder Bones," so-called because one played the tambourine while the other clacked a pair of bones, sat at either end.

During the show's first act the dignified interlocutor asked questions and the sassy end men answered back with puns and double entendres studded with broken pronunciation. Besides their outlandish costumes, the end men sometimes donned "fright wigs" rigged to stand on end when the actors pulled a string. Other props included seltzer bottles to squirt water, exploding cigars, paddles, and whistles to soot the faces of other actors. Interspersing the verbal jousting were nonstop violin, piano, and banjo solos; jokes, comic skits, and satiric lectures; and rousing songs like "Oh, Susanna!" and sentimental ballads like "Old Folks at Home," sung against a background depicting Southern plantation life—cotton patches, levees teaming with cotton bales, steamboats, and happy slaves. An elaborate number ended the first part with the performers clapping, shouting, dancing, and singing to another rousing tune like "Camptown Races" as they circled the stage.

After a brief intermission, the second part of the show called the "olio" began. The "olio" featured short skits like the "wench" number, in which an actor dressed as a buxom woman sang songs in falsetto and acted in sketches with the other actors. Next came a comedy monologue called the "stump speech," in which another actor satirized politicians, celebrities, social issues of the day, and local events. The olio concluded with animal acts, banjo tunes, musicians playing unusual instruments like combs or quills, juggling acts, acrobatics, singing, dancing, and any other kind of fast-paced variety act.

For the finale, the entire troupe parodied one of the operas or concerts touring the country at the time, complete with set and costumes. Then parts from the two preceding acts were repeated followed by a grand finale called a "walk-around."

Since minstrel shows portrayed the South, especially slavery, in a favorable light, they were as popular in the South as they were in the North. The 5 February 1858 edition of the *Augusta (Georgia) Evening Dispatch* told its readers the company presenting *School for Scandal* had no audience "in consequence of the Campbell Minstrels."[29] Richmond's audiences ignored the production of *Monte Cristo* until the manager put some minstrels on the program.[30] In New Orleans, the theater capital of antebellum America, minstrel shows were so popular they were performed in French as well as English.[31] On 20 December 1860 South Carolina's "independence day," the "Original George Christy Minstrels" were entertaining audiences in Charleston. Even on the eve of Richmond's surrender in 1865, "Budd and Buckley's Minstrels and Brass Band" were still being "received nightly with shouts of applause."[32]

The influence of the minstrel show on American music was pervasive. Had it not been for minstrel shows and the musical market they provided, a songwriter like Stephen Foster might have been nothing more than an obscure historical footnote.[33] The minstrel show democratized American music.[34] At the same time it extended what romantic composers across Europe were doing—transforming folk tunes into distinctive national musical styles. Composers like Stephen Foster interwove musical elements from various national and ethnic sources, including African American tunes and musical instruments, and combined them into something uniquely American. Some of the songs written expressly for minstrel shows became American classics, among them, many of Stephen Foster's immortal ballads like "The Old Folks at Home" (also known as "Swanee River" 1851), "My Old Kentucky Home" (1853), and "Old Black Joe"(1860); Dan Emmett's "I Wish I Was in Dixie's Land" (1858), an otherwise banal love song about "Willium," a black lothario and a "deceaber," who made "Old Missus" die from a broken heart; and "The Yellow Rose of Texas," written about a mulatto girl ("the sweetest rose of color this darkey ever knew") for a minstrel show in 1853, which became the marching song of Gen. John Bell Hood's "Texas Brigade."

When minstrel tunes became big hits, publishers cranked up their presses. Songwriters who had nothing to do with minstrelsy wrote similar songs without the Negro dialect. After its debut in the 1840s, the minstrel show dominanted theatrical entertainment in America for the next forty years.

Music scholars often distinguish between minstrel songs and operatic arias and art songs. The former, called "vernacular" or less courteously, "lowbrow," were not self-consciously produced and were sung and played solely as mass entertainment for the working classes; the latter, called "cultivated" or "highbrow," were deliberately created by trained composers and often played by trained performers for sophisticated audiences educated to appreciate their moral and aesthetic attributes.[35] These distinctions did not emerge until the end of the nineteenth century. As noted above, the American public did not differentiate between opera and minstrel tunes as entertainment; it was not uncommon to hear one or the other in the same show.

The next chapter surveys in detail some of the South's main theaters, where the songs and music described in this introduction were heard. The final chapter examines what was perhaps one of the most phenomenal Confederate accomplishments, the growth of its music publishing industry.

CHAPTER 13

Musical Entertainment
In The South

New Orleans was one of the two major entertainment capitals in America before the war, the other being New York. No opera company, English or foreign, no instrumentalist, no singer, no entertainer of stature ignored New Orleans in his or her tour of America.[1]

When it came to opera or concert music, New Orleans was the most sophisticated city in America prior to the war. "Opera," said John Sullivan Dwight, America's foremost music critic, "is probably more an institution in New Orleans than in any of our Atlantic cities."[2] Rossini's *Barber of Seville,* the first Italian opera introduced in America (1825), for example, debuted not in the more populous Northern cities of New York, Boston, or Philadelphia, but in New Orleans. And that was only one of many Italian operas to make their American debuts in New Orleans instead of in the North. On one April night in 1836, opera lovers in New Orleans had their choice of nine different operas.[3]

Operas, a local newspaper observed, "amuse our citizens more than any other form of public amusement—except balls."[4] By the 1840s, a writer in the *New Orleans Delta* beamed: "We have now, in this place, what no city in America, and few cities in the world can boast of, strong [opera] companies in the English, French, and Italian languages, and what is more they are all extremely well patronized."[5] Although opera was popular across the country, another writer boasted that in comparison to New Orleans American audiences elsewhere were apathetic and soulless.[6] The *New Orleans Delta* gloried in the "fondness for the opera [which] has become disseminated throughout our population. . . ."[7]

Although they didn't mingle, opera drew people from all ranks of society, not just the wealthy and socially elite. Operagoers came from every national and racial element in the city, French, American, Spanish, Italian,

German, and Negro, and from every segment of that population, coopers, blacksmiths, shopkeepers, salesmen, clerks, longshoremen, steamboat pilots, stevedores, gamblers, thieves, housewives, quadroon and prostitutes. The latter often sat in box seats reserved in their names, paid for by men who sat in less expensive seats with their wives. Slaves were allowed to go to the opera on Monday and Wednesday nights if they had written permission from their masters; admission—fifty cents, free blacks paid a dollar, the same as whites.[8]

Thursday and Saturday nights were "fashionable nights," and ticket prices were as much as one thousand dollars for reserved season's tickets on those days to keep them that way, although the quality of the performance was no different.[9] On "fashionable nights," women came "attired in Parisian fashion, not over dressed . . . their luxuriant hair tastefully arranged, fastened with ornamental pins and adorned with coloured ribbons or a simple flower"[10] and "moustached and bearded dandies, with Parisian cut coats, and a most undeniable odour of tobacco"[11] wandered the halls or stood in the lobbies ogling the unattached belles during intermissions.[12]

Theaters were generally divided into three sections, the boxes, the pit, and the gallery, sometimes with separate entrances for each. The cheapest seats were in the gallery, the highest balcony in the theater. In the South this part of the theater was reserved for "colored" patrons who were proscribed from sitting elsewhere in the auditorium. In the St. Charles Theatre in New Orleans, free blacks sat in one section of the gallery and slaves in another. Some theaters in the North were also segregated, but there were others which opened their galleries to whites, typically servants and apprentices who couldn't afford any other seats.

Just below the gallery was the "notorious third tier" allocated to prostitutes.[13] The pit was today's orchestra section. Seats here cost more than in the gallery and were occupied by the skilled laborers of the "middling class," although only men could sit there. The most expensive seats were the boxes located above the pit. They were private, comfortable, and expensive, and the only part of the theater in which a woman could sit and retain her respectability.[14] When opera critics mentioned the audiences, they almost always described the wealthy and elite who sat in these seats. But no theater could stay in business without the denizens of the galleries and the pits.

New Orleans's passion for opera is the reason that most of the operatic arias published in the South during the war were issued by music publishers in New Orleans. When the Civil War cut off New Orleans from the

Southern circuit, Richmond and cities like Columbus, Athens, Augusta, Macon, and Atlanta emerged as concert and theatrical centers, albeit never on the same scale as New Orleans.

RICHMOND

Destined to become the Confederacy's political and cultural capital, Richmond emerged as Virginia's entertainment mecca after the American Revolution. Located at the head of the James River, like Rome it was built around seven hills. By 1860 it was one of the most elegant American cities. Because of the large number of Germans settling there in the 1850s, many of the virtuosos touring America included Richmond on their itineraries. The prewar Virginian theater circuit, with its hub in Richmond, included Fredericksburg, Petersburg, Norfolk, Lynchburg, and Alexandria. During the war, only Richmond and Petersburg remained active theatrical centers.

When Richmond became the Confederacy's capital, it was transformed into a bustling metropolis, with a population of about 128,000 in 1864, almost four times greater than its 1861 census.[15] People from all classes converged on the city. Hotels were filled to capacity. Bars were standing room only; seats at the theaters were never empty. For the well-to-do, there was no end to the dinners, balls, soirees, and picnics. In sharp contrast to the sometimes lavish lifestyles of the rich, thousands of others eked out a meager existence and lived in damp basements.

The Richmond Theater at the corner of Seventh and Broad was the city's best-known stage for drama, concert music, and opera. Built in 1819, it was remodeled in 1838 and renamed the Marshall Theater, but most people continued to call it "The Richmond." Many itinerant opera troupes played there before the war.[16] Songs and music from operas popular at "The Richmond" were then sung and played at concerts at the nearby Exchange Hotel by ballad singers and family-group singers like "The Orphean Family," "The Hughes Family" (three adults and three children), "The Distin Family" (a father and his three sons), "The Harmoneans," and "The Nightingale Ethiopians."[17] The "Hungarian Bell Ringers" played there on 20 December 1850 on the same night Jenny Lind was packing audiences in at the Richmond Theater at prices as high as $105 a ticket![18] The Exchange also saw its share of famous concert artists. Virtuoso pianist, Henri Herz, played there in 1847 and again in 1849. Another master pianist, Maurice Strakosch, came to the Exchange in 1851 and 1852; the Germania Band entertained audiences there in 1851. Although much smaller than "The Richmond," the Exchange also saw its share of opera as well.

John Hill Hewitt managed "The Richmond" from October 1861 until it burned down on 2 January 1862.[19] Hewitt and actor Richard D'Orsey Ogden were asleep in the theater when the fire broke out and they almost burned to death. Virtually everything in the theater was lost. Hewitt immediately moved his company to Franklin Hall, popularly known as the "Richmond Varieties," or just the "Varieties," and less than a week after the fire, Hewitt's troupe was entertaining audiences there. Originally a church, the "Varieties" had been converted to a theater to satisfy Richmond's unquenchable appetite for entertainment. The *Richmond Daily Dispatch* congratulated Hewitt for furnishing the public with pleasing performances in spite of extremely annoying circumstances.[20]

The New Richmond Theater reopened on 9 February 1863, with former actor Richard Ogden as manager, composer C. A. Rosenberg as musical director,[21] and new rules for audiences. To cut down on the drunkenness that often ruined performances, liquor would no longer be sold. Smoking was also prohibited, as was placing feet on the back of benches, swearing, and making unnecessary noise. Favorites were no longer to be cheered; those out of favor were not to be booed. The callboy who prepared the stage was no longer to be jeered. The management warned that "order shall be observed";[22] miscreants would be ejected from the theater and thrown in jail.

The theater was packed opening night. The managers had offered a special prize of three hundred dollars for best "Inaugural Poem" for the occasion. The contest was won by Henry Timrod, who with that single prize became the highest paid poet in the Confederacy. After the poem was read by actor Walter Keeble, the whole company came on stage and sang the "Virginia Marseillaise," which was considered more dignified than "Dixie." After the song, the troupe put on a tableau representing the Virginia coat of arms and performed Shakespeare's *As You Like It*.

Despite the theater's efforts to keep standards high, there simply weren't enough good actors or singers in Richmond to satisfy demanding audiences. Except for Sallie Partington. When she sang "My Southern Soldier Boy" in the "Virginia Cavalier," every teenage soldier in the audience thought she was singing just to him; the din of their cheers was deafening.[23]

Equally popular for variety acts was Metropolitan Hall on the north side of Franklin. Originally built as a church, it was converted to a concert

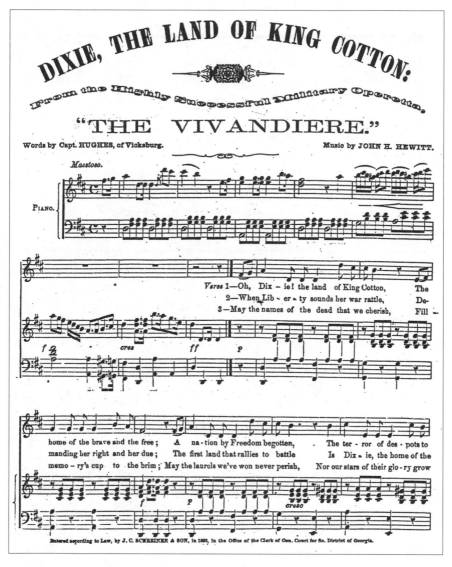

An 1863 Schreiner & Son edition of "Dixie, The Land of King Cotton" from John H. Hewitt's operetta "The Vivandiere."

hall in 1853. With seats for fifteen hundred, it headquartered various minstrel troupes such as "Buckley's Southern Nightingales," which played there from mid-October 1862 to mid-January 1863, and Harry Macarthy, who staged his "Personation Concerts" throughout 1863. The Corinthian Hall (also known as Mechanics Hall Institute) housed several dancing schools and offered concerts. In 1864 it was renamed the Opera House, reflecting the many minstrel shows ("Ethiopian Operas") staged there. In 1865 it burned during the evacuation fire.

Despite the war, Richmond's theaters were always full. Even when the city was on the verge of capture in 1865, diehards still went to the theater although most of Richmond's professional entertainers now served in the army.[24]

CHARLESTON

Charleston was one of the largest cities in the South, with a population of about forty-eight thousand in 1860. Its musical heritage was the oldest in America; among its "firsts" were the first performance of a ballad opera (1735) and creation of the first musical society in America, the St. Cecilia Society (1762).

At the time of the Revolution, Charles Town was America's most sophisticated city, with more professional musicians than any other city in America. The priorities of the *Charleston Daily Courier* couldn't have been clearer when it complained on 23 November 1861 that the recent political excitement concerning South Carolina's impeding secession was keeping audiences away from performances of *The Barber of Seville*.[25] After the Revolution, Charleston lost its musical preeminence when most of the professional musicians who emigrated to America from Europe settled in the North, especially in the middle Atlantic States, where they were more likely to find jobs playing music. These foreign-born musicians generally surpassed native American musicians. As a result, Charleston no longer dominated the country's music industry. Nevertheless, Charleston remained a prominent American musical center and a prewar hub for the southeastern theater circuit and a ceter for musical soirees in the South:

> "The February balls in Charleston," wrote one visitor, "are scarcely less known to fame than the races. The most select and fashionable are those of the Saint Cecilia, and they have been given here from times running back past the memory of all the dancers now

living. . . . They go at ten o'clock and stay until three. The attendance, however, is principally confined to the younger portion of
the fashionable community, who, before setting off for the dance,
see the mammas and papas comfortably to bed."[26]

The "mammas" and "papas," when they weren't comfortably in bed,
were often at the Hibernian Hall, the city's main theater. But on 11
December 1862 a fire, which had nothing to do with the war, destroyed
the Hibernian along with a third of the city. Despite the war, the
theater was remodeled and reopened but it never regained its former
preeminence.

During the first two years of the war, Charleston was all parade. People
entertained themselves and their guests by playing the piano, singing, and
dancing. On one night, a number of officers on General Beauregard's staff
danced the "CanCan" at their headquarters for a group of female visitors.
One of the ladies was taken aback. She had seen the "CanCan" in Paris, she
said, and had since "been trying to forget that I ever did see anything so
purely disgusting."[27]

Elsewhere, amateur concerts raised money for wartime causes. Some of
these were so packed, they were "held over" for several nights. At one concert, the French consul's wife loosed a white pigeon painted with the Confederate colors; everyone thought it a great compliment to the South on
her part. Elegantly uniformed soldiers serenaded Charleston's belles beneath
their windows with sentimental songs and escorted them to dinner parties,
dances, and military balls or lunched with them in nearby camps on "fruit-
cake and champagne." To some Charlestonians, "the war seem[ed] . . . an
incentive to love."[28]

AUGUSTA

Following the historic trade routes established by Georgia's founder, Gen.
James Oglethorpe, a theater circuit extended from Charleston through
towns in Georgia, down to Montgomery and Mobile in Alabama. A
smaller theater circuit in Alabama followed a stagecoach line passing
through smaller towns like Tuskeegee.[29]

Augusta, Georgia, a bustling commercial center with twelve thousand
inhabitants in 1860, a quarter of them slaves, was the smallest of the Southern cities with populations over ten thousand. Yet it had a theater as early
as 1790,[30] private schools where students were taught music, a teacher who

gave violin lessons to the "sons of Augusta's most prominent and respectable citizens," a singing school with more than one hundred boys and girls, an adult chorus that became so popular it formed itself into the Augusta Choral Society, and a "Brahms Band" that gave summer concerts at parades, picnics, and outings.[31]

Despite their enthusiasm for almost all other forms of music, Augusta was too small for many of the touring greats to visit, although violinist Ole Bull performed there in 1852 and pianist Sigismund Thalberg included Augusta in his 1858 Southern tour.[32]

During the war few professional entertainers visited Augusta, but local symphonies offset their absence. In May 1861, "The Confederate Philharmonic Association" gave a concert in Augusta, which combined the "artistic skill of the professional gentlemen belonging to this association with that of lady and gentlemen amateurs."[33]

The Blackmars thought there was more than enough musical interest in Augusta for them to relocate their New Orleans music business there; in April 1863 they began selling sheet music and songsters from their new shop on Broad Street. General Beauregard's sister fled to Augusta from New Orleans and opened a music school. John Hill Hewitt wrote there his "King Linkum The First," a musical burletta. Entertainers also fled to Augusta's relative safety as the Federal noose tightened around the South. Macon songwriter Hermann Schreiner and various other prominent entertainers from other Southern cities journeyed to Augusta to give benefit concerts on behalf of these less fortunate colleagues.[34]

COLUMBUS

Columbus, Georgia, located on the Chattahoochee River, was the largest manufacturing town south of Richmond and a major railroad and shipping center in the South. When showboats began plying the Chattahoochee in the late 1820s, they brought the first professional entertainers to Columbus and other river towns. As Columbus prospered, it became part of a Charleston-Savannah-Columbus-New Orleans theater circuit. A complete circuit, involving steamers, barges, stagecoaches and wagons, took fifty to seventy days to complete.[35]

Despite its size, Columbus had a well-deserved reputation for musical sophistication in the South, which was largely due to the many German immigrants who settled there in the 1840s and 1850s. A sure sign of Columbus's musical stature was Henry Russell's appearance there for a week in November 1843 and his return a month later. Violinist Ole Bull visited

Columbus several times in the 1840s and 1850s, as did pianists Henri Herz and Sigismund Thalberg and contralto Marietta Alboni.

Greater sophistication didn't mean minstrel troupes were any less popular in Columbus then elsewhere in America. The Temperance Hall Theater, built in 1849 to accommodate Columbus's ever increasing audiences, was one of four theaters in the city and the biggest, a hundred feet long, sixty feet wide, and three stories high. Large as it was, it had to be replaced within a few years.

Columbus remained a prominent theatrical center during the war. Harry Macarthy visited frequently as did soprano Charlotte Cushman, the Queen Sisters, the Slomans, and "Blind Tom," whose owners, the Bethunes, lived there. "The only let-up in theater," comments Columbus historian Katherine Mahan, "occurred during the actual siege of Columbus in the Spring of 1865."[36]

MACON

Macon, in the interior of Georgia, was a cotton market prior to the war. By 1860 it had grown to fifteen thousand and was no longer bypassed by traveling stars and music companies. Sigismund Thalberg came to Macon in 1858 for the inaugural concert at Ralston Hall, Macon's new theater. Also on the bill were violinist Henri Vieuxtemps, prima donna Bertha Johansen, and members of the New York Academy of Music.[37] Ole Bull, Adelina Patti, the leading prima donna with the New York Italian Opera Company, Anna Bishop, and pianist Maurice Strakosch played in Macon several times as did many of the major itinerant opera troupes of the time. "Blind Tom" Bethune gave his first concert in Macon in 1855. Many prominent minstrel groups brought their form of entertainment to Macon as well.

During the war, John Schreiner made Macon a prominent center for the South's sheet music industry while his brother Hermann emerged as a major composer. Macon relied on its own local talent for most of its musical entertainment during the hostilities, but the Queen Sisters, "Blind Tom," the Slomans, Ella Wren, and others gave concerts between 1861 and 1863.

ATHENS

Athens, Georgia, about a hundred miles northeast of Atlanta, was a handsome, wealthy community of about four thousand many of them of prominent Confederate stock. In wartime it was an important arsenal for the South, using machinery imported from Europe to manufacture Enfield rifles and ammunition for the Confederate army. The town supported a young lady's seminary, which continued to flourish in spite of the war. Athens, spared many of the privations that plagued other Southern cities, began to enhance Georgia's musical life, although its performers were not always praiseworthy.

The Slomans performed there in 1863 but so did the "Dixie Family," a "seedy-looking man, two women, and an impertinent boy" who advertised they would give a "Grand Concert," part of the proceeds to go to the Ladies' Aid Society. The concert was dreadful. According to the local newspaper, four local black musicians highlighted an otherwise abysmal program. The group took in about two hundred dollars and skedaddled; none of the money went to the Ladies' Aid Society.[38] Most of the city's other musical entertainment was provided by local musicians.

Athens remained largely unscathed by the war until 1865. Even as late as 13 October 1864, Helen Newton felt Athens was "gayer than ever before." She had been to several parties the week before, she said, in which "the young folks danced until four or five in the morning,"—as well as to two musical concerts.[39]

Olivia Newton Cobb, wife of Howell Cobb, one of the original "fire-eaters" from Georgia and a brigadier general in the Confederate army, wrote to her mother-in-law, Lucy Cobb, from Athens five days later. "Athens," she said, "is really as gay as the papers used to say Richmond was last winter. I think there has been at least five dances in town during the last two weeks. . . . I think the girls of the town have gone perfectly crazy on the subject of dancing." Mrs. Cobb also mentioned the concert by the Palmetto Band and added that after the concert there was a dance that lasted until one o'clock.[40] The Slomans were back in 1864. "Blind Tom" Bethune gave concerts for a week in 1864, one night of which was reserved entirely for servants.[41]

MONTGOMERY

Montgomery, Alabama's state capital, was a small quiet town of six thousand poised on seven hills that sloped down to the Alabama River. At the start of the war it was a major depot for tobacco, rice, corn, and cotton, and the first capital of the newly established Confederate States of America. Montgomery pridefully called itself "The Cradle of the Confederacy." Many of its streets were wide and ankle-deep in sand. But in February 1861, people from all over the South converged on Montgomery to watch Jefferson Davis's carriage wind its way from the Exchange Hotel to the white domed

Capitol, escorted by a band playing a new arrangement of an as yet little-known minstrel tune called "Dixie."

Not recognized as a major entertainment center, Montgomery still had a dancing school run by a "Professor and Teacher of Dancing" from New Orleans and Memphis and a theater, which was on the circuit of various concert artists and minstrel troupes, among them violinist Ole Bull (1855), an opera troupe, and a philharmonic orchestra that performed there the following year.

Montgomery also had its local entertainments. A colonel dining in the city in November 1864 related that he was treated to "some extra fine music" after dinner, "according to the Italian, Spanish, and French books, for we had some of each sort done up in true opera fashion, I suppose." But the colonel confessed "it was a *leetle* too foreign for [his] ear," adding that "that was my fault, and not the fault of the music."[42]

ATLANTA

Atlanta, with a population of about six thousand people in 1855, was not one of the South's major musical centers prior to or during the war. Music historian N. Lee Orr attributes its inferior status to its lack of an aristocratic class. Instead, the town was inhabited primarily by middle-class business families, farmers, and workers.[43] Nevertheless, it was visited by some of the touring masters such as pianist Sigismund Thalberg and violinist Henry Vieuxtemps. Atlanta's musical entertainment was limited during the war. The city was visited by the Queen sisters and the Slomans, but most of the city's entertainment during the war was provided by a local group known as the "Atlanta Amateurs."

In 1861 and 1862 slaves and slave owners provided entertainment for blacks by hosting "Negro balls," at various local hotels, permission being given because all monies raised were to go to indigent families of Confederate soldiers. One slave host raised $20 for soldiers' families and $15 for the families of Negro servants attached to the Confederate army. In 1863, however, the white city fathers outlawed the balls, even though they were supervised by white policemen, as a "public nuisance."[44]

MOBILE

Mobile was one of the largest cities of the South during the war with about thirty thousand inhabitants, many of them foreign-born. Bustling with warehouses, businesses, and shops, boasting five hospitals, a Medical College, twenty-four churches, two synagogues, seven public schools, and several private academies, Mobile prided itself on its well-deserved reputation as the most cosmopolitan city in the South, next to New Orleans.[45] Situated at the head of Mobile Bay where two rivers converged, the city was guarded by Forts Gaines and Morgan, which sat at the entrance to the bay, and was considered impregnable during the early years of the war.

Dauphin Street, in Mobile, was home to Joseph Bloch, one of the leading music publishers in the Confederacy. Prior to the war Mobile was a prominent stopover on the Southern opera and concert circuit. The city had a reputation for welcoming theatrical performers. Many of the best and most famous played there and returned again and again. Ole Bull and Maurice Strakosch both performed there, as did several touring opera companies. Jenny Lind performed in 1851 but the price of a seat was so high many couldn't afford to see her. Humorist "Simon Suggs" said he started to hear her but his money gave out.[46] Adelina Patti gave two concerts in Mobile in January 1861, where tickets sold for the unheard of price of six dollars and eight dollars for private boxes. The Queen Sisters were especially popular in Mobile, as they were in the rest of the South; in 1862 they were held over for a whole month "by request of several influential families."[47]

The "Queen Sisters," a family of three girls and three boys, were managed by their father, Alfred Waldron. Waldron dubbed them the "Queen Sisters" because the press kept calling them "little queens." They began as amateurs in Charleston, entertaining audiences with serious drama and songs. By 1862 they were stars. When they played at Franklin Hall that year, John Hill Hewitt managed the Richmond Theater. When Hewitt moved to Augusta, he and Waldron became their managers. Several songs published during the war were either advertised as being sung by "Miss Laura [Waldron], of the Queen Sisters," or were dedicated to her.[48] "Such is their popularity," said the *Savannah Daily Morning News,* "that even lowering skies and threatening gunboats cannot enforce the blockade upon them."[49]

John Sloman was the star performer in Mobile in December 1862. Advertisements billed him as "the popular and well-established comedian, and comic vocalist of the day." Sloman was not only the star performer in three of the plays being offered one night, he also sang the songs during intermission.[50]

MEMPHIS

Memphis emerged as Tennessee's theatrical center in the late 1840s. In 1845 the four hundred seats in Concert Hall were completely sold out when violinist Ole Bull came to town. The clearest indication of Memphis's prominence as a Southern music center was Jenny Lind's concert in 1850, which grossed forty-five hundred dollars in receipts.[51] By 1860 Memphis was the sixth largest city in the South and Tennessee's largest. Its twenty-two thousand inhabitants supported six newspapers, two medical schools, three female seminaries, twenty-one public schools, and a philharmonic orchestra.

On the eve of the Civil War, Memphis was the acknowledged commercial mistress and social gadfly of the Mississippi between St. Louis and New Orleans.[52] Other musical superstars to play in Memphis's theaters were European pianists Leopold De Meyers and Henri Herz, as well as America's own primo virtuoso, Louis Gottschalk, Belgian violinist Henri Vieuxtemps, soprano Adelina Patti, Catherine Hayes, the "Irish Thrush," and scores of minstrel performers,[53] including Dan Emmett,[54] who, a few years later, invented the minstrel show and wrote the South's unofficial anthem, "Dixie."

NASHVILLE

When the Adelphi Theater opened in Nashville in 1850, it had one of the largest stages in America.[55] Built mainly for staging plays, the program changed every day, each offering a variety of songs. The city's other theaters, the Musical Academy and the Female Academy, also entertained at public concerts. Nashville's sizable German population introduced classical works by Haydn and Handel to audiences preferring classical music. In 1859, the Germans organized a Schiller music festival to celebrate the poet's one hundredth anniversary. Luigi Arditi brought his Italian Opera Company to Nashville in 1854.[56] Most theatergoers, however, attended more out of curiosity than appreciation of the music, and the *Nashville Daily Gazette* dutifully educated its readers on what to look and listen for next time out.[57]

But opera took a distant second to singers like Jenny Lind, who came to Nashville in 1851, and other stars like violinist Ole Bull and child prodigy Adelina Patti, who entertained there in 1853. Patti was back again in 1853; Bull returned in 1856. Pianist Sigismund Thalberg and his counterpart on the violin, Henry Vieuxtemps, came to Nashville in 1858.[58] Nashville also figured prominently on the minstrel circuit during the 1850s.[59]

SAVANNAH

Savannah was the oldest, largest, and most populous city (about twenty-two thousand) in Georgia and the state's main seaport and cultural center during the war. The city was settled in 1733. By 1763 it had its own newspaper and theater. Three years later, Savannah had its first "concert of musick."[60] By the 1840s, opera troupes and prominent singers and musicians included it on their itineraries. During the 1850s, the Savannah theater-going public could go to a different play almost every night during the entertainment season, which lasted from November to May.

P. T. Barnum heard about Savannah's appetite for music and demanded twenty thousand dollars to bring Jenny Lind there during her Southern tour. The price was too steep, even for Savannah. If Jenny Lind wouldn't come to Savannah, wealthy admirers from Savannah, Augusta, and even Macon would go to her; many of them made the two-hundred-mile overland trip or the one-hundred-mile sea voyage from Savannah to see her when she came to Charleston.

Savannah entertained up to the eve of the war[61] and didn't pause even for that. Early in 1861 the *Savannah Daily Morning News* commented: "music is rapidly becoming a matter of vast educational importance," and announced a series of upcoming concerts.[62] Those who craved less serious entertainment could watch George Christy's Minstrels.[63] The Bryant Minstrels, the Queen sisters, the Charleston Palmetto Band, "Blind Tom," the Johnston's Minstrels, and the Southern Harmoneons also brought their acts to Savannah during the war. John Hill Hewitt staged his "King Linkum the first," starring the Queen sisters, in Savannah. So attached was Savannah to its entertainment that on 12 January 1865, despite the entry of Sherman's army into the city, many inhabitants turned out for a concert at the Savannah theater by the 33rd Massachusetts Volunteers.[64]

JACKSONVILLE

Florida was not on any major or minor theatrical circuit but still managed to keep abreast of the musical trends going on in the rest of the country.

Jacksonville, Florida, a town of about three thousand people in the 1850s, had little in the way of professional musical entertainment prior to or during the war, but even in a town as small as Jacksonville, the estate of one of its residents contained sixteen violins and eight German flutes when he died in 1835.[65] An item in *The (Jacksonville) News* in 1853 informed readers that a Professor Folsom had pianos, violins, guitars, accordions, and sheet music in stock and also offered lessons to any interested students.[66] Business was brisk and two years later Professor Folsom was still advertising musical instruments and lessons; his success prompted a C. D. Oaks to compete with him.[67]

In 1856 a fire gutted most of the city, putting both men out of business, but in 1857 music teacher-merchant A. A. Ochus intervened, selling pianos, melodeons, guitars, violins, flutes, accordions, and sheet music.[68] Though there were no more than three thousand people in the city, most of them seem to have been playing pianos they bought from Messrs. Folsom, Oaks, and Ochus, because there were at least three piano tuners working either independently or under subcontract to Ochus during this era, although not at the same time.

Although Jacksonville was too small and too out of the way to attract big-name entertainers, its newspapers were filled with items about Ole Bull, Jenny Lind, and other headliners. Jacksonville's citizens followed the itineraries of the superstars and vicariously attended their concerts through their newspapers. Newspapers also explored the powerful effect of opera on audiences. Its elemental appeal, said a journalist for *The (Jacksonian) News,* was the way it spoke "directly and sensibly to the passions and emotions of the heart."[69]

Jacksonville residents, though removed from the main musical centers, sang and played the latest musical pieces in America by sending for them by mail from Northern sheet music publishers and dealers that advertised in the Jacksonville papers.[70] Although Jacksonville did not have a brass band, bands traveling by steamboat, like the Savannah Brass Band, provided concerts and music for large dances.[71] For most dances, Jacksonville's citizens, like those throughout most of the South, danced to the strains of a black fiddler.[72]

With fewer than three thousand people, Jacksonville did not rival Charleston or even Montgomery, but for a frontier town still threatened by Indian raids, it was surprisingly sophisticated when it came to music. And Jacksonville was no different from other frontier towns in the South.

During the war Jacksonville was occupied by Union troops on four different occasions, ending most of its musical activities. But elsewhere in Florida, concerts endured. In April 1864 "Blind Tom" entertained audiences in Tallahassee with Southern songs, ending, as he always did, with his special composition, "The Battle of Manassas."

Susan Bradford Eppes was looking forward to the concert:

> He is too wonderful to miss. . . . His master, Colonel Bethune, is so proud of him and Tom loves him and is so affectionate; just like some sweet-tempered animal that you have petted. . . . How an imbecile (for Tom is plainly that) could ever be taught a connected description of Manassas, is certainly a miracle.[73]

On 9 April 1865, the day of General Lee's surrender, a Tallahassee audience filled to capacity the chamber of the House of Representatives for a concert featuring opera music and tunes like "The Southern Marseillaise," "Une Pluie du Perle," and "Sleeping I Dreamed Love."[74]

HOUSTON

Houston, with a population of nearly five thousand in 1861, was the third largest city in Texas at the start of the war, after San Antonio and Galveston. After the Union navy blockaded Galveston, however, many of that city's residents moved to Houston, whose population swelled.

Houston was not on a major theater circuit prior to the war, but it was visited in 1860 by a few well-known entertainers such as vocalist Anna Bishop (Henry Bishop's wife), considered one of the best female singers of her era. The nationally known Peak Family Swiss Bell ringers and violinist Gustave Kauffman also visited the city.[75] Several professional minstrel troupes such as the Sable Brothers, the Apollo Minstrels, the Congo Minstrels, and the Great Ethiopian minstrels also passed through Houston prior to the war.

Houston music sellers were as well-stocked as any in the latest songs. Even as late as 1864, one of Houston's music stores had a stock of four thousand piano pieces.[76] The best know music seller was the German-born August Sachtleben. Sachtleben had settled in Galveston along with many other German immigrants and had gone into business selling musical instruments and sheet music and had even ventured into the sheet music publishing business with the "Southern Pleiades March and Quickstep"[77] before he was forced to flee to Houton. When he arrived in Houston in December 1861, he placed an ad informing Houston's music-loving community that he was hereby announcing "the removal of his music store from Galvaston to Main Street, Houston, where he would be able to furnish all the latest musical publications of the Southern states and Europe."[77]

During the war, Houston was too remote for professionals to visit. Most of the musical performers who entertained were amateur or semiprofessional groups such as the Confederate Minstrels, who had previously played in Richmond and other Southern cities. As elsewhere in the South, amateur singers and musicians entertained the local citizenry. At one concert, Col. Xavier DeBray played the flute, Col. George Baylor played the violin, and Col. John Baylor played the piano.[78]

CHAPTER 14

Confederate Music Publishers and Their Industry

Song publishing was as patriotic an act as writing or singing songs. But music publishing was also a business, and in both the North and the South, the music publishing business throve during the Civil war.

At the start of the war, sheet music sold for 25 to 50 cents a copy. The cost of printing one hundred copies of a four-page song was about $15 ($2.50 for one hundred sheets of paper, $1.25 for printing, and $3.00 per page for engraving). Publishers expected half their output to flop. Among the thousands of songs published in prewar days, one in ten met expenses and one in fifty was a success (sales of three thousand copies for an instrumental piece, five thousand for a song). Still, profits could be enormous. In the North, the return on a song like George Root's "Tramp, Tramp, Tramp" was $10,000, even though its popularity was cut short by the war's end.[1]

The South had fewer accomplished composers than the North, but it shared inspiration, heartfelt sincerity, and patriotism. As the *Southern Illustrated News* said, Southern songs "compare favorably, in all respects, with any published in the land of wooden nutmegs [that is, the North]."[2] But without a viable outlet, there would have been no way to disseminate the songs. That outlet, of course, was the music publishing industry, which hardly existed in the prewar South. The fledgling music industry more than met its challenge; and even though it, like every other Confederate industry, was plagued by the shortages of raw materials, Confederate music publishers continued to publish songs up to the Confederacy's last desperate days.

Not surprisingly, the Confederacy's primary publishers were located in the South's larger cities—New Orleans, Richmond, Augusta, Savannah, Macon, Charleston, Columbia, and Mobile. With the exception of Columbia, these cities shared the oldest musical traditions in the South. To reach the widest possible markets, music publishers also developed large distribution networks and often listed on the sheet music the stores that carried their publications. The Blackmar brothers, whose main business was located in New Orleans until its capture in 1862, for instance, had a wholesaler in Richmond who distributed their songs to music dealers throughout the South.[3] Publishers also regularly advertised in local newspapers long lists of their sheet music, which the public could buy directly from them by mail.[4]

ORIGINS OF THE SOUTHERN MUSIC PUBLISHING INDUSTRY

America's music publishing industry began after the American Revolution when the Carr family came to America and began selling music from stores they opened in Philadelphia, Baltimore, and New York. The Carrs had been prominent musicians, instrument makers, and music publishers in England for several centuries. When their business declined, Benjamin Carr (1768-1831) sailed to America and set up a "musical repository" in Philadelphia in 1793 from which he sold musical instruments. Not long after that he began publishing original songs and instrumental music, among them the first edition in 1798 of "Hail! Columbia." Not content with merely selling music, the indefatigable Carr worked as a concert pianist and vocalist, conducted the local orchestra, and wrote and arranged his own music.

While Benjamin was creating a music industry in Philadelphia, his father, Joseph, and his brother, Thomas, were doing the same in Baltimore. In 1813 Thomas musically arranged "The Defense of Fort McHenry," rechristened it "The Star-Spangled Banner," and launched what became America's national anthem.

The Carrs also set up a branch in New York that didn't prosper. When James Hewitt (1770-1827) expressed an interest in buying it, they were happy to sell. Hewitt had also emigrated from England, leaving behind a distinguished career as a violinist and music director in the court of King George III. When buisness was too slow to earn a living from just selling musical instruments and sheet music, Hewitt paid his bills by playing the violin, conducting orchestras, organizing subscription concerts for entertainers, and composing and arranging music for an opera company.

Hewitt eventually became one of New York's most prominent citizens, especially after his marriage into one of the city's eminent families. But though his musical talents enriched and honored him, Hewitt detected a palpable prejudice against professional musicians among the elite. When

Hewitt's son, John Hill Hewitt, wanted to follow in his footsteps, he discouraged him. But the younger Hewitt would not be deterred. In 1827 he became the first American to write an international "hit," "The Minstrel's Return from the War." His father had meanwhile died penniless, leaving the family business to his other son, James. James published his brother's song but failed to copyright it. Years later, he estimated that mistake cost them about ten thousand dollars, the equivalent of several million in twentieth-century dollars. John Hill Hewitt wrote many other hit tunes in his life and became the "Bard of the Confederacy," but his music never made him wealthy.

Another pioneer in American music publishing, noteworthy because his enterprise eventually became a leading source of pro-Southern sheet music, was John Cole. Originally from England, Cole and his family moved to Baltimore in 1786 when he was twelve. He was a self-taught musician and worked for a time as Church organist and choirmaster. In 1802 he began compiling and publishing religious tune books, then began writing them as well. In 1822 he started a music publishing business with his son. In 1839 they sold their business to Frederick D. Benteen, who worked as a clerk in another music publishing business in Baltimore owned by George Willig. Benteen borrowed money from Willig, bought all of John Cole's stock, and went into business. He became a successful music publisher in his own right but suffered poor health; in 1862 he sold his business to two of his clerks, William Miller and Joseph R. Beacham, and the firm became Miller & Beacham. Miller and Beacham published the first editions of many of the songs that became the Confederacy's biggest hits, among them James Ryder Randall's "Maryland! My Maryland!" Beacham either quit or died in 1863 and Miller ran the business after that. In 1872 the business was taken over by the Boston firm of Oliver Ditson & Co.

John Siegling founded a business at 69 Broad Street in Charleston in 1819, then moved to King Street at the corner of Beaufain. His son assumed the business in 1858. When the war erupted, his was the oldest music publishing enterprise in America,[5] and he continued to publish songs throughout the war.[6] Siegling's most noteworthy Civil War piece was "The Palmetto State Song," published in December 1860, the first of what was to become the Confederate music collection. The song featured a lithographed cover of South Carolina's secession convention with a dedication to the signers of the secession ordinance.

Up until 1825, only fourteen companies published the 400 pieces of sheet music produced each year in America.[7] Philadelphia was the nation's music publishing center, accounting for most of the country's sheet music. The reason Philadelphia figured so prominently in early American music was that it had the largest local market with about seventy thousand inhabitants. Next came New York (sixty thousand), Boston (twenty-five thousand), Charleston (eighteen thousand), and Baltimore (thirteen thousand).

Several new music publishing firms began business in the South during the 1830s, among them Paul Emile Johns and Benjamin Casey, both in New Orleans, and Samuel Bromberg in Mobile; in the 1840s, William T. Mayo took over Johns's business, Philip P. Werlein opened a music store in Mississippi, George Cole and George Oates both competed in Charleston with John Siegling, and J. W. Randolph started a business in Richmond. Between 1850 and 1861, George Oates closed his business in Charleston and he and his brother relocated to Augusta. That same decade, Philip Werlein, the Blackmar brothers, Louis Grunewald, and Elie and Chassaignac went into the music business in New Orleans; John Burke and John Schreiner both set up shop in Macon; James A. McClure did the same in Memphis;[8] and Joel H. Snow started publishing songs from his shop in Mobile. Despite almost insurmountable obstacles, several other entrepreneurs entered the music publishing business during the war, among them Julian Selby and Blanton Duncan, both in Columbia, South Carolina, George Dunn in Richmond, and John Hill Hewitt in Augusta.

THE SOUTHERN LITHOGRAPHIC INDUSTRY

A lithographic image on the cover of a piece of sheet music automatically increased its sales potential. During the first year of the war, the older firms and the upstarts vied with one another for the most ornately lithographed covers. These covers—many in color—featured generals, statesmen, battle scenes, and even composers, reflecting the Confederacy's ebullient nationalism.

Lithography was invented in Germany by Aloys Senefelder (1771–1834), purely by happenstance. A sometime composer, poet, painter, engraver, and violinist, Senefelder was broke. Without money to buy copper plates for engraving music, he was constantly scavenging for anything smooth and sturdy enough to take an etching. By luck, he found just what he wanted in limestone, and it was free! Limestone's smooth surface produced effects that were impossible with copper plates. Grease and water didn't stick to copper; limestone absorbed both. When Senefelder poured water onto a smooth, flat limestone surface on which he had drawn a picture with a grease pencil, the water permeated all the areas except those lined in grease. When he ran an ink-covered roller over the stone, the grease lines absorbed the ink and the water-soaked stone remained unstained. If the stone was pressed onto a piece of paper, the drawing transferred onto the page. Experimenting further, he created colored pictures by using different stones for different colors.

Senefelder's discovery electrified the art of illustration. First used in England in 1800 for illustrating books, lithography became an art form in its own right by the 1820s, replacing engraved illustrations. The first piece of American sheet music with a lithographed cover ("The Soldier Tired") appeared in 1823. Five years later, fifteen-year-old Nathaniel Currier found employment in a Boston printing shop to learn the art. After a five-year apprenticeship, he left Boston to work with a master lithographer in Philadelphia. In 1834 he moved to New York and partnered a lithography business with James Merritt Ives.

Unlike Currier and Ives, most lithographers of that era designed the covers for America's sheet music without fanfare. Although their creations were displayed as artwork in family parlors across the country, individual lithographers were unheralded. Prior to the war, about a hundred lithographers worked in the American sheet music industry,[9] seven of them in New Orleans.[10] The most prominent lithographers in the Confederacy were George Dunn and E. Crehen in Richmond; Gray and Valory, and Blanton Duncan in Columbia, South Carolina; and J. T. Patterson & Co. in Augusta, Georgia. Some, like Dunn, were also active publishers as well.[11]

A lithographer working for Blanton Duncan recalled the problems Duncan and other lithographers faced in those days. First,

> no two presses were alike. There was an old French one, with its swinging scraper box; a Philadelphia press, with its top lines, on which, in order to get pressure, you had to swing two large balls around till the scraper rested on the tympon, and then pull through; and yet other presses of different make, but not one was to be compared with the hand press of today. We had to make our own printing ink. There was a large room in the building set apart for that purpose, and in it benches were set up with slabs to grind up lamp black. The varnish was made up in a large iron kettle and the lithos had to take turns in superintending it. . . . The ink was only half ground and it was with some difficulty that we could print and keep it on the stone.

The lithographers in Duncan's shop also had a taste for spirits and once he jailed them all for a few days.[12]

Evans and Cogswell was one of the most important lithographers and printers for the Confederacy. The business had been started by Joch C. Walker, who moved to Charleston from New York in 1821. Walker joined with Evans and Cogswell. After Walker died in 1860, the business became Evans and Cogswell. When the war started, the firm printed bonds, stock certificates, and money for the government. To meet the new demands, Evans sailed a blockade-runner to England and Scotland where he hired 10 lithographers and an engraver and bought a number of presses and printing material. The ship docked at Nassau where the lithographers and their equipment were transferred to two blockade-runners that narrowly missed being intercepted by Federal gunboats.

Evans ran the blockade to England several more times and each time he was able to hire a few more lithographers. In 1864 the firm relocated in Columbia, South Carolina. Their printing business was one of the many that were torched in February 1865 when Gen. William T. Sherman burned the city. The owners moved back to Charleston after the war; by December 1865 they were again in business.

In contrast to lithography, engraving involved punching notes and musical notations onto the plates for transcription. The best-known engravers in the Confederate music industry were the Wehrmanns, Henry and his wife Charlotte Marie Clementine. In 1849 they had emigrated from Paris to America and settled in New Orleans. Henry also operated a printing press from their business at 142 Burgundy Street in New Orleans.

The Wehrmanns began engraving music for Southern publishers in the early 1850s. Their first clients were William Mayo and Philip Werlein. During the war they engraved music for virtually every music publisher in the Confederacy. Their sons and daughters figured prominently in New Orleans's musical life in the latter part of the nineteenth century.[13] The other engraver whose name appears on many pieces of Confederate sheet music is W. H. Leeson, but nothing is known of his (or her) background.

By 1863 the South's book and music industries were beginning to founder because printers, engravers, and lithographers enlisted or worked for the government, where they were exempt from military service.[14] Although European and English printers and lithographers were smuggled through the blockade,[15] or were hired in New York and Philadelphia and spirited across Federal lines, they often joined government projects because the pay was much higher than in the music business.

THE PAPER CHASE

The main problem confronting publishers, music and otherwise, however, was paper. In 1861 there were only about fifteen paper mills in the South; most were located in the Carolinas, Georgia, Tennessee, and Virginia.[16] These mills produced seventy-five thousand pounds of paper a day, about half the South's daily consumption, most of which was used for newsprint.[17]

In 1861 there were seventy-five newspapers in Mississippi alone;[18] but by 1864, only forty-one daily newspapers served the entire South.[19] As early as June 1861, the *Richmond Whig* urged Southerners to save their rags for conversion to paper,[20] while *The Southern Cultivator* prodded the Confederacy's paper mills to increase production so "Southern authors [could] write and publish Southern books."[21] By October 1861, the *Atlanta Southern Confederacy* was "curtailed" to half its original size and printed on brown paper.

A breakdown in a mill's machinery, like the one that occurred in Atlanta in January 1862, caused desperation. The *Atlanta Southern Confederacy* alerted its readers to its plight: "The mill which makes our paper is unable, on account of recent damage to the machinery, which cannot be repaired or replaced until the blockade is ended, to make any more paper of our weekly size."[22] Paper had to be smuggled into the South from the North or through the blockade.[23] By 1862 the thin paper was dingier, the newspaper size was smaller, and the ink rubbed off when touched. When there were no more rags, papermakers resorted to cotton, cornhusks, and sunflower stalks.[24]

At first, editors believed the scarcity and skyrocketing cost were due to speculators. In May 1862 the editor of the *Macon Telegraph* shared his exasperation with his readers:

> We are completely puzzled, confounded and destroyed by the unreasonable exactions of the paper mills, against which there is no defence. We must pay what they choose to charge, and may God reward them according to their works. This week they have raised upon us from five to six dollars per ream, and we see no reason why they will not get up to a hundred dollars a ream before the year is out. . . . We see nothing before us or the Southern press in general but certain ruin, if things go on long as they are now traveling.[25]

Paper mills began to succumb by 1863.[26] Georgia's three mills, located near Columbus, Athens, and Augusta, stayed in business longer but not without mishap. The Bath Mill near Augusta, Georgia, which had some government contract work, burned down in 1863, precipitating a crisis for the various newspapers in the area. The May and June 1863 editions of *The Southern Cultivator* informed readers that:

> [the accident] compels us to limit nearly all advertisements, and curtail the size of our sheet. The high price of cotton—great scarcity of rags, and limited capacity of the few papers mills in the Confederacy, may force us to a still further reduction in size; but we are pledged neither to suspend temporarily, nor stop the *Cultivator,* so long as it is possible to procure paper enough to print two pages; and we trust our readers will mind that, if somewhat less in quantity, there is no deterioration in the quality or value of the reading matter which we furnish them.[27]

The mill reopened by November 1864.[28] An editorial in *The Southern Cultivator* for 1 January 1865 assured readers that although circumstances beyond its control had prevented the publisher from supplying the journal as promptly as desired,

> We are happy to state that we have still enough paper for the present year [1865], and if not interrupted by the enemy we will continue to send the paper to all who wish it, so far as we have mail facilities.[29]

Industrial demand for paper always fell far short of supply. In 1864 the *Columbia Daily South Carolinian* reminded readers:

> Don't forget to save your rags; all the paper mills and newspaper publishers are in a strait for the want of material. It costs nothing to save rags and high prices are paid for them. If the money the rags bring in is not an inducement to take care of them, then do it for the purpose of keeping newspapers from suspending. White rags, of course, are preferable, but colored ones will do, to make paper of some sort. Cotton or linen rags of any description will make good paper.[30]

The Southern Cultivator reprinted an editorial from the *Columbus Sun,* which made the same point:

Let the rag bag become a recognized institution in every household. Nothing would tend more to increase the quantity of paper, and cheapen its price, than the general institution of the rag bag. Let every scrap of cloth, rope and thread, refuse cotton, and all waste material, of which either cotton, flax or hemp forms the fibre, be diligently saved, and sold to the paper mills, and paper will become abundant and be furnished at reduced rates.[31]

In 1864, in the preface to his book on the first two years of the war, E. A. Pollard told his readers: "Owing to the extreme scarcity and printing facilities in the Confederacy," he was arranging for the printing of his third volume in England.[32]

Southerners were scolded that they had to save their rags if they wanted to read and write. The publisher of the *Macon Telegraph* asked "all persons in Macon and vicinity having any linen or cotton rags white or colored, to send them to his store, where the highest market prices will be paid for them in goods or cash as may be desired. I will collect them solely for the *Telegraph*."[33]

Without paper, newspaper and book publishers first cut back on size and then simply defaulted.

The *Richmond Examiner,* in 1865, reduced its print from four pages to two. Other newspapers resorted to recycling wallpaper, wrapping paper, or any paper they could procure. Some days the news was printed on blue paper, some days on brown. In October 1864 the *Columbia Daily South Carolinian* apologized to its readers for its shoddy print:

> The difficulty of obtaining paper compels us to this issue to use a much smaller size than usual, and to present to our readers a deformed sheet. We hope in a few days to be able to remedy the difficulty.[34]

Confederate sheet music likewise deteriorated noticeably during the war. In 1861 sheet music was printed on heavy paper. By the second year of the war, the paper was thinner, had shrunk in size, and tore easily. Raw cotton, hemp, and other materials were used as fillers. When lampblack for making ink disappeared, elderberries, green persimmons, pomegranate rind, maple, dogwood, or magnolia bark, and pine needles were ground up for ink. When one color was depleted, the printer dabbed on the next until it too was exhausted, and then utilized whatever was left. To complete an edition of "The Mocking Bird Quickstep," George Dunn used black, brown, and wine-colored ink.[35]

As paper supplies dwindled, prices for songs skyrocketed. In 1861 "The Bonnie Blue Flag," the song that would contend for the Confederacy's unofficial anthem, sold for 40 cents, whereas "The Confederacy March" and "Our First President's Quickstep" each sold for 50 cents. Songs selling for less included "The Southron's Chaunt of Defiance," "God Will Defend the Right," and "Carrie Bell" at 35 cents each, while "Let Me Kiss Him for His Mother" and "I Still See Her in My Dreams" asked for 25 cents. By 1863 the price of sheet music had doubled and, in some cases, tripled. The third edition of "All Quiet along The Potomac Tonight" and the fourth edition of "Rock Me to Sleep Mother" cost $1.00 each; "Mother Oh! Sing Me To Rest" and "Kathleen Mavourneen" were $1.50 each. By 1864 the price of "All Quiet along The Potomac Tonight" rose to $1.50, as did "No One to Love" and "Call Me Not Back from that Echoless Shore." Later that year, Julian Selby was selling songs for $1.50 to $2.50.

In Richmond, publishers West and Johnson decided costs and shortages had escalated beyond their control and they called it quits:

> Wishing to discontinue the sale of sheet music, and having a large stock of excellent music on hand, we will send post paid, to any one remitting us Five Dollars, Twenty Pieces containing:
>
> Variations
> Waltzes
> Polkas,
> Marches,
> or Guitar Music
>
> Great care will be furthered in its selection. Address orders forthwith to West & Johnson.[36]

Other music publishers stepped in. In 1864 H. C. Clarke, a Mobile music dealer, listed the title of over one hundred songs he had just received and was offering for sale at $2.00 a copy.[37] Clarke also advertised the third edition of *The New Confederate Flag Song Book:*

Just Published! *The New Confederate Flag Song Book,* No. 1, Third Edition, enlarged to 80 pages, by the addition of several new and popular songs and ballads, humorous, sentimental and patriotic. The popularity of this Song Book has never been equalled. Over 50,000 copies of the two first editions have been sold. Price $1. H. C. Clarke, Publisher, Mobile Ala."[38]

In October 1863 Macon music publisher John Schreiner could no longer keep up with an inflation that had pushed up costs for paper, ink, and printers' wages over 200 percent. He told his distributors he would no longer preprice his sheet music so that increased costs would not force him to print new covers reflecting higher prices.[39] Even so, Schreiner held down his prices because he had the foresight to buy a large number of cotton bales, which kept his business in paper for two years.[40] As the war dragged on, prices for songs catapulted.

Royalty payments between authors or composers and publishers varied. Usually the publisher bought the music outright and copyrighted it in his own name. In 1864 John Schreiner offered twenty-five pieces of music to anyone who would write an answer to the song, "When This Cruel War Is Over." The winner was "I Remember the Hour When Sadly We parted," which Schreiner then sold for $2.00 a copy.[41] In some cases, an author was paid a royalty on each copy or a percentage of the profits; sometimes the author or composer paid for the printing himself, gave the publisher a discount off the wholesale price, advertised his songs, and sold them directly from his own home, adding postage to the cost. Sometimes jobbers bought music in quantity and sold it to local dealers. Confederate publishers also reprinted many songs originally published in the North, as "Flowers of Song Transplanted to Southern Soil." These transplants allowed Confederate publishers to avoid any copyright or royalty fees.

Publishers also purposely omitted the copyright date on their music to avoid paying royalties. Sometimes publishers dated their music covers but didn't date the music which, in many cases, was written a year or more earlier. Some pieces of music carried two dates—one for the cover and one for the music. Because dates were often omitted or because of this dual dating, many pieces of Confederate sheet music cannot be accurately dated. In some cases where there are no dates, music scholars are able to tentatively date pieces from the numbers and letter codes engravers etched into their plates to accommodate the publishers. The plates, however, were not always engraved with numbers. Occasionally, a publisher used the same music plates but attached new covers or catalogs to them, which might or might not be dated.

No sales records were kept of Confederate sheet music. According to Mildred Staton, "When This Cruel War is Over" had sales of almost a million, and "No One To Love" sold about 100,000 copies.[42] Some songs went through several editions, but the number of copies in an edition isn't known. Assuming an edition for one company was the same as for another (not a very good assumption, but at least a basis for comparing some songs), the most popular songs would be those with the most editions, among them "The Bonnie Blue Flag" (14 editions), "God Save The South" (13 editions), "The Volunteer" (10 editions), "Our First President's Quickstep" (9 editions), "Lorena" (9 editions), "Missouri" (9 editions), "The Brightest Eyes" (8 editions), "The Rock Beside The Sea" (7 editions), "There's Life In The Old Land Yet" (7 editions), "Rock Me To Sleep Mother" (6 editions), "Bonnie Eloise" (6 editions), "All Quiet Along The Potomac Tonight" (6 editions), "The Stars Of Our Banner" (5 editions), "Ever of Thee" (5 editions), "Then You'll Remember Me" (5 editions). "Rock Me To Sleep Mother" was in its fourth edition in June 1863 and in its fifth a month later.[43] "All Quiet Along the Potomac Tonight" was in its third edition in June 1863 and its fourth in January 1864.[44]

MUSIC PUBLISHERS

None of the Confederate music publishers left diaries so that little is known about the business side of music publishing in the Confederacy, or about the personal lives of those who spearheaded that industry. What we do know has been pieced together from the few facts available about some of the better-known publishers.

Armand Blackmar

A Northerner by birth (1826), A(rmand) Edward Blackmar was the leading music publisher in the Confederacy. Blackmar had spent his early years in Vermont and Ohio. In 1845 he moved to Huntsville, Alabama, where he taught piano and violin and moonlighted as an arranger for the local band. In 1852 he moved to Jackson, Mississippi, where he became professor of music at Cenenary College. In 1856 he stopped teaching to enter the music business, selling pianos and other instruments.[45] Moving to Vicksburg in 1858, he partnered with E. D. Patton. The next year his brother Henry Clay (b. 1831) moved South. The brothers bought out Patton's interest and soon began publishing songs with a Blackmar & Bro., Vicksburg, imprint. The Blackmars continued to publish music from their Vicksburg branch until 1862, but less so after 1860, when they started another business in New Orleans at 74 Camp Street, using the imprint A. E. Blackmar & Bro.

Armand Blackmar married in 1860. His wife, Margaret B. Meara, had been working as a governess[46] at a plantation where he had been a music teacher. Their first child was born in 1861, after the war had started; they named her Louisiana Rebel Blackmar.[47]

By April 1862 when the Federals occupied New Orleans, Armand Blackmar was the South's most prominent music publisher, with a distribution network that included Atlanta, Columbia, Goldsboro, Macon, Savannah, Mobile, Montgomery, Raleigh, and Richmond. Blackmar's widespread network kept him under surveillance because it could have been used to pass along espionage as easily as sheet music. Blackmar, like everyone else in New Orleans, had to take an oath of allegiance to the United States in order to stay in business during the occupation. But because he had written and published songs supporting the Confederate cause, especially Harry Macarthy's "The Bonnie Blue Flag," which rivaled "Dixie" as the South's unofficial anthem,[48] Gen. Benjamin "Beast" Butler, the commanding Federal officer, was unforgiving.

To Butler, "The Bonnie Blue Flag" was seditious. He fined Blackmar five hundred dollars for publishing it and imprisoned him on Ship Island for a brief time.[49] Defiant, Blackmar whistled the tune while being escorted to jail.[50]

While Armand was in prison, his brother Henry smuggled as many of their music plates and other supplies as he could out of the city and headed for Augusta. When Armand was finally released from prison, he found the printing presses and other stock which Henry had been forced to leave behind destroyed, undoubtedly under Butler's orders. Undaunted, Blackmar stayed in New Orleans, surreptitiously writing songs under various pseudonyms, among them Ye Comic ("Short Rations"), Dudie Diamonds ("The Gallant Girl That Smote the Dastard Tory, Oh"), A. Pender ("Goober Peas"), and A. E. A. Muse ("My Warrior Boy"). Meanwhile, Henry had started business in Augusta. By June 1862, he was advertising songs for sale at 255 Broad Street. Business was so brisk that five months

later he relocated down the street to 199 Broad Street, below the Bank of
Augusta, and placed an ad in the *Augusta Daily Chronicle and Sentinel* that
the Blackmars were

> now prepared to fill orders for their many popular publications, at
> but a slight advance on former prices. We are now publishing "The
> Bonnie Blue Flag," "The Volunteer," "Missouri," "Maryland, My
> Maryland," etc. and can supply customers with these popular songs
> in large or small quantities. We have also a choice selection of stan-
> dard sheet music.[51]

In 1864 the Augusta shop was celebrated in Edward O. Eaton's "The
199 Broad Street Polka." (Eaton had previously celebrated the firm's New
Orleans location in his "Seventy-Four Camp Street Polka.")

Henry continued to issue music from the Augusta store throughout the
war, except when he was jailed for beating his wife. In 1863 Armand managed to reopen the Blackmar store in New Orleans at 74 Camp Street and
published music again under the imprint of Blackmar & Co. He also temporarily joined with John Schreiner; the two of them jointly issued "Missouri, Bright Land of the West" and "Southern Dixie." The sheet music for
that song gives Mobile as the address for the Blackmars and Montgomery
for Schreiner, although neither had any known publishing activities in
either city. In the fall of 1864, Armand moved his shop to 167 Canal Street
but still used the Blackmar & Co. imprint.

On 10 April 1865, Armand sold the Augusta store's stock of about fifteen
thousand pieces of music and thirty-seven hundred other publications to John
Hill Hewitt for $150,000, about four times what he had paid for it originally,
albeit prior to runaway Confederate inflation.[52] Hewitt had worked for
Henry in Augusta and had even lived in his house. Although he wrote many
songs during this time, he was under contract to John Schreiner in Macon,
and so Blackmar couldn't publish any of those tunes. When he bought the
Blackmar business, news of Lee's surrender hadn't yet reached Augusta.

The Blackmar imprint varied during the war years. In some cases it was
A. E. Blackmar & Bro., Blackmar & Co., or Blackmar Bros. Henry was
always the "Bro." Though Henry was sometimes the local manager,
Armand was always in charge. After the war, the Blackmar brothers argued
and Henry struck off on his own. Perhaps Henry resented always being the
"Bro." in the firm.

Between 1865 and 1868, Armand changed his imprint to A. E. Blackmar and his catalog advertised "A. E. Blackmar (Successor to Blackmar & Bro., and Blackmar & Co.), Music Publisher and Wholesale and Retail Dealer in Pianos, Melodeons, Sheet Music, Instruction Books, & All Kinds of Musical Merchandise." In 1871 Henry swallowed his pride and clerked for his brother. But the siblings quarreled incessantly, and finally parted for good. Henry opened a music store in 1886 at 199 Canal Street, while Armand operated his store at 202 Canal Street; but the two avoided each other.[53]

In the 1870s and 1880s, Armand Blackmar constantly relocated, weaving in and out of partnerships with other music dealers. In 1877 he moved to San Francisco and started business with a Louis Davis. That partnership lasted until 1880 when he returned to New Orleans and clerked for his erstwhile business rival, Philip Werlein.[54] When he wasn't writing songs or publishing those written by others, Armand turned to chess, his other main love, eventually writing a book on the game entitled *Blackmar Gambit*.[55] In 1885 he tried the music business again. Three years later he died.

Philip Werlein

Armand Blackmar's main competitor in New Orleans immediately prior to and during the first two years of the war was the equally patriotic and enterprising Philip Peter Werlein (1812-1885).

Werlein was born in Germany and trained there as a pianist. He emigrated to America in 1831 and settled in Vicksburg where he taught music. Shortly thereafter he moved to Clinton, Mississippi, as head of the music department for the Clinton Female Seminary.[56] In 1842 he moved back to Vicksburg where he sold musical instruments and sheet music. He married Margaret Halsey in 1846.

Werlein's early business ventures were unsuccessful until 1853 when he moved to New Orleans and, in partnership with L. C. Ashbrand, purchased Emile Johns's music business at 93 Camp Street. The following year he bought out William T. Mayo's stock and store on Camp Street and began business on his own.[57] In 1858 he expanded to an adjoining store on Camp Street, and in 1860 he was issuing music from another store on Canal Street.

At the outbreak of the war, Werlein served with the New Orleans Home Guard. When the Federals occupied New Orleans, he refused to take the oath of allegiance to the United States and fled to New Iberia, Louisiana, where he remained for the rest of the war.[58]

Werlein didn't return to the music publishing business until 1865. He was succeeded by his son, Philip (1847–99), and then his grandson. In 1940 Dave Franck bought the Werlein publishing business, but the retail segment remained in the family.[59]

Louis Grunewald

Louis Grunewald's music business was smaller than both the Blackmars' and Werlein's, but was still a major Confederate music publishing outlet during the war. Like Werlein, Grunewald was born in Germany (1827). He came to New Orleans in 1852 and supported himself as an organist at several of the Catholic churches in the city.[60] Four years later, he started business as a music dealer in a small store on Magazine Street. An early photograph reveals his thick mustache melding into a full beard and long sideburns.[61] In 1859 he moved to 214 Constance Street, and then in 1861 to 26 Chartres Street where he stayed until 1863, when he relocated to 129 Canal Street. Unlike his competitors, Armand Blackmar and Philip Werlein, Grunewald did not openly espouse the Confederate cause, and none of his songs was overtly patriotic. As a result, Grunewald stayed open throughout the war.

The "Canal Street March," published in 1864, features a lithographed cover of Grunewald's music house. The firm was one of a number of businesses located in the Touro Building, whose name was located prominently at the top along with the date 1856, when the building was presumably erected. Grunewald occupied all four floors of the Touro Building. The sign "Music Store" hung above the windows on the top floor, above the second, "Piano Ware Rooms," above the third, "Melodeons & Organs," "Music Publishing House" above the ground floor. The show window featured several brass instruments. The caption page had the long title "129 Canal Street Quick March," by Charles Mayer.

Grunewald was a very successful businessman. By the end of the century, his family owned a hotel, an opera house, and many other businesses, besides their prosperous music stores. In 1879 the *Illustrated Visitors' Guide to New Orleans* said of him, "By his energy and perseverance, he has given the music business great prominence in the trade of our city, and made his own establishment the leading business house of the South."[62]

Eugene Chassaignac

Little is known about the French New Orleans music publisher, Eugene Chassaignac (1820–78). He was born in Nantes, France, and studied music with composer H. Halévy. In 1858 he emigrated to New Orleans and, in partnership with Adolphe Elie, started a music publishing business for French composers. The partnership lasted only a short time. A man named Sourdes bought out Elie's share in 1861, and Elie went into business for himself.[63]

During the war, Chassaignac served as a captain with Company F, 1st Regiment, 2nd Brigade, 1st Division, Louisiana Militia, and wrote twelve songs, which his firm published under the Sourdes and Chassaignac imprint.

George Dunn and Julian Selby

George Dunn, about whom almost nothing is known, was a major Richmond lithographer and music publisher during the war. Neither the Virginia archives nor state library mention him. Yet there are several letters by and about him in the correspondence of the Confederate Treasury indicating that he supervised the lithographic designs used in the department's printing of Confederate bonds and paper money.[64]

Shortly after the start of the war, Dunn sailed to England to hire printers and engravers for the Confederate Treasury.[65] He ran the blockade with them and landed in Columbia, South Carolina, to supervise the engraving of Confederate money and bonds.

What he saw he didn't like. The unoriginal designs used for Confederate money were inferior to the engravings used in the North. He prophetically warned the Treasury of the danger of Confederate currency being counterfeited.[66] A day later, Assistant Secretary of the Treasury B. C. Pressley telegraphed Treasury Secretary Christopher Memminger from Charleston, South Carolina, to notify him that he had just seen four counterfeit bills and to relate a complaint from bank tellers that the treasury should have warned them of the problem. Pressley portentously ended his telegram: "Unless something be done especially to allay the fears and to re-create confidence, the credit of Treasury notes will be gone before you are aware of it."[67]

It is unknown why Dunn ceased to work with the Treasury shortly after; he did not surface again until he entered the music publishing and lithography business in Richmond in 1863.

Many of Dunn's songs were published in collaboration with Julian Augustus Selby in Columbia, South Carolina. Selby was born in 1833 on an island off the coast of South Carolina. He attended a private boy's school in Columbia and worked at the *Daily South Carolinian* newspaper. He volunteered to serve in the Confederate army but was persuaded by Dr. Gibbs, his employer, to stay with the paper. Selby also found the time and resources to go into the music business. His best known publication is "All Quiet along the Potomac Tonight."

John Schreiner & Son

Johann Schreiner was yet another German immigrant who became prominent in the Confederate music industry. Schreiner came to America in 1849 along with his son, Hermann, and settled in Macon, Georgia. In 1860 Johann engaged in the music publishing business, using the imprint John Schreiner. In 1861 the imprint became John Schreiner and Sons. If he had more than one son, as the imprint indicates, nothing is known of him. His only known son, Hermann, was a music teacher and arranger.

In December 1861 Hermann moved to Savannah and the Schreiners entered into partnership with a Charles Oxhenius, about whom nothing is known; the partners bought out W. D. Zogbaum's stock at 107 Bryan and 94 St. Julian Streets. Notice of the partnership was published in the *Savannah Daily Morning News*. The business was to be continued at the "well known store of W. D. Zogbaum . . . one of our firm being a professional teacher."[68] The imprint for the new business was "Schreiner & Oxhenius, Congress St." The partnership was brief since the imprint only appears for 1863. For the remainder of the war, the imprint was John Schreiner and Son, Macon and Savannah.

Richard Harwell mentions an undated clipping from the *Savannah Morning News*, which says Hermann Schreiner was in New Orleans buying music at the time of its capture.[69] When Hermann returned to Macon, his father worried about what was going to happen to his own music business, now that New Orleans would no longer be able to supply him with the basic publishing materials. Hermann assured his father all would be well and left for Cincinnati, an empty satchel in hand and a gun in his pocket. Federal agents noticed him but thought he was an Ohioan going about his business buying printing type.

After he crossed back into the South, Hermann was mistaken in Nashville for a Union agent and arrested. His gun was taken from him but he was allowed to keep his satchel. A day later, he was released and he returned to Macon.[70] An interesting story, but probably fanciful.

The Schreiners were in the music publishing business long before 1862. Early in the war, John Schreiner also had a joint venture with D. P. Faulds, in Louisville, Kentucky. "The Song of the Southern Boys," renamed "Cheer, Boys Cheer," carried both their imprints. The Federal occupation

of Kentucky made further contact between the two publishers too danger-
ous for Faulds, so both maintained separate businesses.

In 1863 the Schreiners signed a contract with songwriter John Hill
Hewitt, in which he promised to write for no other music publisher. The
following year, they partnered with Hewitt when he opened his own music
publishing business in Augusta and published ten songs under the imprint
of Schreiner & Hewitt.[71]

Blanton Duncan

Blanton Duncan began publishing sheet music in Columbia, South Carolina, in 1863, after he lost government printing contracts with the Treasury Department.

Before the war, Duncan had been a wealthy landowner in Kentucky. In
1860 as a member of the Kentucky State Executive Committee, he backed
John Bell's unsuccessful bid for the presidency of the United States.[72] When
he joined the 9th Kentucky Confederate Volunteers at the outbreak of the
war he was appointed colonel, but Duncan aspired beyond military service.
Soon after receiving his military commission, he sent a check for five hundred dollars to Treasury Secretary Memminger with the note:

> "Dear Sir, This being my birthday, I know no better way of cele-
> brating it than to enclose you a check for $500, which you will
> invest in the most appropriate manner to aid in the defeat of Lin-
> coln's mercenaries."[73]

Two months later, Duncan was mustered out of the army. On the basis
of his donation, he wrangled an appointment to see Memminger and
wound up with the job of smuggling banknote paper out of Kentucky into
Tennessee.[74] Duncan may have been a patriot, but his patriotism always left
a little room for personal gain. Once he had ingratiated himself with Memminger, he broached a new plan to the treasury secretary for smuggling four
or five engravers and printers out of Philadelphia to work on behalf of the
Confederacy. Disingenuously, Duncan added that he would accept a contract to make sure the work was done properly.[75]

Duncan continued making deals for the Treasury, but he was not very
trustworthy. In November 1861 a John Douglas sent Secretary Memminger
some of the paper he had just received from Duncan with a note stating
that it was "perfectly useless."[76]

By December, Duncan tired of being a small cog in the Treasury Department's wheel and, unbeknownst to Memminger, applied for a contract to do printing work for the government. Belatedly he informed Memminger that he had used him as a reference. The money that went with that job, he told the treasury secretary, would help him support his family during the war, adding that "I cannot practice law, as there is no litigation."[77]

Duncan's name-dropping earned him a contract to print Confederate paper currency and he set up shop in Richmond where he soon offered to undercut other printers.[78] By 1862 Duncan's duplicity was well-known in Richmond. In a letter to his wife, William Preston Johnston (the son of Gen. Albert Johnston) told her that Duncan had sent him a box of peaches, adding that the gift meant Duncan would probably soon be wanting something from him.[79]

In August 1862 a Confederate Treasury agent wrote to Memminger that he had just received from Duncan over half a million one and two dollar bills tinted green. The bills, he said, were supposed to have been tinted black. Duncan had given them a green tinting, claiming it made them more attractive, and had billed the Treasury extra for the ink. The agent agreed they were more attractive, but didn't feel the change warranted Duncan's unauthorized billing.[80]

Meanwhile, Duncan began using government-paid lithographers to produce sheet music covers for a business he had started. One of his first efforts was an illustrated cover with a portrait of Gen. P. G. T. Beauregard for the Blackmar's "The Beauregard Manassas Quick-Step." Although Duncan's name appears as lithographer, the lithographers did the work and Duncan claimed the credit. That way, he kept the Treasury from knowing he was using some of the lithographers to work on his own sheet music business.

In January 1862 Duncan offered to buy all the lithographic presses and stones owned by the government and pay for them in work.[81] In March he offered to take all the presses and printers the Treasury was about to import from England "at cost price," offering to pay whatever it had cost to smuggle the printers through the blockade, and to pay them "large wages". Since he was already working under contract to the Treasury, the profit margin would already have been figured into the agreement; he could only have paid "large wages" to these new lithographers and printers if he could put them to work at jobs in private industry, such as the sheet music trade. He now had sixteen new presses under contract and was sending to New York and Europe for more printers and materials.

One of the reasons Duncan needed to hire more printers was that he had to take whatever equipment he could get and none of his presses were alike; each required a different procedure to get the image onto paper. Under those circumstances, it was more efficient to assign a single printer to each press.

Though business was good, Duncan was unsatisfied. He wanted more printers, more lithographers, more stones, more presses, and he didn't much care how he acquired them. In May 1862 J. T. Patterson, one of Duncan's main competitors, complained to Memminger that Duncan had enticed two of his (Patterson's) lithographers to go to work for Duncan. Duncan denied the accusation. He had nothing to do with their leaving Patterson, Duncan said; in fact, he claimed he was the injured party since his printers had told him that Patterson had tried to get them back by offering them higher wages than Duncan was paying.[82] Meanwhile, Duncan had set up another printing shop in Columbia, South Carolina, in August 1862, and continued to raid other companies, all the while planning his revenge on Patterson. "I determined, if possible, to get even with him," he subsequently admitted to Secretary Memminger, and deviously persuaded the War Department to issue an order to bring all Patterson's printers, between the ages of eighteen and thirty-five, to Richmond to work on his government contracts, under the Conscript Act. All that was needed, he told Memminger, was his approval. Memminger refused.[83] Patterson apparently had other problems working for the government and, in October 1862, gave up his government contract[84] and channeled his resources into doing lithography for various sheet music publishers in the Confederacy.

Patterson was not the only one to be victimized by Duncan. An Edward Keatinge complained Duncan had falsely accused him of treason. Keatinge and a partner were doing government engraving in Columbia and had run afoul of Duncan, who had lured away their workmen and had even tried to burn down their shop. When Duncan's efforts failed to put Keatinge out of business, Keatinge said Duncan had resorted to the treason accusation.[85] Duncan claimed he had affidavits proving Keatinge's disloyalty but would not publicize them because they contained personal information about President Davis. Secretary of the Treasury Memminger knew about Keatinge's Northern background, but nonetheless awarded Keatinge the Treasury's best contract, which Duncan guessed would earn him in the neighborhood of twenty-five thousand dollars a month. In a letter to an unknown correspondent in Richmond, Duncan asked that the affidavits be put in safekeeping and, if the opportunity presented itself, suggested they be shown to Mrs. Davis, who, Duncan said, despised Memminger.[86]

By the middle of 1862, Duncan and Treasury Secretary Memminger were no longer on good terms. In December of that year, Duncan's contract with the Treasury was about to expire and he tried to pressure Memminger into renewing it by telling him that his services were also in demand elsewhere. He had been offered engraving contracts from South Carolina, which were very favorable, but he felt bound to offer his services to the Treasury first.[87] Memminger didn't take the bait. The next year, Duncan was no longer working for the government. Without much else to do, he went into the music publishing business full-time:

> Intending to engage largely in the publication of Music, Vocal and Instrumental, we append a list of pieces, which we shall in a few days commence issuing. Desirous of ascertaining the taste of the public, we ask the favor of Music dealers to suggest other pieces, which would meet with success. We shall endeavor not to compete with other dealers in pieces published by them, and will publish editions of Music for any of them as heretofore. Our terms will be liberal, and the Music will be gotten up in the best style of Lithographing. We have made arrangements to be constantly supplied through the blockade with the latest European Music of merit, and will publish it as soon as received. Not less than 50 copies of a piece will be sold, as we shall only engage in the wholesale business. Terms cash, or 'C.O.D'.[88]

Duncan published several songs, none of them memorable. He was no more a success in the music business than he had been working for the government. In April 1864 he sold his enterprise to Gray and Valory,[89] up until then, sheet music lithographers.

Augustus Sachtleben

Augustus Sachtleben's only known published piece of sheet music during the war was "The Southern Pleiades March and Quickstep," by Edward Wharton. Sachtleben would otherwise go unnoticed except that he was the only known music publisher in Texas. Before moving to Houston he had owned a music store in Galveston, where he operated the largest of the town's three music stores.[90]

Competition was fierce in the frontier town. Whereas Sachtleben claimed to be the sole agent for a number of piano makers, among them Chickering, his competitors, Buttlar and Branard, tried to undermine Sachtleben's credibility by claiming to sell "the only Simon pure Chickering & Sons Pianos." Jabbing at Sachtleben, they warned potential customers to "beware of buying or looking elsewhere for these world renown instruments."[91] The other music dealer in town was Francis D. Allan[92] about whom little is known. Allan remained in business throughout the war and in 1874 published a collection of Confederate songs.[93]

EPILOGUE

At the war's start Southerners ebulliently sensed their destiny. Southern editors invited their readers to share their feelings and sentiments through the "Poet's corner" of their newspapers. Literally thousands of Southerners responded. "Southern independence has struck the lyre as well as unsheathed the sword," said the editor of a collection of these poems published in 1862.[1] *The Southern Illustrated News* had "a flour barrel full of poems" at its disposal.[2]

Although there was no shortage of poems, only a small percentage was ever published as sheet music. "We are receiving too much trash in rhyme," said the editor of the *Southern Literary Messenger.* "Fires are not acessible at this time of the year, and it is too much trouble to tear up poetry. If it is thrown out of the window, the vexatious wind always blows it back."[3] The *Atlanta Southern Confederacy* kindly asked its readers not to send it "any more shabby attempts."[4] Other papers tried to discourage submissions by charging ten cents a line, the going rate for obituaries.[5]

Occasionally, a poem like James Ryder Randall's "My Maryland" plumbed to the core of human experience and stirred the nation. But literary merit aside, that poem became a national favorite only when it was set to music. The same was true for many other poems that were turned into songs during the war. Thousands of others died without the slightest fanfare. In 1866 Thomas Cooper DeLeon claimed he had accumulated over nineteen hundred of them.[6]

More than a hundred years later, it's almost impossible to know which of the thousands of songs struck a responsive chord and which didn't. Songs tied to a current event were usually ephemeral. A song boasting of a victory in 1862 was uninspiring in 1863. The answer to fathoming the past, as far as popular song is concerned, said Richard Harwell, resides in the sheet music produced by the Confederacy's music publishers. Sheet music unlocks not just Southern musical tastes but also the ideas and motives that anchored the new nation, Harwell argued, because sheet music represents the "greatest of all test[s] of popularity . . . publication for profit."[7]

William Mahar cites sales figures for many of the Northern songs he lists in his "top twenty songs of the Civil War," but there are no comparable figures for Southern songs, and he doesn't indicate the criteria for songs with Southern appeal such as "The Bonnie Blue Flag" and "Maryland! My Maryland!"[8] It's impossible to use the "profit motive" to infer popularity, because no sales records were kept of Confederate sheet music. And just because a song was published as sheet music doesn't mean it sold and earned a profit.

An indirect index of profitability, and hence popularity, is the number of editions a publisher issued for a particular song, the assumption being the more editions, the greater the sales. Here too there are basic problems, one of which is we don't know the number of copies in an "edition." Assuming the number in one company's edition equaled that in all others,, not a very good assumption but at least a basis for comparison, the most popular songs in the Confederacy would be those with the most editions.[9]

A slightly different indicator of a song's popularity, and one that probably comes closer to Harwell's suggestion, is the number of different publishers issuing the same song, the assumption here being that the more publishers releasing a particular song, the greater its demand. "Maryland! My Maryland!" for instance, was published in New Orleans, Augusta, and Baltimore; "God Save the South" was printed by publishers in Augusta, Charleston, Macon, Mobile, New Orleans, and Richmond; and "Lorena" was produced separately in Augusta, Danville, Virginia, Macon, Memphis, and New Orleans. The basic problem associated with relying on songs published as sheet music, of course, is that some of the most popular songs may not have appeared in that format; they may simply have been "too popular"—everyone already knew the tune and the words.

Other music historians gauge a song's popularity by counting the number of times it is mentioned in diaries or songsters. The former, however, would have to assume that any such collection of diaries would be representative of all. As to the latter, a survey of eleven Southern songsters[10] indicated that the top twenty songs were "All Quiet Along the Potomac Tonight," "Annie Laurie," "Annie of the Vale," "Bonny Jean," "The Cottage by the Sea," "Ever of Thee," "Fairy Belle," "Her Bright Eyes Haunt

Me Still," "Home Sweet Home," "I See Her Still in My Dreams," "Juanita," "Let Me Kiss Him for His Mother," "My Wife and Child," "Nelly Gray," "Oft in the Stilly Night," "Rock Me to Sleep Mother," "Stonewall Jackson's Way," "We Conquer or Die," "When This Cruel War Is Over," and "Who Will Care for Mother Now?"

There is agreement among all these lists, but different songs will be more or less prominent depending upon which list one relies. Do some or even many of the songs discussed in this book actually reflect widespread Southern feelings during the war? If, for example, Southern songs are quoted as an expression of Southern nationalism, then large numbers of Southerners ought to have bought them as sheet music and correspondingly sung them. Songs have to be examined in their context and should tell the same story as other contemporary sources.[11] Sheet music gathering dust on the shelves of a music publisher or seller doesn't reflect popular taste.

One of the values of examining the Southern war effort in terms of its songs is that the songs written during the war, unlike memoirs, are not colored by later experiences. Songs are of special interest, because they reflect a collective experience, validated by that popularity, and that popularity did not depend on literacy. By recognizing the themes in these songs, we can come closer to understanding the emotional climate at the time; we gain some insight into why the South went to war and how its people coped with the changes it forced upon them.

Songs are multifaceted, however. They not only reflect immediate sensation, but they also voice a subtext of feelings and experiences that are otherwise buried in our unconscious. On an immediate level, the unemotional political differences that divided the North and South hardly appeared in Southern songs, except perhaps in the guise of "southern rights." Instead, Southern songs leveled their emotional barrage on Northern betrayal, perfidy, and aggression. These songs emphasized the insults the South had suffered, thereby providing a moral basis for war.

Beneath these themes was a common tribal sense shared by soldier and civilian alike; by emphasizing their shared resentments as well as their allegiances, these songs enabled people to confront powerful, but otherwise latent feelings. Southerners had always felt loyalty for their local communities; now songwriters directed their loyalties to a wider fraternity. Each Southerner no longer hailed from Henderson, Texas, or Charleston, South Carolina. Instead, he (and she) were part of a tribal "band of brothers (and sisters)" called the Confederacy. This "band" was not an inimical agency controlled by Northern despots, but a clan of like-minded Southerners. Here was an ideal worthy of pride and protection.

Southern songwriters urged soldiers and civilians alike to fight the enemy. Since the nation was an extension of the family, both were made to feel that they were fighting the enemy whether on the field or at home. Everything done in support of the war effort was a collective blow against him.

Consciously or unconsciously, these songs were aimed at raising morale; their overarching motivation was to bolster support for the war effort. At first Confederate songs were ebullient. They imparted the idea that the war would be won by moral and psychological superiority as much as by force of arms. They heralded victories, but also underscored loyalty and sacrifice. When the news from the battlefront was bad, the songs became sadder, more sorrowful, but they urged Southerners to be resolute and defiant rather than despondent. They praised Southern initiative and pluck in the face of scarcity. These morale-building songs must have had some impact since they were sung and remembered by soldiers and civilians alike. Dirges for the prominent fallen military leaders became ever more common. Their intent was not to convey despair, but to affirm their sacrifice and their martyrdom.

Music also tranquilized febrile emotions in the army. No matter how bored, weary, hungry, afraid, or indignant over discipline they were, Johnny Rebs found ways to discharge their pent-up feelings through song. Whether marching and countermarching endless miles, wading swollen rivers, waiting nervously for the enemy to attack, dodging bullets, grouching with their messmates, or crouched around a campfire at night, soldiers either adapted or created a song for every occasion. No day was so dark or gloomy that no one sang. Comic or sentimental, gay or serious, songs were always heard in camp.

Virtually every aspect of the soldier's life found its way into a song. These were clearly more than self-deprecatory recreation. Many of these antimilitarist songs, though seemingly lighthearted, enabled the ordinary soldier to express his resentment and defiance for those in command. These songs, ironic and resentful, were his psychological defense against the indignities he endured from the "brass" and his own fears about his future. They helped him discharge the inner tension that would otherwise have made him so rebellious or so despondent that he would have been unable to function as a soldier. The humor in these songs reveals resilience. These soldiers take their anger in stride and even when they are under stress, their minds are still active and playful, sometimes able to surmount daunting odds.

Singing was more than emotional venting. Through music people interacted with one another, whether they were singing around their parlor pianos or campfires, playing their fiddles or dancing. Singing aloud was a social activity, especially when it occurred in glee clubs. Amateur singing groups, theatricals, and dances offered soldiers and civilians the emotional satisfaction of socializing with others. In camp, men sang, fiddled, and danced not only for sheer enjoyment, but to reaffirm their humanity under conditions that were often inhumane. The respite of lighthearted social activities enabled people to draw close to one another as if they were kin, not strangers thrust together by duty. Like the songs they sang and the letters they wrote, the music of the Civil War both reflected and created emotional bonds between a band of brothers.

APPENDIX A

REGIMENTAL AND BRIGADE BANDS
IN THE CONFEDERACY MENTIONED IN DIARIES,
MEMOIRS OR REGIMENTAL HISTORIES

Alabama:

First Infantry (ten musicians)
Shoaff's (Savannah) Battalion
14th Infantry
22nd Infantry

Arkansas:

3rd Infantry (eighteen musicians)
34th Infantry

Florida:

Joseph Finegan Brigade Band (fourteen musicians)

Georgia:

First Infantry (nine musicians; led by a free black man)
2nd Infantry (twenty-four musicians)
2nd Georgia Battalion
3rd Infantry (twelve musicians)
4th Infantry
5th Infantry (two musicians)
6th Infantry (fifteen musicians)
7th Infantry
8th Infantry (twenty-three musicians)
9th Infantry (eighteen musicians)
10th Infantry (one musician, a black barber)
11th Infantry
12th Infantry

Georgia *continued*:

13th Infantry (one musician)
14th Infantry (two musicians)
15th Infantry (six musicians)
16th Infantry
17th Infantry (two musicians)
18th Infantry
18th Georgia Battalion Field Band (formerly Savannah Volunteer
      Guards' Band, comprised of black musicians led by another
      black, the slave Joe Parkman)
19th Infantry
20th Infantry (fourteen musicians)
21st Infantry
22nd Infantry (two musicians)
23rd Infantry (ten musicians)
24th Infantry
25th Infantry (twenty-five musicians at its peak in 1861)
26th Infantry (three musicians)
27th Infantry
28th Infantry
29th Infantry
30th Infantry
31st Infantry (twenty musicians)
32nd Infantry (four musicians)
34th Infantry (two musicians)
35th Infantry
36th Infantry (two musicians)
37th Infantry (twelve musicians)
38th Infantry (twelve musicians)
39th Infantry (two musicians)
42nd Infantry (six musicians)
43rd Infantry (nine musicians)
44th Infantry (one musician)
46th Infantry (ten musicians)
63rd Infantry

Kentucky:
> 3rd Regiment Mounted Infantry (three musicians)
> 4th Infantry (led by Charles Ward, who composed several songs during
>   the war)
> 7th Regiment Mounted Infantry

Louisiana:
> Washington Artillery Band
> New Orleans Artillery Battalion (eight musicians)
> 4th Infantry
> 8th Infantry
> 19th Infantry
> 20th Infantry
> 26th Infantry
> Randall Lee Gibson Louisiana Brigade Band

Mississippi:
> 3rd Infantry
> 7th Infantry
> 10th Infantry
> 11th Infantry
> 12th Infantry
> 13th Infantry
> 16th Infantry
> 17th Infantry
> 18th Infantry
> 20th Infantry
> 21st Infantry
> 24th Infantry
> 43rd Infantry

Missouri:
> 3rd Infantry (eleven musicians)

North Carolina:
  1st Infantry (five musicians)
  4th Infantry (nineteen musicians)
  6th Infantry (fifteen musicians)
  9th Regiment, 1st North Carolina Cavalry (eleven musicians)
  13th Infantry (twenty-two musicians)
  16th Infantry (eleven musicians)
  17th Infantry
  19th Regiment; 2nd North Carolina Cavalry (eight musicians)
  20th Infantry (ten musicians)
  21st Infantry (also known as 11th North Carolina Band and First
      Battalion Band, fifteen musicians)
  23rd Infantry (six musicians)
  24th Infantry (nineteen musicians)
  25th Infantry
  26th Infantry (fourteen musicians)
  27th Infantry (fourteen musicians)
  32nd Infantry
  33rd Infantry (fifteen musicians)
  42nd Infantry (twenty-three musicians)
  43rd Infantry (fifteen musicians)
  44th Infantry (sixteen musicians)
  46th Infantry (fifteen musicians)
  47th Infantry (three musicians)
  49th Infantry (twenty-four musicians)
  50th Infantry (seventeen musicians)
  52nd Infantry (four musicians)
  53rd Infantry (eleven musicians)
  54th Infantry
  55th Infantry (eight musicians)
  59th Infantry; 4th North Carolina Cavalry (ten musicians)
  66th Infantry (twenty-eight musicians)

South Carolina:
  First Infantry (eleven black musicians, most of them "free persons
      of color")
  2nd Infantry (four musicians)
  5th Infantry (sixteen musicians)
  6th Infantry (fifteen musicians)

South Carolina *continued*:

14th Infantry
15th Infantry
17th Infantry
25th Infantry
29th Infantry

Tennessee:

4th Infantry (fourteen musicians, transferred to 13th Infantry soon
after it was formed in April 1861)
5th Infantry (six musicians)
13th Infantry (fifteen musicians)
17th Infantry
19th Infantry
28th Infantry

Texas:

First Infantry
4th Infantry (thirteen musicians)
5th Infantry (two musicians)
10th Infantry
26th Texas Cavalry
Col. George Wythe Baylor's Regiment
Colonel Robert's Regiment
Col. John Moore's Regiment
Col. William Young's Regiment
Colonel Cooke's Regiment

Virginia:

First Virginia Cavalry
First Infantry
2nd Virginia Cavalry (ten musicians)
5th Infantry (later the "Stonewall Brigade Band")
7th Infantry
10th Infantry (ten musicians)
17th Infantry
19th Infantry (ten musicians)
30th Infantry
48th Infantry

APPENDIX B

IMPRINTS OF SOUTHERN MUSIC PUBLISHERS
C[harles] D. Benson, Nashville, Tennessee
Benson opened in 1858 at 34 Union Street. Between 1860 and 1861 the firm moved to 46 Union Street. No address is listed during the war years. The imprint remained C. D. Benson until 1879 when the firm moved to 126 Church Street and used the imprint Chas. D. Benson.

A[rmand] E. Blackmar, New Orleans, Louisiana
Armand Blackmar opened his first shop in partnership with E. D. Patton, in Vicksburg, Mississippi, in 1858 at Washingston Street under the imprint of A. E. Blackmar & E. D. Patton. The following year, A. E. Blackmar and his brother, H. C. Blackmar, bought out Patton and began publishing under the imprint of Blackmar & Bro. In 1860, the brothers moved to New Orleans.

During 1860 to 1862, the address of the firm was 74 Camp Street and its imprint was A. E. Blackmar & Bro. Between 1863 and 1864 the firm published as Blackmar & Co. from the same address. During the fall of 1864, the firm moved to 167 Canal Street and continued to use the Blackmar & Co. imprint. From 1865 to 1868, the firm published under the name of A. E. Blackmar at the same address. Between 1869 and 1870, the firm's address was another of its entrances, 164 Canal Street. Between 1871 and 1872, the imprint remained A. E. Blackmar but the address was 201 Canal Street. Between 1873 and 1874, the imprint became A. E. Blackmar & Co., at the 201 Canal Street address. In 1875, the firm became Elie & Blackmar and published at 151–153 Canal Street. The following year, the imprint was changed to Blackmar & Finney, at 174 Canal Street.

In 1877 A. E. Blackmar moved to San Francisco and published under the imprints of Blackmar & Davis, and Blackmar & Co. He returned to

New Orleans in 1881 and published under the A. E. Blackmar imprint from various addresses. From 1862 until 1865, the firm also operated at 199 Broad Street in Augusta, Georgia. During this time, the firm published under three imprints: Blackmar & Bro., A. E. Blackmar & Bro., and Blackmar Bros. Edward O. Eaton composed a polka, "The 199 Broad Street Polka" in 1864, in homage to the Augusta location. In 1865 the firm relocated to 255 Broad Street.

J[oseph] Bloch, Mobile, Alabama

Bloch opened his shop at 55 Dauphin Street in Mobile in 1862. Little is known about his firm or its history.

A. Bohne, New Orleans, Louisiana

The firm was located at 118 Rue Du Canal and catered primarily to a French-speaking clientele.

John W. Burke & Co., Macon, Georgia

Burke's address in Macon is unknown. During the war he published under the imprint of John W. Burke. After the war, the imprint was changed to John W. Burke & Co in 1866, then returned to John W. Burke in 1877.

J[ohn] W. Davies & Son, Richmond, Virginia

Davies open in Richmond in 1864 under the imprint of J. W. Davies & Son. The address is unknown. In 1866, the imprint was changed to Davies & Sons and the address was 920 E. Main Street. The firm continued to published from this address under variations of the Davies imprint until the 1880s.

C. T. De Coeniel, Richmond, Virginia

The firm opened in 1863 and published only one song, "God Save the South," which was written by De Coeniel.

B. Duncan and Co., Columbia, South Carolina

The firm mainly provided lithographs for sheet music but in 1863 it attempted to move into publishing sheet music as well. One of its first attempts was "Battery Wagner."

Geo. Dunn & Co., Richmond, Virginia

The firm published under the Geo. Dunn & Compy. imprint. Between 1863 and 1864 it listed its address as Main and 14th Streets. Dunn also lithographed much of its sheet music, as well as covers for other firms.

D[avid] P. Faulds, Louisville, Kentucky

Faulds opened in 1855 and between 1855 and 1856 he used the imprint of D. P. Faulds. Between 1858 and 1860, the imprint was changed to D. P. Faulds & Co. In 1861, the imprint was also D. P. Faulds & Co., and the address was 223 Main Street. Between 1862 and 1864, the imprint reverted to D. P. Faulds and the firm remained at the same address. The firm continued to use the D. P. Faulds name from 1865 to 1894 but moved several times. In 1865 it was located at 70 Main Street.

L[ouis] Grunewald, New Orleans

The firm used the L. Grunewald imprint from 1858, when it was founded, to 1889. In 1861, the address was 67 Chartres Street and 26 Chartres Street. Between 1862 and 1863 it was 26 Chartres Street. The firm did not operate between 1862 and 1863 except for copyrighting a number of songs which were published under the Blackmar imprint. It resumed business in 1863 when it opened at 129 Canal Street.

Henry McCaffrey, Baltimore, Maryland

The firm always published under the imprint of Henry McCaffrey. It opened in 1853 at 189 Baltimore Street and remained there until 1857. Between 1858 and 1859 the address was 209 Baltimore Street; in 1860, 207 Baltimore Street. It did not publish between 1861 and 1863. In 1864 it resumed publishing at 205 Baltimore Street until 1874. It used the 209 Baltimore Street address between 1875 and 1878 and then moved to Charles Street where it remained in business until 1895.

J[ames] A. McClure, Nashville, Tennessee

The firm always used the J. A. McClure imprint. It opened in 1855 at 33 Union Street and published during the war from this address although the address was not listed on its music sheet. In 1870, its sheet music had 36 Union Street as its address. In 1874 it moved to Cherry Street but in 1877 moved back to Union Street.

Miller & Beacham, Baltimore, Maryland

The firm took over the business of F. D. Benteen in 1838. It began publishing under the Miller & Beacham imprint in 1853 and used it until 1864. Between 1853 and 1859 it was located at 181 Baltimore Street. In 1860 it relocated to 10 N. Charles Street and remained there until 1872, although the imprint was changed in 1865 to Wm. C. Miller.

J. W. Randolph, Richmond, Virginia

The firm used the J. W. Randolph imprint from the time of its opening in 1849 until 1865. It was located at 121 E. Main Street prior to the war. Its address during the war is unknown.

J[ohn] C. Schreiner & Son, Macon and Savannah, Georgia

Schreiner published under several imprints. Between 1860 and 1861, the firm published under the name John Schreiner, Cotton Street, Macon, Georgia. Between 1862 and 1864 the address was the same but the imprint changed to J. C. Schreiner & Son. Between 1863 and 1865, the John C. Schreiner & Son imprint was used and the address was listed as Congress Street. In 1868, the firm began publishing under the imprint of Hermann L. Schreiner.

Julian A. Selby, Columbia, South Carolina

Selby published in conjunction with Geo. Dunn & Company. It did, however, occasionally publish under its own imprint.

J[oel] H. Snow, Mobile, Alabama

The firm opened in 1860 at 29 Dauphin Street and remained at this address until 1874. From 1860 to 1869 it used the imprint of J. H. Snow. Variations of the Snow imprint were used until 1895.

Sourdes and Chassaignac, New Orleans

During the war the firm was located at Chartres Street. It catered primarily to French-speaking customers.

Tripp & Cragg, Louisville, Kentucky

The firm opened in 1857 at 109 4th Street. During the war its address was 321 4th Street. The imprint was Tripp & Cragg until 1865 when it became Louis Tripp.

P[hilip] P. Werlein, New Orleans

Werlein went into the music business in Vicksburg in 1842. In 1853 he moved to New Orleans and began publishing under the imprint of Ash–brand & Werlein, at 93 Camp Street. From 1854 to 1861, the imprint was P. P. Werlein and the address was listed variously as 5 or 7 Camp Street. In 1861, the address was 3 and 5 Camp Street and 172 Canal Street. Werlein also published under the imprint of P. P. Werlein & Halsey, at 3 and 5 Camp Street between 1861 and 1862. Halsey was the maiden name of his wife. In 1862 the firm went out of business and did not reopen until after the war in 1865.

G[eorge] Willig, Jr., Baltimore, Maryland

The firm relocated several times along Baltimore Street from 1823 to 1857. In 1858 its address was 1 N. Charles Street and it remained there during the war.

NOTES

INTRODUCTION

1. The role of Civil War films and documentaries on the American psyche is examined in William C. Davis's *The Cause Lost: Myths and Realities of the Confederacy* (Lawrence: University Press of Kansas, 1996), 191–205, and Jim Cullen, *The Civil War in Popular Culture: A Reusable Past* (Washington, D.C.: Smithsonian Institute Press, 1995).
2. This is no less true of its depiction in movies and documentaries; see Davis, *Cause Lost,* 200.
3. Bruce Catton, *Prefaces to History* (Garden City, N.Y.: Doubleday, 1970), 2.
4. Don Campbell, *The Mozart Effect* (New York: Avon Books, 1997); Susanne Katherina Langer, *Philosophy in a New Key: A Study in the Symbolism of Reason, Rite, and Art* (Cambridge: Harvard University Press, 1957).
5. On music's ability to enhance memory, see Campbell, *Mozart Effect,* 74–75.
6. Charles A. Kupchan, "Introduction: Nationalism Resurgent," in *Nationalism and Nationalities in the New Europe,* ed. Charles A. Kupchan (Ithaca, N.Y.: Cornell University Press, 1995), 4.
7. Ibid.
8. Carol Ryrie Brink, *Harps in the Wind: The Story of the Singing Hutchinsons* (New York: Macmillan Co., 1947), 207–11.
9. Dennis S. Lavery and Mark H. Jordan, *Iron Brigade General: John Gibbon, a Rebel in Blue* (Westport, Conn.: Greenwood Press, 1993), 31–34.
10. Lincoln repeatedly said that he had no desire to interfere with slavery in the states where it existed. In the Ottawa, Ilinois, debate with Stephen Douglas, in 1858, he explicity denied being an Abolitionist, and expressed the view that if he could free all the slaves, his first impulse would be to send them to Liberia. Although morally opposed to the institution of slavery, Lincoln readily acknowledged that the "great mass of white people," himself included, would not tolerate making former slaves politically and socially their equals. See Roy P. Basler, ed., *Abraham Lincoln: His Speeches and Writings* (New York: DaCapo Press, n.d.), 442–44.
11. On Civil War songs as propaganda, see James Stone, "War Music and War Psychology in the Civil War," *Journal of Abnormal Social Psychology* 36 (1941): 543–60.
12. Mildred Lewis Rutherford, *The South in History and Literature* (Atlanta: Franklin Turner Co., 1907), 254.
13. John Smith Kendall, *The Golden Age of the New Orleans Theater* (Baton Rouge: Louisiana State University Press, 1952), 498.
14. John Thomas Scharf, *The History of Maryland from the Earliest Period to the Present Day* (Baltimore: J. B. Piet, 1879), 2:527.

16. Brander Matthews, "Control of the Baltimore Press during the Civil War," *Maryland Historical Magazine* 36 (1941): 164.

17. Drew Gilpin Faust, *The Creation of Confederate Nationalism* (Baton Rouge: Louisiana State University Press, 1988).

18. *Southern Literary Messenger* 33 (October 1861): 353.

19. J. Schlesinger, "How Can I Leave Thee Gallopade" in *Southern Flowers (Fleurs du Sud): a Selection of Favorite Pieces Arranged for the Piano-Forte and Respectfully Dedicated to the Young Ladies of the Sunny South* (Mobile, Ala.: Joseph Block, 1861).

20. *Southern Illustrated News,* 5 December 1863, 4:4.

21. For a collected overview of these explanations, see Kenneth M. Stampp, ed., *The Causes of the Civil War* (New York: Touchstone Books, 1986).

22. Quoted in Max Wilk, *They're Playing Our Song* (New York: Athenaeum, 1973), 7.

23. Quoted in Lehman Engle, *Their Words Are Music: The Great Theatre Lyricists and Their Music* (New York: Crown, 1975), 9.

24. Bruce Catton, *The Coming Fury* (Garden City, N.Y.: Doubleday & Co., 1961); see also Catton, *Prefaces.*

PART 1

1. South Carolina's batteries, commanded by Brig. Gen. Pierre Gustave Toutant Beauregard, opened fire on the fort on April 12. Ironically, Beauregard had been the fort's commanding officer's (Mr. Robert Anderson's) pupil at West Point. On 14 April 1861, Anderson surrendered. The following day Lincoln called for seventy-five thousand volunteers to subdue the "rebellion" and recapture the fort. For details of the events surrounding these events, see Robert Hendrickson, *Sumter, the First day of the Civil War* (Chelsea, Mich.: Scarborough House, 1990) and Catton, *The Coming Fury.*

2. Douglas J. Cater, *As It Was: Reminiscences of a Soldier of the Third Texas Cavalry and the Nineteenth Louisiana Infantry* (Austin: Statehouse Press, 1990), 62.

3. Ibid., 70. Motives for volunteering have recently been examined in detail in James McPherson's *For Cause and Comrades: Why Men Fought in the Civil War* (New York: Oxford University Press, 1997).

4. William Andrew Fletcher, *Rebel Private Front and Rear* (Washington, D.C.: Zenger Pub. Co., 1985), 6–7.

5. Ibid.

6. John Keegan, *Face of Battle* (New York: Viking Press, 1976), 164–65.

7. Simpson to sister, 14 July 1861, in Guy R. Everson and Edward H.Simpson, eds., *Far, Far from Home: The Wartime Letters of Dick and Tully Simpson, Third South Carolina Volunteers* (New York: Oxford University Press, 1994), 4. Simpson was the son of South Carolina Congressman Richard F. Simpson, one of the signers of the South Carolina Ordinance of Secession. He enlisted in the 3rd Carolina Volunteers.

8. C. C. D. "The Stonewall Banner" (Richmond: J. W. Randolph, 186–).

9. Capt. E. Lloyd Wailes (Kirk's Ferry Rangers), "Confederate Song" (tune, 'Bruce's Address'), in William Long Fagan, ed., *Southern War Songs: Camp-Fire, Patriotic, and Sentimental* (Atlanta: M. T. Richardson, 1892).

10. A Lady of Richmond, "God Will Defend the Right" (New Orleans: Blackmar & Co., 186–).

11. Fred A. Shannon, ed., "The Civil War Letters of Sergeant Onley Andrus," *Illinois Studies in the Social Sciences* 28, #4 (1947): 25–26.

12. Don E. Fehrenbacher, *Constitutions and Constitutionalism in the Slaveholding South* (Athens, Ga.: University of Georiga Press, 1989), 59.

13. On the hardships Southern civilians endured during the war, see Charles W. Ramsdell, *Behind the Lines in the Southern Confederacy* (Baton Rouge: Louisiana State University Press, 1944). For hardships specifically related to the Federal occupation, see Stephen

V. Ash, *When the Yankees Came: Conflict and Chaos in the Occupied South, 1861–1865* (Chapel Hill: University of North Carolina Press, 1965); Mark Grimsley, *The Hard Hand of War: Union Military Policy toward Southern Civilians 1861–1865* (Cambridge: Cambridge University Press, 1995).

14. In a long speech he gave to the Senate on 10 January 1861, regarding South Carolina's secession, Jefferson Davis painstakingly argued that secession was constitutionally justifiable because according to the compact theory of government, any allegiance Americans owed to the United States was through their individual states. See Dunbar Rowland, ed., *Jefferson Davis, Constitutionalist: His Letters, Papers, and Speeches* (Jackson: Mississippi Deptartment of Archives and American History, 1923), 5: 26.

15. Eric J. Hobsbawm, "Some Reflections on Nationalism," in *Imagination and Precision in the Social Sciences,* ed. Thomas J. Nossiter, Albert H. Hanson, and Stein Rokkan (London: Farber and Farber, 1972), 392.

16. Douglas Southall Freeman, *R. E. Lee, a Biography* (New York: Charles Scribner's Sons, 1934–35), 1:418.

17. On the absence of Southern nationalism at the beginning of the war, see Emory M. Thomas, *The Confederate Nation, 1861–1865* (New York: Harper and Row, 1979); Paul D. Escott, *After Secession: Jefferson Davis and the Failure of Confederate Nationalism* (Baton Rouge: Louisiana State University Press, 1978); Richard E. Beringer et al., *Why The South Lost the Civil War* (Athens, Ga.: University of Georgia Press, 1986); Drew Gilpin Faust, *The Creation of Confederate Nationalism* (Baton Rouge: Louisiana State University Press, 1988).

18. Edward Pessen, "How Different from Each Other Were the Antebellum North and South?" *American Historical Review* 85 (1980): 1122, 1149, 1247.

19. Charles Edward Merriam, "The Political Philosophy of John C. Calhoun," in *Studies in Southern History and Politics* ed. William A. Duning, (New York: Columbia University Press, 1914), 319–38.

20. H. Kohn, *Prophets and Peoples: Studies in 19th Century Nationalism* (New York: Macmillan Co., 1946); Boyd C. Shafer, *Nationalism: Myth and Reality* (New York: Harcourt Brace, 1955).

21. See Daniel W. Crofts, *Reluctant Confederates: Upper South Unionists in the Secession Crisis* (Chapel Hill, N.C.: University of North Carolina Press, 1989)

22. Carlton McCarthy, *Detailed Minutiae of Soldier Life in the Army of Northern Virginia, 1861–1865* (1888; reprint, New York: Time-Life Books, 1982), 3.

23. Dusan Kecmanovic, *The Mass Psychology of Ethnonationalism* (New York: Plenum Press, 1996), 12.

24. Fletcher Melvin Green, "Johnny Reb Could Read," in *Democracy in the Old South and Other Essays by Fletcher Melvin Green,* ed. J. Isaac Copeland (Nashville: Vanderbilt University Press, 1969).

25. *Southern Literary Messenger* 38 (May 1864): 315.

26. Faust, *The Creation of Confederate Nationalism,* 18.

27. Ibid.

CHAPTER 1

1. Quoted by Richard E. Beringer, "Confederate Identity and the Will to Fight," in *On the Road to Total War: The American War and the German Wars of Unification 1861–1871,* ed. Stig Forster and Jorg Nagler (New York: Cambridge University Press, 1997), 78.

2. On the symbolic importance of these flag presentations, see Richard Rollins, *Damned Red Flags* (Redondo Beach, Calif.: Rank and File Publications, 1997), esp. 11–15.

3. Frank Moore, *The Rebellion Record: A Diary of American Events* (New York: G. P. Putnam, 1861–68), 1:164.

4. On the role of geographical features affecting the character of the two sections, see Thomas Govan, "Americans below the Potomac," in *The Southerner as American,* ed.

Charles Grier Sellers et al. (Chapel Hill: University of North Carolina Press, 1960), 21–23.

5. On the nationalistic significance of place names, see Wilbur Zelinsky, *Nation into State: The Shifting Symbolic Foundations of American Nationalism* (Chapel Hill: University of North Carolina Press, 1988), ch. 4.

6. Anna K. Hearn, "The Flag of the South" (Nashville: C. D. Benson & Co., 1861); Will S. Hays, "My Southern Sunny Home!" (New Orleans: Blackmar and Co., 1864); "Chivalrous C.S.A." in Fagan, *Southern War Songs,* 78.

7. Captain G. Griswold and J. W. Groschel, "National Hymn" (Mobile: J. H. Snow, 1862).

8. E. M. Thompson and J. A. Butterfield, "The South Our Country" (New Orleans: A. E. Blackmar & Bro., 1861).

9. Laura Lorrimer and J. W. Groschel, "Alabama" (Mobile, Ala: J. H. Snow, 1861).

10. Charlie Wildwood and John H. Hewitt, "The South" (Columbia, S.C.: Julian A. Selby, 1863).

11. Several other songs also describe the Southern landscape, for example, H. H. Strawbridge's "Confederate Land," "Southern Song of Freedom," and Susan A. Tally's "Rallying Song of the Virginians," in Fagan, *Southern War Songs,* 12, 48, 55.

12. Most of these songs, however, do not create attachments to any scenic part of the South. Childhood memories of babbling brooks are not recalled to create a nostalgic sense of belonging to the land and the past. Missing is any landscape-as-heritage nostalgia. There is no national ethos comparable to the compositions by English songwriters whose songs were reprinted by Confederate music publishers, such as "Cottage by the Sea" by J[ohn] R[odgers] Thomas (New Orleans: Blackmar and Co., 186–):

> Childhood's days now pass before me,
> Forms and scenes of long ago,
> Like a dream they hover o'er me,
> Calm and bright as evenning's glow;
> Days that knew no shade of sorrow,
> When my young heart, pure and free,
> Joyful hail'd each coming morrow,
> In the cottage by the sea.

For Thomas and other English songwriters, the landscape is archetypically British; it defines England (see David Lowenthal, "European and English Landscapes as National Symbols," in *Geography and National Identity,* ed. David Hooson (Oxford, U.K.: Blackwell Publishers, 1994), 22.

13. P. W. H. T., "Southern Dixie" (Montgomery, Ala: Schreiner & Son; Mobile, Ala: Blackmar & Bro., 1863).

14. John Hill Hewitt, "Dixie, the Land of King Cotton" (Macon and Savannah: John C. Schreiner & Son, 186–).

15. On the differences between patriotism and nationalism, see Kecmanovic, *Mass Psychology,* 13.

16. Alice Rhine and H. Walther, "Our Country's Call" (New Orleans: P. Werlein & Halsey, 1861); Thompson and Butterfield, "The South Our Country," dedicated "To the Citizens of the South"; A Baltimorean [Earnest Halphin] and M. L. Reeves, "God Save the South! The Confederate National Hymn" (New Orleans: P. Werlein & Halsey, 1862).

17. Eric Hobsbawm, *Nations and Nationalism since 1780: Programme, Myth, Reality* (Cambridge: Cambridge University Press, 1990), 390.

18. C. D. Benson, "Secesh Battle Flag March" (Nashville: C. D. Benson, 1861).

19. Harry Macarthy, "The Bonnie Blue Flag" (New Orleans: A. E. Blackmar & Bro.; Vicksburg: Blackmar & Bro., 1861). "The Bonnie Blue Flag" is the subject of chapter 3.

20. F. W. Rosier and Mrs. Rosier, "Virginian Marseillaise" (Richmond: Geo. Dunn & Co.; Columbia, S.C.: J. A. Selby, 1863); see also Wm. B. Harrell, "Up with The Flag" (Richmond: Geo. Dunn & Co.; Columbia, S.C.: J. A. Selby, 1863); "Oh, hasten, brothers, the proud foe to meet."
21. James Sloan Gibbons and L. O. Emerson, "We Are Coming Father Abr'am" and C. E. Pratt and Frederick Buckley, "We'll Fight for Uncle Abe," in Irwin Silber's ed., *Songs of the Civil War* (New York: Bonanza Books, 1960), 104–10. Many of the Northern songs cited in this book are reprinted in Paul Glass and L. C. Singer eds., *Singing Soldiers* (New York: DaCapo Press, 1988). Since this book is concerned primarily with Southern songs, citations of southern sheet music are from original sheet music and songsters.
22. Hobsbawm, *Nations and Nationalism,* 75.
23. Quoted by Rollin G. Osterweis, *Romanticism and Nationalism in the Old South,* 1949. (reprint Baton Rouge: Louisiana State University Press, 1971), 79.
24. A lady of Kentucky [Mrs. Catherine Anne Ware Warfield] and A. E. Blackmar, "The Southron's Chaunt of Defiance" (New Orleans: A. E. Blackmar & Bro., 1864). The two regions were in fact settled by people from different regions in England. The Britons who started the Massachusetts Bay colony, for instance, came primarily from a narrow, sixty-mile radius in East Anglia, and many of those who later settled in Massachusetts lived in East Anglia before emigrating. These people also were primarily austere, morally rigid Puritans. By contrast, the people who settled on the eastern seaboard in the South came mainly from the southern and western parts of England, and had a long tradition of hierarchical society. On these and other differences between the North and South, see David Hackett Fischer, *Albion's Seed: Four British Folkways in America* (New York: Oxford University Press, 1989) passim; Thomas Sowell, *Conquests and Cultures: An International History* (New York: Basic Books, 1998), 70–82.
25. "The legend of the Virginia cavalier," Fischer says, "was no mere romantic myth. In all of its major parts, it rested upon a solid foundation of historical fact." (See Fisher, *Albion's Seed,* 225.) On the South's "cavalier" image of itself, see William R. Taylor, *Cavalier and Yankee* (New York: G. Brazilier, 1961); G. Tindall, "Mythology, A New Frontier in Southern History" in *The Idea of the South: Pursuit of a General Theme,* ed. Frank E. Vandiver (Chicago: Chicago University Press, 1964), 1–15.
26. Eric H. Walther, *The Fire-Eaters* (Baton Rouge: Louisiana State University Press, 1992, 187).
27. J. Woodburn, "The Warrior's Farewell" (Richmond: J. W. Davies & Sons, 186–).
28. "Chivalrous C.S.A."
29. Quoted by Richard N. Current, "God and the Strongest Battalions," in *Why the North Won the Civil War,* ed. David Herbert Donald (New York: Touchstone, 1996), 23.
30. [Halphin] and Reeves, "God Save the South!"
31. "Another Yankee Doodle," in Fagan, *Southern War Songs,* 15. Many Southern songs used the tune of "Scots wha hae wi' Wallace bled," not so much because of its melody, but because they likened themselves to the Scots led by William Wallace and Robert the Bruce against the English (see Josiah Pittman, Colin Brown, Charles Mackay, and Myles Birket Foster, *The Songs of Scotland* [London: Boosey and Co., 1877]).
32. Osterweis, *Romanticism and Nationalism,* 41–53. Based on an analysis of the number of times various novels are mentioned in Civil War letters and diaries, David Kaser found that Scott was the "all-around favorite," followed by James Fenimore Cooper, Victor Hugo, Edward George Bulwer-Lytton, Charles Dickens, George Eliot, and William Makepeace Thackeray (*Books and Libraries in Camp and Battle* [Westport, Conn.: Greenwood Press, 1984], 18).
33. Diary entry, 23 May 1862, William C. Davis, ed., *Diary of a Confederate Soldier: John S. Jackman of the Orphan Brigade* (Columbia: University of South Carolina Press, 1990), 38.
34. Simpson to sister, 28 April 1863, in Everson and Simpson, *Far, Far from Home,* 221.

35. Mark Twain, *Life On The Mississippi,* 332–33, 374–376, quoted in Osterweis, Romanticism and Nationalism, 49–50.

36. "The Southern Soldier Boy, Song, As Sung by Miss Sallie Partington in 'The Virginia Cavalier' at the Richmond New Theater" (Richmond: Geo Dunn & Compy.; Columbia, S.C.: Julian A. Selby, 1863). The South's cherished image of itself as a land of cavaliers was well known to Northern songwriters who mocked these portraits of Southern chivalry, once the tide had turned against the South. "We'll Fight for Uncle Abe," for example, taunts the Confederates now that Vicksburg has been captured: "You may talk of Southern chivalry / And cotton being king, / But I guess the war is done, / You'll think another thing." (Pratt and Buckley, "We'll Fight for Uncle Abe.") In "The Fall of Charleston," the narrator gloats over the Yankees' route of "the chivalry of sixty-one" (see Silber, *Songs of the Civil War,* 264–67), while "Jeff in Petticoats" by George Cooper and Henry Tucker (New York: W. A. Pond & Co., 1865) sarcastically lampoons Jeff Davis as "You flow'r of chivalree.'" (See Silber, *Songs of the Civil War,* 343.) "The Battle Cry of Freedom" can be found on 17–19 in Silber, *Songs of the Civil War,* and on 36–37, in Glass, *Singing Soldiers.*

37. Rowland, *Jefferson Davis, Constitutionalist,* 5:24. On Davis's nationalistic ideology, see Paul Escott, *After Secession.*

38. "Southern War Cry," in *Hopkins' New Orleans 5 Cent Song Book* (New Orleans: John Hopkins, 1861); Fagan, *Southern War Songs,* 35.

39. A Clergyman of the Episcopal Church, "Southrons Attend" (New Orleans: Ph. P. Werlein; Nashville: J. A. M'Clure, 186–).

40. [Halphin] and Reeves, "God Save the South!"

41. Fagan, *Southern War Songs,* 71.

42. Anon., "Rebel is a Sacred Name." In Hubner, Charles William, *War Poets of the South and Confederate Camp-Fire Songs* (Atlanta: Chas. P. Byrd, n.d.), 40.

43. *Richmond Examiner,* 4 April 1861.

44. "Riding a Raid" (Richmond: J. W. Randolph, 186–).

45. On Stuart, see chapter 6, "Jefferson Davis and His Generals."

46. Steven M. Stowe, *Intimacy and Power in the Old South: Ritual in the Lives of the Planters* (Baltimore: Johns Hopkins University Press, 1987), 7–8.

47. Rowland, *Jefferson Davis, Constitutionalist,* 5:84. On the Southern honor code, see Bertrand Wyatt-Brown, *Southern Honor* (New York: Oxford University Press, 1982).

48. Rowland, *Jefferson Davis, Constitutionalist,* 5:104.

49. Frank Moore, *Rebel Rhymes and Rhapsodies* (New York: G. Putnam, 1864), 8–9.

50. "The Wearing of the Gray," see Glass, *Singing Soldiers,* 292–94.

51. Harry B. Macarthy, "The Volunteer; or, It Is My Country's Call" (Augusta: Blackmar & Bro., 1861).

52. Lieut. H. H. Strawbridge and Capt. Eug. Chassaignac, "Confederate Land!" (New Orleans: Chassaignac, 1861).

53. [Halphin] and Reeves, "God Save the South!"

54. Henry Russell, "Cheer, Boys Cheer" (Nashville and Memphis: Jas. A. McClure, 1861).

55. H. W., "Carolina's Sons" (Wilmington, N.C.: T. S. Whitaker, 1861).

56. George C. Rable, *Civil Wars: Women and the Crisis of Southern Nationalism* (Urbana: University of Illinois Press, 1989); Drew Gilpin Faust, *Mothers of Invention: Women of the Slaveholding South in the American Civil War* (Chapel Hill: University of North Carolina Press, 1996); Elizabeth Fox-Genovese, *Within the Plantation Household: Black and White Women in the Old South* (Chapel Hill, N.C.: University of North Carolina Press, 1988).

57. Dorothy Stanley, ed., *The Autobiography of Sir Henry Morton Stanley* (Boston: Houghton Mifflin Co., 1909), 165.

58. Ibid.

59. George F. Root, "The Battle Cry of Freedom" (Chicago: Root and Cady, 1862). Root wrote two versions of the song. The first was a rallying song for the home front; the

second for the battlefront. The song was so popular, it inspired a Southern version by Wm. S. Barnes and Hermann L. Schreiner, "The Battle-Cry of Freedom" (Macon and Savannah, Ga.: J. C. Schreiner & Son, 1864): "Our Dixie forever, she's never at a loss / Down with the eagle and up with the cross. / We'll rally round the bonny flag, we'll rally once again. / Shout, shout the battle cry of Freedom." George F. Root was one of the most prolific and popular songwriters prior to and especially during the Civil war. On Root's career and influence on American music, see his autobiography, *The Story of a Musical Life* (Cincinnati: John Church, 1891); "Biographies of American Musicians, Number Twenty: Dr. G. F. Root," *Brainard's Musical World* 16 (1879): 82–83; W. Birdseye, "America's Song Composers, II: George F. Root," *Potter's American Monthly* 12 (1879): 145–48; Brander Matthews, "Geo. F. Root, Mus. Doc," *Music: A Monthly Magazine* 8 (1895): 502–9; Coonley, "George F. Root and His Songs," *New England Magazine* 13 (1896): 555–70; D. J. Epstein, "The Battle Cry of Freedom," *Civil War History* 4 (1958): 307–18; H. L. Jillson, " The Vacant Chair': The Hero and the Author of the Song," *New England Magazine* 16 (1897): 131–45.

60. Pratt and Buckley, "We'll Fight for Uncle Abe." See Silber, *Songs of the Civil War,* 109–10; Glass, Singing Soldiers, 123.

61. "The Why and the Wherefore"; see Silber, *Songs of the Civil War,* 41–42.

62. Abraham Lincoln, speech delivered at Springfield, Illinois, 16 June 1858; reprinted in Basler, *Abraham Lincoln,* 372.

63. Harrison Millard, "The Flag of Columbia"; see Glass, *Singing Soldiers,* 12–14.

64. Lincoln to Alexander H. Stephens, 20 December 1860, in Basler, *Abraham Lincoln,* 568.

65. Bruce Catton, *The Coming Fury,* 84–85, 114.

66. Macarthy, "The Bonnie Blue Flag."

67. Dr. J. Mathews and Theodore von La Hache, "The Volunteers [sic] Farewell; or, Farewell My Dearest Katie" (New Orleans: P. Werlein & Halsey, 1862).

68. Theodore Von La Hache, "I Would Like to Change My Name," 5th ed. (Augusta: Blackmar & Bro, 1862).

69. L. M., "Southern Song," in Fagan, *Southern War Songs,* 99.

70. Benson, "Secesh Battle Flag March."

71. Francis Fernandez, "Tillie's Waltz" (New Orleans: L. Grunewald, 1861).

72. Hewitt, "Dixie, the Land of King Cotton."

73. Root, "The Battle Cry of Freedom."

74. Millard, "The Flag of Columbia."

75. On the different interpretations of "liberty," see Randall C. Jimerson, *The Private Civil War* (Baton Rouge: Louisiana State University Press, 1988), 16–18, 32–34.

76. Address at Sanitary Fair, 18 April 1864, in Basler, *Abraham Lincoln.*

77. Earl J. Hess, *Liberty, Virtue, and Progress: Northerners and Their War for the Union* (New York: Fordham University Press, 1997), 7.

78. Rowland, *Jefferson Davis, Constitutionalist,* 5:28–29.

79. Quoted by Hess, *Liberty, Virtue, and Progress,* 16.

80. Rowland, *Jefferson Davis, Constitutionalist,* 5:72.

81. Catton, *Coming Fury,* 85.

82. Quoted by Escott, *After Secession,* 101. On the relationship between slavery and antebellum Southern nationalism, see John McCardell, *The Idea Of A Southern Nation: Southern Nationalists and Southern Nationalism 1830–1860* (New York: W. W. Norton, 1979), 85–90, 136–37.

83. Basler, *Abraham Lincoln,* 442–44. Andrus Onley, whose appreciation of Southern tenacity was previously noted, was equally candid about his animosity toward blacks (see Shannon, "Civil War Letters," 27–29).

84. Larry M. Logue, "Who Joined the Confederate Army? Soldiers, Civilians, and Communities in Mississippi," *Journal of Social History,* 27 (1993): 611–23.

85. P. E. C., "Song of the Southern Soldier," in Fagan, *Southern War Songs,* 78.

86. L. M., "Southern Song."
87. Benjamin F. Butler, *Butler's Book* (Boston: A. M. Thayer & Co., 1892), 256–64.
88. Rud Adam, "The Contraband's Hotel" (Nashville and Memphis: J. A. McClure, 1862).
89. E. A. Benson, "Poor Oppressed; or, The Contraband Schottisch" (Nashville: C. D. Benson, 186–).
90. Charlie L. Ward, 4th Ky. Regt., C.S.A., "I'm Coming to My Dixie Home" (Columbia: B. Duncan & Co., 1861).
91. "John Brown's Body"; see: Glass, *Singing Soldiers,* 7. The same tune was used for "The Battle Hymn of the Republic."
92. Jesse Hutchinson, "The Liberty Ball"; see Silber, *Songs of the Civil War,* 98.
93. Col. J. L. Geddes, "The Bonnie Blue Flag with Stripes and Stars"; see Glass, *Singing Soldiers,* 19.
94. Like many Southern leaders, James Chesnut, Jr., who had represented South Carolina in the U.S. Senate, believed the Union would not oppose secession. Chesnut said he would drink all the blood spilled in the contest.
95. Stiles, *Four Years under Marse Robert* (New York: Neale Pub. Co., 1903), 350.
96. John H. Hewitt, "You Are Going to the Wars, Willie Boy!" (Macon and Savannah: John C. Schreiner & Son, 1863).
97. Rhine and Walther, "Our Country's Call."
98. Martin Crawford, "Confederate Volunteering and Enlistment in Ashe County, North Carolina, 1861–1862," *Civil War History,* 37 (1991): 29–50.
99. Ibid.
100. Logue, "Confederate Army."
101. Faust, *Mothers,* 12–18.
102. See note 68.

CHAPTER 2

1. *Confederate Veteran* 20 (1912): 158–59. Many of the details of this story, however, have been challenged by E. Stockton, "Didn't Sing 'Dixie' When Home Was Burning," *Confederate Veteran* 28 (1912): 260; see also Douglas Southall Freeman, *Lee's Lieutenants: A Study in Command* (New York: Charles Scribner's Sons, 1942–44), 1:128, 413; 3:571.
2. The role of national anthems in nationalistic movements is discussed at length by Joseph Zikmund, "National Anthems as Political Symbols," *Australian Journal of Politics and History* 15, no. 3 (1969): 73–80. Other good surveys include Zelinsky's *Nation into State,* 171–74; Malcolm Boyd, "National Anthems," in *The New Grove Dictionary of Music and Musicians,* ed. Stanley Sadie (London: Macmillan, 1980), 13:46–75.
3. Richard Grant White, *National Hymns: How They Are Written and How They Are Not Written: A Lyric and National Study for the Times* (New York: Rudd and Carleton, 1861), 65–66.
4. "The Star Spangled Banner" was not officially adopted as the anthem of the United States until 1931.
5. "National Songs," *Columbia Daily South Carolinian,* 24 January 1864, reprinted in Jay Broadus Hubbell, ed., *The Last Years of Henry Timrod, 1864–1867* (Durham, N.C.: Duke University Press, 1941), 140–43.
6. Henry Timrod to Rachel Lyons. Quoted in William Moss, *Confederate Broadside Poems: An Annotated Descriptive Bibliography Based on the Collection of Z. Smith Reynolds Library of Wake Forest University* (Westport, Conn.: Meckler Co., 1988), 13.
7. Ibid.
8. Referring to the popularity of the tune, the *New York Commercial Advertiser,* 1861, said, "The pen drops from the fingers of the plodding clerk, spectacles from the nose and the paper from the hands of the merchant, the needle from the nimble digits of the maid or matron, and all hands go hobbling, bobbling in time with the magical music of

'Dixie'." Quotation reprinted on the last page of A. W. Muzzy and Dan D. Emmett, "Dixie Unionized" (New York: Firth, Pond & Co., 1861).

9. Long after the war, Lt. Gen. John Brown Gordon (C.S.A.) reflected that "these are the words . . . and the only words, which are inseparably associated with the great song and great struggle" (United Daughters of the Confederacy, "Joint Committee Appointed to Consider and Report on a Selection of New Words for 'Dixie'"; Opelika, Ala., 1904. Boston Public Library, Boston, Mass., 3, hereafter shortened to "Joint Committee.")

10. Hans Nathan's *Dan Emmett and the Rise of Early Negro Minstrelsy* (Norman: University of Oklahoma Press, 1962) is the most thorough biography of Emmett's life; Charles Burleigh Galbreath's *Daniel Decatur Emmett: Author of "Dixie"* (Columbus: Fred J. Heer, 1904) is also worth consulting.

11. A copy of the playbill appears in Nathan, *Emmett*, 246. For a description of a typical walk-around, see idem, "Emmett's Walk-Arounds: Popular Theater in New York," *Civil War History* 4 no. 3 (1958): 213–224; idem, "Dixie," *Musical Quarterly* 35 (1949): 60–84. For minstrel shows and their influence, see chapter 13.

12. When the Confederacy adopted "Dixie" as its unofficial anthem, Unionists accused Emmett of Southern sympathies and treason. Some even hinted he might look best hanging from a scaffold (Galbreath, *Daniel Decatur Emmett*, 21). Months into the war, Emmett said he had second thoughts about writing the song. One night a friend of his on furlough caught up with Emmett while the songwriter was in a bar with some of his other friends and told the group that the Confederates seemed to have adopted "Dixie" as their national anthem. Emmett is reported to have replied, "Yes: and if I had known to what use they were going to put my song, I will be damned if I'd have written it!" (Thomas Cooper DeLeon, *Belles, Beaux, and Brains of the 60s*, 1909; reprint,(New York: Arno Press, 1974, 359). But by 1863, his loyalties no longer in doubt, Emmett expressed pride in having written the song. In June of that year, Emmett, Stephen Foster, and Foster's friend, Brickett Clarke, were eating in the Collamore House at Broadway and Spring Street in New York, when a regimental band playing "Dixie" passed by. The ensuing conversation between Emmett and Foster was recorded by Clarke in his diary:

> "Your song," said Foster.
> "Yes," replied Emmett.
> A short time later, another regimental band passed by playing "The Old Folks at Home."
> "Your song," said Emmett.
> "Yes," answered Foster.

Clarke recalled standing there, "between the parents of the two most popular songs this or any other country has ever produced," in *St. Louis Post Dispatch's Sunday Magazine*, 24 May 1908.

13. Nathan, *Emmett*, 288–89 contains a copy of the contract. The first authorized edition, June 1860, was entitled, "I Wish I Was in Dixie's Land. Written and Composed expressly for Bryant's Minstrels By Dan. D. Emmett. Arranged For the PianoForte by W. L. Hobbs." (New York: Firth, Pond & Co., 1860). The caption title was "Dixie's Land." A copy is in the Madison branch of the Library of Congress. Even though he had a prolific writing career, Emmett never acquired any real business sense. He received less than one thousand dollars in royalties for his songs, and three hundred dollars of that came from the sale of the copyright for "Dixie." (He would have died in abject poverty except for a five-dollar-a-week pension awarded him by the Actor's Fund of America when some New York members discovered his plight.)

14. *Dwight's Journal of Music*, 8 December 1860, 291.

15. Henry Clay Whitney, *Life on the Circuit with Lincoln,* (Boston: Estes and Lauriat, 1892), 87. A day after Robert E. Lee surrendered the Army of Northern Virginia (9 April 1865), Abraham Lincoln appeared before a cheering crowd gathered around the White House. Among the minions was a band. When he finished speaking, Lincoln asked it to play "Dixie," declaring the song had always been one of his favorites. Whimsically he added, "our friends across the river have appropriated it to their own use during the last four years . . . But (with Lee's surrender) I think we have captured it. At any rate, I conferred with the Attorney General this morning, and he expressed the opinion that 'Dixie' may fairly be regarded as captured property." There are several variations of this story, but all substantially agree. See Carl Sandburg, *Abraham Lincoln: The Prairie Years and the War Years* (New York: Hartcourt Brace, 1954), 3:808; *Louisville Herald,* Tuesday, 4 June 1907; Whitney, *Life on Circuit,* 87.

16. Hy Rumsey and W. W. Newcomb organized the Rumsey & Newcomb Minstrels in 1857.

17. The reception of "Dixie" at the Variety Theater comes from a Dr. G. Kane, in the *Richmond Dispatch,* 19 March 1893, and in the *New York World,* 1893. These descriptions are reprinted in *Southern Historical Society Papers* 21 (1893): 212–14 and Galbreath, *Daniel Decatur Emmett,* 20. Kane mistakenly credited the lead to Susan Denim.

18. Edgar Porter, "The Original Dixon's Line; or Dixey Land with Original Words" (Philadelphia: William H. Coulston, 1860).

19. J. Newcomb, W. H. Peters, and J. C. Viereck, "I Wish I Was in Dixies [*sic*] Land" (New Orleans: P. Werlein & Halsey, 1861).

20. A. W. Riecke, "Dixie," *Confederate Veteran* 12 (1904): 39, mistakenly credited Rumsey and Newcomb for introducing "Dixie" in Charleston, but advertisements in the *Charleston Daily Courier* (14 December 1860) and the *Charleston Mercury* (19 December 1860) showed that the Christy troupe was the only minstrel show playing at the time.

21. *Augusta Chronicle and Sentinel,* Sunday Morning, 17 February 1861.

22. "Wife Urged Playing of Melody during Inauguration of Jeff Davis," *Birmingham News,* 2 November 1924.

23. John Tasker Howard, *Our American Music* (New York: Thomas Crowell, 1958), 257. G. A. Kane credited the quickstep arrangement to Romeo Menri, bandleader of the New Orleans Washington Artillery; see *Southern Historical Society Papers,* 1893, 21, 212–14.

24. *Augusta Chronicle And Sentinel,* 20 February 1861, 2.

25. Arnold, quoted in *Birmingham News,* 2 November 1924. Twenty-five years after his inauguration, Davis once again stood outside the Capitol in Montgomery and tried to speak to the cheering crowds. But just as he began, "the crazy brass band, which had gone into the hotel struck up 'Dixie'", and completely drowned him out. No one could get the band to stop and Davis was escorted to his room." (*New York World,* 28 April 1886); Rowland, *Jefferson Davis, Constitutionalist,* 9:421.

26. Henry Hotze, "Three Months in the Confederate Army: The Tune of Dixie," *The Index* 1 (26 June 1862): 140. Many others have shared Hotze's puzzlement over the song's popularity and have tried to explain it, for example, Nathan, *Emmett,* 247–8; Sigmund Gottfried Spaeth, *A History of Popular Music in America* (New York: Random House, 1948), 142. Such efforts are doomed. If someone could explain why one tune sticks in the mind and another doesn't, that same person would be able to manufacture popular tunes at will. Scholars of music are rarely songwriters and vice versa.

27. *Memphis Appeal,* 18 December 1861.

28. Capt. Hughes and John H. Hewitt, "Dixie, the Land of King Cotton" (Macon and Savannah: John C. Schreiner & Son, 1864). The words appeared in the Memphis Appeal, 18 December 1861.

29. These and the other remaining verses have an interesting social foundation rarely recognized in discussions of the song: Minstrel songs, like "Dixie," typically depicted slavery in a favorable light and were anti-Abolitionist. At the same time, slavery was

incompatible with Victorian attitudes about love and family since slaves could be bought, thus undermining marriage and destroying families. Minstrelsy countered this criticism, writes Alexander Saxton (*The Rise and Fall of the White Republic* [New York: Verso, 1990] 177–79) by ridiculing these Victorian ideals among blacks. Instead of idealizing women and romantic love, minstrel songs demeaned them, especially where blacks were concerned. This is the basis for Emmett's description of the lothario and his romantic conquests in the second and remaining verses of "Dixie." On Victorian culture in America, see Daniel Walker Howe, ed., *Victorian America* (Philadelphia: University of Pennsylvania Press, 1976); Anne C. Rose, *Victorian America and the Civil War* (New York: Cambridge University Press, 1992). Jacqueline S. Bratton, *The Victorian Popular Ballad* (Totowa, N.J.: Rowman and Littlefield, 1975) examines the impact of Victorian culture specifically on music.

30. Charles W. Hutson, "Reminiscences," 68, Southern Historical Collection no. 362, University of North Carolina, Chapel Hill.

31. Hotze, "Three Months," 140.

32. Charles Goolrick, "He Didn't Like 'Dixie'!" *Virginia Cavalcade* 9 (1960): 5–10.

33. For a full-length biography about Pike, see Walter Lee Brown, *A Life of Albert Pike* (Fayetteville: University of Arkansas Press, 1997).

34. Albert Pike and J. C. Vierick, "The War Song of Dixie" (New Orleans: P. Werlein & Halsey, 1861). The song first appeared in the *Natchez Courier,* 30 April 1861.

35. H. S. Stanton and A. Noir, "Dixie War Song" (Augusta: Blackmar & Bro.; New Orleans: Blackmar & Co., 1861). "A. Noir" was the pseudonym for Armand Blackmar, the publisher. With a substitution of "Texas" for "Dixie," Stanton's song became "Awake! To Arms in Texas!" (see Fagan, *Southern War Songs,* 166–67; Francis D. Allan, *Allan's Lone Star Ballads: A Collection of Southern Patriotic Songs Made during Confederate Times* (Galveston: J. D. Sawyer, 1874).

36. P. W. H. T., "Southern Dixie"(Montgomery, Ala.: Schreiner & Son; Mobile, Ala: Blackmar & Bro., 1863).

37. Quoted by F. Moore, *Rebellion Record* 1:92.

38. [Halphin] and Reeves, "God Save the South!" Halphin was a pseudonym for George H. Miles (1824–71), a professor of English literature in Maryland. For biographical information about Miles, see Edwin Anderson Alderman, Joel Chandler Harris, and Charles William Kent, eds., *Library Of Southern Literature* (New Orleans: Martin and Hoyt, 13 vols., 1908–1913). 8:3641–43.

39. Review from unidentified newspaper reprinted in Frank Moore, *The Civil War in Song and Story* (New York: F. Collier, 1889), 360.

40. Earnest Halphin C.S.A. and C. T. DeCoeniel, "God Save the South!" (Richmond: C. T. DeCoeniel, 1862).

41. D[aniel] D. Emmett and C. S. Grafulla, "I'm Going Home to Dixie" (New York: Pond & Co., 1861).

42. Daniel D. Emmett, "Away Down South in Dixie," *New York Clipper,* 6 April 1872, reprinted in Nathan, *Emmett,* 286–87.

43. Quoted in F. Moore, *Rebellion Record,* vol. I. 1:113.

44. William Howard Russell, *My Diary: North And South* (Philadelphia: Temple University Press, 1988), ch. 38.

45. Hotze, "Three Months," 140.

46. According to Hans Nathan, Emmett's biographer, the first recorded mention of "Dixie" occurs in 1850 in a play, "United States Mail and Dixie in Difficulties," put on by the Sabine Minstrels of Portsmouth where "Dixie" refers to a Negro. If "Dixie" were a common name for Negroes in the mid-1800s, Emmett's "Dixie's Land" may have been another way of saying "Land of the Negro" (Nathan, *Emmett,* 265). At that time, however, Dixie was not as yet a common term. In March 1859, a short time before he wrote "Dixie," Emmett used "Dixie's Land" in the last stanza of another

song, "Johnny Roach": "Gib me de place called 'Dixie's Land,'/Wid hoe and shubble in my hand." "Dixie" was therefore a definite place in Emmett's own mind before he wrote the song for the Bryant show, and as Emmett himself said, when he wrote "Dixie" he meant the South. DeLeon, *Belles,* 359, has an anecdote in which Emmett allegedly expressed a slight regret at having written "Dixie" when the song seemed destined to become the Confederate anthem. (See note 12).

47. Quoted in Nathan, *Emmett,* 271.

48. Emmett and Grafulla, "I'm Going Home to Dixie."

49. Muzzy and Emmett, "Dixie Unionized."

50. "The New Dixie! The True 'Dixie' for Northern Singers," broadside, Essex Institute, Salem, Mass., n.d.

51. Quoted by Richard Barksdale Harwell, *Confederate Music* (Chapel Hill: University of North Carolina Press, 1950), 4. The reference to Bryant reflects the continued performance of the song and its associated "walk about" in the Bryant Minstrel show, which was still performing the act in New York at the time.

52. Nathan, *Emmett,* 264. Nathan documented the phrase "Dixie's Land" in an early New York children's game, "Tom Tiddler's Ground," but discounts this evidence because a chorus from Emmett's song is quoted in another version of this game.

53. Mildred Lewis Rutherford, "Miss Rutherford's Scrap Book," 8:10; *Confederate Veteran* 22 (1914): 139.

54. Galbreath, *Daniel Decatur Emmett,* 19; *St. Louis Post-Dispatch,* Sunday Magazine, 24 May 1908. Werlein later offered Emmett five dollars for the copyright (Emmett in letter to *New York Clipper,* 6 April 1872, reprinted in Nathan, *Emmett,* 288). Werlein's misappropriation didn't bother Emmett since he dedicated "I'm Going Home to Dixie," which he wrote the following year, "To P. Werlein of New Orleans."

55. *Birmingham News,* 2 November 1924. Arnold's version of this story is preserved in a mural on the third floor of the Alabama Department of Archives and History Building in Montgomery.

56. On an earlier occasion, however, Arnold claimed to have heard Emmett sing "Dixie" at the New Montgomery Theater when John Wilkes Booth starred at its opening in 1860. DeLeon, *Belles,* 357, notes that the theater burned down in January 1859 and was not rebuilt until 1865. DeLeon claims Arnold himself never told the story about Emmett's copying "Dixie" from the wall of the theater.

57. *Birmingham News,* 2 November 1924.

58. *St. Louis Post-Dispatch,* Sunday Magazine, 24 May 1908.

59. This song is examined in detail in chapter 8.

60. Howard, *Our American Music,* 702; Spaeth, *History of Popular Music,* 158; *Louisville Courier-Journal,* 24 July 1907; E. G. Johnson, "Way Down South in Dixie Land," *Louisville Courier-Journal,* 29 May 1898. Hays's legacy with respect to modern country music has been ably chronicled by Bill C. Malone, *Singing Cowboys and Musical Mountaineers: Southern Culture and the Roots of Country Music* (Athens: University of Georgia Press, 1993), 60–66.

61. A friend of Hays, Young E. Allison, said Hays had a somewhat superior estimation of his (Hays's) work and, that like many artists he knew, may have deceived himself into thinking he wrote the song. (Letter to Albert Mathews, 17 August 1915, Allison Papers, Filson Club Historical Society.)

62. Hays, quoted in *Louisville Herald* (May 1907), "Filson Club Members Decide Credit of Authorship of 'Dixie' Belongs to Col. Will S. Hays."

63. Ibid.

64. The *Louisville Courier-Journal,* 24 December 1909, quoting O. G. T. Sonneck, chief of the division of music at the Library of Congress. At one time even President Theodore Roosevelt expressed an interest in seeing "Dixie" become the national anthem of the United States (*Literary Digest,* 26 July 1913, 135).

65. "W. S. Hays," Western Kentucky University.
66. Firth's interview with Fauld's story was reprinted by John Tillery Lewis, *Origin of Dixie,* in a promotion pamphlet published by E. Witzman & Co., Pianos, Organs and Music, Memphis, n.d., 10–13.
67. William Shakespeare Hays, Manuscripts Section, Kentucky Building, Western Kentucky University, Bowling Green.
68. Ibid.
69. Howard L. Sacks and Judith R. Sacks, *Way Up North in Dixie: A Black Family's Claim to the Confederate Anthem* (Washington, D.C.: Smithsonian Institute, 1993).
70. Anon., "Joint Committee," *Confederate Veteran* 12, no. 5 (1904): 215. These efforts to adopt a "new Dixie" are chronicled in John A. Simpson's, "Shall We Change the Words of 'Dixie'?" *Southern Folklore Quarterly* 45 (1981): 19–40.
71. *Billboard,* 16 January 1904.
72. *Confederate Veteran* 11, no. 11 (1903): 487; see also, *Confederate Veteran* 12, no. 5 (1904): 215; 12, no. 2 (1904): 66.
73. "Joint Committee," 3. Gordon may have lost some sleep over giving the UDC his support. He was actually an admirer of Emmett's. When Emmett toured the South in 1895, he introduced him to audiences in Nashville and then visited him later at his home in Mt. Vernon (Galbreath, *Daniel Decatur Emmett,* 33–34). Given the choice between offending the UDC and his friendship for Emmett, he chose the members but may have felt that he still retained his integrity by supporting Emmett's chorus.
74. Ibid.
75. *Confederate Veteran* 12, no. 9 (1904): 432; UDC Joint Committee. In his *War Songs and Poems of the Southern Confederacy, 1861–1865* (Philadelphia: Winston, 1904), Henry Marvin Wharton included Emmett's "Dixie" under the title, "The Original 'Dixie'" but did not mention Emmett as its author. Wharton's introduction states "We all know the air, but how few have seen the original song! There have been many versions, but we give here the original one, from which they all sprang," 59.
76. The four prominent Confederate societies were the United Daughters of the Confederacy, the United Confederate Veterans Association, the Sons of Veterans and Other Organizations, and the Confederated Southern Memorial Associations.
77. *Nashville Banner,* 16 June 1904, quoted in Simpson, "Shall We Change," 33.
78. *Confederate Veteran* (December 1904) 12, no. 12, 591. The President of the Tennessee chapter of the UDC later claimed that the national UDC would never have given its support to a "new Dixie" if they had been aware of General Cabell's passion for the old version (see J. A. Simpson, "Shall We Change," 34).
79. The "Joint Committee" never met.
80. *Confederate Veteran* 12, no. 10 (1904): 501.
81. Minutes of the 12th UDC convention, quoted in J. A. Simpson, "Shall We Change," 36–37.
82. *Louisville Courier-Journal,* 16 June 1905, quoted in J. A. Simpson, "Shall We Change," 36.
83. Sam Dennison, *Scandalize My Name: Black Imagery in American Popular Music* (New York: Garland Pub. Inc., 1982), 188.

CHAPTER 3

1. *Confederate Veteran* 19 (1911): 478. An item in *Confederate Military History,* 9:452, says that Mrs. Smyth gave the flag to a C. R. Dickson, who presented it to Barry as a gift from her; see also, M. L. Crimmins, "The Bonnie Blue Flag," *Frontier Times* 17 (1940): 323–25. The flag itself was made by a Miss Em Lou Cadwallader.
2. *Confederate Veteran* 36 (1928): 209; the *Arkansas Gazette* (17 April 1904, p. 7, col. 6) says Macarthy was asked by his friend, Judge Wiley Harris, a member of the Mississippi secession convention, to write a song marking the occasion and that he did so within the hour.

3. *Confederate Veteran* 19 (1911): 478.
4. *Arkansas Gazette,* 17 April 1904, 7:6.
5. The earliest copyrighted version of "The Bonnie Blue Flag" does not have an illustrated cover, simply states, "Written By Harry Macarthy," and does not have a plate number. All other versions carry the dedication to Albert Pike and a reference to Macarthy's "Personation Concerts." This version also spells Blackmar incorrectly ("A. E. Blackuear [*sic*] & Bro.") and has the copyright in Macarthy's name on the caption page (see note 14).
6. John Smith Kendall, "New Orleans' Musicians of Long Ago," *Louisiana Historical Quarterly* 31 (1948): 2–21.
7. Statement in catalog on back page of Theodore von La Hache, "Confederates' Polka March" (New Orleans: Blackmar and Bro., 1862).
8. *Confederate Veteran* 19 (1911): 478; 3 (1905): 216; Rutherford, *South in History,* 14:6086.
9. A Louisiana Artillery Man, "Reminiscences of New Orleans, Jackson, and Vicksburg," *Confederate Annals* 1, no. 2 (1883): 48–49.
10. The incident involving Booth is contained in Kendall's *Golden Age,* 498.
11. Macarthy's chronology is incorrect. South Carolina seceded first (20 December 1860), followed by Mississippi (9 January 1861), and then Alabama (11 January 1861), Georgia (19 January 1861), Louisiana (26 January 1861), Texas (7 February 1861), Virginia (17 April 1861), Arkansas (6 May 1861), Tennessee (6 May 1861), and North Carolina (20 May 1861). The original lyrics composed in Jackson could only have had the first two verses and chorus since, at the time Macarthy wrote the song, only South Carolina and Mississippi had seceded. As new stars were added to the banner, new versions quickly followed. Eventually the single star in "The Bonnie Blue Flag" grew to thirteen when Macarthy added Missouri and Kentucky, although the official flag of the Confederacy had only eleven.
12. Although northern Missouri was firmly under Union control, parts of the southern area of the state were pro-Southern and were considered part of the Confederacy by the Confederate Congress. The Kentucky state legislature voted to stay in the Union, but an independent convention from 18 to 20 November 1861 voted to depose the state legislature and form a provisional government, which then appealed for inclusion and was accepted into the Confederate States of America.
13. Edward Young McMorries, *History of the First Regiment Alabama Volunteer Infantry C.S.A.* (Montgomery, Ala: Brown Printing Co., 1904), 52; Mary Lasswell, ed., *Rags and Hope–The Recollections of Val C. Giles: Four Years with Hood's Brigade Fourth Texas Infantry, 1861–1865* (New York: Coward-McCann, Inc., 1961), 90–91.
14. Macarthy's connection with Pike has never been explained. One of the earliest editions had two crossed flags in the center with a blue flag and single star on the left and the Stars and Bars with eleven stars and three stripes on the right. Harry Dichter and Elliot Shapiro (*Handbook of Early American Sheet Music, 1768–1889* [1941; reprint, New York: Dover Publications, 1977], 119) argue that this could not have been the first edition since it bore music plate numbers (either 46 or 57), whereas a less ornate edition with a typeset cover had no plate number.
15. J. C. Viereck, "The Bonnie Blue Flag as a Quickstep" (New Orleans: Blackmar & Co.; Augusta: Blackmar & Bro., 1862). Miller & Beacham (Baltimore, 1862) published another variation "composed and arranged for the piano-forte" with a cover featuring the flag with its single star. John Schreiner, the Macon, Georgia music publisher, issued the song with a different set of words by Robert Carlin in 1863, a surgeon in the 5th Georgia Infantry, under the title, "Southern Constellation."
16. Devereaux D. Cannon, *The Flags of the Confederacy: An Illustrated History* (Memphis: St. Lukes Press and Broadfoot Publishing, 1988), 35–58; G. Ward Hubbs, "Lone Star Flags and Nameless Rags," *Alabama Review* 39, no. 4 (1986): 275.

17. Mrs. C. Sterett and M. H. Frank, "Reply to the Bonnie Blue Flag" (New York: S. T. Gordon, 1863).

18. *Arkansas Gazette,* 17 April 1901, 7:6; cf. DeLeon, *Belle,* 356.

19. Item in *Charlotte (N.C.) Observer,* in Valentine Museum, ca. 4 November 1900; see also DeLeon, *Belles,* 356.

20. *New Orleans Daily States,* 25 November 1888, 8:5.

21. *Memphis Daily Appeal,* 28 December 1858, 3:1.

22. *Arkansas Gazette,* 26 February 1859, 2:1.

23. Pike's own "The War Song of Dixie," was the main rival of Emmett's "Dixie" (see chapter 1).

24. *Daily Picayune,* letter dated 3 August, printed 6 August 1861, 2:6, and reprinted for several days more.

25. *New Orleans Daily Crescent,* 10 August 1861, 1:3; *Daily Picayune,* 10 August 1861, 2:5.

26. *New Orleans Daily Crescent,* 8 August 2:1; 17 August 1861. Macarthy had written "The Volunteer: or It Is My Country's Call" soon after the Confederate victory at First Manassas (20 July 1861) as a tribute to the Southern soldier. The song became so popular the Blackmar's eventually issued it in six separate editions.

27. *Daily Picayne,* 8 August 1861, 4:2; Morning, 9 August 1861, 2:5

28. *Daily Picayne,* Saturday, 10 August 1861, afternoon edition, 1:2.

29. *Daily Picayne,* 27 September 1861, 2:11; 13 October 1861, 2:3.

30. Grady McWhiney, *Braxton Bragg and Confederate Defeat* (New York: Columbia University Press, 1969) 1:183.

31. Lasswell, *Rags and Hope,* 53.

32. James R. Randall papers, letter dated Wilmington, 6 December 1863, (Southern Historical Collection, University of North Carolina).

33. Ibid.

34. The *Macon Daily Confederate,* 12 April 1864, 2:2.

35. *New Orleans Daily States,* 25 November 1888, 8:5.

36. Hewitt's career is examined later in this chapter.

37. After the dinner, Randall wrote to his fiancé that he found the company disagreeable, especially Lottie, who he said was "very coarse and not pretty." (Wilmington, 18 March 1864, Randall papers).

38. Quoted by Richard Barksdale Harwell, "The Star of the Bonnie Blue Flag," *Civil War History* 4, no. 30 (1958): 289–290. The accusation was false—Macarthy was born in England and never renounced his citizenship. Confederate veterans from Arkansas said Macarthy enlisted in an Arkansas unit but was discharged (*Confederate Veteran* 9 [1901]: 213; 19 [1911]: 478; 23 [1915]: 470–71).

39. The parody accused Macarthy of "stirring the rebels up" and "tickling them with praise," only to "fill [his] purse." Hewitt also dismissed "The Bonnie Blue Flag" and "Missouri" as "wishy-washy" and "clap-trap." (John Hill Hewitt, Manuscript, Special Collections, Emory University, Atlanta, 291).

40. Harry Macarthy, *His Book of Original Songs, Ballads, and Anecdotes, as Presented by the Author In His Well-Known Personation Concerts* (Indianapolis: Indiana State Sentinel, 1888). The book also contains some of Macarthy's songs. It is very rare. Two copies are located in the rare book room of the Library of Congress.

41. Ibid. Entry, 12 February 1867.

42. *Jefferson (Texas) Times And Republican,* 2 March 1870; *Vicksburg Herald,* 29 March 1870; *Springfield (Illinois) Daily State Journal,* 12 May 1870; notices in Macarthy, *His Book,* 28, 30.

43. Thomas Allston Brown, *A History of the New York Stage from the First Performance in 1732 to 1901* (New York: Dodd, Mead & Co., 1903), 1:354; *Confederate Veteran* 9 (1901): 213; 19 (1911): 478.

44. *New Orleans Daily States,* 15 November 1888, 2:1.

45. *Richmond Dispatch,* Sunday, 17 June 1900.
46. Quoted in *Arkansas Gazette,* 17 April 1904, 7:6.
47. A bibliography of Hewitt's songs as well as all of his other compositions, plays, and writings is contained in Frank W. Hoogerwerf, *John Hill Hewitt: Sources and Bibliography* (Atlanta: Emory University, 1981).
48. Hewitt to Beauregard, 14 October 1862, quoted in William Craig Winden, "The Life and Music Theater Work of John Hill Hewitt" (Ph.D. diss., University of Illinois, 1972), 20.
49. See Winden, "Life and Music," passim.
50. Hewitt, manuscript, quoted in John Howard Tasker, "The Hewitt Family in American Music," *Musical Quarterly* 17 (1931): 34. Hewitt's biographer, William Winden ("Life and Music," 26), says the song was the "mystery tune" on a popular radio program in the 1940s, and a contestant won more than thirty thousand dollars for correctly identifying it.
51. Mrs. M. E. Hewitt and W[illiam] V[incent] Wallace, "Sleeping I Dream'd Love" (Macon, Ga.: John W. Burke, 186–); Mrs. Mary E. Hewitt and Wm. Vincent Wallace, "Softly Ye Night Winds" (Macon, Ga.: John W. Burke, 186–). William Vincent Wallace was a prominent Irish composer. Mrs. Hewitt apparently felt more comfortable setting words to his music than asking her husband to collaborate on her songs.
52. *Savannah Daily Morning News,* 19 March 1863, 2:3.
53. Music historian John Howard Tasker ("Hewitt Family") felt Hewitt's place in American music was very much overrated by his admirers.

CHAPTER 4

1. Quoted by F. Moore, *Rebellion Record,* 1:80.
2. Ibid.
3. Quoted by Brander Matthews, "The Songs of the War," *Century Magazine* 34 no. 4 (1887): 621.
4. Ibid.
5. *Sic Semper Tyrannis* (Thus Always to Tyrants), Virginia's state motto, shouted by John Wilkes Booth as he jumped to the floor of Ford's Theater after assassinating Lincoln.
6. Harrison mentions introducing Jennie to the song in a letter he wrote in 1867; see Daniel E. Sutherland, *The Confederate Carpetbaggers* (Baton Rouge: Louisiana State University Press, 1988), 41.
7. The tune itself is older than anyone realizes. Originally written in England in the twelfth century by an Oxford deacon, it made its way to Germany and became the tune for "Tannenbaum, O Tannenbaum" and "Lauriger Horatius," the song Hetty Cary found in the Yale songbook. See Spaeth, *History of Popular Music,* 144–45.
8. Quoted by Matthews Page Andrews, 145–46. Thomas W. Hall, publisher of *The South,* the newspaper "My Maryland" appeared in, was imprisoned in Fort Warren for spreading "seditious sentiments." (Matthews Page Andrews, "History of 'Maryland! My Maryland!'" in *Library of Southern Literature,* ed. Edwin Anderson Alderman, Joel Chandler Harris, and Charles William Kent (New Orleans: Martin & Hoyt Co., 1909), 16:68.
9. A Baltimorean in Louisianna [*sic*] and C[harles] E[llerbock], "Maryland, My Maryland" (Baltimore: Miller & Beacham, 1861).
10. Kate Elony Baker Staton, *Old Southern Songs of the Period of the Confederacy: The Dixie Trophy Collection* (New York: Samuel French, 1926), 199–200.
11. Matthews, "Songs of the War," 622; see also Charles William Hubner, *War Poets Of The South* (privately published, n.d.), 199–201.
12. Gary W. Gallagher, ed., *Fighting for the Confederacy: The Personal Recollections of General Edward Porter Alexander* (Chapel Hill: University of North Carolina Press, 1989), 62.
13. Quoted by Ruth Scarborough, *Belle Boyd: Siren of the South* (Macon, Ga.: Mercer University Press, 1983), 78.

14. James R. Randall, "Maryland! My Maryland!" (Baltimore: George Willig, 1862).
15. For example, Jas. [*sic*] R. Randall and P[hilip] W[erlein], "Maryland, [My] Maryland" (New Orleans: P. Werlein & Halsey, 1862); J. R. Randall and a Lady of Baltimore, "Maryland, My Maryland" (Nashville and Memphis: J. A. McClure, 1861). Although the song was a hit across the South, neither Randall nor any publisher had taken the trouble to copyright it. Armand Blackmar realized that although it was too late to copyright the song, there was still money to be made from Randall's endorsement. By 1862 Blackmar's editions of the song carried this statement, "Having disposed of the copy-right of my poem, Maryland! My Maryland!' to Messrs. Blackmar & Bro., I hearby certify that their edition is the only one that has my sanction and approval.—Jas. R. Randall. (Jas. [*sic*] R. Randall and a Lady of Baltimore, "Maryland! My Maryland!" [Augusta, Ga.: Blackmar & Bro.; New Orleans: Blackmar & Co., 1862].) Blackmar's ploy worked. His competitors stopped printing any more editions.
16. *Richmond Daily Examiner,* 6 January 1864.
17. James Cephas Derby, *Fifty Years among Authors: Books and Publishers* (New York: G. W. Carleton & Co., 1884), 665. Although "My Maryland" made him famous, all Randall ever received for writing it was a hundred dollars in Confederate money from Armand Blackmar, which he used to buy himself a much needed suit of clothes. (Randall, Letters, 5 and 14 February 1864.)
18. Derby, *Fifty Years,* 664.
19. Randall, Letter to his wife, 6 December 1863.
20. Randall, Letter dated 6 January 1905.
21. James I. Robertson, *The Stonewall Brigade* (Baton Rouge: Louisiana State University Press, 1963), 154.
22. William Miller Owen, *In Camp and Battle with the Washington Artillery of New Orleans* (Boston: Ticknor and Co., 1885), 240.
23. John S. Robson, *How a One-Legged Rebel Lives* (reprint, Mattituck, N.Y.: Amereon House Ltd., 1997), 118.
24. Quoted by Alfred Hoyt Bill, *The Beleaguered City: Richmond, 1861–1865* (New York: Alfred A. Knopf, 1946), 150.
25. *Southern Historical Society Papers* 47 (1930): 120.
26. Ibid.
27. Septimus Winner, "Maryland, My Maryland (A Northern Reply)"; see Glass, *Singing Soldiers,* 24.
28. "Answer to 'My Maryland'"; see Silber, *Songs of the Civil War,* 73.
29. George F. Root, *The Story of a Musical Life* (Cincinnati: John Church, 1891).
30. Claude-Joseph Rouget de Lisle, "La Marseillaise (Caption title: 'The Southern Marseillaise')" (New Orleans: A. E. Blackmar & Bro; Charleston: H. Siegling, 1861).
31. For example, Miss M. A. Doyle, "The Southern Marseillaise Hymn" (Nashville and Memphis: J. A. McClure, 1861); Mis. [*sic*] L. Fanshaw, "Southern Marseillaise" (New Orleans: P. Werlein & Halsey, 1861).
32. Rosier and Rosier, "Virginian Marseillaise."
33. Quoted in Derby, *Fifty Years,* 665.
34. Letter dated 16 July 1888, Special Collections, Duke Library, Durham, N.C..
35. Letter dated 6 January 1905, Special Collections, Duke Library.
36. Derby, *Fifty Years,* 664.
37. DeLeon, *Belles,* 364.
38. Spaeth, *History of Popular Music,* 145.

CHAPTER 5

1. After it formally seceded, South Carolina abandoned that earlier flag and adopted as its official flag a banner of red silk with a blue cross in its middle, inside of which were fifteen stars, one for each of the slaveholding states. The center of the cross contained one star much larger than the rest, representing South Carolina. The left-hand corner bore

a palmetto, the state's emblem, the top right-hand corner a crescent. George Henry Preble, *History of the Flag of the United States of America, and of the Naval and Yacht-Club Signals, Seals and Arms, and Principal National Songs of the United States, with a Chronicle of the Symbols, Standards, Banners, and Flags of Ancient and Modern Nations* (Boston: James R. Osgood and Co., 1880), 498.

2. Louisiana's first secession flag had fifteen stars and a pelican. An argument soon broke out as to the appropriateness of that bird as a state symbol. The pelican, complained those who disapproved, was unsightly, filthy in its habits, and cowardly in its nature—hardly a worthy symbol. Louisiana subsequently adopted a multicolored flag with thirteen stripes and a single, pale yellow, five-pointed star in its center.

3. A letter to the *Louisville Courier-Journal* (2 June 1980) credits Nicola Marschall with the design. A monument was erected to Marschall in Marion, Alabama, in 1936, honoring him as "the father of the Stars and Bars." Marschall was born in Prussia and immigrated to the United States in 1849. He had studied art in Italy and Germany, and after settling in Marion, taught art, music, and languages to daughters of wealthy plantation owners. Marschall enlisted in the Confederate army when Alabama seceded, but before he went to war, a wife of a Marion planter asked him to design a flag for the Confederate states. After the war, Marschall married one of his former pupils and moved to Louisville, where he worked as a portrait artist. He died in 1917.

4. Quoted in Preble, *History of the Flag,* 444.

5. The *Charleston Daily Courier,* Friday, 19 April 1861, 2:4.

6. Preble, *History of the Flag,* 449–52.

7. 3 May 1861; quoted in Preble, *History of the Flag,* 453.

8. Ibid.

9. Ibid., 404.

10. *Hopkins' New Orleans 5 Cent Song Book,* 12–13; see also, Earle Leighton Rudolph, *Confederate Broadside Verse* (New Braunfels, Texas: Book Farm, 1950), nos. 133, 223, 295.

11. Gen. John A. Dix was commanding officer of the Middle Department. This law is mentioned in a broadside entitled "William Price" in Rudolph, *Confederate Broadside Verse,* no. 315.

12. For different versions of the Barbara Fritchie story, see Preble, *History of the Flag,* 485–91.

13. The *Richmond Dispatch* (7 December 1861) admitted as much in its editorial: "We know the flag we had to fight; yet, instead of getting as far from it, we were guilty of the huge mistake of getting as near to it as possible." Quoted by Frederick Cocks Hicks, *The Flag of the United States* (Washington, D.C.: W. F. Roberts, 1926), 402 (hereafter cited as *Flag of the U.S.*).

14. Ella D. Clark and J. R. Boulcott, "Adieu to The Star Spangled Banner Forever" (New Orleans: P. Werlein & Halsey, 1861).

15. The "Stars and Bars" in Moore, *Rebel Rhymes,* 127. The flag that now symbolizes the United States was born out of the Revolution. On 14 June 1777, while fighting for its independence, the new American Congress resolved "that the flag of the thirteen United States be thirteen stripes, alternate red and white; that the union [the area in the top left-hand corner] be thirteen stars, white in a blue field, representing a new constellation." When England and the United States signed the peace treaty of 1783, the "Stars and Stripes" was recognized as the banner of the new republic and took its place alongside the banners of the other nations of Europe whose representatives had assembled in Paris to witness that treaty. For a history of colonial and revolutionary flags, and possible precursors of the "stars and stripes," see Milo Milton Quaife, Melvin J. Weig, and Roy E. Appleman, *The History of the United States Flag, from the Revolution to the Present: Including a Guide to Its Use and Display* (New York: Harper and Bros., 1961); Hicks, *Flag of the U.S.,* passim.

16. *Richmond Dispatch,* 7 December 1861, quoted by Hicks, *Flag of the U.S.,* 158–60.

17. Harry Macarthy, "Origin of the Stars and Bars" (New Orleans: A. E. Blackmar & Bro., 1861). The same song was also published under the title, "Our Flag and Its Origin" (New Orleans: A. E. Blackmar & Bro., 1861).
18. Preble, *History of the Flag,* 402–4.
19. Ibid., 511.
20. Genl. M. Jeff Thompson and Theod. Von La Hache, "The New Red, White, and Blue" (New Orleans: A. E. Blackmar & Bro.; Vicksburg: Moody & Kuner, 1862). Thompson (1826–76) was a former mayor of St. Joseph, Missouri. At the outbreak of the war he organized a battalion and led it south. He served primarily in the Trans-Mississippi Army.
21. P. E. Collin and Newton Fitz, "The Banner of the South" (Mobile, Ala: J. H. Snow, 1861).
22. Quoted in Scot M. Guenter, *The American Flag* (Rutherford, N.J.: Farleigh Dickinson University Press, 1990), 74–75.
23. Samuel L. Hammond and J. P. Caulfield, "Our Southern Flag" (Charleston: Geo. F. Cole, 1861).
24. Mrs. C. D. Elder and Sig. G. George, "The Confederate Flag!" (New Orleans: A. E. Blackmar & Bro., 1861).
25. Rev. T. B. Russell, "Hurrah for Our Flag!" (Macon, Ga.: J. W. Burke, 1864).
26. E. V. Sharp and J[ohn] H. Hewitt, "Flag of the Sunny South" (Augusta, Ga.: J. H. Hewitt, 186–).
27. M. F. Bigney and Alice Land, "The Stars of Our Banner" (Augusta: Blackmar & Bro., 1861).
28. M. F. Bigney and J. C. Viereck, "The Flag of the Free Eleven" (New Orleans: P. Werlein & Halsey, 1861).
29. Robt. F. Carlin, "Southern Constellation (tune of 'The Bonnie Blue Flag')" (Vicksburg, Miss: Blackmar & Bro.; Montgomery, Ala: Schreiner & Sons, 1863). Carlin was a surgeon in the 5th Confederate Regiment, C.S.A.
30. Elder and George, "The Confederate Flag."
31. C. H. Mueller, "The Palmetto Song" (Nashville and Memphis: J. A. McClure, 186–).
32. Hermann L. Schreiner, "Secession Quickstep" (Macon, Ga.: John Schreiner and Sons, 186–).
33. Wm. H. Hartwell, "Confederates' Grand March" (New Orleans: A. E. Blackmar & Bro., 1861).
34. Ibid; at the head of the title: "Fifty Thousand."
35. Ibid; at the head of the title: "4th Edition" (lithographed date is 1862).
36. Lena Lyle, "The Song of the South" (Nashville and Memphis: Jas. A. M'Clure, 1861).
37. See chapter 4.
38. James Harrold, "Surgeons Of The Confederacy," *Confederate Veteran* 40, no. 5 (1932): 173.
39. Charles T. Beauman, "Confederate Battle Flag March" (Nashville: C. D. Benson, 186–).
40. Hermann L. Schreiner, "Battle Flag Grand March," listed in Werlein & Halsey's catalog under "Marches and Quicksteps" (New Orleans: P. Werlein & Halsey, 1862).
41. Hermann L. Schreiner, "Battle-Flag Polka" (Macon and Savannah: John C. Schreiner & Son, 1863).
42. R. H. D. and James Pierpont, "Our Battle Flag!" (New Orleans: P. Werlein & Halsey, 1862).
43. Henry St. Tucker, "The Cross of the South" (Baltimore: Henry McCaffrey, 1861).
44. Charles Ellerbrock, "The Southern Cross" (Baltimore: Henry McCaffrey, 1861).
45. *Richmond Dispatch,* 7 December 1861.
46. Quoted by Preble, *History of the Flag,* 526.
47. Subaltern, "The Star Spangled Cross and the Pure Field of White" (Richmond: Geo. Dunn & Compy.; Columbia, S.C.: Julian A. Selby, 1864).

48. Edmond B. Newmann, "Battery Wagner" (Columbia, S.C.: Duncan and Co., 1863); Hartwell, "Confederates' Grand March"; E. O. Eaton, "I Dream of Thee" (Augusta: Blackmar & Bro., 1864); Edward O. Eaton, "Never Surrender" (Augusta: Blackmar & Bro., 1863); Lyle, "The Song of the South." A song recorded by Moore, in his *Rebel Rhymes,* 107–8, with the ubiquitous "Southern Cross" title, may also have been written for the "stainless banner," since it urges Southerners to "Salute thy cross of stars!" and looks forward to the day when "Thy stainless field shall empire wield."

49. Preble, *History of the Flag,* 530.

50. Father J. Abram Ryan and Theodore Von La Hache, "The Conquered Banner" (New Orleans: A. E. Blackmar, 1866).

51. Ibid.

52. Quoted by Hubbs, "Lone Star Flags," 271.

53. *New York Times,* 8 December 1996, late edition, sec. 4:5; 28 December 1996, 4:6; *Jet,* 20 January 1997, 15–16; *U.S. News and World Report,* 10 March 1997, 13; *Wall Street Journal,* 4 February 1997, A20.

CHAPTER 6

1. Wilbur Zelinsky, *Nation into State: The Shifting Symbolic Foundaitons of American Nationalism* (Chapel Hill: University of North Carolina Press, 1988), 20. The term and general discussion of "eidolons" in this chapter is based on Zelinsky.

2. Alfred F. Toulmin, "Confederacy March" (Baltimore: George Willig, 1861); Mary Kelly, "Jefferson Davis March" (Baltimore: George Willig, 1861).

3. C[arl] [W.] Sabatier, "Jefferson Davis, First President of the Confederate States of America" (New Orleans: P. P. Werlein & Halsey, 1861); Mrs. Flora Byrne, "President Jefferson Davis Grand March" (New Orleans: P. P. Werlein & Halsey, 1861); J. E. Gleffer, "Grand March of the Southern Confederacy" (New Orleans: P. P. Werlein & Halsey, 1861).

4. P. Rivinac, "Our First President's Quickstep" (New Orleans: A. E. Blackmar and Bro., 1861). Rivinac, the piece's composer, was a pianist from Louisiana about whom little is known, although he wrote many wartime tunes. In his diary, Sgt. Edwin H. Fay, who served with the Minden Rangers, a Louisiana cavalry company in Van Dorn's Division, wrote that Rivanic was "the most accomplished pianist I ever heard play"; Bell I. Wiley, ed., *This Infernal War: The Confederate Letters of Sgt. Edwin H. Fay* (Austin: University of Texas Press, 1958), 305.

5. Elder and George, "The Confederate Flag!"

6. P. E. Collins, and William Herz, "The Southern Battle Song" (Mobile, Ala: J. H. Snow, 1861).

7. Macarthy, "The Bonnie Blue Flag"; "The Southern Wagon: Respectfully Hitched Up for the President, Officers, and Men of the Confederate Army (tune of 'Wait for the Wagon')" (Mobile: Joseph Bloch, 1862).

8. "The Song of the Exile," in Fagan, *Southern War Songs,* 245.

9. "Yankee Vandals," in Fagan, *Southern War Songs,* 314.

10. Zelinsky, *Nation into State,* 10.

11. Silber, *Songs of the Civil War,* 89.

12. J. P. McRebel and F. Bartensetin, "The Abe-iad" (Alexandria, Va: John H. Parrott, 1861).

13. On his way to Washington to take office as president, Lincoln made a number of speeches en route. In Columbus, Ohio, he addressed the state legislature. Despite the fact that six states had seceded and had chosen a president for their Confederacy, Lincoln downplayed the looming showdown between the North and the South by assuring everyone that "there is nothing going wrong." Nothing had yet happened "that

really hurts anybody . . . nobody is suffering anything." Confederate songwriters latched onto the phrase and in "There's Nothing Going Wrong, Dedicated to Old Abe,'" ridiculed his complacency:

> THERE'S a general alarm,
> The South's begun to arm,
> And every hill and glen
> Pours forth its warrior men;
> Yet, "There's nothing going wrong,"
> Is the burden of my song.

> Six States already out,
> Beckon others on the route;
> And the cry is "Still they come!"
> From the Southern sunny home;
> Yet, "There's nothing going wrong,"
> Is the burden of my song.

Fort Sumter's surrender and the defeat at Manassas triggered two other Confederate songs featuring Lincoln's comment "nobody's hurt": "The Song of the Exile," in Fagan, *Southern War Songs* ("Fort Sumter's taken and nobody's hurt!" / Fight away. . . .) and "Nobody's hurt is easy spun, / But the Yankees caught it at Bull Run", R. E. Holtz, "We'll Be Free in Maryland," in Fagan, *Southern War Songs.*

14. "The Song of the Exile," in Fagan, *Southern War Songs,* 245.
15. Dr. Woodcock and J[acob] Schlesinger, "The Hobbie" (Mobile, Ala: Joseph Bloch, 1861).
16. Cooper and Tucker, "Jeff in Petticoats" in Silber, *Songs of the Civil War,* 343–45. The cover for the song shows Davis in women's clothes, still wearing his own boots, with his bonnet fallen off. In the background a Federal officer is pointing a gun at him while Varina, his wife, is running toward the officer, ostensibly to keep him from firing. Davis's capture and his alleged disguise is discussed in detail in Burke Davis's *The Long Surrender* (New York: Random House, 1985), 141–58.
17. John H. Hewitt, "King Linkum the First: A Musical Burletta"; but there were exceptions: "The Despot's Song" by "Ole Secesh" is anything but humorous, describing Lincoln "With a beard that was filthy and red / His mouth with tobacco bespread." See Nora F. M. Davidson, *Cullings From the Confederacy.* (Washington, D.C.: Rufus H. Darby Co., 1903), 122.
18. The *(Richmond) Magnolia Weekly* 1 (11 July 1863): 232, quoted in Ellen Cullen, *The Civil War in American Drama before 1900* (Rhode Island: Brown University, 1990), 20.
19. The *Index,* 3 (24 September 24 1863): 347, quoted in Cullen, *Civil War Drama,* 20.
20. "Old Abe Lincoln Came Out of the Wilderness," in Silber, *Songs of the Civil War,* 94–95.
21. The tune has been traced back to 1858 when it was originally called, "Down in Alabam" and described an "old hoss" that "came tearin' out de wilderness" (Spaeth, *History of Popular Music,* 135).
22. Jesse Hutchinson, "Lincoln and Liberty," in Silber, *Songs of the Civil War,* 96–97. Jesse Hutchinson was one of the members of the singing Hutchinsons (see the introduction).
23. James Sloan Gibbons and L. O. Emerson, "We Are Coming Father Abr'am;" Septimus Winner, "Abraham's Daughter (She Is the Child of Abraham)"; Pratt and Buckley, "We'll Fight for Uncle Abe"; see Silber, *Songs of the Civil War,* 99–101, 104–10.
24. Macarthy, "The Bonnie Blue Flag."
25. Anon., *The Southern Wagon Respectfully Hitched up for the President, Officers, and Men of the Confederate Army* (Mobile, Ala.: Joseph Block, 1862).

26. Macarthy, "The Volunteer; or, It Is My Country's Call"; Miss Victoria C., "The Beauregard; or, Fort Sumter Polka March" (New Orleans: privately published, ca. 1861).

27. J. B. Hawkins, "The Minute Men" (Nashville: Jas. A. McClure, 1861).

28. H. N. Hempsted, "Mason & Slidell Quick Step, Respectfully Dedicated to Messrs. Mason & Slidell, Out [sic] Southern Ministers to England forcibly taken from the British Steamer *Trent*" (Nashville: C. D. Benson, 1861).

29. Klubs and Ducie Diamonds, "The Gallant Girl That Smote the Dastard Tory Oh!" (New Orleans: A. E. Blackmar, ca. 1862). Klubs is believed to be a pseudonym for James R. Randall.

30. Hawkins, "The Minute Men."

31. E. M., "Our Queen Varine" (London: C. Dondsdale, n.d.). The cover for the song has a "Stars and Bars" with only seven stars, indicating that it was written after Davis's election as president of the Confederacy in February 1861, and before April 1861.

32. Miss Victoria C., "The Beauregard; or Fort Sumter Polka March."

33. Chas. Lenschow, "Beauregard's March" (Baltimore: Miller and Beacham, 1861); S. C., "Salut a Beauregard" (Baltimore: Miller & Beacham, 1862).

34. Mrs. V. G. Cowdin, "Gen. Beauregard's Grand March" (New Orleans: A. E. Blackmar & Bro., 1861).

35. O. M. and Elizabeth Sloman, "Sumter: A Ballad of 1861 (Charleston, S.C.: H. Siegling; New Orleans: A. E. Blackmar & Bro., 1861).

36. Beauregard's eidolonic stature was also reflected in sheet music published in border states in addition to Maryland. In Kentucky, for example, he was celebrated in Eugene Beauvais's "Beauregard's Grand March" (Louisville: Tripp and Cragg, 1861).

37. Macarthy, "The Volunteer; or It is my Country's Call."

38. A. Noir, "The Beauregard Manassas Quick-Step" (New Orleans: A. E. Blackmar & Bro., 1861).

39. Ibid.

40. J. A. Rosenberger, "Beauregard Bull Run Quick Step" (New Orleans: P. P. Werlein & Halsey, 1862).

41. F. E. D. and H. D., "Beauregard: A Southern Song" (New Orleans: Blackmar & Co., 186–).

42. Jas. R. Randall and Edward O. Eaton, "There's Life in the Old Land Yet" (New Orleans: A. E. Blackmar & Bro., 1862).

43. In addition to the pieces already cited, Beauregard's name appears in sheet music in either the title or dedication in Knabe, "Beauregard's Polka" (Baltimore: George Willig, 1862); [Joseph] Ascher, "Gen'l Beauregard's Grande Polka Militaire!" (New Orleans: P. P. Werlein & Halsey, 1861); E. Heineman, "Genl. Beauregard's Grand March" (New Orleans: P. Werlein & Halsey, 1861); E. Heineman, "Gen. Beauregard's Grand March" (Macon, Ga.: John C. Schreiner and Son, 186–); Miss C. Mcconnell, "A Tribute to Beauregard" (New Orleans: Blackmar & Co., 1861); "Southern Victory Polka March" (Mobile, Ala.: J. H. Snow, 1861); J. R. Stevenson, "Those Sabbath Bells!" (Baltimore: Miller & Beacham, 1862).

44. [Hermann] L. Schreiner, "Beauregard's Charleston Quickstep (at head of title: 'To the Hero of Shiloh & Charleston')" (Macon and Savannah: J. C. Schreiner & Son, 1863).

45. Theo. Von La Hache, "Elegy on the Death of Mme. G. T. Beauregard (the cover has a lithograph of a coffin with a cross on the lid in foreground, resting on a beach, and a steamboat in the distance)" (New Orleans: Louis Grunewald, 1864); Octavie Rome, "A la MÇmoire de Madame G. T. Beauregard" (New Orleans: privately published, 1864).

46. Hermann L. Schreiner, "Gen. Lee's Grand March: (at head of title) To General Robert E. Lee, Commander-in-Chief of the Army of the Confederate States" (Macon & Savannah: John C. Schreiner & Son, 1863); J. C. Vierick, "Genl. R. E. Lee's Grand March" (New Orleans, privately published, 1863); Charles Young, "Genl. Rob't E. Lee's Quick March" (New Orleans: Blackmar & Co.; Augusta, Ga.: Blackmar & Bro.

1863). A note in the Blackmar catalog accompanying an edition of "Harry Macarthy's Songs & Ballads" warns music lovers "Be careful to ask for Young's composition, to avoid getting a Lee's March by an anonymous writer;" J. W. Evans, "The Lee Schottis-che" (Richmond: J. W. Davies and Sons, 186–).

47. Miss R. Stakely, "The Sword of Gen. Lee" (Louisville: Louis Tripp, ca. 1867); Moina [Father A. J. Ryan] and E. Louis Ide, "Sword Of Robert Lee" (Baltimore: George Willig and Co., 1867); Moina and Henry Weber, "Sword of Robert Lee" (Nashville: Jas. A. McClure, 1867).

48. E. C. E. Vile, "The Stonewall Jackson Grand March" (Nashville and Memphis: Jas. A. M'Clure, 1862). Jackson himself was credited in 1862 with writing a poem entitled "My Wife and Child" which was turned into a song after his death, but in a letter dated 17 November 1862, Jackson said a mistake had been made and that the real author was John [*sic*] R. Jackson, who had served as a field officer in a Southern regiment during the Mexican War. Jackson erred somewhat (cf. *Savannah Daily Morning News,* 26 August 1863, 2:2). The author was Henry Rootes Jackson (1820-98). Henry Jackson also had a distinguished career. Born in Athens, Georgia, he graduated from Yale in 1839, prac-ticed law in Savannah, and was subsequently appointed U.S. attorney for the District of Georgia. In 1849, he was elected to the supreme court for the District of Georgia. After serving as a colonel in the Mexican War, he was appointed American ambassador to Austria. During the Civil War he served as a brigadier general in the Confederate army. During Cleveland's administration he was U.S. minister to Mexico. "My Wife and Child" was but one, albeit the best, of his many poems. (See Mildred Lewis Rutherford, *American Authors: a Handbook of American Literature from Early Colonial to Living Writers* [Atlanta: Franklin Printing and Publishing Co., 1894], 523; "General H. R. Jackson's Poems," *Confederate Veteran* 11 [1903]: 164). Whether they were unaware of the facts, or knew them and ignored them in favor of boosting sales, George Dunn and Julian Selby pooled resources and issued a musical version of the song in 1863, crediting "the late lamented hero, General Stonewall' Jackson," as author ("My Wife and Child" [Rich-mond: Geo. Dunn & Compy.; Columbia, S.C.: Julian A. Selby, 1863].) The cover has two men in a thoughtful pose at the top of page; Jackson is mounted on a pedestal in the middle and beneath: *"Dulce et decore est pro patria mori"* ("It is sweet and seemly to die for one's country"). The quotation is from Cicero.

49. "Stonewall Jackson's Way!" (Richmond: J. W. Randolph, 1863). The caption page has: "Found on a Confederate Sergeant of the old Stonewall Brigade taken at Winchester, Va." The same song, published independently by both George Willig and Miller and Beacham, has 1862 imprints.

50. Union general Nathaniel Prentiss Banks.

51. Quoted in Francis Trevelyan Miller, *The Photographic History of the Civil War* (New York: Review of Reviews Co., 1911), 9:86, 88.

52. Charles Young, "Stonewall Jackson's Grand March" (New Orleans and Augusta, Ga.: Blackmar & Co., 1863).

53. Hermann L. Schreiner, "'Stonewall' Jackson's Grand March" (Macon and Savannah: J. C. Schreiner & Son, 1863).

54. "Stonewall Jackson's Midnight Review Grand March" (New Orleans: Louis Grunewald, 1863).

55. Thomas Cooper DeLeon, *Four Years in Rebel Capitals: An Inside View of Life in the Southern Confederacy: From Birth to Death* (Mobile, Ala: Gossip Printing Co., 1890), 296.

56. C[harles] Nordendorf, "The Stonewall Brigade" (Danville, Va: Charles Nordendorf, 1863).

57. L. Rieves and B. A. Whaples, "'Stonewall' Jackson's Prayer" (New York: Blelock & Co., 1864).

58. There were two Sweeneys in Stuart's camp, Sam Sweeney, who played the banjo, and his cousin, Bob Sweeney, who played the violin. After Stuart's death at Yellow Tavern,

Sam Sweeney served under Gen. Fitzhugh Lee, until he (Sweeney) died of smallpox at Hanover Court House (Robert J. Trout, ed., *Riding with Stuart: Reminiscences of an Aide-de-Camp by Captain Theodore Stanford Garnett* [Shippensburg, Pa.: White Mane Pub. Co., 1994], 30–31).

59. "Riding a Raid." The cover has a lithograph of Stuart on horseback.

60. Ibid.

61. In June 1862, as part of a reconnaissance mission, Stuart led his cavalry completely around Gen. George McClellan's army.

62. John S. Wise, *The End of an Era* (Boston: Houghton, Mifflin and Co., 1902), 335–37.

63. Earnest Halphin, "Coming at Last!" (Baltimore: Miller & Beacham, 1862).

64. C[harles] C. Nordendorf, "Southern Troopers, Dedicated to Genl. J. E. B. Stuart, and his Gallant Soldiers" (Danville, Va.: C. C. Nordendorf, 186–).

65. E. M., "A Confederate Raid" (London: C. Londdale, n.d.). The song is dedicated "To General J. E. B. Stuart of the Confederate Cavalry." The cover, in color, features the Stars and Bars with seven stars.

66. William Wilis Blackford, "The Cavalier's Glee," in D. L. Cary, *Confederate Scrap Book,* (Richmond: J. L. Hill Printing Co., 1893), 205; Fagan, *Southern War Songs,* 261. Blackford was Stuart's engineer officer since June 1862. He was appointed a major in 1864.

67. "Stuart!" (New Orleans: Blackmar & Co., 186–). The caption page has an 1863 copyright in Georgia.

68. "How Are You? John Morgan: Comic Song: A Sequel to Here's Your Mule" (Nashville: C. D. Benson, 1864). The cover has a picture of Morgan escaping from the Columbus prison on a mule.

69. Eugene Raymond (music by Daniel Decatur Emmett), "Three Cheers for Our Jack Morgan!" (Augusta: Blackmar & Bro., 1864).

70. "John Morgan March (listed on cover page of Southern Cheer Boys'" (Macon: Schreiner and Son, 186–); "John Morgan Polka (listed on cover page of 'Gallopade')" (Nashville and Memphis: Jas. A. M'Clure, 1862); A. Davis, "John Morgan's Bride Polka," (New Orleans: P. P. Werlein & Halsey, 1863); C. D. Benson, "Capt. John Morgan Schottisch," (below title: 'Now you'v [sic] got him. Now you haven't.')" (Nashville: C. D. Benson, 1862); C. L. Peticolas, "Gen'l Morgans Grand March" (lithographed portrait of Morgan on cover)" (Richmond: Geo. Dunn & Co.; Columbia, S.C.: Julian Selby, 1864).

71. John Jacob, "Gen. Ben. McCullough's [sic] Grand March" (New Orleans: Louis Grunewald, 1861); "Oak Hill Polka: Dedicated to Gen. Ben. McCulloch (listed on cover page for 'Gallopade')" in "M'Clure's Collection of National Melodies" (Nashville and Memphis: Jas. A. M'Clure, 1862).

72. Rivinac, "Gen. Bragg's Grand March" (New Orleans: A. E. Blackmar & Bro., 186–); "The Song of the Exile," in Fagan, *Southern War Songs.*

73. "Forrest Polka (listed on title page of 'Southern Cheer Boys')" (Macon: Schreiner & Son, ca. 1861); E. C. E. Vile, "The Forrest Schottisch" (Nashville: Jas. A. McClure, 1863).

74. "General Forrest—A Confederate," *Confederate Veteran* 14 (1906): 299.

75. C. D. Benson, "Gen. A. Sidney Johnson's [sic] Grand March" (Nashville: C. D. Benson, 1861).

76. Adolphus Brown, "Genl. Joseph E. Johnston Manassas Quick March." (New Orleans: A. E. Blackmar & Bro., 1861). The cover has a lithographic portrait of Johnston. Johnston, who was called "Uncle Joe" by the Army of Tennessee, was fondly extolled in a parody to the "Yellow Rose of Texas," which the Army of Tennessee sang after the disastrous Nashville campaign in 1864 when their ranks were ravaged by their commander, reckless John Bell Hood: "And now I'm going southward, / For my heart is full of woe; / I'm going back to Georgia, / To find my Uncle Joe."

77. John Prosinger, "Pickets [sic] Charge March" (Columbus, S.C.: B. Duncan & Co., 186–).

78. C. Young, "Gen. Longstreet's Grand March"(New Orleans: Blackmar & Co.; Augusta: Blackmar & Bro., 186–); Hermann L. Schreiner, "Gen. Mercer's Grand March!" (Macon: John C. Schreiner & Son, 186–); T. J. Martin, "Gen'l Persifor F. Smith's March" (Nashville: C. D. Benson, 186–).

79. Charlie L. Ward, "Gen. Breckenridge's[*sic*] Grand Waltz" (Nashville and Memphis: Jas. A. McClure, 1862).

80. Lizzie C. Orchard, "Maj. General Hampton's Quickstep" (Columbia, S.C.: privately published, 186–). Capt. Wm. Henry Capers, "The Winder Galop" (Columbia, S.C.: B. Duncan & Co., 186–). The cover has a face-and-shoulder portrait of Winder.

81. [C. Young], "Lexington Quickstep: Dedicated to Gen. Price (listed on cover page for 'Gallopade')" (Nashville and Memphis: Jas. A. M'Clure, 1862); C[harles] Chakyde, "Old Dominion March: Dedicated to General William Smith, Governor of Virginia" (Richmond: C. Nordendorf, 1863); Jas. A. McClure, "Song of the Southern Boys: Cheer, Boys, Cheer (at head of title: 'To Gen. F. K. Zollicoffer of Tennessee')" (Nashville and Memphis: Jas. A. McClure, 1861); F. Sulzner, "Leesburg March: Dedicated to Gen. Evans" (Nashville and Memphis: Jas. A. M'Clure, 1861); John H. Hewitt, "The Stonewall Quickstep: Composed and Dedicated to Lt. Gen. Ewell and 'Stonewall Brigade'" (Macon and Savannah: John C. Schreiner and Son, 1863).

82. Jo. Benson, "Belmont Quick Step: Respectfully Dedicated To Gen. Leonidas Polk, Gen. B. F. Cheatham, Gen. Gideon J. Pillow" (Nashville: C. D. Benson, 1861). The Battle of Belmont, in which the Confederates turned back a Federal force led by Ulysses Grant, was fought near the town of that name in Missouri on 7 November 1861.

83. J. Willard, "Magruder's March" (Baltimore: George Willig, 1862).

84. R. E. Holtz, "We'll Be Free in Maryland," in Fagan, *Southern War Songs,* 49.

85. D. M. W., "My Texas Land" in Allan, *Allan's Lone Star Ballads.* (Galveston: J. D. Sawyer, 1874).

86. A Texian, "Johnny B. Magruder," in Allan, *Collections of Southern Songs,* 89.

87. See Allan, *Collections of Southern Songs,* 11–12, 26–27, 42–43, and passim.

88. G. Orloff, "Ashby Galop" (Baltimore: Miller & Beacham, 1861). Ashby, who led Stonewall Jackson's cavalry forces in the Shenandoah Valley, was killed in June 1862. In "Stonewall Jackson's Way," there is a line, "pay off Ashby's score." DeLeon, *Four Years in Rebel Capitals,* 296, said he had dozens of dirges devoted to Ashby.

89. A Lady of Kentucky and J. E. Smith, "You Can Never Win Us Back: Dedicated to Mosby and His Men (minor variation of 'The Southrons' Chaunt of Defiance')" (Richmond: J. W. Davies & Sons, 1864).

90. Charlie L. Ward, "Kentucky Battle Song" (Columbia, S.C.: B. Duncan & Co., 1863); Henry Schoeller, "Soldier's Greeting: March Militaire: Dedicated to Maj. Genl. Richard H. Anderson of Stateburg, S. C." (Augusta, Ga.: Blackmar and Bro., 186–). Schoeller was a music teacher in Columbia, S.C. (*Columbia Daily Southern Carolinian,* 25 October 1864, cited by Alice Washburne, *A Descriptive Catalog of Confederate Music in the Duke Library Collection.* Durham, N.C., 1936, 236); Mrs. J. H. News, "Southern Shout: Dedicated to Brig. Gen. Harry T. Hays, of La.," in *New and Beautiful Music for the Piano* (catalog on last page of "I Would Like To Change My Name") (Augusta, Ga.: Blackmar & Bro., 1864).

91. A. Lubuscher and A. S. Bykowsky, "Col. J. J. Thornton's March" (Nashville: C. D. Benson, 186–).

92. Mrs. E. B., "Louisiana Guard March: Dedicated to Capt. G. A. Breaux [*sic*]" (New Orleans: P. P. Werlein & Halsey, 1861); Lieut. R. J. Alexander and E[dward] O. Eaton, "Orleans Cadet's Quick Step (cover has lithograph of Dreux)" (New Orleans: A. E. Blackmar & Bro.,1861); Theo Schoeheit, "Lt. Col. Dreux Funeral March" (New Orleans: P. Werlein & Halsey, 1861); James R. Randall and G[eorge] M. Loening, "Elegy on the Death of Lt. Col. Dreux" (New Orleans: privately published by James Randall, 1861). The song was subsequently reissued by Werlein and Halsey under its

imprint. Another elegy, "Col. Bond's Funeral March," was written by Hermann Schreiner for a much lesser known but popular local hero. See "Col. Bond's Funeral March," listed in *Popular Music* in the catalog under "Marches & Quicksteps" on the last page of "The Soldier's Grave" (Macon, Ga.: John C. Schreiner And Son, 186–).

93. E. King and F[itz] W[illiam] Rosier, "The Alabama: Respectfully Dedicated to the Gallant Captain Semmes, His Officers, and Crew; and to the Officers and Seamen of the C. S. Navy" (Richmond: Geo. Dunn & Compy., 1864).

CHAPTER 7

1. G. W. Jamison and Jacob Schlesinger, "Trust to Luck Alabama" (Mobile: Joseph Bloch, 186–).
2. A. W. Morse, "The Soldiers [*sic*] Mission" (New Orleans: P. P. Werlein, 1861).
3. H. W. and T. S. Whitaker, "Carolina's Sons" (New Orleans: A. E. Blackmar & Bro., 1861).
4. Charlie Wildwood and John H. Hewitt, "The South" (Columbia, S.C.: Julian A. Selby, 1863).
5. A. E. A. Must and A. E. Blackmar, "My Warrior Boy" (New Orleans: A. E. Blackmar, 1864).
6. S. F. Cameron, "God Save the Southern Land" (Richmond: Geo. Dunn & Compy., 1864).
7. James Pierpont, "We Conquer or Die" (New Orleans: P. P. Werlein and Halsey, 1861).
8. The skirmish at Big Bethel on 9 to 10 June 1861, for example, was celebrated in "General Butler," written to the tune of "Yankee Doodle," and "Great Big Bethel Fight," written to the tune of "Dixie." In that melee, the first land battle of the war, several thousand Federals under Gen. Benjamin Butler attacked less than one thousand Confederates under Gen. John Magruder at Big Bethel Church near Yorktown, Virginia, and were driven back with about seventy killed and wounded, compared with less than ten casualties for the Confederates. Broadsides marking the victory are listed in Esther Parker Ellinger, *The Southern War: Poetry of the Civil War* (1918; reprint, New York: Burt Branklin, 1970); Rudolph, *Confederate Broadside Verse*; and Moss, *Confederate Broadside Poems*.
9. "Flight of Doodles," in Fagan, *Southern War Songs,* 66–67. Enumerating the exploits of each state, however, indicates that for the author, the Confederacy was not yet fighting as a nation, but as a collection of individual states.
10. "Another Yankee Doodle" in Fagan, *Southern War Songs,* 27.
11. [J] Viereck, "Battle of Manassas," listed in the catalog on the last page of "Gen'l Beauregard's Grande Polka Militaire!" (New Orleans: P. P. Werlein & Halsey, 1861); S. Schlesinger, "Manassas Polka" (Mobile, Ala.: Joseph Bloch, 186–); B. R. Scott, "Evening at Manassas," listed in the catalog on the last page of "I'd Be a Star" (New Orleans: A. E. Blackmar & Bro., 186–); [Fourrier], "Victory of Manassas Grand March," listed on the title page for "Inauguration March of Our First President" (New Orleans: P. P. Werlein & Halsey, 1862); Mrs. C. McC., "Our Triumph at Manassas: Fantaisie Mazurka" (New Orleans: P. P. Werlein & Halsey, 186–); Geo. M. Taylor, "Manassas Quickstep" (Nashville and Memphis: J. A. McClure, 186–); Adolphus Brown, "Genl. Jospeh E. Johnston Manassas Quick March" (New Orleans: A. E. Blackmar & Bro., 1861).
12. Coralie Buard, "Oak Hill March Triomphale" (New Orleans: Sourdes & Chassaigac, 1862); "Oak Hill Polka" (Nashville and Memphis: Jas. A. M'Clure, 1862). Oak Hill (also called Wilson's Creek), fought on 10 August 1861, was the next large battle after First Manassas. Though outnumbered by about ten thousand to five thousand, Union general Nathaniel Lyon attacked the Confederates near Springfield, Missouri, on an incline called "Oak Hill" and was beaten back.

13. "Belmont Quick Step" (Nashville: C. D. Benson, 1861). At Belmont, Missouri, Gen. U. S. Grant sent about three thousand Federals from Cairo to capture Columbus, Kentucky. On the way the Federals encountered Confederates under Gen. Leonidas Polk, who crossed from Kentucky and turned the Union flank, forcing Grant to retreat.
14. E. C. E. Vile, "Shiloh Victory Polka" (Nashville and Memphis: Jas. A. McClure, 186–).
15. William Shakespeare Hays, "The Drummer Boy of Shiloh" (Augusta, Ga.: Blackmar & Bro., 1863). The battle of Shiloh and its "drummer boy" are examined in detail in chapter 12.
16. John R. Thompson, "Richmond Is a Hard Road To Travel" (New Orleans and Augusta: Blackmar & Co., 1863).
17. Edward O. Eaton, "Never Surrender Quick Step" (Augusta, Ga.: Blackmar & Bro., 1863).
18. John A. Augustin and Edward O. Eaton, "We'll Die, but Never Surrender" (New Orleans: A. E. Blackmar & Bro., 186–). Both men were members of the Orleans Cadets, Dreux Battalion.
19. Fr. C. Mayer, "Boys, Keep Your Powder Dry" (Augusta, Ga.: Blackmar & Bro., 1863).
20. Carrie B. Sinclair and Clarke E. Ilsley, "The Soldier's Suit of Grey" (Augusta, Ga.: Blackmar & Bro., 1864).
21. Carrie B. Sinclair, "The Homespun Dress," in *The Jack Morgan Songster* (Fayetteville, N.C.: Branson & Farrar, 1864).
22. D. W. Jones, "My girl with the Home-spun Dress," listed on last page of "I'd Be A Star" (Augusta, Ga.: A. E. Blackmar & Bro., 1864).
23. Many women, however, shunned homespun clothes since weaving was formerly work done by slaves. Likewise, husbands serving in the army wrote to their wives that such work was beneath their dignity. See Faust, *Mothers,* 45–47. Faust writes that a study of wartime textiles indicates that relatively few white women did in fact make homespun. Privileged women imported it from blockade-runners or purchased it behind enemy lines. On the other hand, they did learn to sew and knit (Ibid., 48–50).
24. Chas. Lever and Edward O. Eaton, "Camp-fire Song" (Augusta, Ga.: Blackmar & Bro., 1864).
25. John H. Hewitt and Clark E. Isley, "Yes We Think of Thee at Home, Answer to Do They Think of Me at Home" (Augusta, Ga.: Blackmar & Bro., 1864).
26. Mrs. M. W. Stratton and Henry Schoeller, "Keep Me Awake, Mother!" (Augusta, Ga.: Blackmar & Bro., 1863).
27. M. F. Bigney and Stephen Glover, "The Southron's Watchword!" (Augusta, Ga.: Blackmar & Bro.; New Orleans: Blackmar & Co., 1861).
28. "The March of the Southern Men" (Richmond: Geo. Dunn & Compy.; Columbia, S.C.: Julian A. Selby, 1863).
29. C. C. Mera, "No Surrender" (Richmond: Geo. Dunn & Compy.; Columbia, S.C.: Julian A. Selby, 1864).
30. *Confederate Veteran* 9 (1901): 399. There is also an undated newspaper clipping on the debate dated 25 March 1901, "About the Song of 'The Homespun Dress'", in the Richmond Museum of Confederacy.

PART 2

1. Cage to wife, in T. H. Williams, ed., "The Civil War Letters of William L. Cage (Barksdale Brigade)," *Louisiana Historical Quarterly* 39 (1956): 113–130.
2. Frank Moore, *Anecdotes, Poetry, and Incidents of the War: North and South* (New York: G. P. Putnam, 1866), 76.
3. Ernest L. Abel and Barbara E. Buckley, *The Handwriting on the Wall* (Westport, Conn.: Greenwood Press, 1977).

4. John Brown Gordon, *Reminiscences of the Civil War* (New York: Charles Scribner's Sons, 1904), 173. For the lighter side of war, see Benjamin LaBree, *Camp Fires of the Confederacy* (Louisville, Ky.: Courier-Journal Printing Co., 1898); F. Moore, *Civil War in Song*; William Watson, *Life in the Confederate Army: Being the Observations and Experiences of an Alien in the South during the American Civil War* (New York: Scribner and Welford, 1888), 234–35; Joseph T. Durkein, ed., *John Dooley, Confederate Soldier: His War Journal* (Notre Dame: University of Notre Dame, 1963), 60–62; Bell I. Wiley, *The Life of Johnny Reb* (Baton Rouge: Louisiana University Press, 1984), 162–64; Larry J. Daniel, *Soldiering in the Army Of Tennessee: A Portrait of Life in a Confederate Army* (Chapel Hill: University of North Carolina Press, 1991), 83–94; B. Crammer, "The Civil War Had Its Jokes, Too," *San Jose Stud* 1 (1975): 87–92.

5. Gordon, *Reminscences of Civil War*, 173.

6. William B. Jones, *Under The Stars And Bars: A History of the Surrey Light Artillery* (Dayton, Ohio: Morningside Bookshop, 1975), 82, 140.

7. L. J. Daniel, *Soldering in the Army*, 52.

8. Albert T. Goodloe, *Confederate Echoes* (Washington, D.C: Zenger Pub. Co., 1983), 144–145.

9. Diary entry 20 September 1863, in William C. Davis, ed., *Diary of a Confederate Soldier*, 88. The phrase "numbered with the slain" was taken from the popular war tune, "Just Before the Battle Mother."

10. Ronald L. Davis, *A History of Music in American Life* (Malabar, Fla.: Kreiger Publishing Co., 1982), 1:43.

11. Ibid.

12. Lewis Gaston Leary, *The Book-Peddling Parson: An Account of the Life and Works of Mason Locke Weems: Patriot, Pitchman, Author, and Purveyor of Morality to the Citizenry of the Early United States of America* (Chapel Hill, N.C.: Algonquin Books, 1984), 149.

13. Mary Anna Morrison Jackson, *Life and Letters of General Thomas J. Jackson*. (New York: Harper and Bros., 1892), 21.

14. Joyce H. Cauthen, *With Fiddle and Well-Rosined Bow: Old-Time Fiddling in Alabama* (Tuscaloosa: University of Alabama Press, 1989), 10–11. On fiddling in the early South, see also Albigence Waldo Putnam, *History of Middle Tennessee; or Life and Times of Gen. James Robertson* (Nashville: A. W. Putnam, 1859); Ivan M. Tribe, *Mountaineer Jamboree: Country Music in West Virginia* (Lexington: University Press of Kentucky, 1984); Bill C. Malone, *Country Music U.S.A.* (Austin: University of Texas Press, 1985). Dena J. Epstein, *Sinful Tunes and Spirituals: Black Folk Music to the Civil War* (Urbana: University of Illinois Press, 1977) and Eileen Southern, *The Music of Black Americans: A History* (New York: W. W. Norton, 1971) contain interesting information on fiddling by slaves.

15. Margaret Hindle Hazen and Robert M. Hazen, *The Music Men: An Illustrated History of Brass Bands in America, 1800–1920* (Washington, D.C.: Smithsonian Institution Press, 1987), 7.

16. Quoted by Henry A. Kmen, *Music in New Orleans: The Formative Years, 1791–1841* (Baton Rouge: Louisiana State University Press, 1966), 212.

17. During the American Revolution, private civilian bands provided the music for ceremonial displays; after the performance, the musicians went home. One of the few regiments in the Continental army with its own military band was the 2nd Virginia, boasting four clarinets, two bassoons and three horns (G. P. Carroll, "The Band Musick of the Second Virginia Regiment," *Journal of Band Research* 11 [n.d.]: 16). Payment and upkeep for the band during the Revolution came out of the pockets of the regiment's officers, a practice that continued into the Civil War. Some state militias allowed men to fulfill their military obligations by playing in their unit's band.

18. Quoted by Hazen and Hazen, *Music Men*, 2–3, 44.

19. Quoted Wiley, *Life of Johnny Reb*, 379 n. 5.

20. Walter Lord, ed., *The Fremantle Diary: Being the Journal of Lieutenant Colonel James Arthur Lyon Fremantle, Coldstream Guards: On His Three Months in the Southern States* (Boston: Little, Brown, 1954).

21. Louis C. Elson, *The National Music of America and Its Sources* (Boston: Page, 1900), 259.

22. Stone, "War Music."

23. Ibid.

24. On romanticism, with special emphasis on its musical expression, see Kenneth Blanchard Klaus, *The Romantic Period in Music* (Boston: Allyn and Bacon, 1970); Arnold Whittall, *Romantic Music: A Concise History from Schubert to Sibelius* (London: Thames and Hudson, 1987). The Romantic influence on American music can be found in Gilbert Chase, *America's Music: From the Pilgrims to the Present* (Urbana: University of Illinois Press, 1987), 266–319; Charles Hamm, *Yesterdays: Popular Song in America* (New York: W. W. Norton, 1979), 62–88, 187–200; idem, *Music in the New World* (New York: W. W. Norton, 1983), 195–229; R. L. Davis, *History of Music*, 1:122–38; Hugh Wiley Hitchcock, *Music in the United States: A Historical Introduction* (Englewood Cliffs, N.J.: Prentice-Hall, 1988), 43–53.

25. On the preoccupation with death in nineteenth-century America, see Charles O. Jackson, ed., *Passing: The Vision of Death in America* (Westport, Conn.: Greenwood Press, 1977). The erotic love-death theme is clearly developed by Rudolph Binion, in *Love beyond Death: The Anatomy of a Myth in the Arts* (New York: New York University Press, 1993).

26. *The Army Songster: The Bonnie Blue Flag Song Book* (Augusta, Ga.: A. E. Blackman, n.d.); *The Jack Morgan Songster;* and *The Stonewall Song Book, 11th edition!—Enlarged! Being a Collection of Patriotic, Sentimental, and Comic Songs* (Richmond: West & Johnston, 1865). The flower metaphor was subsequently copied by American songwriters. Early in his career, for example, George F. Root wrote "Rosalie, the Prairie Flower" who lived:

> On the distant prairie,
> Where the heather wild
> In its quiet beauty lived and smiled.

Since Root never lived "on the distant prairie" he was obviously relying for his information about the "heather wild" on British composers like Moore (George F. Root, "Rosalie, the Prairie Flower" [Boston: Nathan Richardson, 1855]).

27. Poe's ideas on beauty are contained in his essays, "The Philosophy of Composition," in James Albert Harrison, ed., *The Complete Works of Edgar Allan Poe* (New York: Society of English and French, 1902), 193–208, and "The Poetic Principle," reprinted in Frederick Clarke Prescott, ed., *Selections from the Critical Writings of Edgar Allan Poe* (New York: Gordian Press, 1981), 228–256. The psychological basis of the death theme in parlor songs is examined in Jon W. Finson's *The Voices That Are Gone* (New York: Oxford University Press, 1994), chapter 3; and by Nicholas E. Tawa, "Songs of the Early Nineteenth Century. Part 1: Early Song Lyrics and Coping with Life," *American Music* 13 (1995): 1–26.

28. Stephen C. Foster, "I See Her Still in My Dreams" (Macon, Ga.: John C. Schreiner & Son, ca. 1862); idem, "Lula Is Gone!" (Macon, Ga.: John C. Schreiner & Son, ca. 1862); idem, "Parthenia to Ingomar" (Macon, Ga.; John C. Schreiner & Son, ca. 1862); idem, "Why No One to Love?" (Richmond: Geo. Dunn & Compy.; Columbia, S.C.: Julian A. Selby, ca. 1862); idem, "Come Where My Love Lies Dreaming" (Macon and Savannah: John C. Schreiner & Son, 1863); idem, "Fairy-Belle" (Augusta, Ga.: Blackmar & Bro., ca. 1863).

29. See Russell Lynes, *The Domesticated Americans* (New York: Harper & Row, 1963), 138; an enjoyable peep into American foibles as reflected in the rooms in which they lived.

30. Arthur Loesser, *Men, Women, and Pianos* (New York: Simon and Schuster, 1954), 511–12.

31. *New Orleans Daily Picayune,* Friday, 17 May 1861, 3:3.
32. *New Orleans Daily Picayune,* 28 May 1861, 3:4.
33. *Memoirs of Mollie McDowell* (Bastrop, Texas: 1978), 32.
34. Ibid., 32–33.
35. Gerry Van der Heuvel, *Crowns of Thorns and Glory: Mary Todd Lincoln and Varing Howell Davis: The Two First Ladies of the Civil War* (New York: Dutton, 1988), 58, 159; C. Vann Woodward, ed., *Mary Chesnut's Civil War* (New Haven: Yale University Press, 1981), 433–434.
36. Root, *Story of Life.*
37. Loesser, *Men, Women, and Pianos,* 508.
38. Peggy C. Boudreaux, "Music Publishing in New Orleans," (master's thesis, University of Southwestern Louisiana, 1977), 55.
39. *National Cyclopedia of American Biography* (Clifton, N.J.: J. T. White, 1984), 24:430.
40. Harwell, *Confederate Music,* 29.
41. *Augusta Daily Constitutionalist,* 9 July 1863, 2.
42. Nordendorf published several songs during the war, which he sold from his office, among them "Lorena, a Brilliant Study for the Piano" (Danville, Va.: C. Nordendorf, 1864). Nordendorf, an Austrian by birth, served in the Austrian army as a military engineer. In 1862 he left military service, and in 1863 he emigrated to Virginia and took a job as a music teacher at Danville Methodist Female College (now called Stratford College). When his engineering background was discovered, however, he was immediately called upon to construct defenses for Danville and its prison camp. After completing this task, he was called upon to plan field fortifications for Richmond. While engaged in these engineering jobs, he wrote numerous songs, several of which were dedicated to Confederate generals, for example, "The Stonewall Brigade" (Danville, Va.: C. Nordendorf, 1863) and "Old Dominion March" (Richmond: Nordendorf, 1863). He also wrote a number of songs about the anguish and personal tragedies experienced by Southerners during the later years of the war. After the war he continued writing songs extolling Confederate generals (for example, "General Robert E. Lee's Grand Quickstep" [Lynchburg: C. Nordendorf, 1866]). In 1867 he set Father Abram Ryan's "The Sword of Robert E. Lee" (Lynchburg: C. Nordendorf, 1867), one of the most popular of the postwar songs in the South, to music. In 1871 he moved to Petersburg where he started a short-lived periodical, *The Weekly Fireside,* devoted to musical compositions. In 1876 he moved to Richmond and in 1882 initiated yet another periodical, his most successful, *The Monthly Fireside,* featuring poems, essays, and songs. The magazine continued to be published until 1884. At the same time, he continued teaching music and selling music and musical instruments at the Richmond Music Exchange. Nordendorf remained poverty-stricken for most of his life and at the time of his death at forty-four years of age, he left only $150.49 to his estate (A. L. Hall, "Charles Chaky De Nordendorf: Soldier-Songster of the Confederacy," *Virginia Cavalcade* 24 [1974]: 41–47).
43. Schlesinger also composed several tunes during the war, among them, "Manassas Polka" (Mobile, Ala: Joseph Bloch, 186–).
44. Hartwell became bandleader for the 16th Mississippi Volunteers in 1861. Hartwell's "Confederates' Grand March" was issued four separate times by Blackmar & Bro. in New Orleans.
45. For an in-depth examination of the influence of female seminaries on music in nineteenth century America, see Judith Tick, *American Women Composers before 1870* (Ann Arbor: UMI Research Press, 1983), 33–56.
46. *Augusta Daily Consitutionalist,* 7 March 1862, 2:3.
47. *Augusta Daily Constitutionalist,* 22 January 1862, 2.
48. *Arkansas Gazette,* 15 September 1860, 3:5.
49. For a detailed discussion of the musical characteristics of parlor songs, see Nicholas E. Tawa, *Sweet Songs for Gentle Americans: The Parlor Song in America, 1790–1860*

(Bowling Green: Bowling Green University Popular Press, 1980), 158–197; a more brief, but worthwhile, summary is given by Perry, "Sex and Sentiment in America," *Journal of Popular Culture* 6 (1972–73): 45. For parlor music in general, Tawa is unparalleled. In addition to Perry, the topic is well covered by R. Davis, "Sentimental Songs in Antebellum America," *Southwest Review* 61 (winter 1976): 50–65.

CHAPTER 8

1. Simpson to sister, 18 June 1862, in Everson and Simpson, *Far, Far from Home,* 129. Many books describe the life of the ordinary soldier. The seminal works on the subject are by Wiley: *Life of Johnny Reb* (1943) and *The Life of Billy Yank* (1952; reprint, Baton Rouge: Louisiana State University Press, 1978). More recent surveys include James I. Robertson's *Soldiers Blue And Gray* (Columbia: University of South Carolina Press, 1988); Reid Mitchell's *Civil War Soldiers* (New York: Viking Press, 1988); Joseph Allen Frank and George A. Reaves, *Seeing the Elephant: Raw Recruits at the Battle of Shiloh* (Westport, Conn.: Greenwood Press, 1989).

2. Durkein, *John Dooley,* 59–60.

3. Benjamin Taylor, *Pictures of Life in Camp and Field* (Chicago: S. C. Griggs & Co., 1888), 93.

4. A new edition of *Infantry Tactics* was published in 1861 for the Confederate army by S. H. Goetzel & Co. in Mobile, Alabama. William Joseph Hardee (1815–73) had been a cavalry officer in the U.S. Army and was commandant of cadets at West Point when the war broke out. When his native state of George seceded, Hardee resigned his commission in the U.S. army, joined the Confederacy, and was appointed brigadier general.

5. Quoted in Harry H. Hall, ed., *A Johnny Reb Band from Salem: The Pride of Tarheelia* (Raleigh: North Carolina Confederate Centennial Commission, 1963), 64–65. The *Macon Telegraph* (5 October 1861, 1) thought its readers would be interested in knowing how their husbands and sons lived in camp and described twelve of the most common tunes that regulated their lives. The tunes have been recorded on compact disc and cassette: J. Pollard, "The Civil War Bugler" (Rome, Ga.: 1988); Kelly Grant, "Civil War Bugler" (Portland, Ore.: Rainbow Recording Studios, 1989); Frederick Fennell, "The Civil War: Its Music and Its Sounds" (New York: Mercury Records, 1990).

6. James Grant Wilson, *General Grant* (New York: D. Appleton and Co., 1897), 31.

7. The timetable described in this chapter is generally based on Watson's *Life in Confederate Army,* 148.

8. Wise, *End of an Era,* 254; John David Billings, *Hardtack and Coffee; or, The Unwritten Story of Army Life* (Boston: George M. Smith and Co., 1888), 164–169; Charles William Bardeen, *A Little Fifer's War Diary* (Syracuse, N.Y.: C. W. Bardeen, 1910), 79.

9. G. Haven, "Camp Life at the Relay," *Harper's New Monthly Magazine* 24 (1861–62): 631. There were at least three roll calls a day, one at "reveille," one at "retreat," and one at "tattoo."

10. Butterfield's account of how he came to write the new tune can be found in Julia Lorrilard S. Butterfield, ed., *A Biographical Memorial of General Daniel Butterfield* (New York: Grafton Press, 1904), 48–49.

11. In the British army, the regiment's youngest drummer boy would administer as well a ritual farewell kick to the miscreant (Lewis S. Winstock, *Songs and Music of the Redcoats: A History of the War Music of the British Army* [London: Leo Cooper, 1970], 95.) The "Rogue's March" goes back at least to the 1790s and may have been originally called "Cuckolds Come Dig," a tune drummers played in Edinburgh when prostitutes were driven out of the city (ibid., 97). Although adopted from the British, the ceremonial degradation associated with the tune during the Civil War far exceeded similar British traditions (ibid.).

12. Edwin Porter Thompson, *History of the Orphan Brigade* (1898; reprint, Dayton, Ohio: Morningside Books, 1995), 73–74.

13. William L. Gammage, *The Camp, the Bivouac, and the Battle Field: Being a History of the Fourth Arkansas Regiment, from Its First Organization down to the Present Date* (Little Rock: Arkansas Southern Press, 1958), 17–18.

14. About two thousand men were executed in the Confederate army for desertion. (Robert E. L. Krick, *Parker's Virginia Battery C.S.A.* (Berryville, Va.: Virginia Book Co., 1975), 4.

15. H. H. Hall, *Johnny Reb Band*, 25.

16. William Bircher, *A Drummer-Boy's Diary: Comprising Four Years of Service with the Second Regiment Minnesota Veteran Volunteer, 1861 to 1865* (St. Paul: St. Paul Book and Stationery Co., 1888), 179–80.

17. A. Moore, *The Louisiana Tigers; or, The Two Louisiana Brigades of the Army of Northern Virginia, 1861–1865* (Baton Rouge: Ortlieb Press, 1961), 275. A mass execution occurred in 1863 when 30 men from two North Carolina regiments deserted. Several were killed trying to get back home; 10 were taken prisoner and were shot to death in the presence of the whole division, with 150 men assigned to the firing squad. The execution gloomed the entire army, recalled John Casler of the Stonewall Brigade, since that many men had never been executed at one time before. These examples didn't keep men from deserting, said Casler, "for I believe the more they shot, the more deserted, and when they did desert, they would go to the enemy" (John Overton Casler, *Four Years in the Stonewall Brigade* [Marietta, Ga.: Continental Book Co., 1951] 190).

18. Herbert E. Valentine, Diary and letters, (Manuscripts Section, Essex Institute, Salem), 17.

19. Owen, *Camp and Battle*, 435. For the complete text, see Willard Allison Heaps and Porter W. Heaps, *The Singing Sixties* (Norman: University of Oklahoma Press, 1960), 129.

20. The first known use of field music by European armies occurred at the Battle of Bouvines in 1214 when trumpets were used to signal French cavalrymen to charge German infantry. By the sixteenth century, European armies were fighting to the sound of drums, fifes, trumpets, and bugles (see Raoul F. Camus, *Military Music of the American Revolution* [Chapel Hill: University of North Carolina Press, 1976], 6ff). *The British Rules and Ordynaunces for the Warre,* written in 1544, called upon "every horseman at the fyrst blaste of the trumpette [to] saddle or cause to be saddled his horse, at the seconde to brydell, [and] at the thirde to leape on his horsebacke, to wait on the kyng, or his lorde or capitayne" (quoted in Stanley Sadie, ed., "Military Calls," in *The New Grove Dictionary of Music and Musicians* [New York and London: Macmillan Pub., 1980], 316). By the 1600s every soldier in the British army was required "diligently [to] observe and learn the distinct and different sounds of Drums, Fifes, and Trumpets, that he may know to answer and obey each of them in time of service" (Ibid). In the 1700s when warfare and maneuvers became more sophisticated, drummers and other field musicians were expected to be adept. Field musicians were outfitted in distinct uniforms and were paid more and enjoyed a higher rank than ordinary enlisted men, a custom still observed during the American Civil War.

21. Francis Alfred Lord and Arthur Wise, *Bands and Drummer Boys of the Civil War* (South Brunswick, N.J.: Thomas Yoseloff, 1966) 52, 200; William C. Davis, *Touched by Fire: A Photographic Portrait of the Civil War* (Boston: Little, Brown and Co., 1985), 1:112; John Esten Cooke, *Wearing of the Gray* (New York: E. B. Treat & Co., 1969), 369. Confederate officers were also not above recruiting Yankee prisoners as field musicians. At Andersonville prison in southwestern Georgia, the 2nd Georgia Guard Regiment at the prison offered a Federal drummer parole from that hell on condition he join their unit. But as horrible as prison life at Andersonville was, the drummer refused (B. P. Ferguson, "Bands Of The Confederacy: An Examination of the Musical and Military Contributions of the Bands and Musicians of the Confederate States of America" [Ph.D. diss., North Texas State University, 1987], 71–72). Another drummer and another fifer, however, decided to take the offer and were marched five miles to

serenade a lady who had given the regiment a flag (Ovid L. Futch, *History of Anderson-ville Prison* [Gainsville: University of Florida Press, 1968], 114).

22. The Civil War drum was a wooden-shelled single-rope-tension snare instrument, 10 inches to 12 inches high and 15 inches to 16 inches in diameter, with a sheepskin head. Confederate drums bore an eagle on their fronts, with the Stars and Bars on the eagle's chest and a banner at its feet which read, "Confederate States of America." A blue background indicated an infantry unit; red, the artillery. The company letter and the regimental number were painted under the arms in a scroll. Some Confederate drums also had a state flag or floral pattern on their sides.

Since army life was so dependent on the drum, army regulations, up to 1841, explicitly required drummers to give their instruments proper care and maintenance. When not in use, a drum's cords were to be slackened and the drum was to be protected against the weather, preferably by storing it in a case. When he wasn't beating his drum on the march, the drummer slung it from his shoulder by a cloth or leather sling; hence the drum's nickname, "side drum". During the Civil War, dozens of drum makers in the North manufactured about thirty-two thousand drums for the Union army (G. Craig Caba, *United States Military Drums, 1845–1865: A Pictorial Survey* [Harrisburg, Pa.: Civil War Antiquities Ltd., 1977], 135–37) at a cost of $5.50 each (*General Orders of the War Department, Embracing the Years 1861, 1862, and 1863,* ed. T. M. O'Brien and O. Diefendorf [Newark: Derby and Miller, 1864], 5 November 1861; 9 December 1862). Because the Southern quartermaster general had no national drum manufacturers to call upon, music stores in the South that had formerly only sold or repaired musical instruments made in the North went into the drum-making business. (See letter from Rudolph Siegling, 16 January 1936, cited in Alice Washburne, "A Descriptive Catalogue of Con-federate Music in the Duke University Collection" (master's thesis, Duke University, 1936), 18. Or drummers and tanners made them from skins and wood (McHenry Howard, *Recollections of a Maryland Confederate Soldier and Staff Officer under Johnston, Jackson, and Lee* [Repr. Wilmington, N.C.: Broadfoot Pub. Co., n.d.], 85).

Bass drums, much larger and heavier than side drums, were introduced into the Amer-ican army in the early nineteenth century and were used primarily by regimental bands. "Kettledrums" or "barrel" drums, measuring about 24 inches x 24 inches, were less common because of their inordinate size, especially in the fast-moving Confederate army.

The 27th Arkansas had a kettledrum in its band (Silas Claiborn Turnbo, *History of the Twenty-Seventh Arkansas Confederate Infantry* [Fayetteville: University of Arkansas Press, 1989], 81) as did the "Orphan Brigade" ("We soon after got a kettle-drum, which was rattled to perfection," Diary entry, 5 October 1861, in Davis, *Diary of a Confederate Sol-dier,* 20). An Atlanta drum maker advertised them for sale early in the war (*Atlanta Daily Intelligencer,* 18 June 1861, 2:4). For photographs of several Union drums and details of drum making, see Robert Joseph Garofalo and Mark Elrod, *A Pictorial History of Civil War Era Musical Instruments and Military Bands* (Charleston, W.Va.: Pictorial Histories Publishing Co., 1985), 35–52.

First used by the ancient Greeks, fifes did not come to prominence as musical instru-ments in the military until the fifteenth century when Swiss mercenaries began using them along with their drums to add melody to field calls. Eventually they were adopted by other European armies for the same purpose.

The fife used by Americans during the Revolution and the Civil War was a one-piece wooden flutelike instrument, about sixty centimeters long with six finger holes. Even though fifes only cost about forty-five cents (*General Orders of the War Department,* 5 November 1861; 8 December 1862), there were relatively few fifers in the Confeder-ate army.

23. *New Orleans Daily Picayune,* 12 May 1861, 4:5; 2 May 1861, 2:5; 8 June 1861, 3:3. Many of the drums used in the Confederate army belonged to local and state militias

that flourished in the South during the first half of the nineteenth century. These drums were all made in the North and were easily obtainable prior to the war. When these militia units joined the Confederate army, they brought their drums with them and Federal designs were simply covered over with Southern insignia. (Union "eagle drums" bore an eagle with the Stars and Stripes emblazoned on its chest and a banner bearing the motto "*E Pluribus Unum*" grasped firmly in its beak.)

24. Bardeen, *Little Fifer's Diary,* 127.
25. Harry M. Kieffer, *Recollections of a Drummer Boy* (Boston: Ticknor and Co., 1889), 111.
26. Describing the murderous twenty-hour battle at the "Bloody Angle" at Spotsylvania (12 May 1864), some years later, Col. A. T. Watts remembered a Mississippi drummer boy, Max Fronthall, who "though insignificant in appearance, had the heart of a lion. For several hours he stood at the immediate point of contact, amid the most terrific hail of lead, and coolly and deliberately loaded and fired without cringing" (Harry Simon-hoff, *Jewish Participants in the Civil War* (New York: Arco Publishing Co., 1963), 263–64.
27. *Savannah Daily Morning News,* 9 December 1862, 2; Ibid., 10 February 1863, 2.
28. The bugle is shorter than the trumpet and often had two coils whereas the trumpet usually had only one. Because of its longer length, the trumpet had a louder, more pen-etrating sound. Since it had more brass, a trumpet cost more ($2.88 compared to a bugle's $2.66; *General Orders of the War Department,* 5 November 1861; 9 December 1862).
29. *Army Regulations Adopted for Use of The Army of the Confederate States* (New Orleans: Bloomfield and Steel, 1861). By June 1864, official pay was raised to eighteen dollars for drummers and fifers and nineteen dollars for cavalry buglers.
30. Cater, *As It Was,* 141–42.
31. Quoted by Camus, *Military Music,* 9.
32. Ferguson, "Bards of the Confederacy," 58.
33. In rare cases, "principal musicians" or drum majors in the Confederate army were trained at the U.S. military music facilities, known as "Schools for Practice." *The Drum-mer's and Fifer's Guide,* the manual used at these schools, was cowritten by George B. Bruce and Daniel Decatur Emmett (1862. Reprint, New York: W. A. Pond, 1885). Emmett had been a fifer in the U.S. army long before the war and like many field musicians, was underage when he served. Later on in life, he went on to write "Dixie," the unofficial anthem of the Confederacy (see chapter 2).
34. Delavan S. Miller, *Drum Taps in Dixie: Memories of a Drummer Boy, 1861–1865* (Water-town, N.Y.: Hungerford-Holbrook Co., 1905), 22; Diary entry, 5 October 1861, in Davis, *Diary of Confederate Soldier,* 20.
35. An English Combatant, *Battle-Fields of the South, from Bull Run to Fredericksburg: With Sketches of Confederate Commanders, and Gossip of the Camps* (New York: John Bradburn, 1864); *Civil War Times Illustrated,* April 1984, 308. Caffey was one of a number of officers trained in the English army who observed the war from the Confederate side. He and the other English officers may have been more critical of musicians in the Confederate Army than were their own officers because they were used to better-trained musicians.
36. E. P. Thompson, *History of Orphan Brigade,* 201.
37. Quoted in John Gilchrist Barrett, *The Civil War in North Carolina* (Chapel Hill: Uni-versity of North Carolina Press, 1963), 24.
38. English Combatant, *Battle-Fields of the South,* 310.
39. John Esten Cooke, *Outlines from the Outpost* (Chicago: R. R. Donnelley & Sons Co., 1961).
40. English Combatant, *Battle-Fields of the South,* 309.
41. For further information on Crouch, see chapter 12.
42. D. S. Miller, *Drum Taps,* 106–7.

CHAPTER 9

1. Thomas Lightfoot to cousin, 29 May 1861, in Annette Tapert, ed., *The Brothers' War* (New York: Times Books, 1988), 7.
2. W. B. Jones, *Under the Stars and Bars,* 82, 140.
3. A. Winters, "Gay and Happy" (Augusta, Ga.: Blackmar & Bro., 1863).
4. F. Jay Taylor, ed., *Reluctant Rebel: The Secret Diary of Robert Patrick, 1861–1865* (Baton Rouge: Lousiana State University Press, 1959).
5. Edwin Fay to wife, 21 April 1862, in Wiley, *This Infernal War,* 38.
6. For humor in the British army during the Boer and later wars, see R. Palmer, *What a Lovely War: British Soldiers' Songs from the Boer War to the Present Day* (London: Michael Joseph, 1990).
7. "The Brass-Mounted Army," in Silber, *Songs of the Civil War,* 198–200.
8. McMorries, *History of the First Regiment,* 51. The brass buttons heralded in the song were the insignia of rank. Confederate generals and staff officers wore bright gilded convex buttons, with an eagle with outstretched wings in the center. The larger button was an inch in diameter, the smaller, half an inch. Lower-ranking artillery, cavalry, and infantry officers wore slightly smaller, plain gilt buttons, with a large raised letter in the center—"A" for artillery, "I" for infantry, and so on. Buttons worn by enlisted men in all branches except the artillery had no design and bore only the number of their regiment; in the artillery, privates and officers wore similar-looking buttons. Many states, however, had their own designs for their buttons. (*New Orleans Picayune,* 25 May 1861.) On buttons and uniforms in general, see Philip J. Haythornthwaite, *Uniforms of the Civil War* (New York: Sterling Publishing Co., 1990).
9. A. Growler, "The Officers of Dixie," in *The New Confederate Flag Song Book,* no. 1 (Mobile, Ala.: H. C. Clark, 1863), 29; Fagan, *Southern War Songs,* 301.
10. Diary entry, 30 August 1862, in Durkein, *John Dooley,* 23.
11. Goodloe, *Confederate Echoes,* 138.
12. Milton Barrett to his sister and brother, 21 February 1863, in J. Roderick Heller and Carolynn Ayres Heller, eds., *The Confederacy Is on Her Way up the Spout: Letters to South Carolina, 1861–1865* (Athens: University of Georgia Press, 1992), 90.
13. Daniel Robinson Hundley, *Social Relations in Our Southern States* (New York: Arno Press, 1973), 269.
14. Quoted in Grady McWhiney, *Cracker Culture: Celtic Ways in the Old South* (Tuscaloosa: University of Alabama Press, 1990), 128.
15. Hundley, *Social Relations,* 269.
16. W. B. Jones, *Under the Stars and Bars,* 147.
17. James W. Silver, ed., *A Life for the Confederacy: As Recorded in the Pocket Diaries of Pvt. Robert A. Moore: Co G. 17th Mississippi Regiment Confederate Guards, Holly Springs, Mississippi* (Wilmington, N.C.: Broadfoot Publishing Co., 1987).
18. Alexander Hunter, *Johnny Reb and Billy Yank* (New York: Neale Publishing Co., 1905), 159; cf. Silver, *Life for the Confederacy,* 294.
19. Silver, *Life for the Confederacy,* 292; cf. Fletcher, *Rebel Private,* 66–67.
20. Quoted in LaBree, *Camp Fires of the Confederacy,* 369.
21. "The Brass-Mounted Army." In most cases, drunkenness was punished with confinement in the guardhouse. Sometimes, however, harsher punishments like "bucking and gagging"—being tied in an awkward position with a bayonet positioned in the mouth—were administered (see Daniel, *Soldering in the Army,* 102–3).
22. John Overton Casler, *Four Years in the Stonewall Brigade,* 56–57; Hunter, *Johnny Reb and Billy Yank,* 159.
23. Charles L. Ward, "Think of Your Head in the Morning" (Columbia, S.C.: B. Duncan & Co., 1863). The song was reprinted in *Songs of Humor and Sentiment* (Richmond: J. W. Randolph, 1863) under the title "Tom Jennings' Headache."

24. C. D. Benson, "Here's Your Mule: Comic Camp Song and Chorus" (Nashville: C. D. Benson, 1862); W. W. Carnes, "Here's Your Mule," *Confederate Veteran* 37 (1929): 373–374.

25. Bromfield Lewis Ridley, *Battles and Sketches of the Army of Tennessee* (Mexico, Mo.: Missouri Printing and Publishing Co., 1906), 633–34.

26. A. Pinder and P. Nutt, "Goober Peas" (New Orleans: A. E. Blackmar, 1866).

27. E. Heinemann, "Here's Your Mule Schottisch" (New Orleans: P. P. Werlein and Halsey, 1862). Since Werlein went out of business after the Federal occupation of the city in April 1862, the song had to have been written before then.

28. McPherson, *For Cause and Comrades*, 102; L. J. Daniel, *Soldering in the Army*, 127–30.

29. *The Punch Songster: A Collection of Familiar and Original Songs and Ballads* (Richmond: Punch Office, 1864); *The General Lee Songster: Being a Collection of the Most Popular Sentimental, Patriotic, and Comic Songs* (Macon and Savannah: John C. Schreiner & Son; Augusta, Ga.: Schreiner & Hewitt, 1865) (contents page lists copyright of 1864).

30. W. P. Jones, *Under the Stars and Bars*, 164.

31. A Lady [Mary Ann Webster Longborough], *My Cave Life in Vicksburg* (New York: Appleton, 1864), 119.

32. James Stevens, "Hostages to Hunger," *Tennessee Historical Quarterly* 48 no. 3 (1989): 131–43.

33. W. C. Davis, *Diary of Confederate Soldier*, 3, 45.

34. Casler, *Four Years in the Stonewall Brigade*, 78.

35. J. Kaiser, "Letters from the Front," *Journal of Illinois State Historical Society* 56 (1963): 158.

36. F. J. Taylor to friend, 11 February, 1863, in F. J. Taylor, *Reluctant Rebel*, 91.

37. Casler, *Four Hears in the Stonewall Brigade*, 208.

38. De Leon, *Four Years in Rebel Capitals*, 307–308; De Leon, *Belles*, 274.

39. Pea bread was a combination of ground peas mixed with cornmeal to add bulk to bread. Vicksburg surrendered on 4th July 1863.

40. O. Dalsheimer, "A life on the Vicksburg bluff," 1863, in Paul Glass and Louis Singer, eds., *Singing Soldiers* (New York: Da Capo, 1988), 211–13.

41. Pinder and Nutt, "Goober Peas."

42. The song wasn't published until after the war, but the last lines ("I wish the war was over . . .") indicate it was sung before then.

43. Ye Tragic and Ye Comic, "Short Rations" (Augusta, Ga.: Blackmar & Bro., 1864).

44. The paper shortage and its impact on the Confederate music industry are examined in chapter 14.

45. Carlton McCarthy, "Camp Fires of the Boys in Gray," *Southern Historical Society Papers* 1 (1876): 80.

46. Thomas P. Lowry, *The Story the Soldiers Wouldn't Tell* (Mechanicsburg, Pa.: Stackpole Books, 1994); cf. L. J. Daniel, *Soldering in the Army*, 98–99.

47. Lowry, *Story the Soldiers* passim.

CHAPTER 10

1. Hunter, *Johnny Reb and Billy Yank*, 26.

2. John Gilchrist, *Civil War in North Carolina* (Chapel Hill: University of North Carolina Press, 1963), 24.

3. F. J. Taylor, *Reluctant Rebel*, 29.

4. Cater, *As It Was*, 82.

5. Diary entry, Tuesday, 13 January 1863, in F. Jay Taylor, *Reluctant Rebel*, 77.

6. Ibid.

7. LaBree, *Camp Fires of the Confederacy*, 115–116.

8. George Dallas Mosgrove, "Following Morgan's Plume through Indiana and Ohio," *Southern Historical Society Papers* 23 (1907): 118–119.

9. Quoted by Silber, *Songs of the Civil War,* 236; see also McMorries, *History of the First Regiment,* 52.

10. Lasswell, *Rags and Hope,* 171–72.

11. Samuel R. Watkins, *Co. Aytch: Maury Grays First Tennessee* (Nashville: Cumberland Presbyterian Publishing House, 1882), 51. About 10 percent of the approximately fifteen hundred pieces of sheet music published in the South during the Civil War was dance music, usually bearing titles paying tribute to some state ("Alabama Secession Gallop"), military hero ("The Stonewall Quickstep"), military unit ("Washington Artillery Band Polka") or battle, especially First Manassas ("The Manassas Polka").

12. J. Cannon, *Inside of Rebeldom: The Daily Life of a Private in the Confederate Army* (Washington, D.C.: National Tribune, 1900), 90; Silver, *A Life for the Confederacy,* 66. Not all Southerners were enamored with dancing. Some churches totally opposed it. A spokesman for the Second Presbyterian Church in Knoxville, Tennessee, saw dancing as a Yankee ploy: "The Church does not allow its members to dance, and we have known instances of the church having members up for violating its religious rules . . . this behavior might be all right in Massachusetts to get votes but not in Tennessee." The principal of the Knoxville Female Academy felt balls and public dancing parties were "criminal in [their] tendencies, as well as injurious to progress in study," and promised to expel anyone caught at them. (*Knoxville American Statesman,* 6 July 1853, *Knoxville Register,* 23 January 1850, quoted in E. K. Crews, "A History of Music in Knoxville, Tennessee, 1781 to 1910" [Ph.D. diss., Florida State University, 1961], 58). But these feelings were definitely in the minority. Much more common was the opinion expressed by the *Nashville Daily Gazette* in 1853: "the youth of our cities commence business life so early and frequently devote themselves to it with such fixed intensity, that exhilarating amusement is necessary to their physical and mental health, and, of all amusements, dancing is the most inspiring and the least injurious. It brings our young men under the gentle, softening, humanizing influence of the more beautiful and holier portion of creation and thus profitably occupies the hours which might otherwise be spent in less innocent relaxation" (quoted in Francis Garvin Davenport, *Cultural Life in Nashville on the Eve of the Civil War* [Chapel Hill: University of North Carolina Press, 1941], 165).

13. John Brickell, *The Natural History of North Carolina* (New York: Johnson Reprint Corp., 1969), 40; Rosalie Roos, *Travels in America 1851–1855* (Carbondale: Southern Illinois University Press, 1982), 92.

14. Cater, *As It Was,* 55. On the different dances popular in the nineteenth century, see Ronald Pearsall, *Victorian Popular Music* (Detroit: Gale Research Co., 1973), chap. 12.

15. W. J. Florence and T. Comer, "The Captain with His Whiskers" (Richmond: J. W. Randolph, 186–). Officers and enlisted men sported beards not because it was the style, or because a beard was manly, but because beards were recommended as a way of protecting them against the elements. The *Southern Military Manual* for 1861 ([New Orleans: H. P. Lathrop, 1861], ch. 19, 113) advised readers to "let the whole beard grow, but not longer than some three inches. This strengthens and thickens its growth, and thus makes a more perfect protection for the lungs against dust, and of the throat against winds and cold in winter, while in summer a greater respiration of the skin is induced, with an increase of evaporation, hence greater coolness of the parts on the outside, while the throat is less feverish, thirsty and dry." Mindful of the health-related benefits of wearing a beard, many officers sported luxuriant beards that were also very stylish, prompting the popular wartime song about beards.

16. On the tradition of the "professor of music" in early America, see D. Maurer's article by that name in *Musical Quarterly* 36 (1950): 511–524.

17. Kmen, *Music in New Orleans,* 5; cf. Liliane Crete, *Daily Life in Louisiana, 1815–1830* (Baton Rouge: Louisiana State University Press, 1981), 202–14.

18. Crete, *Daily Life in Louisiana,* 203.

19. Mrs. Matilda Charlotte Houstoun, *Texas and the Gulf of Mexico; or, Yachting in the New World* (Philadelphia: G. B. Zeiber, 1845), 1:162.

20. *Memoirs of Mollie McDowall,* 1978.
21. Norman D. Brown, ed., *Journey to Pleasant Hill: The Civil War Letters of Captain Elijah Petty: Walker's Texas Division, C.S.A.* (San Antonio: University of Texas Institute of Texan Cultures, 1982), 314.
22. James Huffman, *Up and Downs of a Confederate Soldier* (New York: Wm. E. Rudge's Sons, 1940) 81–82.
23. Maj. William A. Smith, *The Anson Guards: Company C, Fourteenth Regiment North Carolina Volunteers, 1861–1865* (Charlotte, N.C.: Stone Publishing Co., 1914), 163.
24. Cater, *As It Was,* 82.
25. W. A. Smith, *Anson Guards,* 163; cf. Daniel E. Sutherland, *Reminiscences of a Private: William E. Bevens of the First Arkansas Infantry, C.S.A.* (Fayetteville: University of Arkansas Press, 1992), 37.
26. W. W. Parker, "How The Southern Soldiers Kept House during the War," *Southern Historical Society Papers* 23 (1895): 327.
27. Casler, *Four Years in the Stonewall Brigade,* 327.
28. F. S. Daniel, *Richmond Howitzers in the War* (1891; reprint, Gaithersburg, Md: Butternut Press, n.d.), 45–47.
29. Gordon, *Reminscences of Civil War,* 107–8.
30. Heros von Borcke, *Memoirs of the Confederate War for Independence* (Edinburgh: W. Blackwood, 1866), 1:193–197.
31. Mrs. Burton Harrison, *Recollections Grave and Gray* (New York: C. Scribner's Sons, 1911), 130.
32. DeLeon, *Belles,* 196–197; idem, *Four Years in Rebel Capitals,* 154.
33. De Leon, *Four Years in Rebel Capitals,* 154.
34. Ibid.
35. Owen, *In Camp and Battle,* 299.
36. Harrison, *Recollections Grave and Gray,* 50.
37. DeLeon, *Belles,* 217, 222; idem, *Four Years in Rebel Capitals,* 201–202; Harrison, *Recollections Grave and Gray,* 129–130.
38. Rose, *Victorian America,* 124–25.
39. J. McArthur, "Those Texians Are Number One Men," *Southwestern Historical Quarterly* 95 (1991–92): 492–494.
40. Lasswell, *Rags and Hope,* 53; Borcke, *Memoirs of War for Independence,* 2:173–174. See also "Theatrical in the Army," in *Southern Illustrated News,* 1864, reprinted in Harwell, *Confederate Reader,* 273–275.
41. Harold B. Simpson, *Hood's Texas Brigade: Lee's Grenadier Guard* (Dallas, Texas: Alcor Publishing Co., 1983), 68–69.
42. Owen, *In Camp and Battle,* 205; cf. Ex-boy [Royall W. Figg], *Where Men Only Dare to Go! or, The Story of a Boy Company (C.S.A.)* (Richmond: Whitten and Shepperson, 1885), 95.
43. Ex-boy, *Where Men Dare,* 95.
44. Casler, *Four Hears in the Stonewall Brigade,* 204–5; cf. Marshall Moore Brice, *The Stonewall Brigade Band* (Verona, Va.: McClure Printing Co., 1967), 39–40.
45. LeGrand James Wilson, *Confederate Soldier* (Memphis: Memphis State University, 1973), 149.
46. Gilbert Moxley Sorrel, *Recollections of a Confederate Staff Officer* (Jackson, Tenn.: McCowat-Mercer Press, Inc., 1958), 51–52.
47. Gordon, *Reminscences of Civil War,* 99.
48. Fitzgerald Ross, *Cities and Camps of the Confederate States* (Urbana: University of Illinois Press, 1958), 166–167.
49. Sweeney had been a private in one of Stuart's regiments. When Stuart learned of Sweeney's talents on the banjo, he detached him to his personal staff. Sweeney played the banjo "with amazing cleverness [and] knew sentimental, bibulous, martial, nautical, comic

songs . . . [and] was carried about with him by the General everywhere," said Stuart's staff officer, Heros Von Borcke *Memoirs of War for Independence,* 1:270–271; cf. William Willis Blackford, *War Years with Jeb Stuart* (New York: Charles Scribner's Sons, 1945), 50–51. Besides Sweeney, Stuart had two fiddlers in his entourage and Mulatto Bob, his personal servant, "who worked the bones with the most surprising and extraordinary agility, and became so excited that both head and feet were in constant employment, and his body twisted about so rapidly and curiously that one could not help fearing that he would [dislocate] his limbs and fly to pieces in the midst of the breakdown" (Borcke, *Memoirs of War for Independence,* 1:270–71.

50. Borcke, *Memoirs of War for Independence,* 1:270–271.
51. Lasswell, *Rags and Hope,* 78–80.
52. Ibid, 83. For other anecdotes about singing generals, see Wise, *End of an Era,* 336–337; Philip Van Doren Stern, *An End to Valor: The Last Days of the Civil War* (Boston: Houghton Mifflin Co., 1958), 125; Arthur Crew Inman, ed., *Soldier of the South: General Pickett's War Letters to His Wife* (Boston: Houghton Mifflin Co., 1928), 128, 130, 132; M. A. M. Jackson, *Life and Letters,* 184.
53. Woodward, ed., *Mary Chesnut's Civil War,* 504, 509; Wise, *End of an Era,* 335–337.
54. W. Lord, *Fremantle Diary,* 28.
55. Varina Davis, *Jefferson Davis: Ex-President of the Confederate States of America* (New York, Belford Co., 1890), 304.
56. W. B. Jones, *Under the Stars and Bars,* 162.
57. Ibid., 20, 23; cf. Durkein, ed., *John Dooley,* 84.
58. McCarthy, "Camp Fires," 80.
59. Cater, *As It Was,* 30–31. Teachers in the South taught their pupils to read music using shape notes. In place of standard round notes, "shape" notes were either square, round, triangular, or diamond-shaped, and each shape had the syllable "fa," "sol,""la," or "me" attached to it, depending on its position on the scale. Because of this schema, shape-note singing was also called "fasola" singing. The shape note system originated in New England in the early 1700s, and though it was largely replaced in the North in the early 1800s by the modern musical scale, it continued to exist alongside the modern notation in the South.
60. The classic treatment of white spirituals is George Pullen Jackson's *White Spirituals in the Southern Uplands: The Story of the Fasola Folks, Their Songs, Singing, and "Buckwheat Notes"* (Chapel Hill: University of North Carolina Press, 1933). The most memorable of these was the Great Revival of 1801. Over twenty-five thousand people from what was then the rural parts of America (Ohio, Kentucky, Indiana) drove, in some cases hundreds of miles, to pray and sing hymns together in Kentucky. They prayed individually by day, and collectively at night around huge roaring campfires where preachers exhorted them to publicly declare their faith while thousands of voices sang "Roll Jordan," "Satan's Kingdom," and other spirituals. Slaves didn't take part in these fiery confessions but slave owners brought them along to these "Great Awakenings" so that they could be redeemed by their presence. The slaves stayed in their own quarters and learned the white spirituals sung at these meetings, later altering them to reflect their own experiences.
61. W. B. Jones, *Under the Stars and Bars,* 162–63.
62. Durkein, *John Dooley,* 54–55, 59.
63. Byron Farwell, *Stonewall: A Biography of General Thomas J. Jackson* (New York: W. W. Norton, 1992), 125.
64. Rose, *Victorian America* (1992).
65. On Victorian America's penchant for communal leisure activities, see ibid., 123–134.
66. June Kimble, "The 14th Tenn. Glee Club." Confederate Museum, Richmond, n.d.; J. H. Jones, "The Rank and File at Vicksburg," *Publications of the Mississippi Historical Society* 7 (1906): 26.

67. J. H. Jones, "Rank and File," 26.
68. W. C. Davis, *Diary of Confederate Soldier,* 3; Parker, "Southern Soldiers," 318–328.
69. Henry C. Work, "Kingdom's Coming; or The Song of the Contraband, As Sung by the First Tennessee Opera Troupe" (Augusta, Ga.: Blackmar & Bro.). (Originally published in Chicago in 1862.)
70. *Richmond Whig,* 10 February 1864.
71. Sara Agnes Rice Pryor, *Reminiscences of Peace and War* (New York: Macmillan Co., 1905), 263–64.
72. Woodward, *Mary Chesnut's Civil War,* 15 January 1864.
73. Owen, *In Camp and Battle,* 299.
74. DeLeon, *Four Years in Rebel Capitals,* 351; Wise, *End of an Era,* 336.
75. Henry Kyd Douglas, *I Rode with Stonewall: Being Chiefly the War Experience of the Youngest Member of Jackson's Staff from the John Brown Raid to the Hanging of Mrs. Surratt* (Chapel Hill: University of North Carolina Press, 1940), 322.
76. Pryor, *Reminiscences,* 327.

CHAPTER 11

1. Hunter, *Johnny Reb and Billy Yank,* 101–102.
2. Parker, "Southern Soldiers," 327; C. S. Avery, "Sketch of Rockbridge Artillery," *Southern Historical Society Papers* 23 (1895): 121.
3. Lasswell, *Rags and Hope,* 69.
4. W. B. Jones, *Under the Stars and Bars,* 216.
5. McCarthy, *Detailed Minutiae,* 45–46; cf. John H. Worsham, *One of Jackson's Foot Calvary: His Experiences and What He Saw during the War, 1861–1865; Including a History of "F Company," Richmond, Va., 21st Regiment Virginia Infantry, Second Brigade, Jackson's Division, Second Corps, A. N. Va.* (1912; reprint, Wilmington, N.C.: Broadfoot Publishing Co., 1991), 156–158; Goodloe, *Confederate Echoes,* 105–107, 109–116.
6. McCarthy, *Detailed Minutiae,* 52.
7. Lasswell, *Rags and Hope,* 191.
8. English Combatant, *Battle-Fields of the South,* 309.
9. Ibid.
10. C. D. Grace, "Rodes' Division at Gettysburg," *Confederate Veteran* 5 (1897): 614.
11. Jacob Hoke, *The Great Invasion of 1863; or, General Lee in Pennsylvania* (Dayton, Ohio: W. J. Shuey, 1888), 135.
12. Quoted by R. E. Myers, *The Zollie Tree* (Louisville: Filson Club Press, 1964), 59.
13. J. W. Reid, *History of the Fourth Regiment of S.C. Volunteers* (Dayton, Ohio: Morningside Bookshop, 1975), 60.
14. Washington Ives to sister, 20 October 1862, Letters, Florida State Archives, Gainesville.
15. Edward Parsons Tobie, *History of the First Maine Cavalry, 1861–1865* (Boston: Emery and Hughes, 1887), 392.
16. U.S. War Department, *The War of the Rebellion: A Compilation of Official Records of the Union and Confederate Armies* (Washington, D.C.: Government Printing Office, 1880–1901), series T, vol. 11, pt. 1, 458–59; hereafter cited as *O.R.*; Richard Wheeler, *Sword over Richmond: An Eyewitness History of McClellan's Peninsula Campaign* (New York: Harper & Row, 1986), 157–58.
17. W. Lord, *Fremantle Diary,* 260.
18. Thomas Cooper DeLeon said that he had no less than forty-seven melodies and dirges on Stonewall Jackson, several dozen on Turner Ashby, and a score on Jeb Stuart. (*Four Years in Rebel Capitals,* 296-297.)
19. Casler, *Four Years in the Stonewall Brigade,* 157; Goolrick, "He Didn't Like Dixie!" 5–10; Lenoir Chambers, *Stonewall Jackson* (New York: W. Morrow, 1959), 2:442–58.
20. Quoted by Goolrick, "He Didn't Like," 6.

20a. Louise Wigfall Wright, *A Southern Girl in '61: The Wartime Memoirs of a Confederate Senator's Daughter* (New York: Doubleday, Page & Co., 1905), 125–26.

21. Woodward, *Mary Chesnut's Civil War,* 22 July 1861, 107.

22. *Army Regulations,* sect. 75, art. 32.

23. Casler, *Four Years in the Stonewall Brigade,* 218–19.

24. The band was originally from Staunton, Virginia. At the outbreak of the war, many of the musicians in the band enlisted as the 5th Virginia Regimental Band. In March 1863, the band was combined with other regimental bands in its brigade into the First Brigade Band, which was then dubbed the "Stonewall Brigade Band." The original band remained with the brigade for the entire four years of the war. When Lee surrendered at Appomattox on 9 April 1865, the band members were allowed to keep their instruments as part of the surrender terms. These pieces are currently on display at the Stonewall Brigade Band hall in Staunton. See Brice, *Stonewall Brigade Band* cf. W. J. Worsham, *The Old Nineteenth Tennessee Regiment, C.S.A. June 1861 April 1865* (Knoxville, Tenn.: Paragon Printing Co., 1902), 17; Casler, *Four Years in the Stonewall Brigade,* 48. J. A. Hiner, "The Stonewall Brigade Band," *Confederate Veteran* 8 (1900): 304. See also Robertson, *Stonewall Brigade,* 47; Farwell, *Stonewall, 125; cf. M. A. M. Jackson,* Life and Letters, *184.*

25. Wilson, *Confederate Soldier,* 149.

26. The regimental band of the 26th North Carolina Infantry was composed mainly of Moravians from Salem, North Carolina. The band remained with the 26th throughout the war and was captured with it on the retreat from Petersburg. Most of what is known about it, and Confederate bands in general, comes from a diary kept by Julius Leinbach (1834-1930), its cornetist, edited by H. H. Hall, *Johnny Reb Band.* Letters written by J. Edward Peterson, another member of the 26th North Carolina Regimental Band, are located at the Moravian Music Center, Winston-Salem, N.C. Excerpts of these letters can be found in J. Edward Peterson, "A Bandsman's Letters to Home from the War," *Moravian Musical Journal* 36, no. 1 (1991): 5–8.

27. H. H. Hall, *Johnny Reb Band,* 96.

28. Ibid.

29. Casler, *Four Hears in the Stonewall Brigade,* 48; Ella Lonn, *Foreigners in the Confederacy* (Gloucester, Mass.: Peter Smith, 1965); Cater, *As It Was,* 179.

30. Xavier B. Debray, "A Sketch of Debray's 26th Regiment of Texas Cavalry," *Southern Historical Society Papers* 13 (1885): 157.

31. Robertson, *Stonewall Brigade,* 34.

32. Watkins, *Co. Aytch,* 50.

33. George M. Neese, *Three Years in the Confederate Horse Artillery* (New York: Neale Publishing Co., 1911), 186-87. For Southern reactions to Northern bands passing through their towns, see Katherine Macbeth Jones, *When Sherman Came* (Indianapolis: Bobbs Merrill Co., 1964), 7.

34. Inman, *Pickett's Letters,* 44–45.

35. W. Lord, *Freemantle Diary,* 239–240.

36. Edwin C. Bearss, ed., *A Louisiana Confederate: Diary of Felix Pierre Poche* (Natchitoches, La.: Northwestern State University Press, 1972), 12.

37. William H. Tunnard, *Southern Record: The History of the Third Regiment, Louisiana Infantry* (Dayton, Ohio: Morningside Books, 1970), 43.

38. W. A. Smith, *Anson Guards,* 229.

39. H. H. Hall, *Johnny Reb Band,* 57

40. Walter Clark, *Histories of the Several Regiments and Battalions from North Carolina in the Great War, 1861–1865* (Goldsboro, N.C.: Nash Brothers, 1901). 2:399.

41. George Anson Bruce, *The Twentieth Regiment of Massachusetts Volunteer Infantry, 1861–1865* (Boston: Houghton-Mifflin Co., 1906), 396.

42. Cooke, *Wearing Gray,* 368.

43. Worsham, *Jackson's Foot Cavalry,* 68–69; Frank M. Mixson, *Reminiscences of a Private (Company # 1st) S.C. Vols.* (Columbia, S.C.: Hagoods State Co., 1910), 37–38; James Dinkins, *By an Old Johnnie: Personal Recollections and Experiences in the Confederate Army, 1861–1865* (Cincinnati: Robert Clarke Co., 1897), 76–77.

44. H. A. Hall, *Johnny Reb Band,* passim.

45. Casler, *Four Years in the Stonewall Brigade,* 210.

46. Valentine, *Diary and letters,* 161.

47. S. Millet Thompson, *Thirteenth Regiment of New Hampshire Volunteer Infantry in the War of the Rebellion, 1861–1865* (Boston: Houghton Mifflin and Co., 1888), 369.

48. Tobie, *First Maine Cavalry,* 392.

49. Ferguson, "Bands of the Confederacy" places the number somewhat higher. See appendix A for a listing of known Confederate bands. In 1798 the U.S. Marine Corps became the first branch of the U.S. military service to staff a band with its own military personnel. The U.S. Military Academy at West Point followed in 1815; the Naval Academy delayed until 1852. By 1832 regimental bands could have up to 10 musicians plus a chief musician. In addition to their musical duties, bandsmen received military training and had to serve in the ranks if they were needed. The number of bandsmen allotted per regiment was boosted twice more, first to 16 during the Mexican War of 1847, and then to 24 in 1857. On 22 July 1861, the U.S. Congress approved a band of up to 24 musicians for each Federal regiment. There was no problem filling that quota. When Federal bands were at their peak in 1861, 143 of the 200 regiments in the Army of the Potomac had a band. (Kenneth E. Olson, *Music and Musket: Bands and Bandsmen of the American Civil War* [Westport, Conn.: Greenwood Press, 1981], 72.) The entire Union army had a total of 2,494 regiments (Frederick H. Dyer, *A Compendium of the War of the Rebellion* [New York: Thomas Yoseloff, 1959], 1:37), creating a potential 39,904 musicians in blue (Olson, *Music and Musket,* 76). Once the enormous cost of maintaining these bands was realized, there was a drastic reduction in the number of Union regiments permitted to have them.

50. Quoted by Barrett, *Civil War in North Carolina,* 24.

51. An English Combatant, *Battle-fields of the South,* 309–10.

52. The only Confederate cavalry regiments to have their own bands were the 1st and 2nd Virginia Cavalry, the 1st, 2nd and 4th North Carolina Cavalry (9th, 19th, 59th North Carolina Regiments), and the 3rd and 7th Kentucky Regiments. Being a bandsman in a cavalry regiment had its challenges in more ways than one. Not only was it difficult to play while riding a horse, there were also mundane problems to contend with, like getting the slide of a trombone tangled in blackberry vines as the musician rode by (Fairfax Davis Downey, *Clash Of Cavalry: The Battle of Brandy Station, June 9, 1863* [New York: David McKay Co., 1959], 7).

53. See appendix A.

54. L. J. Daniel, *Soldering in the Army,* 91.

55. General Orders nos. 15 and 48, July 1861; *O.R.,* Series III, vol. 1, 373–74.

56. *O.R.,* Series III, vol. 1, 728.

57. *O.R.,* Series III, vol. 1, 596–97.

58. *O.R.,* Series III, vol. 2, 336.

59. *O.R.,* Series III, vol. 2, 270–79.

60. Garofalo and Elrod, *Pictorial History,* 53.

61. *Savannah Morning News,* 10 February 1863, 2. The ad ran for several editions.

62. Silver, *Life for the Confederacy,* 55.

63. Ibid., 292.

64. Lonn, *Foreigners,* 257.

65. Free black musicians played in a number of different drum corps in the Confederate army. A black barber, George Douglas, led the 10th Georgia Volunteer (Company A) Drum Corps. (R. Lockwood Tower, ed., *A Carolinian Goes to War: The Civil War*

Narrative of Arthur Middleton Manigualt, Brigadier General, C.S.A. [Charleston: University of South Carolina Press, 1983], 5.) The 18th Georgia Battalion Field Band was originally a four-man fife and drum corps made up of black musicians, two of them slaves, the other two freemen. At its peak, the band had six black musicians. (L. Henderson, *Roster of the Confederate Soldiers of Georgia, 1861–1865* [Hapeville, Ga.: Longino & Porter, Inc., 1955–64], 150.) Another black man, Alexander Harris, led the First Georgia Volunteer Drum Corps. Harris had been a member of the Savannah Republican Blues prior to the war. When that militia unit enlisted, Harris followed them. He is listed in the roster as "not mustered but in service," meaning not formally enlisted in a unit, a concession to whites who resented the idea of a black man enlisting in their units (L. Henderson, *Roster*).

66. McCarthy, *Detailed Minutiae*, 52.
67. John G. Pressley, "The Wee Nee Volunteers of Williamsburg District, South Carolina, in the First (Hagood's) Regiment," *Southern Historical Society Papers* 26 (1888): 173.
68. McMorries, *History of the First Regiment*, 51.
69. Quoted by Wiley, *Life of Johnny Reb*, 157.
70. H. H. Hall, *Johnny Reb Band*, 65.
71. DeLeon, *Four Years in Rebel Capitals*, 70.
72. Ross, *Cities and Camps*, 40.
73. W. Lord, *Fremantle Diary*, 58.
74. An English Combatant, *Battle-Fields of the South*, 300.
75. DeLeon, *Four Years in Rebel Capitals*, 70.
76. Betsy Fleet and John D. Fuller, eds., *Green Mount: A Virginia Plantation Family during the Civil War: Being the Journal of Benjamin Robert Fleet and Letters of His Family* (Charlottesville: University Press of Virginia, 1962), 337.
77. DeLeon, *Four Years in Rebel Capitals*, 70.
78. D. S. Miller, *Drum Taps*, 175.

CHAPTER 12

1. [George F. Root], "Just before the Battle Mother" (Richmond: J. W. Davies & Sons, 186).
2. Rose, *Victorian America*.
3. Ted Barclay to sister, 14 July 1861, in Charles W. Turner, ed., *Ted Barclay, Liberty Hall Volunteers: Letters from the Stonewall Brigade* (Natural Bridge Station, Va.: Rockbridge Publishing Co., 1992), 94.
4. Joseph M. Goff and Clarke Ilsey, "Kiss Me before I Die, Mother!" (Augusta, Ga.: Blackmar & Bro., 186-); M[atthias] Keller, "Mother, Oh! Sing Me to Rest (Richmond: Geo. Dunn & Compy.; Columbia, S.C.: Julian A. Selby, 186-); Mrs. M. W. Stratton and Jos. Hart Denck, "Keep Me Awake! Mother (Macon, Ga.: John C. Schreiner & Son, 1863); Florency Percy and John H. Hewitt, "Rock Me to Sleep, Mother" (Columbia, S.C.: Julian A. Selby, 1862); Stephen Glover, "Mother! Can This the Glory Be?" (Mobile, Ala.: J. H. Snow, 1862); Joseph Hart Denck, "Mother Is the Battle Over?" (Columbia, S.C.: Blanton Duncan, 186-).
5. E. Bowers and Henry Tucker, "Dear Mother I've Come Home to Die" (Richmond: Geo. Dunn & Compy., 186-).
6. Charles Carroll Sawyer and C. F. Thompson, "Who Will Care for Mother Now?" (Richmond: George Dunn and Compy., 1863). In addition to writing songs, Sawyer also published music in Brooklyn, New York.
7. Charles Carroll Sawyer, "Mother Would Comfort Me" (Augusta, Ga.: Blackmar & Bro., 186-).
8. Charles Carroll Sawyer, "When This Cruel War Is Over" (Richmond: Geo. Dunn & Compy., 1864).

9. Heaps and Heaps (*Singing Sixties,* 224) state that the song so deadened morale that some generals forbade its singing in camp, but they do not document this statement. One such "answer" was John Hill Hewitt and Hermann L. Schreiner's "When upon the Field of Glory" (Macon, Ga.: J. C. Schreiner & Son, 1864):

> Weep no longer, dearest,
> Tears are now in vain. . . .
> When this cruel war is over,
> We may meet again.

10. Quoted in William Smyth Babcock Matthews, *A Hundred Years of Music in America* (Chicago: L. Howe, 1889), 74.
11. Silber, *Songs of the Civil War,* 117.
12. William S. Hays, "The Drummer Boy of Shiloh" (Louisville: D. Faulds, 1862).
13. Shiloh inspired the war's first antiwar song, "The Battle of Shiloh Hill." Written by M. B. Smith, a soldier serving with the 2nd regiment, Texas volunteers, to the tune of the "Wandering Sailor," it described the carnage from the perspective of the actual fighters, and was too graphic to be turned into sheet music:

> Come all you valiant solders, and a story I will tell,
> It is of a noted battle you all remember well;
> It was an awful strife, and will cause your blood to chill,
> It was the famous battle that was fought on Shiloh Hill!
>
> The battle it raged on, though dead and dying men
> Lay thick all o'er the ground, on the hill and on the glen.
> And from their deadly wounds their blood ran like a rill
> Such were the mournful sights that I saw on Shiloh Hill.
>
> Before the day was ended the battle ceased to roar,
> And thousands of brave soldiers had fell to rise no more;
> They left their vacant ranks for some other ones to fill,
> And now their moldering bodies all lie on Shiloh Hill.

(Fagan, *Southern War Songs,* 326–27.) On Shiloh's impact on the South, see Wiley Sword, *Shiloh: Bloody April* (New York: Morrow, 1974).
14. [William S. Hays] and Clarke Ilsey, "The Drummer Boy of Shiloh" (Augusta, Ga.: Blackmar & Bro., 1863). Songs about drummer boys faded from the public mind after the war, and their place in the conflict was forgotten until the next decade when Eastman Johnson (1824–1906) painted "The Wounded Drummer Boy." That painting, one of the best-known Civil War pictures of the late nineteenth century, shows a drummer boy beating the calls as he is being carried on the shoulder of an older comrade. Johnson is said to have witnessed the scene at the battle of Antietam. The painting was first exhibited at the National Academy in 1872 and the catalog explained that "a drummer boy was disabled by a shot in the leg. As he lay upon the field he called to his comrades, 'Carry me, and I'll drum her through!' They tied up his wound, a big soldier took him upon his shoulders, and he drummed through the fight." *Civil War Times Illustrated* 3, no. 1 (1964): 1.
15. Michael Barton, *Goodmen: The Character of Civil War Soldiers* (University Park: Pennsylvania State University Press, 1981), 57–62.
16. Henry C. Work, "Little Major" (Cleveland: S. Brainard's Sons, 1862); see Silber, *Songs of the Civil War,* 120.
17. Woodward, *Mary Chesnut's Civil War,* 370.

18. Ibid.
19. Marrie Revenel De La Coste and John H. Hewitt, "Somebody's Darling" (Macon and Savannah: John Schreiner and Son, 1864).
20. A. E. A. Muse, "My Warrior Boy" (New Orleans: A. E. Blackmar, 1864); Henri Fourrier, "La jeune Mere louisianaise; Ou, hymne au drapeau confedere (New Orleans: Henri Fourrier, 1861); Haynes Bayly and Hermann L. Schreiner, "The Mother of the Soldier Boy" (Macon and Savannah: J. C. Schreiner & Son, 1864).
21. John Pond Ordway, "Let Me Kiss Him for His Mother" (New Orleans: Blackmar Bro., 1861). (For its impact on the home front, see John F. Marszalek, ed., *Diary of Miss Emma Holmes* [Baton Rouge: Louisiana State University Press, 1979], 91.)
22. Denck, "Mother Is the Battle Over?"
23. Alice Hawthorne, "What Is Home without a Mother?" (Augusta, Ga.: Blackmar & Bro., ca. 1863).
24. F. J. Taylor, *Reluctant Rebel,* 92.
25. [Henry S. Washburn] and George F. Root, "The Vacant Chair" (Richmond: Davies & Sons, 186-).
26. See H. L. Jillson, "The Vacant Chair," *The New England Magazine* 16 (1897): 131–145.
27. Ibid.
28. For the story behind "The Girl I Left behind Me" see chapter 2.
29. J. Dickson Bruns and John H. Hewitt, "I Am Fondly Dreaming of Thee" (Richmond: Geo. Dunn & Company, ca. 1862); George Linley Foley Hall, "Ever of Thee" (Augusta, Ga.: Blackmar & Bro., ca. 1863). The latter was so popular, authorship was claimed by several songwriters. The controversy is described by Shaf J. A. Fitzgerald in *Stories of Famous Songs* (Philadelphia: J. B. Lippincott Co., 1898), 1:90–104. Confederate publishers issued nine editions of the song (five are no longer extant) and it was reprinted in eight different songsters: *Army Songster, Bonnie Blue Flag Song Book, The Carolina Songsters* (Stanton, Va.: n.p., 1863), *The General Lee Songster: Being a Collection of the Most Popular, Sentimental, Patriotic, and Comic Songs* (Macon and Savannah: John C. Schiner [*sic*] & Son; Augusta: Schneiner [*sic*] & Hewitt, 1865 [contents page lists copyright of 1864]), *Songs of Humor And Sentiment, Jack Morgan Songster, The Stonewall Song Book: Being a Collection of Patriotic, Sentimental and Comic Songs* 2nd ed. (Richmond: West & Johnson, 1865), *The Stonewall Song Book: Being a Collection of Patriotic, Sentimental, and Comic Songs,* 11th edition—Enlarged! (Richmond: West & Johnston, 1865); see the bibliography for a listing of the many songsters published in the South during the war. Fred Buckley and E. Clarke Ilsley, "I Am Dreaming Still of Thee" (Augusta, Ga.: Blackmar and Bro., ca. 1862); Stephen Foster, "I See Her Still in My Dreams" (Augusta, Ga.: Blackmar & Bro., ca. 1863); J. E. Carpenter and W. T. Wrighton, "Her Bright Smile Haunts Me Still" (Richmond: Geo. Dunn & Compy., 1864); Giorgio Stigelli, "The Brightest Eyes" (Macon, Ga.: John C. Schreiner & Son, ca. 1862).
30. Trout, *Riding with Stuart,* 61.
31. Cabaniss, *Civil War Journal,* 16 January 1864; Woodward, *Mary Chesnut's Civil War,* 356.
32. Thomas Dunn and Nelson Kneass, "Ben Bolt; or, Oh! Don't You Remember (Augusta, Ga.: Blackmar & Bro., ca. 1863); Lady John Montague-Douglas [Alicia Ann Scott], "Annie Lawrie" [*sic*] (Augusta, Ga.: Blackmar & Bro., ca. 1863). The original Annie Laurie was the daughter of Sir Robert Laurie, first baronet of the Maxwelton family, which was created in 1685. She was renowned for her beauty and was courted by a Mr. Douglas. Although she promised to marry Douglas, she instead married a Mr. Ferguson. Douglas wrote a poem about the reneged promise that is almost identical to the present version by Lady Scott; George Morris and J. R. Thomas, "Annie of the Vale" (Richmond: Geo. Dunn & Compy., 1864); W. W. Fosdick and George R. Poulton, "Aura Lee, or, the Maid with Golden Hair" (Richmond: Geo. Dunn & Compy.,

1864); Stephen Glover, "The Song of Blanche Alpen" (Augusta, Ga.: Blackmar & Bro., ca. 1863); B. F. Woolf and Fred Buckley, "Darling Little Blue-Eyed Nell" (Augusta, Ga.: Blackmar & Bro.; and Blackmar & Co., New Orleans, ca. 1863); George W. Elliott and J. R. Thomas, "Bonny Eloise" (Augusta, Ga.: Blackmar and Bro., ca. 1863); Capt. W. C. Capters and Theodore Von La Hache, "Carrie Bell" (Augusta, Ga.: Blackmar & Bro., 1861); G. M. Wickliffe and E. K. Cole, "Carrie Vaughan" (Augusta, Ga.: Blackmar Brothers, 1864); Charlie Wildwood and John Hill Hewitt, "Claribel" (Savannah, Augusta, and Macon: John C. Schreiner & Sons, 1866); Ernst W. Muller, "Ellen Bayne" (New Orleans: P. P. Werlein & Halsey, 1861); Dr. A. L. Green, "Gentle Nettie Moore" (Macon, Ga.: John W. Burke, 1862); Mrs. A. B. Crawford and Frederick Nicholls Crouch, "Kathleen Mavourneen" (Augusta, Ga.: Blackmar and Bro., ca. 1863); W. L. Gammage and J. E. T., "Lillie Terrell" (Augusta, Ga.: Blackmar & Co., ca. 1863); Stephen Foster, "Lula Is Gone" (Macon, Ga.: John C. Schreiner & Son, ca. 1863); C. Jefferys and Sydney Nelson, "Mary of Argyle" (Richmond: Geo Dunn & Compy., 1864); Hermann L. Schreiner, "Minnie Lee" (Macon and Savannah: J. C. Schreiner & Son, 1864); Amelia and Jason H. Newman, "Nelly Was Bright and Happy" (New Orleans: P. P. Werlein & Halsey, 1861).

33. "Mavourneen" is the anglicized Gaelic, *mo mhuirmin,* my sweetheart (Joseph Roach, "Barnumizing Diaspora: the 'Irish Skylark' Does New Orleans," *Theatre Journal* 50 (1998): 39–51. In addition to the Blackmars in Augusta, the song was also issued during the war by George Dunn in Richmond, Julian Selby in Columbia, John Schreiner in Macon, Jason McClure in Nashville, and Philip Werlein and Louis Grunewald in New Orleans. It also appeared in *The Army Songster, The Bold Soldier Boy's Song Book,* and *The New Confederate Flag Song Book.*

34. After the war, life for Crouch was austere. He died in 1896. Fighting against him during the war was another Irishman, James Marion Roche, whose favorite song while he was growing up in Ireland was Crouch's "Kathleen Mavourneen." Years later, when he heard Crouch was destitute, he changed his name to Crouch and became the composer's adopted son so he could take care of him (*Richmond Observer,* 20 August 1896).

35. " Ben Bolt': Something about the Authors of Words and Music of the Famous Song," *Brainard's Musical World* 32 (1895): 117–18; "The Story of Old Ben Bolt," *American Art Journal* 61 (1893): 458–59.

36. Alice Hawthorne, "Listen to the Mocking Bird" (Augusta, Ga.: Blackmar and Bro., 1864).

37. Cooke, *Wearing Gray,* 366–67.

38. The words and original arrangement for "Mockingbird" were Winner's but the melody was by Dick Milburn, a black street entertainer in Philadelphia, known as "Whistling Dick." Milburn earned a little money by entertaining passersby with his whistling. One of his best tunes imitated a mockingbird. Winner heard him whistling it one day and developed it into "Listen to the Mocking Bird" (Charles Eugene Claghorn, *The Mocking Bird: The Life and Diary of Its Author, Sep. Winner* (Philadelphia: Magee Press, 1937), 28–29.

39. Hon. Mrs. Caroline Norton, "Juanita" (Macon, Ga.; John C. Schreiner & Son, ca. 1862).

40. *The Army Songster, The Beauregard Songster Being a Collection of Patriotic, Sentimental, and Comic Songs, The Most Popular of the Day* (Macon and Savannah: John C. Schreiner & Son, 1864); *The Bold Soldier Boy's Song Book,* and *The Carolina Songster.* Norton's other songs issued by Confederate publishers included "The Officer's Funeral," "Bingen on the Rhine," "Would I Were with Thee" and "The Murmur of the Shell."

41. J[oseph] P[hilip] Knight, "The Yellow Rose of Texas" (Macon, Ga.: John Schreiner and Son, ca. 1863).

42. Bromfield Lewis Ridley, *Battles and Sketches of the Army of Tennessee* (Mexico, Mo.: Missouri Printing and Publishing Co., 1906), 439.

43. Martha Anne Turner, *The Yellow Rose of Texas: Her Saga and Her Song: With the Santa Anna Legend* (Austin: Shoah Creek Pub., 1976).

44. Woodward, *Mary Chesnut's Civil War,* 457, 722.

45. Basil Wilson Duke, *Reminiscences* (Garden City, N.Y.: Doubleday, Page & Co., 1911), 287.

46. Ibid, 287–88.

47. Rev. Henry D. L. Webster and J[oseph] P[hilbrick] Webster, "Lorena" (New Orleans: A. E. Blackmar & Bro., 186–).

48. James H. McNeilly, "The Story of Lorena, *Confederate Veteran* 23 (1915): 211.

49. "Paul Vane; or, Lorena's Reply" (Macon, Ga.: John Schreiner, 1863).

50. Lasswell, *Rags and Hope,* 80.

51. George Linley and Charles Osborne, "Bonny Jean" (Augusta, Ga.: Blackmar & Bro., 186–).

52. Lasswell, *Rags and Hope,* 78–79.

53. "Home, Sweet Home" was so well know that its lyrics were never published in sheet music in the Confederacy. On the theme of the exile, see Phil Eva, "Home Sweet Home? The 'Culture of Exile' in Mid-Victorian Popular Song," *Popular Music* 16 (1977): 131–50.

54. Lasswell, *Rags and Hope,* 104.

55. S. M. Thompson, *Thirteenth Regiment,* 61.

56. Stone, "War Music," 36, 543–60.

57. Lasswell, *Rags and Hope,* 209–10.

58. Mixson, *Reminiscences of a Private,* 37–38; cf. Worsham, *Old Nineteenth,* 68–69.

59. Sorrel, *Recollections,* 153.

60. Joseph A. Brown, *Memoirs of a Confederate Soldier* (Abingdon, Va.: Forum Press, 1940), 43–44.

61. For the popularity of "Home, Sweet Home" in the British army, see Palmer, *Lovely War,* 56.

62. C. F. Thompson and C[harles] C[aroll] Sawyer, "Who Will Care for Mother Now" (Richmond: Geo. Dunn & Co.; Columbia, S.C.: Julian A. Selby, 1863); Charles Caroll Sawyer, "Mother Would Comfort Me (If She Were Here)" (Augusta, Ga.: Blackmar & Bro., 186–.)

63. William Thomas Wrighton, "The Dearest Spot of Earth to Me Is Home" (Augusta, Ga.: Blackmar & Bro., ca. 1863).

64. Hermann L. Schreiner, "Take Me Home" (Macon and Savannah: J. C. Schreiner & Son, 1864); Charlie L. Ward, "My Natal Home" (Columbia, S.C.: B. Duncan & Co., 1862); E. Bowers and Henry Tucker, "Dear Mother, I've Come Home To Die (Richmond: Geo. Dunn & Co.; Columbia, S.C.: Julian A. Selby, 186–); T. Paine, "The Old Cabin Home," (Macon and Savannah: J. C. Schreiner & Son; Augusta, Ga.: Schreiner & Hewitt, ca. 1863); John H. Hewitt, "The Dear Ones at Home" (Augusta, Ga.: Blackmar and Bro., 1863); Will S. Hays, "My Sunny Southern Home" (New Orleans: Blackmar and Co., 1864); Charles Jefferys, "Home to Our Mountains" (New Orleans: P. P. Werlein & Halsey, 1861); Harry A. Barcley and S. Schlesinger, "The Old House by the Bay" (Mobile, Ala.: Joseph Bloch, 1861); F. B. Gordon and Francis Abt, "When the Swallows Homeward Fly" (Richmond: J. W. Davies & Sons, 186–).

65. H. E. Grannis, "Do They Miss Me at Home?" (Augusta, Ga.: Blackmar & Bro., 1863).

66. J. E. Carpenter and C. W. Glover, "Do They Think of Me at Home?" (New Orleans: Blackmar & Bro.; Augusta: Blackmar & Bro., 186–); John Hill Hewitt, "Yes We Think of Thee at Home" (Augusta, Ga.: Blackmar & Bro., ca. 1863).

67. Walter Kittredge, "Tenting on the Old Camp Ground," in Silber, *Songs of the Civil War,* 183–184. The author, Walter Kittredge, offered the song to a Boston publisher for fifteen dollars but was turned down. Another publisher bought it and sold ten thousand copies in the first three months. On Kittredge, see Gordon Hall Gerould, "'Tenting on

The Old Camp Ground,' and its Composer," *New England Magazine* 20 (1899): 723–731.

68. Henry C. Work, "Brave Boys Are They" (Augusta, Ga: Blackmar & Bro., 1864).

PART 3

1. Walt Whitman, "I Hear America Singing," in *Leaves of Grass* (Repr. Boston: Thayer and Eldridge, 1860), 195–96.

2. Walt Whitman, "Proud Music of the Storm," in *Leaves of Grass,* 358.

3. *Charleston Daily Courier,* 23 November 1860, 1:5.

4. N. Lee Orr, *Alfredo Barili and the Rise of Classical Music in Atlanta* (Atlanta: Scholars Press, 1995), 6. On the popularity of opera in antebellum America, see John Dizikes, *Opera in America: A Cultural History* (New Haven: Yale University Press, 1991).

5. The most popular of the "Englishizers" was musician-composer Henry Rowley Bishop, John Howard Payne's collaborator on "Home, Sweet Home" (see chapter 12). Bishop not only popularized Italian opera by his unrestrained translations, he also created or removed characters or story lines from the original. It was his "Englishized" versions of Bellini's *La sonnambula,* Mozart's *The Marriage of Figaro* and *Don Giovanni,* and Rossini's *Barber of Seville,* not the originals, that endeared those operas to both Britons and Americans. These "manglings offended purists"; but Queen Victoria, along with the rest of the English-speaking world, was so appreciative of his "operas for the people" that she knighted Bishop, the first musician to be so honored.

6. Composers like Bellini wrote operas whose main characters were ordinary people caught up in tragic events not of their own making. Bellini said his intention was to "draw tears, inspire terror, [and] make people die, through singing." Composer Gaetano Donizetti said he wrote opera with strong love themes, "because without it subjects are cold" and the more violent the love theme, the better. (Quoted in D. David Charlton, "Romantic Opera: 1830–1850," in *Romanticism,* ed. Gerald Abraham, [Oxford: Oxford University Press, 1990], 90, 142, 147). Among the "Englishized" opera tunes published in the South during the war are C. Jefferys and Vincenzo Bellini's "Hear Me, Norma" (Richmond: J. W. Davies and Sons, ca. 1862); C. Jefferys and Gaetano Donizetti, "The Child of the Regiment" (Macon, Ga.: John C. Schreiner & Son, ca. 1862); C. Jefferys and Giuseppe Verdi, "Ah! I Have Sigh'd to Me" (New Orleans: P. P. Werlein & Halsey, ca. 1861). Donizetti's "The Child of the Regiment" was included in *The Beauregard Songster;* his "It is Better to Laugh Than Be Sighing" and "Make Me No Gaudy Chaplet," from *Lucrezia Borgia,* were included in *The Army Songster* and the *Humor and Sentiment* Songster; Verdi's "Ah! I Have Sighed to Rest Me" was reprinted in *The Bold Soldier Boy's Song Book.*

7. Susan Eppes, *Through Some Eventful Years* (Macon, Ga.: J. W. Burke, 1926), 262, 266.

8. On the spread of German music to America and its influence, see Hamm *Music,* 205–208; idem, *Yesterdays,* 187–200, 260–61, 222; "Dwight's Journal of Music," 10 April 1852, reprinted in Irving Sablosky, *What They Heard: Music in America, 1852–1881,* from the pages of *Dwight's Journal of Music* (Baton Rouge: Louisiana State University Press, 1986), 17–22; Hitchcock, *Music in the United States,* 46ff; Howard, *Our American Music,* 211–218. On the German influence in Stephen Foster's music, see Hamm, *Yesterdays,* 222–23.

9. Heaps and Heaps, *Singing Sixties,* 7.

10. Julian Mates, *America's Musical Stage: Two Hundred Years of Musical Theatre* (Westport, Conn.: Greenwood Press, 1985), 24.

11. On theatrical activities in the South during the war, see the four-part series by Terry Theodore, "The Confederate Theatre: Theatre Personalities and Practices During the Confederacy," *Lincoln Herald* 76, no. 4 (1974): 187–195; 77, no. 1 (1975): 33–41.

12. Ibid., 77 (1975): 33–41; Mates, *America's Musical Stage,* 22.

13. Quoted by Lawrence W. Levine, *Highbrow, Lowbrow* (Cambridge: Harvard University Press, 1988), 90.

14. Larry Willoughby, *Texas Rhythm, Texas Rhyme* (Austin Texas Monthly Press, 1984), 3; Katherine K. Preston, *Opera on the Road* (Urbana: University of Illinois Press, 1993), 550.

15. *Musical Review,* 17 August 1854, 289, quoted in Preston, *Opera,* 279.

16. Lorna Walsh, "The Antics of Ante-bellum Virtuosi," *Etude* 35 (1917): 381–382. Not everyone was impressed. "Fire-eater" Edmund Ruffin attended a concert given by pianist Sigismund Thalberg and violinist Henri Vieuxtemps in Richmond in 1858. Although he praised their "execution," Ruffin said their music was mainly "flourishes to show off their wonderful skill." He himself would have preferred "simple airs correctly and plainly played," and he ventured that half the audience would likewise have preferred hearing an "ordinary fiddler playing common reels, and Yankee Doodle." He would not have them pandering to bad taste by playing Yankee Doodle, he said, but there were thousands of beautiful and simple airs that would pleasure their audiences (William Kauffman Scarborough, ed., *The Diary of Edmund Ruffin* (Baton Rouge: Louisiana State University Press, 1972), 10 January 1858, 1:143).

17. Harry R. Edwall, "Some Famous Musicians on the Memphis Concert Stage prior to 1860," *West Tennessee Historical Society Papers* 5 (1961): 90–105; Walsh, "Antics," 381–82.

18. *New Orleans Weekly Picayune,* 3 March 1851, 4.

19. Henri Herz, *My Travels in America* (Madison: University of Wisconsin Press, 1963), 38.

20. Ibid., 28–29.

21. Hamm, *Music,* 220. The most famous of the European orchestras to tour America was led by French composer-conductor Louis-Antoine Jullien (1812–60). To keep his audiences' attention, he combined polkas and quadrilles with music by Mozart and Beethoven, interspersing extravagant special effects to give audiences the spectacles they craved. Jullien believed in showmanship. For his most spectacular number, "The Fireman's Quadrille," Jullien created a mock though totally realistic fire, complete with flames and firemen in full regulation attire bursting on stage and splintering false wooden panels with their axes.

22. The definitive biography for "Blind Tom" is Geneva Handy Southall's *Blind Tom: The Post-Civil War Enslavement of a Black Musical Genius* (Minneapolis: Challenge Productions, 2 vols., 1979–1983), from which most of this biographical sketch has been taken.

23. On minstrel shows and their influence on American music, see Nathan, *Emmett*; Robert C. Toll, *Blacking Up: The Minstrel Show in Nineteenth-Century America* (New York: Oxford University Press, 1974); Carl Frederick Wittke, *Tambo And Bones: A History of the American Minstrel Stage* (Westport, Conn.: Greenwood Press, 1968); Chase, *America's Music,* 232–247; Hitchcock, *Music,* 102–113; Hamm, *Music,* 76–82, 182–188, 255–258; idem, *Yesterdays,* 108–140; R. L. Davis, *History of Music,* 203–26.

24. Crude and mainly negative stereotypical images of the Irish were similarly fodder for America's entertainment industry; see William H. A. Williams, *'Twas Only an Irishman's Dream* (Urbana: University of Illinois Press, 1996). The role of the blackfaced minstrel as the symbolic scapegoat, the black clown from the lowest stratum of society whose pretensions are obviously beyond his reach, is deftly presented by Gary D. Engle, ed., *This Grotesque Essence: Plays from the American Minstrel Stage* (Baton Rouge: Louisiana State University Press, 1978), xxvi–xxvii. Finson's, *Voices,* chap. 5, is likewise illuminating. For a bitter denunciation of the minstrel show as embodying and preserving racism, see Eric Lott, *Love and Theft: Blackface Minstrelsy and the American Working Class* (New York: Oxford University Press, 1993). For a more balanced assessment, see Roger D. Abrahams, *Singing the Master: The Emergence of African American Culture in the Plantation South* (New York: Pantheon Books, 1992), 131–53. Saxton's *Rise and Fall,* 165–182, discusses the minstrel show in its political and cultural context.

25. *Republican Banner and Nashville Whig,* 9 June 1858, quoted in Davenport, *Cultural Life,* 158.
26. Quoted in Toll, *Blacking Up,* 31.
27. Phineas Taylor Barnum, *Struggles and Triumphs; or, Forty Years' Recollections of P. T. Barnum* (New York: Macmillan, 1930), 50.
28. See chapter 2, "To Live and Die in Dixie."
29. Wittke, *Tambo and Bones,* 60.
30. Kay DeMetz, "Minstrel Dancing in New Orleans' Nineteenth Century Theatres," *Southern Quarterly* 20 (1982): 32–33.
31. Wittke, *Tambo and Bones,* 83. On antebellum minstrel shows in Memphis, see Harry R. Edwall, "The Golden Era of Minstrelsy in Memphis: A Reconstruction," *West Tennessee Historical Society Papers* 9 (1955): 29–47.
32. Ridley, *Battles and Sketches,* 439.
33. The most recent Foster biography is Ken Emerson's, *Doo-Dah! Stephen Foster and the Rise of American Popular Culture* (New York: Simon and Schuster, 1997). Emerson says Foster wrote for the minstrel stage, but his music publisher, C. D. Benteen, published his songs as "plantation melodies" to distinguish them from the more common "Ethiopian" minstrel pieces (156–57). Most of Foster's songs, however, were published by Firth and Pond in New York. In 1850 Firth and Pond offered Foster a contract to write songs fulltime. Foster accepted, although at first he asked that his name not appear on the song covers "owing to the prejudice against them by some, which might injure my reputation as a writer of another style of music, that is, sentimental parlor songs." By 1852 Foster was devoting himself to the "Ethiopian business without fear or shame with the intention of establish[ing] my name as the best Ethiopian songwriter." (Letter to E. P. Christy, dated 25 May 1852, quoted by John Howard Tasker, *Stephen Foster: America's Troubadour* [New York: T. Y. Crowell, 1953], 196.) The other standard source for Foster is William W. Austin's, *"Susanna," "Jeanie," and "The Old Folks at Home": The Songs of Stephen C. Foster from His Time to Ours* (New York: Macmillan, 1975).
34. Minstrel shows, Saxton (*Rise and Fall,* 175) argues, reinforced the Jacksonian democratic principles of egalitarianism, nationalism and white supremacy, and were oriented toward Democratic party policy which opposed temperance, welcomed European immigration, and favored territorial expansion.
35. Levine, *Highbrow, Lowbrow,* passim.

CHAPTER 13

1. On opera and classical music in New Orleans, see Kmen, *Music in New Orleans;* Robert Clemens Reinders, *A Social History of New Orleans* (Austin: University of Texas, 1957), 138ff; Kendall, *Golden Age,* 2ff; Ronald L. Davis, *A History of Opera in the American West* (Englewood Cliffs, N.J.: Prentice-Hall, 1965), 1–19; Dizikes, *Opera in America,* 120–22; Virginia Westbrook, "Old New Orleans and the Opera," (Howard-Tilton Memorial Library, Tulane University, New Orleans, n.d.); John H. Baron, "Vieuxtemps (and Ole Bull) in New Orleans," *American Music,* summer 1990, 210–23).
2. Quoted in Kendall, *Golden Age,* 2.
3. Kmen, *Music in New Orleans,* 141–142.
4. Ibid., 142.
5. Ibid., 151.
6. Ibid.
7. *New Orleans Weekly Delta,* 3 April 1853, quoted in Reinders, *Social History,* 541.
8. In Natchez, Mississippi, free blacks paid seventy-five cents and slaves paid fifty cents. At that time a dollar bought a night and day's lodging at Natchez's best hotel, plus three meals or two gallons of the best peach brandy. (Linda Virginia Hamil, "A Study of Theatrical Activity in Natchez, Mississippi from 1800–1840," Master's diss., University

of Mississippi, 1976, 21.) For theater practices in general, see James Dormon, *Theater in the Ante Bellum South, 1815–1861* (Chapel Hill: University of North Carolina Press, 1967). On theatrical activities in the South during the war, see the four-part series by Theodore, "Confederate Theatre" 76, no. 4 (1974): 187–95; 77, no. 1 (1975): 33–41.

9. Kendall, *Golden Age,* 540.

10. Charles Lyell, *A Second Visit to the United States of North America* (New York: Harper and Bro., 1849), 2:115.

11. Edward Robert Sullivan, *Rambles and Scrambles in North and South America* (London: R. Bentley, 1852), 223.

12. Eliza Ripley, *Social Life in Old New Orleans* (New York: D. Appleton and Co., 1912), 66.

13. On the assignment of prostitutes to the third tier and its impact on the theater's acceptance and support, see Claudia D. Johnson, "That Guilty Third Tier: Prostitution in Nineteenth Century American Theaters," in *Victorian America,* ed. Daniel Walker Howe (Philadelphia: University of Pennsylvania, 1976).

14. Preston, *Opera,* 32–33.

15. Virginius Dabney, *Richmond* (Charlottesville: University Press of Virginia, 1990), 182.

16. See Albert Stoutamire, *Music of the Old South* (Rutherford, N.J.: Fairleigh Dickinson University Press, 1972); Preston (*Opera,* 542–51) catalogs all the English opera companies playing in Richmond from 1847 to 1860.

17. Stoutamire, *Music of Old South,* 192.

18. Ibid., 192, 208.

19. An article in the *Richmond Daily Dispatch* (3 January 1862, 2:2) reviewed the history of the theater.

20. Ibid., 27 January 1862, 2:3.

21. Ibid., 11 February 1862, 2:4.

22. Ibid.

23. Sallie Partington, also an accomplished dancer, set up a dancing school in Richmond in 1864 (Theodore, "Confederate Theater" 77, no. 1 (1975): 41; "The Southern Soldier Boy, Song, as Sung by Miss Sallie Partington in, 'The Virginia Cavalier' at the Richmond New Theater" (Richmond: Geo Dunn & Compy.; Columbia, S.C.: Julian A. Selby, 1863). The "Virginia Cavalier" is specifically mentioned by Capt. Robert Park (12th Alabama Infantry) in his diary, 8 February 1862, as one of the plays he saw at the Richmond Theater (Diary of Capt. Robert Emory Park, Southern Historical Society Papers, 1896, vol. 26, 3).

24. Cf. DeLeon, *Belles,* 196–197; DeLeon, *Four Years in Rebel Capitals,* 154.

25. R. L. Davis, *History of Music,* 48; *Charleston Daily Courier,* 23 November 1860, 1:5.

26. J. Milton Mackie, *From Cape Cod to Dixie and the Tropics,* (1864; Repr. New York: Negro University Press, 1968), 99–100.

27. Quoted by Walter J. Fraser, *Charleston! Charleston! The History of a Southern City* (Columbia: University of South Carolina Press, 1989), 257.

28. Marszalek, *Diary of Holmes,* 44, 86, 91, 97, 120, 138–39, 141, 277–79, 296–97, 299, 332, 351, 359.

29. Henry W. Adams, *Montgomery Theater, 1822–1835* (Tuscaloosa: University of Alabama Press, 1955), 5.

30. Monique Davis Boyce, "The First Forty Years of the Augusta, Georgia, Theater," (master's thesis, University of Georgia, 1957), 40–41.

31. Florence F. Corley, *Confederate City: Augusta, Georgia, 1860–1865* (Columbia: University of South Carolina Press, 1960), 14; John W. Wagner, "Some Early Musical Moments in Augusta," in *Music in Georgia,* ed. Frank W. Hoogerwerf (New York: Da Capo Press, 1984), 305–10.

32. Corley, *Confederate City,* 14; Wagner, "Musical Moments," 305–310. For English opera troupes playing in Augusta prior to the war, see Preston, *Opera,* 542–51.

33. *Augusta Chronicle and Sentinel,* 5 May 1861.
34. Corley, *Confederate City,* 74; *Augusta Chronicle and Sentinel,* 16 June 1864.
35. Katherine Hines Mahan, "History of Music in Columbus, Georgia, 1828–1928" (Ph.D. diss., Florida State University, 1967), 11.
36. Ibid., 108; William Osler Langley, "The Theater in Columbus, Georgia, 1828–1878" (master's thesis, Auburn University, 1937), 92–113.
37. Walter E. Steinhaus, "Music in the Cultural Life of Macon, Georgia, 1823–1900" (Ph.D. diss., Florida State University, 1973), 63–64.
38. Kenneth Coleman *Confederate Athens* (Athens: University of Georgia Press, 1967), 59.
39. Ibid., 102.
40. Ibid., 109.
41. Ibid., 147.
42. Minnie Clare Boyd, *Alabama in the Fifties: A Social Study* (New York: Columbia University Press, 1931), 226; music comments quoted by Walter Fleming, *Civil War and Reconstruction in Alabama* (New York: Peter Smith 1949), 241.
43. On Atlanta during the war, see James M. Russell, *Atlanta, 1847–1890: City Building in the Old South and the New* (Baton Rouge, Louisiana State University Press, 1988), 108–12; Orr, *Alfredo Barili,* 63–65.
44. Orr, *Alfredo Barili,* 63–65; Russell, *Atlanta 1847–1890,* 110.
45. Arthur W. Bergeron, *Confederate Mobile* (Jackson: University of Mississippi, 1991), 4.
46. Quoted in M. C. Boyd, *Alabama,* 227–28.
47. The *Mobile Daily Advertiser and Chronicle,* 14 May 1862, quoted in Bergeron, *op. cit.,* 65.
48. For example, Frederick Loenigsberg, "Keep Me Awake! Mother": As Sung by Miss Laura, of the "Queen Sisters" (at head of title: To Miss Laura Waldron, "Queen Sisters") (Macon, Ga.: John C. Schreiner & Son, 1863); D. Ottolengui and Hermann L. Schreiner, "The Soldier's Grave" as Sung with Unbounded Applause, by Miss Laura, of the "Queen Sisters"! (Macon, Ga.: John C. Schreiner & Son, 186–).
49. *Savannah Daily Morning News,* 7 November 1862, 2:2.
50. *Mobile Daily Advertiser and Chronicle,* 16 December 1862, advertisement reprinted in Bergeron, *op. cit.,* figure 4.
51. Charles C. Ritter, "The Theater in Memphis, Tennessee, from Its Beginning to 1859" (Ph.D. diss., University of Iowa, 1956), 109.
52. Gerald Mortimer Capers, *Biography of a River Town: Memphis, Its Heroic Age* (Chapel Hill: University of North Carolina, 1939), 44–45.
53. On theater in Memphis, see Edwall, "Famous Musicians," 5, 90–105; Ritter, "Theater in Memphis," 326–373.
54. See newspaper item from *Memphis Daily Eagle,* 28 March 1849, quoted in Edwall, "Famous Musicians," 44; see also Ritter, "Theater in Memphis," 73–74.
55. Davenport, *Cultural Life,* 119.
56. Luigi Arditi's (1825–1903) best-known composition, "Il Bacio" (The Kiss) was published before the war in New Orleans, with words in English, German and French, by Louis Grunewald. During the war, J. H. Snow published it in 1863 in Mobile.
57. *Nashville Daily Gazette,* 30 May 1854, quoted in Davenport, *Cultural Life,* 141.
58. Davenport, *Cultural Life,* 150–51.
59. Ibid., 154.
60. Wyoline Hester, "The Savannah Stage" (master's thesis, Alabama Polytechnical Institute, 1930), 2–3.
61. Elvena M. Green, "Theatre and Other Entertainments in Savannah, Georgia, 1818–1865" (Ph.D. diss., University of Iowa, 1971), 2:438–546.
62. *Daily Morning News,* 31 January 1861, 2:2.
63. See also *Daily Morning News,* 8 January 1861, 2:2; 12 August 1861, 2:2; 23 June 1862, 2:2; 19 June 1862, 2:3.

64. The *Jackson Courier,* 9 July 1835, in Grier M. Williams, "A History of Music in Jacksonville, Florida, from 1822 to 1922" (Ph.D. diss., Florida State University, 1957), 6.

65. The *Jacksonville News,* 1 January 1835, in Williams, "Music in Jacksonville," 7.

66. Williams, "Music in Jacksonville," 8.

67. Ibid., 8–9.

68. The *Jacksonville News,* 20 October 1855, quoted in Williams, "Music in Jacksonville," 17.

69. Williams, "Music in Jacksonville," 20.

70. The *Jacksonville News,* 18 June 1847; Williams, "Music in Jacksonville," 26.

71. Williams, "Music in Jacksonville," 25–26.

72. The *Florida Republican,* 11 November 1852, in Williams, "Music in Jacksonville," 28.

73. John Edwin Johns, Florida during the Civil War (Gainesville: University of Florida Press, 1963), 173; Susan Bradford Eppes, *Through Some Eventful Years* (Repr. Gainesville: University of Florida Press, 1968), 233.

74. Ibid.

75. Donald Wagner Pugh, "Music in Frontier Houston, 1836–1876" (Ph.D. diss., University of Texas, 1970), 50.

76. Ibid., 72.

77. Edward Wharton, "Southern Pleiades March and Quickstep" (Galveston: Sachtleben, 1861).

78. Quoted by Paul A. Levengood, "In the Absence of Scarcity: The Civil War Prosperity of Houston, Texas," *Southwestern Historical Quarterly* 101, 1998: 404.

CHAPTER 14

1. Root, *Story of Life,* 151.

2. *Southern Illustrated News,* 5 December 1863. Prior to the war, a Southern book was a "dreg" in the market, said the editor of the *Southern Illustrated News* on 20 September 1862. Now, he beamed, Southern books were eagerly sought after.

3. See advertisement, *Southern Illustrated News,* 5 December 1863, 4:4.

4. For example, *Southern Illustrated News,* 26 September 1863, 8:4; 5 December 1863, 4:4.

5. It was not the first music publishing firm in Charleston, however. That distinction went to Philip Muck, who started business in 1803 but closed in 1822.

6. Oscar Sonneck's *Bibliography of Early Secular American Music,* published in 1905 (reprint, New York: Da Capo Press, 1964) and updated by Richard J. Wolfe, *Secular Music in America, 1800–1825* (New York: New York Public Library, 1964), and Dichter and Shapiro's *Early American Sheet Music* are the two major sources for information on sheet music publishing in the east up to the first quarter of the nineteenth century.

7. In 1905 the business's name changed to the Siegling Music House, a name that persisted until its demise.

8. McClure opened his music store, at 360 Main Street, on 8 December 1858. The advertisement for the store's opening claimed his stock of pianos, melodeons, violins, flutes, accordions, music books and sheet music was the "largest and best assorted stock ever offered in this city" (*Memphis Daily Appeal,* 9 December 1858, 1:6).

9. Edith A. Wright and Josephine A. McDevitt, "Lithographers before 1870," *Antiques,* 1922, 18, 342.

10. William A. Grice, *New Orleans Merchant's Diary and Guide* (New Orleans: Grice, 1858), 30.

11. Lesser-known lithographers included a D. Simon, who worked for Bromberg and Son in Mobile; W. H. Leeson, who worked for J. Manouvrier and Co. in New Orleans and various other publishers both as a lithographer and an engraver; T. Sinclair, who worked for Bromberg and Co. in Mobile; and R. H. Howell of Milledgeville, Georgia, who worked for John Burke in Macon. Lithographers in border states such as John

Slinglandt in Louisville and A. Hoen & Co. in Baltimore also managed to engrave for Confederate music publishers.

12. Washburne, "Descriptive Catalogue," 32.
13. Kendall, "New Orleans' Musicians Quarterly," 20; Boudreaux, "Music Publishing in New Orleans," 34–41.
14. Duncan to Memminger, 9 January 1862; Raphael P. Thian, *Correspondence with the Treasury Department of the Confederate States of America, 1861–1865* (Washington, D.C.: n.p., 1880), 5:466; Duncan to Memminger, 19 April 1862, ibid., 5:527.
15. Duncan to Memminger, 17 March 1862, ibid., 5:497.
16. *Southern Illustrated News,* 14 March 1863.
17. Joel Munsell, *The Chronology of the Origin and Progress of Paper and Papermaking* (New York: Garland Publishers, 1980), 156; the Richmond typefoundry was the only one of its kind in the South (*Winston Salem People's Press,* Friday, 1 November 1861, 4:3).
18. *Richmond Examiner,* 4 February 1864, quoted in Washburne, "Descriptive Catalogue," 38.
19. *Columbia Daily South Carolinian,* 17 January 1864, quoted in Washburne, "Descriptive Catalogue," 41.
20. *Richmond Whig,* 7 June 1861, 2:3.
21. *The Southern Cultivator,* November 1861, 291.
22. *Atlanta Southern Confederacy,* 15 January 1862, quoted in Michael T. Parrish and Robert M. Willingham, *Confederate Imprints: A Bibliography of Southern Publications from Secession to Surrender: Expanding and Revising the Earlier Works of Marjorie Crandall and Richard Harwell* (Austin: Jenkins Publising Co., 1984), 12.
23. See Thian, *Correspondence with Treasury,* 5:309; *Daily Chronicle and Sentinel,* 30 December 1864, quoted by Washburne, "Descriptive Catalogue," 42.
24. The resourcefulness of the South in finding substitutes for everything, including paper and ink, is ably told in Mary Elizabeth Massey's *Ersatz in the Confederacy* (Columbia: University of South Carolina Press, 1952).
25. Reprinted in *The Southern Cultivator,* 20, no. 5 (May 1862): 111; 20, no. 6 (June 1862): 1–2.
26. Advertisement in *Southern Illustrated News,* 14 March 1863, in Washburne, "Descriptive Catalogue," 39.
27. *The Southern Cultivator,* 33, no. 5 (May 1863); 31, no. 6 (June 1863).
28. *Columbia Daily South Carolinian,* 8 October 1864.
29. *The Southern Cultivator,* 23, no. 1 (1 January 1865).
30. *Columbia Daily South Carolinian,* 27 April 1864.
31. *The Southern Cultivator,* 21, no. 5 (May 1863): 88; 21, no. 6, (June 1863): 2.
32. E. A. Pollard, *The Rival Administrations: Richmond and Washington in December 1863* (Privately published: Richmond, 1864).
33. *Macon Telegraph,* 23 September 1863, 2:4.
34. Ibid., 11 October 1864, quoted in Washburne, "Descriptive Catalogue" 38–39.
35. J. A. Rosenberger, "The Mocking Bird Quickstep" (Richmond: Geo. Dunn & Compy., 1864).
36. *Southern Illustrated News,* Saturday, 11 July 1863, vol. II, 8:4.
37. Ibid.
38. *The Confederate Spirit and Knapsack of Fun,* 23 July 1864.
39. Broadside quoted in Harwell, *Confederate Music,* 18. The price marks refer to the publisher's code that was often printed on the cover in the form of a five pointed star with a number inside. A $2^1/2$ inside the star, for example, meant twenty-five cents. The dealer's discount was based on this price.
40. Hewitt, Manuscript, quoted by Harwell, *Confederate Music,* 18.
41. *Southern Illustrated News,* 10 April 1864.
42. Kate Elony Baker Staton, *Old Southern Songs of the Period of the Confederacy* (New York: Samuel French, 1926), 142–43.

43. *Columbia Daily South Carolinian,* 28 July 1863, in Washburne, "Descriptive Catalogue," 53.
44. *Columbia Daily South Carolinian,* 28 June 1863, 14 January 1864, in Washburne, "Descriptive Catalogue," 52–53.
45. Dorothy Blackmar, "Armand Edward Blackmar," Special Collections, Howard Tilton Memorial Library, Tulane University, New Orleans, n.d., 1.
46. Ibid., 4.
47. Boudreaux, "Music Publishing in New Orleans," 57.
48. Blackmar bought the rights to the song from Macarthy for a five-hundred-dollar piano (Kendall, *Golden Age,* 17).
49. Mildred Lewis Rutherford, *The South In History And Literature* (Atlanta: Franklin Turner Co., 1907), 254.
50. Kendall, *Golden Age,* 18.
51. *Augusta Daily Chronicle and Sentinel,* 17 October 1862.
52. Blackmar's music stock at the time of sale is reprinted by Harwell, *Confederate Music,* 21.
53. Boudreaux, "Music Publishing in New Orleans," 59.
54. Ibid.
55. Blackmar, "Armand Edward Blackmar," 4.
56. *National Cyclopedia of American Biography,* 24: 420.
57. The acquisition of Mayo's stock is mentioned in a letter signed "J. S. B." published in *The Musical World and New York Musical Times,* 14 (2 April 1853): 211.
58. Boudreaux, "Music Publishing in New Orleans," 43.
59. Ibid., 43–54.
60. Ibid., 72.
61. J. Curtis Waldo, *Illustrated Visitors' Guide to New Orleans* (New Orleans: Waldo, 1879), 115.
62. Ibid.
63. *New Orleans Bee,* 20 September 1861, 1:9.
64. Thian, *Correspondence with Treasury,* 5:185–86.
65. Gemmell and McFarlane to C. G. Memminger, 3 July 1861, in Thian, *Correspondence with Treasury,* 5:510.
66. Dunn to Pope, 19 August 1862, in Thian, *Correspondence with Treasury,* (appendix) 5:599–600.
67. Pressley to Memminger, 20 August 1862, in Thian, *Correspondence with Treasury,* (appendix) 5:601. Ironically, the North failed to undermine the South's economy through counterfeiting for the simple reason that the Northern engravers were much better at their job and their handiwork was easy to spot compared with the less skilled efforts of the Southern engravers (John Wilkerson, *Narrative of a Blockade Runner* (New York: Sheldon & Co., 1877), 130.
68. *Savannah Daily Morning News,* 9 December 1862, 2.
69. Instead of buying music from Blackmar, Hermann was negotiating a publishing agreement. The Schreiners and the Blackmars had jointly published four songs ("Le Boifeuillet," "Missouri," "Southern Constellation," and "Southern Dixie"). A fifth song, "Nobody Hurt," by Hermann Schreiner had the John C. Schreiner & Sons imprint pasted over the A. E. Blackmar, New Orleans imprint.
70. Undated clipping from *The Musical Courier* (Hewitt, Manuscript), quoted in Harwell, *Confederate Music,* 17.
71. "Evergreen Waltz," "The Gipsey Countess," "I've Brought Thee an Ivy Leaf," "Leonora, or Affection Waltz," "Morning Star Waltz," "The Mother of the Soldier Boy," "The Old Cabin Home," "Some One to Love," "Somebody's Darling," "The Song of Blanche Alpen,"and "The Vacant Chair"; Hewitt published "Flag of the Sunny South" under his own imprint.
72. Letter, 18 August 1860, Blanton Duncan, Miscellaneous Papers, Filson Club Historical Society, Louisville.

73. Duncan to Memminger, Winchester, 2 July 1861, Thian, *Correspondence with Treasury,* 5:185.
74. Duncan to Memminger, 3 September 1861, ibid., 5:309; 8 September 1861, ibid., 5:321.
75. Duncan to Memminger, 8 September 1861, ibid., 5:321–22.
76. Douglas to Memminger, 5 November 1861, ibid., 5:425–26.
77. Duncan to Memminger, 5 December 1861, ibid., 5:437.
78. Duncan to Memminger, 10 February 1862, ibid., 5:486.
79. Johnston to his wife, Rosa, 1 August 1862, Johnston Family Papers, Filson Historical Society, Louisville.
80. Treasury agent to Memminger, 22 August 1862, Thian, *Correspondence with Treasury,* 5:601–2.
81. Duncan to Memminger, 6 January 1862, ibid., 5:102.
82. Duncan to Memminger, 24 May 1862, ibid., 5:552.
83. Duncan to Memminger, 10 June 1862, ibid, 5:563.
84. Evans and Cogswell to Patterson, 24 October 1862, ibid., 5:654.
85. Keating to Memminger, 23 October 1862, ibid., 5:656–57.
86. Duncan to unknown correspondent, Columbia, S.C., 20 June 1863 (Johnston Family Papers).
87. Duncan to Memminger, 26 December 1862, Thian, *Correspondence with Treasury,* 5:700.
88. This advertisement, dated 27 July 1863, was included on the back page of several of Duncan's published songs (for example, "Battery Wagner").
89. *Columbia Daily South Carolinian,* 15 April 1864, quoted by Harwell, *Confederate Music,* 15.
90. *Galveston Civilian and Gazette,* 8 June 1861, 3:6.
91. Ibid.
92. Ibid., 23 April 1861, 3:4.
93. Allan, *Lone Star Ballads.*

EPILOGUE

1. Bohemian [W. G. Shepperson] *War Songs of the South* (Richmond: West and Johnson, 1862), 3, 5–6.
2. Quoted in E. Merton Coulter, *Confederate States of America* (Baton Rouge: Louisiana State University Press, 1950), 509.
3. *Southern Literary Messenger,* July 1863, 447.
4. *Atlanta Southern Confederacy,* quoted in Coulter, *Confederate States,* 509.
5. Coulter, *Confederate States,* 509.
6. DeLeon, *Four Years in Rebel Capitals,* 295.
7. Harwell, *Confederate Music,* 7.
8. William Mahar, "March to the Music," *Civil War Times Illustrated,* 23 (1984): 13–16, 41–44.
9. See Chapter 14.
10. *Army Songster; Beauregard Songster* (Macon and Savannah, Ga.: John C. Schreiner & Son, 1864); *Bonnie Blue Flag Song Book; Carolina Songsters; The Dixie Land Songster* (Augusta, Ga.: A. E. Blackmar, 1863); *General Lee Songster; Songs of Humor and Sentiment; Jack Morgan Songster; New Confederate Flag Song Book; Southern Soldier's Prize Songster: Containing Martial and Patriotic Pieces, (Chiefly Original) Applicable to the Present War* (Mobile, Ala.: W. F. Wisely, 1864); *Stonewall Song Book,* 2nd ed.
11. Paul Charosh, "Studying Nineteenth-Century Popular Song," *American Music* 15 (winter 1997): 479–93.

BIBLIOGRAPHY

PRIMARY SOURCES
Diaries and Letters
Allison, Young E. Papers. Filson Club Historical Society, Louisville.

Duncan, Blanton. Miscellaneous Papers. Filson Club Historical Society, Lousiville.

Hays, William Shakespeare. Manuscripts Section. Kentucky Building, Western Kentucky University, Bowling Green.

Ives, Washington. Letters. Florida State Archives. Gainesville.

Johnston Family Papers. Filson Club Historical Society, Lousiville.

Peterson, J. Edward (26th North Carolina Regimental Band). Letters. Moravian Music Center, Winston-Salem.

Randall, James R. Letters. Southern Historical Collection. University of North Carolina, Chapel Hill.

Valentine (23rd Rgt, Mass Volunteers), Herbert E. Diary and letters. Essex Institute, Manuscripts Section. Salem.

Unpublished Manuscripts and Typescripts
Blackmar, Dorthy. "Armand Edward Blackmar." Special Collections. Howard Tilton Memorial Library. Tulane University, New Orleans, n.d.

Hewitt, John Hill. Manuscripts. Special Collections. Emory University, Atlanta.

Hutson, Charles W. "Reminiscences." University of North Carolina, Chapel Hill. Southern Historical Collection, no. 362.

Kimble, June. "The 14th Tenn. Glee Club." Confederate Museum, Richmond, n.d.

Randall, James Ryder. Letters. Special Collections. Duke University, Durham, N.C.

Westbrook, Virginia. "Old New Orleans and the Opera." Howard-Tilton Memorial Library. Tulane University, New Orleans, n.d.

United Daughters of the Confederacy. Joint Committee Appointed to Consider and Report on a Section of New Words for "Dixie." Opelika, Ala., 1904. Boston Public Library, Boston, Mass.

Government Publications

Army Regulations Adopted for Use of the Army of the Confederate States. New Orleans: Bloomfield and Steel, 1861.

General Orders of the War Department, Embracing the Years 1861, 1862, and 1863. Arranged by T. M. O'Brien and O. Diefendorf. New York: Derby and Miller, 1864.

Hardee, W. J. *Rifle and Light Infantry Tactics: For the Exercise and Manoeuvres of Troops When Acting as Light Infantry or Riflemen: Prepared under the Direction of the War Department.* Philadelphia: Lippincott, Grambo & Co., 1855.

————. *Rifle and Infantry Tactics, Revised and Improved.* Mobile, Ala.: S. H. Goetzel & Co., 1861.

Public Laws of the Confederate States of America, Passed at the First Session of the First Congress, 1862. Edited by Matthews. Richmond: J. M. and R. M. Smith, 1862.

Regulations for the Army of the Confederate States, 1864. Revised and Enlarged with a New and Copius Index. Third and Only Reliable Edition: In Which Are Corrected Over 3,000 Important Errors Contained in the Editions Published by West & Johnston. Richmond: J. W. Randolph, 1864.

Southern Military Manual: Containing All the Confederate Military Laws, Articles of War, Army Regulations, Field Artillery; Mahan's Treatise on the Effects of Musketry and Artillery, and the Means of Directing the Fire As to Obtain the Best Results; Hardee's Manual of Arms, Fully Illustrated; Military Ordinances of Louisiana and Mississippi; Uniforms; Military Maxims of Napoleon I; Health Hints for Volunteers, Etc. New Orleans: H. P. Lathrop, 1861.

Thian, Raphael P. *Correspondence with the Treasury Department of the Confederate States of America, 1861–1865.* Vol. 5. Washington, D.C.: Gov't. Printing Office, 1880.

U.S. War Department. *The War of the Rebellion: A Compilation of Official Records of the Union and Confederate Armies.* Washington, D.C.: Government Printing Office, 1880–1901.

———. *Revised Regulations for the Army of the United States, 1861.* Philadelphia: J. G. L. Brown, 1861.

Newspapers and Magazines
Arkansas Gazette
Atlanta Daily Intelligencer
Augusta Chronicle and Sentinel
Augusta Daily Constitutionalist
Birmingham News
Charleston Daily Courier
Charlotte (N.C.) Observer
Columbia Daily South Carolinian
Confederate Annals
Confederate Military History
Confederate Spirit and Knapsack of Fun
Confederate Veteran
Dwight's Journal of Music
The Index
Jet
Literary Digest
Louisville Courier-Journal
Louisville Herald
Macon Daily Confederate
Macon Telegraph
Memphis Daily Appeal
New Orleans Daily Crescent
New Orleans Daily Picayune
New Orleans Daily States
New York Commercial Advertiser
New York Times
Richmond Dispatch
Richmond Examiner
Richmond Magnolia Weekly
Richmond Whig
Savannah Daily Morning News
Savannah Republican
Southern Illustrated News
Southern Literary Messenger

St. Louis Post-Dispatch
U.S. News and World Report
Wall Street Journal
Winston-Salem (N.C.) People's Press

Songsters

Allen's Lone Star Ballads: A Collection of Southern Patriotic Songs. No. 1. Galveston and Houston: Francis D. Allen, 1863.

The Army Songster: Dedicated to the Army of Northern Virginia. Richmond: Geo. L. Bidgood, 1864.

The Beauregard Songster. Being A Collection of Patriotic Sentimental and Comic Songs the Most Popular of the Day. Macon and Savannah, Ga.: John C. Schreiner & Son, 1864.

Bohemian (W. G. Shepperson) War Songs of the South. Richmond: West & Johnson, 1862.

The Bold Soldier Boy's Song Book. Richmond: West & Johnston, n.d.

The Bonnie Blue Flag Song Book. Augusta, Ga.: A. E. Blackmar, n.d.

The Carolina Songster Containing a Splendid Collection of Original and Selected Songs. Stanton, Va.: n.p., 1865.

The Cotton Field Melodies. Augusta, Ga.: A. E. Blackmar, 1863.

The Dixie Land Songster. Augusta, Ga.: A. E. Blackmar, 1863.

The General Lee Songster: Being a Collection of the Most Popular Sentimental, Patriotic and Comic Songs. Macon and Savannah: John C. Schreiner [*sic*] & Son; Augusta, Ga.: Schreiner & Hewitt, 1865 (contents page lists copyright of 1864).

Hopkins' New Orleans 5 Cent Song Book. New Orleans: John Hopkins, 1861.

The Jack Morgan Songster. Fayetteville, N.C.: Branson & Farrar, 1864.

The New Confederate Flag Song Book, no. 1. Mobile, Ala.: H. C. Clark, 1863.

The Punch Songster: A Collection of Familiar and Original Songs and Ballads. Richmond: Punch Office, 1864.

Songs of Humor and Sentiment. Richmond: J. W. Randolph, 1863.

Songs of Love and Liberty. Fayetteville, N.C.: Branson & Farrar, 1864.

Songs of the South. Richmond: J. W. Randolph, 1862.

Songs of the South. Richmond: J. W. Randolph, 1863.

The Southern Soldier's Prize Songster: Containing Martial and Patriotic Pieces, (Chiefly Original) Applicable to the Present War. Mobile, Ala.: W. F. Wisely, 1864.

The Stonewall Song Book: Being a Collection of Patriotic, Sentimental and Comic songs. 2nd ed. Richmond: West & Johnston, 1865.

The Stonewall Song Book: Being a Collection of Patriotic, Sentimental, and Comic Songs. 11th edition!—Enlarged! Richmond: West & Johnston, 1865.

Postwar Anthologies and Facsimilies

Allan, Francis D. Allan's Lone Star Ballads: A Collection of Southern Patriotic Songs Made During Confederate Times. Galveston: J. D. Sawyer, 1874.

Bruce, George B. and Daniel D. Emmett Drummer's and Fifer's Guide. 1862. Repr., New York: W.A. Pond, 1895.

Daniel, L. C. Confederate Scrap Book. Richmond: privately published, 1893.

Davidson, N. F. M. Cullings from the Confederacy: A Collection of Southern Poems, Original and Others, Popular during the War Between the States, and Incidents and Facts Worth Recalling, 1862–1866: Including the Doggerel of the Camp, As Well As Tender Tribute to the Dead. Washington, D.C.: Rufus H. Darby Printing Co., 1903.

Ellinger, Esther Parker. The Southern War: Poetry of the Civil War. 1918. Reprint, New York: Burt Franklin, 1970.

Fagan, William Long, ed. Southern War Songs: Camp-Fire, Patriotic, and Sentimental. New York: M. T. Richardson, 1892.

Glass, Paul, and Louis C. Singer, ed. Singing Soldiers. New York: Da Capo Press, 1988.

Hubner, Charles William. War Poets of the South and Confederate Camp-Fire Songs. Atlanta: Chas. P. Byrd, n.d.

Macarthy, Harry His Book of Original Songs, Balladas, and Anecdotes, As Presented by the Author in His Well-Known Presentation Concerts. Indianapolis: Indiana State Sentinel, 1898.

Pittman, Josiah, Colin Brown, Charles Mackay, and Myles Birket Foster. The Songs of Scotland. London: Boosey and Co., 1877.

Silber, Irwin, ed. Songs of the Civil War. New York: Bonanza Books, 1960.

Staton, Kate Elony Baker. Old Southern Songs of the Period of the Confederacy: The Dixie Trophy Collection. New York: Samuel French, 1926.

Wharton, Henry Marvin. War Songs and Poems of the Southern Confederacy, 1861–1865. Philadelphia: Winston, 1904.

SECONDARY SOURCES
Periodicals

Anon. "Biographies of American Musicians: Dr. G.F. Root." Brainard's Musical World 16, 1979: 82–83.

Anon. "Ben Bolt: Something about the Authors of Words and Music of the Famous Song." Brainard's Musical World 32, 1895: 117–18.

Anon. "The Story of Old Ben Bolt." *American Journal* 61, 1893: 458–59.

Avery, C. S. "Sketch of Rockbridge Artillery." *Southern Historical Society Papers* 23 (1895): 98 125.

Barbee, D. R. "Who Wrote Dixie?" *Musical Digest* 30 (1948): 6–9.

Baron, John H. "Vieuxtemps (and Ole Bull) in New Orleans." *American Music* 8, 1990: 210–23.

Birdseye, W. "America's Song Composers, II: George F. Root." *Potter's American Monthly* 12 (1879): 145–48.

Boyce, Joseph. "Cockrell's Brigade Band at Franklin." *Confederate Veteran* 20 (1911): 271.

Bradwell, I. G. "Carlos Maximilian Cassni, Our Old Bandmaster." *Confederate Veteran* 34 (1926): 333–34.

Carnes, W. W. "Here's Your Mule." *Confederate Veteran* 37 (1929): 373–74.

Carroll, G. P. "The Band Musick of the Second Virginia Regiment." *Journal of Band Research* 22 (n.d.): 16.

Charosh, Paul. "Studying Nineteenth-Century Popular Song." *American Music* 15 (winter 1997): 479–93.

Civil War Times Illustrated 3, no. 4 (1964): 22.

Confederate Veteran 2 (1901): 464; 19 (1911): 5; 20 (1911) 271; 34 (1926): 333.

Coonley. "George F. Root and His Songs." *New England Magazine* 13 (1896): 555–70.

Crammer, B. "The Civil War Had Its Jokes Too." *San Jose Studies* 1, 1975: 87–92.

Crawford, Martin. "Confederate Volunteering and Enlistment in Ashe County, North Carolina, 1861–1862." *Civil War History* 37 (1991): 29–50.

Crimmins, M. L. "The Bonnie Blue Flag." *Frontier Times* 17 (1940): 323–25.

Cunningham, S.A. "Daniel D., Daniel Decatur Emmett, Author of Dixie." *Confederate Veteran* 1 (1893): 139.

———. "Daniel Decatur Emmett, Author of Dixie." *Confederate Veteran* 6 (1898): 2.

———. "Daniel D. Emmett." *Confederate Veteran* 13 (1905): 432.

———. "Letter." *Confederate Veteran* 1, no. 4 (1893): 101–2.

———. "Monument to the Composer of Dixie Land." *Confederate Veteran* 24 (1916) 52.

———. "When the Band First Played Dixie." *Confederate Veteran* 34 (1926): 234.

Davis, R. "Sentimental Songs in Antebellum America." *Southwestern Historical Quarterly* 80 (winter 1976): 50–65.

Debray, Xavier B. "A Sketch of Debray's 26th Regiment of Texas Cavalry." *Southern Historical Society Papers* 13 (1885): 157.

DeMetz, Kay. "Minstrel Dancing in New Orleans' Nineteenth Century Theatres." *Southern Quarterly* 20 (1982): 28–39.

Edwall, H. R. "The Golden Era of Minstrelsy in Memphis: A Reconstruction." *West Tennessee Historical Society Papers* 9 (1988): 29–47.

Edwall, Harry R. "Some Famous Musicians on the Memphis Concert Stage Prior to 1860." *West Tennessee Historical Society Papers* 5 (1951): 90–105.

Epstein, D. J. "The Battle Cry of Freedom." *Civil War History* 4 (1958): 307–18.

Eva, Phil. "Home Sweet Home? 'The Culture of Exile' in Mid-Victorian Popular Song." *Popular Music* 16 (1977): 131–50.

Fennell, Frederick. "The Civil War: Its Music and Its Sounds." *Journal of Band Research* 4 (1968): 36; 5 (1968): 8; 5 (1969): 4; 6 (1969): 46.

French, J. M. "Tenting on the Old Camp Ground." *Granite State Monthly* 61 (1929): 123–27.

Gerould, Gordon Hall. "'Tenting on the Old Camp Ground' and its Composer." *New England Magazine* 20 (1899): 723–31.

Goolrick, Charles. "He Didn't Like 'Dixie'!" *Virginia Cavalcade* 9 (1960): 5–10.

Grace, C. D. "Rhode's Division at Gettysburg." *Confederate Veteran* 5 (1897): 614–15.

Hainer, J. A. "The Stonewall Brigade Band." *Confederate Veteran* 8 (1900): 304.

Hall, A. L. "Charles Chaky De Nordendorf: Soldier-Songster of the Confederacy." *Virginia Cavalcade* 24 (1974): 41–47.

Harrold, James. "Surgeons of the Confederacy." *Confederate Veteran* 40 (1932): 173.

Harwell, Richard Barksdale. "The Star of the Bonnie Blue Flag." *Civil War History* 4, no. 3 (1958): 285–90.

Haven, G. "Camp Life at the Relay." *Harper's New Monthly Magazine* 24 (1861–62): 631.

Hiner, J. A. "The Stonewall Brigade Band." *Confederate Veteran* 8 (1900): 304.

Hotze, Henry. "Three Months in the Confederate Army: The Tune of Dixie." *The Index* 1 (1862): 140.

Hewitt, John Hill. "King Linkum The First: A Musical Barletta." *Emory University Publications* 4, no. 1, 1947.

Hoole. W. Stanley. "The Antebellum Charleston Theater: Charleston The-
    atricals During the Tragic Decade." *Journal of Southern History* 11
    (1945): 538–47.
Howard, John. "The Hewitt Family in American Music." *Musical Quarterly*
    17 (1931): 25–39.
Hubbs, G. Ward "Lone Star Flags and Nameless Rags." *Alabama Review* 39,
    no. 4 (1986): 271–301.
Jillson, H. L. "'The Vacant Chair': The Hero and the Author of the Song."
    New England Magazine 16 (1897): 131–45.
Jones, J. H. "The Rank and File at Vicksburg." *Publications of the Mississippi
    Historical Society* 7 (1910): 17–31.
Kaiser, J. "Letters from the Front." *Journal of Illinois State Historical Society* 56
    (1963): 158.
Kendall, John Smith. "New Orleans Musicians of Long Ago." *Louisiana
    Historical Quarterly* 31 (1948): 2–21.
"Kirkland's Brigade, John Franklin Hoke's Division, 1864–1865." *Southern
    Historical Society Papers* 23 (1895): 165.
Leinbach, J. "Regiment Band of the Twenty Sixth North Carolina." Edited
    by D. McCorkle. *Civil War History* 4, no. 3 (1958): 225–236.
Levengood, Paul A. "In the Absence of Scarcity: The Civil War Prosperity
    of Houston, Texas." *Southwestern Historical Quarterly* 101 (1998):
    401–31.
Logue, Larry M. "Who Joined the Confederate Army? Soldiers, Civilians,
    and Communities in Mississippi." *Journal of Social History* 27 (1993):
    611–23.
Louisiana Artillery Man. "Reminiscences of New Orleans, Jackson, and
    Vicksburg."
Confederate Annals 1, no. 2 (1883): 48–49.
Mahar, William. "March to the Music." *Civil War Times Illustrated* 23
    (1984): 13–16, 41–44.
Matthews, Brander. "Control of the Baltimore Press during the Civil War."
    Maryland Historical Magazine 36 (1941): 164.
———. "Geo. F. Root, Mus. Doc." *Music: A Monthly Magazine* 8 (1895):
    502–9.
———. "The Songs of the War." *Century Magazine* 34, no. 4 (1887):
    619–29.
Maurer, D. "Professor of Music," *Musical Quarterly* 36 (1950): 511–24.

Maury, D. H. "Defence of Spanish Fort." *Southern Historical Society Papers* 39 (1914): 136.

McArthur, J. "Those Texians Are Number One Men." *Southwestern Historical Quarterly* 95 (1991–92): 492–494.

McCarthy, Carleton. "Camp Fires of the Boys in Gray." *Southern Historical Society Papers* 1 (1876): 76–89.

McNeilly, James H. "The Story of Lorena." *Confederate Veteran* 23 (1915): 24.

Mosgrove, George Dallas. "Following Morgan's Plume through Indiana and Ohio." *Southern Historical Society Papers* 23 (1907): 110–21.

Nathan, Hans. "Dixie." *Musical Quarterly* 35 (1949): 60–84.

————————. "Emmett's Walk-Arounds: Popular Theatre in New York." *Civil War History* 4, no. 3, (1958): 213–24.

Park, Robert Emory. "War Diary of Capt. Robert Emory Park, Twelfth Alabama Regiment." *Southern Historical Society Papers* 26 (1898): 1–31.

Parker, W. W. "How the Southern Soldiers Kept House during the War." *Southern Historical Society Papers* 23 (1895): 318–30.

Pessen, Edward. "How Different From Each Other Were the Antebellum North and South?" *American Historical Review* 85 (1980): 1112–1247.

Peterson, J. Edward. "A Bandsman's Letters to Home from the War." *Moravian Musical Journal* 36, no. 1 (1991): 5–8.

Pressley, John G. "The Wee Nee Volunteers of Williamsburg District, South Carolina, in the First Hagood's Regiment." *Southern Historical Society Papers* 16 (1888): 116–180.

Roach, Joseph. "Barnumizing Diaspora: The 'Irish Skylark' Does New Orleans." *Theatre Journal* 50 (1998): 39–51.

Robinson, R. V. "Confederate Copyright Entries." *William and Mary Quarterly* 16 (1936): 248 66.

Shannon, Fred A., ed. "The Civil War Letters of Sergeant Onley Andrus." *Illinois Studies in the Social Sciences* 28, no. 4 (1947).

Simpson, John A. "Shall We Change the Words of 'Dixie'?" *Southern Folklore Quarterly* 45 (1981): 19–40.

Smith, H. A. "The Author of 'Dixie.'" *Confederate Veteran* 40 (1932): 17–20.

St. Clair, C. E. "Letter." *Confederate Veteran* 19, no. 6 (1911): 271.

Stevens, John K. "Hostages to Hunger: Nutritional Night Blindness in Confederate Armies." *Tennessee Historical Quarterly* 48, no. 3 (1989): 131–43.

Stackton, E. "Didn't Sing 'Dixie' When Home Was Burning." *Confederate Veteran* 20 (1912): 260.

Stone, James, "War Music and War Psychology in the Civil War." *Journal of Abnormal Social Psychology* 36 (1941): 543–60.

Tasker, John Howard. "The Hewitt Family in American Music." *Musical Quarterly* 17 (1931): 31–39.

Tawa, Nicholas E. "Songs of the Early Nineteenth Century. Part 1: Early Song Lyrics and Coping with Life." *American Music* 13 (1995): 1–26.

Theodore, Terry. "The Confederate Theatre: Personalities during the Confederacy." *Lincoln Herald* 76, no. 4 (1974): 187–95; 77, no. 1 (1975): 33–41; 77, no. 2 (1975) 102–14; 77, no. 3 (1975): 158–67.

Walsh, Lorna. "The Antics of Ante-bellum Virtuosi." *Etude* 35 (1917): 381–82

Williams, T. H., ed. "The Civil War Letters of William L. Cage (Barksdale Brigade)." *Louisiana Historical Quarterly* 39 (1956): 113–30.

Wright, Edith and McDevitt, Josephine A. "Lithographers before 1870." *Antiques* 18 (1922): 341–44.

Zikmund, Joseph. "National Anthems as Political Symbols." *Australian Journal of Politics and History* 15, no. 3 (1969): 73–80.

Dissertations

Boudreaux, Peggy C. "Music *Publishing in New Orleans.*" Master's thesis, University of Southwestern Louisiana, 1977.

Boyce, Monique Davis. "The First Forty Years of the Augusta, Georgia, Theater." Master's thesis, University of Georgia, 1957.

Bufkin, William A. "Union Bands of the Civil War: Instrumentation and Score Analysis." Ph.D. diss., Louisiana State University, 1973.

Crews, E. K. "A History of Music in Knoxville, Tennessee, 1791 to 1910." Ph.D. diss., Florida State University, 1961.

Ferguson, Ben P. "The Bands of the Confederacy: An Examination of the Musical and Military Contributions of the Bands and Musicians of the Confederate States of America." Ph.D. diss., North Texas State University, 1987.

Green, Elvena M. "Theatre and Other Entertainments in Savannah, Georgia, 1818–1865." Ph.D. diss., University of Iowa, 1971.

Hamil, Linda Virginia. "A Study of Theatrical Activity in Natchez, Mississippi from 1800–1840." Master's thesis, University of Mississippi, 1976.

Hester, Wyoline, "The Savannah Stage." Master's thesis, Alabama Polytechnical Institute, 1930.

Langley, William Osler. "The Theater In Columbus, Georgia, 1828–1878." Master's thesis, Auburn University, 1937.

Mahan, Katherine Hines. "History of Music in Columbus, Georgia, 1828–1928." Ph.D. diss., Florida State University, 1967.

Pugh, Donald Wagner. "Music in Frontier Houston, 1836–1876." Ph.D. diss., University of Texas, 1970.

Reinders, Robert Clemens. "A Social History of New Orleans, 1850–1860." Ph.D. diss., University of Texas, 1957.

Ritter, Charles C. "The Theatre in Memphis, Tennessee from Its Beginning to 1859." Ph. D. diss., University of Iowa, 1956.

Steinhaus, Walter E. "Music in Cultural Life of Macon, Georgia 1823–1900." Ph.D. diss., Florida State University, 1973.

Washburne, Alice. "A Descriptive Catalog of Confederate Music in the Duke University Collection." Master's thesis, Duke University, 1936.

Williams, Grier W. "A History of Music in Jacksonville, Florida, from 1822 to 1922." Ph D. diss., Florida State University, 1957.

Winden, Craig. "The Life and Musical Theater of John Hill Hewitt." Ph.D. diss., University of Illinois, 1973.

General Works

Abel, Ernest L., and Barbara E. Buckley. *The Handwriting on the Wall.* Westport, Conn.: Greenwood Press, 1977.

Abrahams, Roger D. *Singing the Master: The Emergence of African American Culture in the Plantation South.* New York: Pantheon Books, 1992.

Adams, Henry W. *Montgomery Theater, 1822–1835.* Tuscaloosa: University of Alabama Press, 1955.

Alderman, Edwin Anderson, Joel Chandler Harris, and Charles William Kent, eds. *Library of Southern Literature.* Atlanta: Martin & Hoyt Co., 1909.

Andrews, Matthews Page. "History of 'Maryland! My Maryland!'" In *Library of Southern Literature,* edited by Edwin Anderson Alderman, Joel Chandler Harris, and Charles William Kent. New Orleans: Martin & Hoyt Co., 1909.

———. "James Ryder Randall." In *Library of Southern Literature,* Vol. 10, edited by Edwin Anderson Alderman, Joel Chandler Harris, and Charles William Kent. New Orleans: Martin & Hoyt Co., 1909.

Ash, Stephen V. *When the Yankees Came: Conflict and Chaos in the Occupied South, 1861–1865.* Chapel Hill: University of North Carolina Press, 1965.

Austin, William W. *"Susanna," "Jeanie," and "The Old Folks at Home": The Songs of Stephen C. Foster from His Time to Ours.* New York: Macmillan, 1975.

Bailey, F. A. *Class and Tennessee's Confederate Generation.* Chapel Hill: University of North Carolina Press, 1987.

Bardeen, Charles William. *A Little Fifer's War Diary.* Syracuse, N.Y.: C. W. Bardeen, 1910.

Barnum, Phineas Taylor. *Struggles and Triumphs; or, Forty Years' Recollections of P. T. Barnum.* New York: Macmillan, 1930.

Barrett, John Gilchrist. *The Civil War in North Carolina.* Chapel Hill: University of North Carolina Press, 1963.

Barton, Michael. *Goodmen: The Character of Civil War Soldiers.* University Park: Pennsylvania State University Press, 1981.

Basler, Roy P., ed. *Abraham Lincoln: His Speeches and Writing.* New York: Da Capo Press, n.d.

Bearss, Edwin C., ed. *A Louisiana Confederate: Diary of Felix Pierre Poche.* Natchitoches, La.: Northwestern State University Press, 1972.

Bergeron, Arthur W. *Confederate Mobile.* Jackson: University of Mississippi, 1991.

Beringer, Richard E., et. al. *Why the South Lost the Civil War.* Athens: University of Georgia Press, 1986.

———. "Confederate Identity and the Will to Fight." In *On the Road to Total War: The American Civil War and the German Wars of Unification, 1861–1871,* edited by Stig Forster and Jorg Nagler. New York: Cambridge University Press, 1997.

Bill, Alfred Hoyt. *The Beleaguered City: Richmond, 1861–1865.* New York: Alfred A. Knopf, 1946.

Billings, John David. *Hardtack and Coffee; or, The Unwritten Story of Army Life.* Boston: George M. Smith and Co., 1888.

Binion, Rudolph. *Love beyond Death: The Anatomy of a Myth in the Arts.* New York: New York University Press, 1993.

Bircher, William. *A Drummer Boy's Diary: Comprising Four Years of Service with the Second Regiment Minnesota Veteran Volunteers, 1861 to 1865.* St. Paul: St. Paul Book and Stationery Co., 1889.

Blackford, William Willis. *War Years with Jeb Stuart.* New York: Charles Scribner's Sons, 1945.

Borcke, Heros von. *Memoirs of the Confederate War for Independence.* Edinburgh: W. Blackwood, 1866.

Boyd, Malcolm. "National Anthems." In *The New Grove Dictionary of Music and Musicians,* edited by Stanley Sadie. Vol. 13. London: Macmillan, 1980.

Boyd, Minnie Clare. *Alabama in the Fifties: A Social Study.* New York: Columbia University Press, 1931.

Bratton, Jacqueline S. *The Victorian Popular Ballad.* Totowa, N.J.: Rowman and Littlefield, 1975.

Breuilly, John. "Nationalism and the State." In *Nationalism: The Nature and Evolution of an Idea,* edited by Eugene Kamenka. Canberra: Australian National University Press, 1973.

Brice, Marshall Moore. *The Stonewall Brigade Band.* Verona, Va.: McClure Printing Co., 1967.

Brickell, John. *The Natural History of North Carolina.* New York: Johnson Reprint Corp., 1969.

Brink, Carol Ryrie. *Harps in the Wind: The Story of the Singing Hutchinsons.* New York: Macmillan Co., 1947.

Brown, Joseph A. *The Memoirs of a Confederate Soldier.* Abingdon, Va.: Forum Press, 1940.

Brown, Norman D., ed. *Journey to Pleasant Hill: The Civil War Letters of Captain Elijah P. Petty: Walker's Texas Division, CSA.* San Antonio: University of Texas Institute of Texan Cultures, 1982.

Brown, Thomas Allston. *History of the American Stage: Containing Biographical Sketches of Nearly Every Member of the Profession That Has Appeared On the American Stage, from 1733 to 1870.* Vol. 1. New York: Dick and Fitzgerald, 1870.

———. *A History of the New York Stage from the First Performance in 1732 to 1901.* Vol. 1. New York: Dodd, Mead & Co., 1903.

Brown, Walter Lee., *A Life of Albert Pike.* Fayetteville: University of Arkansas Press, 1997.

Bruce, George Anson. *The Twentieth Regiment of Massachusetts Volunteer Infantry, 1861–1865.* Boston: Houghton Mifflin, Co., 1906.

Bryan, T. Conn. *Confederate Georgia.* Athens: University of Georgia Press, 1955.

Butterfield, Julia Lorrilard S., ed. *A Biographical Memorial of General Daniel Butterfield.* New York: Grafton Press, 1904.

Caba, G. Craig. *United States Military Drums, 1845–1865: A Pictorial Survey.* Harrisburg, Pa.: Civil War Antiquities Ltd., 1977.

Cabaniss, Jim R., ed. *Civil War Journal and Letters of Serg. Washington Ives, 4th Florida, CSA.* Tallahassee, Fla.: J. R. Cabaniss, 1987.

Campbell, Don. *The Mozart Effect.* New York: Avon Books, 1997.

Camus, Raoul F. *Military Music of the American Revolution.* Chapel Hill: University of North Carolina Press, 1976.

Cannon, Devereaux D. *The Flags of the Confederacy: An Illustrated History.* Memphis: St. Lukes Press and Broadfoot Publishing, 1988.

Cannon, J. P. *Inside of Rebeldom: The Daily Life of a Private in the Confederate Army.* Washington, D.C.: National Tribune, 1900.

Capers, Gerald Mortimer. *Biography of a River Town: Memphis, Its Heroic Age.* Chapel Hill: University of North Carolina, 1939.

Cary, D. L. *Confederate Scrap Book.* Richmond: J. L. Hill Printing Co., 1893.

Casey, S. *Infantry Tactics: For the Instruction, Exercise, and Manoeuvres of the Soldier, A Company, Line of Skirmishers, Battalion, Brigade, or Corps D'Armee.* New York: D. Van Nostrand, 1863.

Casler, John Overton. *Four Years in the Stonewall Brigade.* Marietta, Ga.: Continental Book Co., 1951.

Cater, Douglas J. *As It Was: Reminiscences of a Soldier of the Third Texas Cavalry and the Nineteenth Louisiana Infantry.* Austin: Statehouse Press, 1990.

Catton, Bruce. *The Coming Fury.* Garden City, N.Y.: Doubleday & Co., 1961.

_____. *Prefaces to History.* Garden City, N.Y.: Doubleday, 1970.

Cauthen, Joyce H. *With Fiddle and Well-Rosined Bow: Old-Time Fiddling in Alabama.* Tuscaloosa: University of Alabama Press, 1989.

Chambers, Lenoir. *Stonewall Jackson.* Vol. 2. New York: W. Morrow, 1959.

Charlton, D. David. "Romantic Opera: 1830–1850." In *Romanticism, (1830–1890).* Oxford: Oxford University Press, 1990.

Chase, Gilbert. *America's Music: From the Pilgrims to the Present.* Urbana: University of Illinois Press, 1987.

Claghorn, Charles Eugene. *The Mocking Bird: The Life and Diary of Its Author, Sep. Winner.* Philadelphia: Magee Press, 1937.

Clark, Walter. *Histories of the Several Regiments and Battalions from North Carolina in the Great War 1861–65.* Vols. 2 and 5. Goldsboro, N.C.: Nash Brothers, 1901.

Coleman, Kenneth. *Confederate Athens.* Athens: University of Georgia Press, 1967.

————, ed. *Confederate Athens, 1861-1865: As Seen through Letters in the University of Georgia Libraries.* Athens: University of Georgia Press, 1969.

Cooke, John Esten. *Outlines from the Outpost.* Chicago: R. R. Donnelley & Sons Co., 1961.

————. *Wearing of the Gray.* New York: E. B.Treat & Co., 1969.

Corley, Florence F. *Confederate City: Augusta, Georgia, 1860–1865.* Columbia: University of South Carolina Press, 1960.

Coulter, E. Merton. *Confederate States of America.* Baton Rouge: Louisiana State University Press, 1950.

Crete, Liliane. *Daily Life in Louisiana, 1815–1830.* Baton Rouge: Louisiana State University Press, 1981.

Crofts, Daniel W. *Reluctant Confederates: Upper South Unionists in the Secession Crisis.* Chapel Hill: University of North Carolina Press, 1989.

Cullen, Ellen. *The Civil War in American Drama before 1900.* Providence: Brown University, 1990.

Cullen, Jim. *The Civil War in Popular Culture. A Reusable Past.* Washington, D.C.: Smithsonian Institution Press, 1995.

Current, Richard N. "God and the Strongest Battalions." In *Why the North Won the Civil War,* edited by David Herbert Donald. New York: Touchstone, 1996.

Dabney, Virginius. *Richmond.* Charlottesville: University Press of Virginia, 1993.

Daniel, F. S. *Richmond Howitzers in the War.* 1891. Reprint, Gaithersburg, Md.: Butternut Press, n.d.

Daniel, Larry J. *Soldiering in the Army of Tennessee: A Portrait of Life in a Confederate Army.* Chapel Hill: University of North Carolina Press, 1991.

Davenport, Francis Garvin. *Cultural Life in Nashville on the Eve of the Civil War.* Chapel Hill: University of North Carolina Press, 1941.

Davis, Burke. *The Long Surrender.* New York: Random House, 1985.

Davis, Ronald L. *A History of Music in American Life.* Vol. 1. Malabar, Fla.: Kreiger Publishing Co., 1982.

———. *A History of Opera in the American West.* Englewood Cliffs, N.J.: Prentice-Hall, 1965.

Davis, Varina. *Jefferson Davis: Ex-President of the Confederate States of America.* New York: Belford Co., 1890.

Davis, William, C. *The Cause Lost: Myths and Realities of the Confederacy.* Lawrence: University Press of Kansas, 1996.

———, ed. *Diary of a Confederate Soldier: John S. Jackman of the Orphan Brigade.* Columbia: University of South Carolina Press, 1990.

———, ed. *Touched by Fire: A Photographic Portrait of the Civil War.* Boston: Little, Brown and Co., 1985.

DeLeon, Thomas Cooper. *Belles, Beaux, and Brains of the 60s.* 1909. Reprint, New York: Arno Press, 1974.

———. *Four Years In Rebel Capitals: An Inside View of Life in the Southern Confederacy: From Birth to Death.* Mobile, Ala.: Gossip Printing Co., 1890.

Dennis, Frank Allen, ed. *Kemper County Rebel: The Civil War Diary of Robert Masten Holmes.* Jackson: University and College Press of Mississippi, 1973.

Dennison, Sam. *Scandalize My Name: Black Imagery in American Popular Music.* New York: Garland Publishing, 1982.

Derby, James Cephas. *Fifty Years among Authors: Books and Publishers.* New York: G. W. Carleton & Co., 1884.

Dichter, Harry, and Elliott Shapiro. *Handbook of Early American Sheet Music, 1768–1889.* 1941. Reprint. New York: Dover Publications, 1977.

Dinkins, James. *By an Old Johnnie: Personal Recollections and Experiences in the Confederate Army, 1861–1865.* Cincinnati: Robert Clarke Co., 1897.

Dizikes, John. *Opera in America: A Cultural History.* New Haven: Yale University Press, 1991.

Doob, Leonard, W. *Patriotism and Nationalism: Their Psychological Foundations.* New Haven: Yale University Press, 1964.

Dormon, James H. *Theater in the Ante Bellum South, 1815–1861.* Chapel Hill: University of North Carolina Press, 1967.

Douglas, Henry Kyd. *I Rode With Stonewall: Being Chiefly the War Experiences of the Youngest Member of Jackson's Staff from the John Brown Raid to the Hanging of Mrs. Surratt.* Chapel Hill: University of North Carolina Press, 1940.

Downey, Fairfax Davis. *Clash of Cavalry: The Battle of Brandy Station, June 9, 1863.* New York: David McKay Co., 1959.

Duke, Basil Wilson. *Reminiscences.* Garden City, N.Y.: Doubleday, Page & Co., 1911.

Duncan, E. *Letters of General J. E. B. Stuart to His Wife.* Vol. 1. Atlanta: Emory University Publications, 1943.

Durkein, Joseph T., ed. *John Dooley, Confederate Soldier: His War Journal.* Notre Dame: University of Notre Dame Press, 1963.

Dyer, Frederick H. *A Compendium of the War of the Rebellion.* Vol. 1. New York: Thomas Yoseloff, 1959.

Elson, Louis C. *The National Music of America and Its Sources.* Boston: Page, 1900.

Emerson, Ken. *Doo-Dah! Stephen Foster and the Rise of American Popular Culture.* New York: Simon and Schuster, 1997.

Engel, Lehman. *Their Words Are Music: The Great Theatre Lyricists and Their Music.* New York: Crown, 1975.

Engle, Gary D., ed. *This Grotesque Essence: Plays from the American Minstrel Stage.* Baton Rouge: Louisiana State University Press, 1978.

English Combatant. *Battle-Fields of the South, from Bull Run to Fredericksburg: With Sketches of Confederate Commanders, and Gossip of the Camps.* New York: John Bradburn, 1864.

Eppes, Susan Bradford. *Through Some Eventful Years.* 1926. Reprint, Gainesville: University of Florida Press, 1968.

Epstein, Dena J. P. *Sinful Tunes and Spirituals: Black Folk Music to the Civil War.* Urbana: University of Illinois Press, 1977.

Escott, Paul D. *After Secession: Jefferson Davis and the Failure of Confederate Nationalism.* Baton Rouge: Louisiana State University Press, 1978.

Everson, Guy R., and Edward H. Simpson Jr., eds. *Far, Far from Home: The Wartime Letters of Dick and Tully Simpson, Third South Carolina Volunteers.* New York: Oxford University Press, 1994.

Ex boy [Figg, Royall W.]. *Where Men Only Dare to Go!; or, The Story of a Boy Company (C.S.A.).* Richmond: Whitten and Shepperson, 1885.

Farwell, Byron. *Stonewall: A Biography of General Thomas J. Jackson.* New York: W. W. Norton, 1992.

Faust, Drew Gilpin. *The Creation of Confederate Nationalism.* Baton Rouge: Louisiana State University Press, 1988.

———. *Mothers of Invention: Women of the Slaveholding South in the American Civil War.* Chapel Hill: University of North Carolina Press, 1996.

Fehrenbacher, Don E. *Constitutions and Constitutionalism in the Slaveholding South.* Athens: University of Georgia Press, 1989.

Finson, Jon W. *The Voices That Are Gone.* New York: Oxford University Press, 1994.

Fischer, David Hackett. *Albion's Seed: Four British Folkways in America.* New York: Oxford University Press, 1989.

Fleet, Betsy, and John D. P. Fuller, eds. *Green Mount: A Virginia Plantation Family during the Civil War: Being the Journal of Benjamin Robert Fleet and Letters of His Family.* Charlottesville: University Press of Virginia, 1962.

Fleming, Walter. *Civil War and Reconstruction in Alabama.* New York: Peter Smith,1949.

Fletcher, William Andrew. *Rebel Private Front and Rear.* Washington, D.C.: Zenger Pub. Co., 1985.

Fox-Genovese, Elizabeth. *Within the Plantation Household: Black and White Women in the Old South.* Chapel Hill: University of North Carolina Press, 1988.

Frank, Joseph Allen, and George A. Reaves. *Seeing the Elephant: Raw Recruits at the Battle of Shiloh.* Westport, Conn.: Greenwood Press, 1989.

Fraser, Walter J. *Charleston! Charleston! The History of a Southern City.* Columbia: University of South Carolina Press, 1989.

Freeman, Douglas Southall. *Lee's Lieutenants: A Study in Command.* Vols. 1 and 3. New York: Charles Scribner's Sons, 1942–44.

———. *R. E. Lee, A Biography.* New York: Charles Scribner's Sons, 1934–35.

Futch, Ovid L. *History of Andersonville Prison.* Gainesville: University of Florida, 1968.

Galbreath, Charles Burleigh. *Daniel Decatur Emmett: Author of "Dixie."* Columbus, Ohio: Fred J. Heer Press, 1904.

Gallagher, Gary W. *The Confederate War.* Cambridge: Harvard University Press, 1997.

———, ed. *Fighting for the Confederacy: The Personal Recollections of General Edward Porter Alexander.* Chapel Hill: University of North Carolina Press, 1989.

Gammage, William L. *The Camp, the Bivouac, and the Battle Field: Being a History of the Fourth Arkansas Regiment, from Its First Organization down to the Present Date.* Little Rock: Arkansas Southern Press, 1958.

Garofalo, Robert Joseph, and Mark Elrod. *A Pictorial History of Civil War Era Musical Instruments and Military Bands.* Charleston, W.Va.: Pictorial Histories Publishing Co., 1985.

Gilchrist, John. *Civil War in North Carolina.* Chapel Hill: University of North Carolina Press, 1963.

Goodloe, Albert T. *Confederate Echoes.* Washington, D.C.: Zenger Pub. Co., 1983.

Gordon, John Brown. *Reminiscences of the Civil War.* New York: Charles Scribner's Sons, 1904.

Govan, Thomas P. "Americans below the Potomac." In *The Southerner As American,* edited by Charles Grier Sellers, et al. Chapel Hill: University of North Carolina Press, 1960.

Green, Fletcher Melvin. "Johnny Reb Could Read." In *Democracy in the Old South and Other Essays by Fletcher Melvin Green,* edited by J. Isaac Copeland. Nashville: Vanderbilt University Press, 1969.

Grice, William A. *New Orleans Merchant's Diary and Guide.* New Orleans: Grice, 1858.

Grimsley, Mark. *The Hard Hand of War: Union Military Policy toward Southern Civilians, 1861–1865.* Cambridge: Cambridge University Press, 1995.

Guenter, Scot M. *The American Flag.* Rutherford, N.J.: Farleigh Dickinson University Press, 1990.

Hall, Harry H., ed. *A Johnny Reb Band from Salem: The Pride of Tarheelia*. Raleigh: North Carolina Confederate Centennial Commission, 1963.

Hamm, Charles. *Music in the New World*. New York: W. W. Norton, 1983.

————. *Yesterdays: Popular Song in America*. New York: W. W. Norton, 1979.

Harrison, Mrs. Burton. *Recollections Grave and Gray*. New York: C. Scribner's Sons, 1911.

Harrison, James Albert, ed. *The Complete Works of Edgar Allan Poe*. New York: Society of English and French, 1902.

Harwell, Richard Barksdale. *Confederate Music*. Chapel Hill: University of North Carolina Press, 1950.

————, ed. *Destruction and Reconstruction: Personal Experiences of the Late War*. New York: Longmans, Green and Co., 1955.

————, ed. *The Confederate Reader*. New York: Longmans, Green and Co., 1957.

Haythornthwaite, Philip J. *Uniforms of the Civil War*. New York: Sterling Publishing Co. 1990.

Hazen, Margaret Hindle, and Robert M. Hazen. *The Music Men: An Illustrated History of Brass Bands in America, 1800–1920*. Washington, D.C.: Smithsonian Institution Press, 1987.

Heaps, Willard Allison, and Porter W. Heaps. *The Singing Sixties*. Norman: University of Oklahoma Press, 1960.

Heller, J. Roderick, and Carolyn Ayres Heller, eds. *The Confederacy Is on Her Way up the Spout: Letters to South Carolina 1861–1865*. Athens: University of Georgia Press, 1992.

Henderson, G. *History of the 3rd, 7th, 8th, and 12th Kentucky CSA*. Louisville: C. T. Dearing Printing Co., 1911.

Henderson, Harry McCorry. *Texas in the Confederacy*. San Antonio: Naylor Co., 1955.

Henderson, L. *Roster of the Confederate Soldiers of Georgia, 1861–1865*. Hapeville, Ga.: Longino & Porter, Inc., 1955–1964.

Hendrickson, Robert. *Sumter, The First Day of the Civil War*. Chelsea, Mich.: Scarborough House, 1990.

Hermann, Isaac. *Memoirs of a Veteran Who Served as a Private in the 60's in the War between the States: Personal Incidents, Experiences, and Observations*. Atlanta: Byrd Printing Co., 1911.

Herz, Henri. *My Travels in America*. Repr. Madison: University of Wisconsin Press, 1963.

Hess, Earl J. *Liberty, Virtue, and Progress: Northerners and Their War for the Union.* New York: Fordham University Press, 1997.

Hewitt, John Hill. *Shadows on the Wall; or, Glimpses of the Past: A Retrospect of the Past Fifty Years.* New York: AMS Press, 1971.

———. *War: A Poem with Copious Notes on the Revolution of 1861–1862.* Richmond: West and Johnston, 1862.

Hewitt, Lawrence L. *Port Hudson: Confederate Bastion on the Mississippi.* Baton Rouge: Louisiana State University Press, 1987.

Hicks, Frederick Cocks. *The Flag of the United States.* Washington, D.C.: W. F. Roberts, 1926.

Hitchcock, Hugh Wiley. *Music in the United States: A Historical Introduction.* Englewood Cliffs, N.J.: Prentice-Hall, 1974.

Hobsbawm, Eric J. *Nations and Nationalism since 1780: Programme, Myth, Reality.* Cambridge: Cambridge University Press, 1990.

———. "Some Reflections on Nationalism." In *Imagination and Precision in the Social Sciences,* edited by Thomas J. Nossiter, Albert H. Hanson, and Stein Rokkan. London: Farber and Farber, 1972.

Hoke, Jacob. *The Great Invasion of 1863; or, General Lee in Pennsylvania.* Dayton, Ohio: W. J. Shuey, 1888.

Hoogerwerf, Frank W. *John Hill Hewitt: Sources and Bibliography.* Atlanta: Emory University, 1981.

———, ed. *Music in Georgia.* New York: Da Capo Press, 1984.

Hoole, William Stanley. *The Ante-bellum Charleston Theatre.* Tuscaloosa: University of Alabama Press, 1946.

Hoole, William Stanley and Addie Shirley Hoole. *Confederate Norfolk: The Letters of a Virginia Lady to the Mobile Register 1861–1862.* University, Ala.: Confederate Pub. Co., 1984.

Houstoun, Mrs. Matilda Charlotte. *Texas and the Gulf of Mexico; or, Yachting in the New World.* Philadelphia: G. B. Zeiber, 1845.

Howard, John Tasker. *Our American Music.* New York: Thomas Y. Crowell, Co., 1958.

———. *Stephen Foster: America's Troubadour.* New York: Thomas Y. Crowell Co., 1962.

Howard, McHenry. *Recollections of a Maryland Confederate Soldier and Staff Officer under Johnston, Jackson, and Lee.* Repr. Wilmnington, N.C.: Broadfoot Pub. Co., n.d.

Howe, Daniel Walker, ed. *Victorian America.* Philadelphia: University of Pennsylvania Press, 1976.

Hubbell, Jay Broadus, ed. *The Last Years of Henry Timrod, 1864–1867.* Durham, N.C.: Duke University Press, 1941.

Hubner, Charles William. *War Poets of the South.* Privately published, n.d..

Huffman, James. *Up and Downs of a Confederate Soldier.* New York: Wm. E. Rudge's Sons, 1940.

Hundley, Daniel Robinson. *Social Relations in Our Southern States.* New York: Arno Press, 1973.

Hunter, Alexander. *Johnny Reb and Billy Yank.* New York: Neale Publishing Co., 1905.

Inman, Arthur Crew, ed. *Soldier of the South: General Pickett's War Letters to His Wife.* Boston: Houghton Mifflin Co., 1928.

Jackson, Charles O., ed. *Passing: The Vision of Death in America.* Westport, Conn.: Greenwood Press, 1977.

Jackson, George Pullen. *White Spirituals in the Southern Uplands: The Story of the Fasola Folk, Their Songs, Singings, and "Buckwheat Notes."* Chapel Hill: University of North Carolina Press, 1933.

Jackson, Mary Anna Morrison. *Life and Letters of General Thomas J. Jackson.* New York: Harper and Bros., 1892.

Jimerson, Randall C. *The Private Civil War.* Baton Rouge: Louisiana State University Press, 1988.

Johns, John Edwin. *Florida during the Civil War.* Gainesville: University of Florida Press, 1963.

Johnson, Claudia D. "That Guilty Third Tier: Prostitution in Nineteenth Century American Theaters." In *Victorian America,* edited by Daniel Walker Howe. Philadelphia: University of Pennsylvania, 1976.

Joint Committee Appointed to Consider and Report on a Selection of New Words for "Dixie." *A Collection of Dixies.* Opelika, Alabama: n. p., 1904.

Jones, Katherine Macbeth. *When Sherman Came.* Indianapolis: Bobbs Merrill Co., 1964.

Jones, William B. *Under the Stars and Bars: A History of the Surrey Light Artillery.* Dayton, Ohio: Morningside Bookshop, 1975.

Kaser, David. *Books and Libraries in Camp and Battle.* Westport, Conn.: Greenwood Press, 1984.

Kecmanovic, Dusan. *The Mass Psychology of Ethnonationalism.* New York: Plenum Press, 1996.

Keegan, John. *The Face of Battle.* New York: Viking Press, 1976.

Kendall, John Smith. *The Golden Age of the New Orleans Theater.* Baton Rouge: Louisiana State University Press, 1952.

Kieffer, Harry M. *Recollections of a Drummer Boy.* Boston: Ticknor and Co., 1889.

Klaus, Kenneth Blanchard. *The Romantic Period in Music.* Boston: Allyn and Bacon, 1970.

Kmen, Henry A. *Music in New Orleans: The Formative Years, 1791–1841.* Baton Rouge: Louisiana State University Press, 1966.

Kohn, Hans. *Prophets and Peoples: Studies in 19th Century Nationalism.* New York: Macmillan Co., 1946.

Krick, Robert E. L. *Parker's Virginia Battery C.S.A.* Berryville, Va.: Virginia Book Co., 1975.

Kupchan, Charles A. "Introduction: Nationalism Resurgent." In *Nationalism And Nationalities in the New Europe,* edited by Charles A. Kupchan. Ithaca, New York: Cornell University Press, 1995.

LaBree, Benjamin. *Camp Fires of the Confederacy.* Louisville, Ky.: Courier-Journal Printing Co., 1898.

Lady [Mary Ann Webster Longborough]. *My Cave Life in Vicksburg.* New York: Appleton, 1864.

Langer, Susanne Katherina. *Philosophy in a New Key: A Study in the Symbolism of Reason, Rite, and Art.* Cambridge: Harvard University Press, 1979.

Lasswell, Mary, ed. *Rags and Hope: The Recollections of Val C Giles: Four Years with Hood's Brigade Fourth Texas Infantry, 1861–1865.* New York: Coward-McCann, 1961.

Lavery, Dennis S., and Mark H. Jordan. *Iron Brigade General: John Gibbon, a Rebel in Blue.* Westport, Conn: Greenwood Press, 1993.

Leary, Lewis Gaston. *The Book-Peddling Parson: An Account of the Life and Works of Mason Locke Weems: Patriot, Pitchman, Author, and Purveyor of Morality to the Citizenry of the Early United States of America.* Chapel Hill, N.C.: Algonquin Books, 1984.

Levine, Lawrence W. *Highbrow, Lowbrow.* Cambridge: Harvard University Press, 1988.

Lewis, John Tillery. *Origin of Dixie.* Memphis: E. Witzman & Co., n.d.

Lewis, L. *Captain Sam Grant.* Boston: Little, Brown and Co., 1950.

Loesser, Arthur. *Men, Women, and Pianos.* New York: Simon and Schuster, 1954.

Lonn, Ella. *Foreigners in the Confederacy.* Gloucester, Mass.: Peter Smith, 1965.

Lord, Francis Alfred, and Arthur Wise. *Bands and Drummer Boys of the Civil War.* South Brunswick, N.J.: Thomas Yoseloff, 1966.

Lord, Walter, ed. *The Fremantle Diary: Being the Journal of Lieutenant Colonel James Arthur Lyon Fremantle, Coldstream Guards: On His Three Months in the Southern States.* Boston: Little, Brown, 1954.

Lott, Eric. *Love and Theft: Blackface Minstrelsy and the American Working Class.* New York: Oxford University Press, 1993.

Lowenthal, David. "European and English Landscapes as National Symbols." In *Geography and National Identity,* edited by David Hooson. Oxford, England: Blackwell, 1994.

Lowry, Thomas P. *The Story the Soldiers Wouldn't Tell.* Mechanicsburg, Pa.: Stackpole Books, 1994.

Lyell, Charles. *A Second Visit to the United States of North America.* Vol. 2. New York: Harper and Bro., 1849.

Lynes, Russell. *The Domesticated Americans.* New York: Harper & Row, 1963.

Macarthy, Harry. *His Book of Original Songs, Ballads, and Anecdotes: As Presented by the Author in His Well-Known Personation Concerts.* Indianapolis: Indiana State Sentinel, 1888.

Mackie, J. Milton. *From Cape Cod to Dixie and the Tropics.* 1864. Repr. New York: Negro University Press, 1968.

Malone, Bill C. *Country Music, U.S.A.* Austin: University of Texas Press, 1985.

———. *Singing Cowboys and Musical Mountaineers: Southern Culture and the Roots of Country Music.* Athens: University of Georgia Press, 1993.

———. *Southern Music, American Music.* Lexington: University Press of Kentucky, 1979.

Manarin, Louis H. *North Carolina Troops.* Raleigh: State Department of Archives and History, 1966–87.

Manarin, Louis H., and Lee A. Wallace. *Richmond Volunteers: The Volunteer Companies of the City of Richmond and Henrico Country, Virginia, 1861–1865.* Richmond: Westover Press, 1969.

Marszalek, John F., ed. *Diary of Miss Emma Holmes.* Baton Rouge: Louisiana State University Press, 1979.

Massey, Mary Elizabeth. *Ersatz In The Confederacy.* Columbia: University of South Carolina Press, 1952.

Mates, Julian. *America's Musical Stage: Two Hundred Years of Musical Theatre.* Westport, Conn.: Greenwood Press, 1985.

Matthews, William Smyth Babcock. *A Hundred Years of Music in America.* Chicago: G. L. Howe, 1889.

McCardell, John. *The Idea of a Southern Nation: Southern Nationalists and Southern Nationalism, 1830–1860*. New York: W. W. Norton, 1979.

McCarthy, Carlton. *Detailed Minutiae of Soldier Life in the Army of Northern Virginia, 1861–1865*. Reprint, New York: Time-Life Books, 1982.

McMorries, Edward Young. *History of the First Regiment Alabama Volunteer Infantry C.S.A.* Montgomery, Ala.: Brown Printing Co., 1904.

McPherson, James M. *For Cause and Comrades: Why Men Fought in the Civil War.* New York: Oxford University Press, 1997.

McWhiney, Grady. *Braxton Bragg and Confederate Defeat*. Vol. 1. New York: Columbia University Press, 1969.

————. *Cracker Culture: Celtic Ways in the Old South*. Tuscaloosa: University of Alabama Press, 1990.

Merriam, Charles Edward. *The Political Philosophy of John C. Calhoun* in Dunning, William A., ed. *Studies in Southern History and Politics*. New York: Columbia University Press, 1914.

Miller, Delavan S. *Drum Taps in Dixie: Memories of a Drummer Boy, 1861–1865*. Watertown, N.Y.: Hungerford-Holbrook Co., 1905.

Miller, Francis Trevelyan, ed. *The Photographic History of the Civil War.* 10 vols. New York: Review of Reviews Co., 1912.

Mitchell, Reid. *Civil War Soldiers.* New York: Viking Press, 1988.

Mixson, Frank M. *Reminiscences of a Private. (Company # 1st) S. C. Vols.* Columbia, S.C.: Hagoods State Co., 1910.

Moore, A. *The Louisiana Tigers; or, The Two Louisiana Brigades of the Army of Northern Virginia, 1861–1865*. Baton Rouge: Ortlieb Press, 1961.

Moore, Frank. *Anecdotes, Poetry, and Incidents of the War: North and South.* New York: G. P. Putnam, 1866.

————. *The Civil War in Song and Story*. New York: P. F. Collier, 1889.

————. *Personal and Political Ballads*. New York: George P. Putnam, 1864.

————. *The Rebellion Record: A Diary of American Events*. Vol. 1–10. New York: G. P. Putnam, 1861–1863.

————. *Rebel Rhymes and Rhapsodies.* New York: G. P. Putnam, 1864.

Moss, William. *Confederate Broadside Poems: An Annotated Descriptive Bibliography Based on the Collection of Z. Smith Reynolds Library of Wake Forest University.* Westport, Conn.: Meckler Co., 1988.

Munsell, Joel. *The Chronology of the Origin and Progress of Paper and Papermaking.* New York: Garland Publishers, 1980.

Myers, R. E. *The Zollie Tree.* Louisville: Filson Club Press, 1964.

Nathan, Hans. *Dan Emmett and the Rise of Early Negro Minstrelsy.* Norman: University of Oklahoma Press, 1962.

National Cyclopedia of American Biography. Vol. 24. Clifton, N.J.: J. T. White, 1984.

Neese, George M. *Three Years in the Confederate Horse Artillery.* New York: Neale Pub. Co., 1911.

Olson, Kenneth E. *Music and Musket: Bands and Bandsmen of the American Civil War.* Westport, Conn.: Greenwood Press, 1981.

Orr, N. Lee. *Alfredo Barili and the Rise of Classical Music in Atlanta.* Atlanta: Scholars Press, 1995.

Osterweis, Rollin G. *Romanticism and Nationalism in the Old South.* 1949. Reprint, Baton Rouge: Louisiana State University Press, 1971.

Owen, William Miller. *In Camp and Battle with the Washington Artillery of New Orleans.* Boston: Ticknor and Co., 1885.

Palmer, R. *What a Lovely War: British Soldiers' Songs from the Boer War to the Present Day.* London: Michael Joseph, 1990.

Parrish, Michael T., and Robert M. Willingham. *Confederate Imprints: A Bibliogaphy of Southern Publications from Secession to Surrender: Expanding and Revising the Earlier Works of Majorie Crandall and Richard Harwell.* Austin: Jenkins Publ. Co., 1984.

Pearsall, Ronald. *Victorian Popular Music.* Detroit: Gale Research Co., 1973.

Pollard, E. A. *The Rival Administrations: Richmond and Washington in December 1863.* Richmond: privately published, 1863.

Porter, General Horace. *Campaiging with Grant.* Bloomington: Indiana University Press, 1961.

Preble, George Henry. *History of the Flag of the United States of America, and of the Naval and Yacht-Club Signals, Seals and Arms, and Principal National Songs of the United States, with a Chronicle of the Symbols, Standards, Banners, and Flags of Ancient and Modern Nations.* Boston: James R. Osgood and Co., 1882.

Prescott, Frederick Clarke, ed. *Selections from the Critical Writings of Edgar Allan Poe.* New York: Gordian Press, 1981.

Preston, Katherine K. *Opera on the Road.* Urbana: University of Illinois Press, 1993.

Pryor, Sara Agnes Rice. *Reminiscences of Peace and War.* New York: Macmillan Co., 1905.

Putnam, Albigence Waldo. *History of Middle Tennessee; or Life and Times of Gen. James Robertson.* Nashville: A. W. Putnam, 1859.

Quaife, Milo Milton, Melvin J. Weig, and Roy E. Appleman. *The History of the United States Flag, from the Revolution to the Present: Including a Guide to Its Use and Display.* New York: Harper & Bros., 1961.

Rable, George C. *Civil Wars: Women and the Crisis of Southern Nationalism.* Urbana: University of Illinois Press, 1989.

Ramsdell, Charles W. *Behind the Lines in the Southern Confederacy.* Baton Rouge: Louisiana State University Press, 1944.

Reid, J. W. *History of the Fourth Regiment of S.C. Volunteers.* Dayton, Ohio: Morningside Bookshop, 1975.

Ridley, Bromfield Lewis. *Battles and Sketches of the Army of Tennessee.* Mexico, Mo.: Missouri Printing and Publishing Co., 1906.

Ripley, Eliza. *Social Life in Old New Orleans.* New York: D. Appleton and Co., 1912.

Robertson, James I. *Soldiers Blue and Gray.* Columbia: University of South Carolina Press, 1988.

———. *The Stonewall Brigade.* Baton Rouge: Louisiana State University Press, 1963.

Robson, John S. *How a One-Legged Rebel Lives.* Reprint, Mattituck, N.Y.: Amereon House Ltd., 1997.

Rollins, Richard. *Damned Red Flags.* Redondo Beach, Calif.: Rank and File Publications, 1997.

Roos, Rosalie. *Travels in America, 1851–1855.* Carbondale: Southern Illinois University Press, 1982.

Root, George F. *The Story of a Musical Life.* Cincinnati: John Church, 1891.

Rose, Anne C. *Victorian America and the Civil War.* New York: Cambridge University Press, 1992.

Ross, Fitzgerald. *Cities and Camps of the Confederate States.* Urbana: University of Illinois Press, 1958.

Rowland, Dunbar, ed. *Jefferson Davis, Constitutionalist: His Letters, Papers, and Speeches.* Vols. 5 and 9. Jackson: Mississippi Department of Archives and American History, 1923.

Rudolph, Earle Leighton. *Confederate Broadside Verse.* New Braunfels, Texas: Book Farm, 1950.

Russell, James Michael. *Atlanta, 1847–1890: City Building in the Old South and the New.* Baton Rouge: Louisiana State University Press, 1988.

Russell, William Howard. *My Diary: North and South.* Philadelphia: Temple University Press, 1988.

Rutherford, Mildred Lewis. *American Authors: A Handbook of American Literature from Early Colonial to Living Writers*. Atlanta: Franklin Printing and Publishing Co., 1894.

————. *The South in History and Literature*. Vol. 14. Atlanta: Franklin Turner Co., 1907.

Sablosky, Irving. *What They Heard: Music in America 1852–1881, From the Pages of Dwight's Journal of Music*. Baton Rouge: Louisiana State University Press, 1986.

Sacks, Howard L., and Judith R. Sacks. *Way Up North in Dixie: A Black Family's Claim to the Confederate Anthem*. Washington, D.C.: Smithsonian Institute Press, 1993.

Sadie, Stanley, ed. *The New Grove Dictionary of Music and Musicians*. New York and London: Macmillan Pub., 1980.

Salley, Alexander Samuel. *South Carolina Troops*. Columbia, S.C.: R. L. Bryan Co., 1913.

Sandburg, Carl. *Abraham Lincoln: The Prairie Years and the War Years*. New York: Harcourt Brace, 1954.

Saxton, Alexander. *The Rise and Fall of the White Republic*. New York: Verso, 1990.

Scarborough, Ruth. *Belle Boyd: Siren of the South*. Macon, Ga.: Mercer University Press, 1983.

Scarborough, William Kauffman, ed. *The Diary Of Edmund Ruffin*. Vol. 1. Baton Rouge: Louisiana State University Press, 1972.

Scharf, John Thomas. *The History of Maryland from the Earliest Period to the Present Day*. Vol. 2. Baltimore: J. B. Piet, 1879.

Schuricht, Hermann. *History of the German Element in Virginia*. Baltimore: Theo. Kroh & Sons, 1898.

Shafer, Boyd. C. *Nationalism: Myth and Reality*. New York: Harcourt Brace, 1955.

Silver, James W., ed. *A Life for the Confederacy. As Recorded in the Pocket Diaries of Pvt. Robert A. Moore: Co G. 17th Mississippi Regiment Confederate Guards, Holly Springs, Mississippi*. Wilmington, N.C.: Broadfoot Pub. Co., 1987.

Simonhoff, Harry. *Jewish Participants in the Civil War*. New York: Arco Publishing Co., 1963.

Simpson, Harold B. *The Bugle Blows Softly. The Confederate Diary of Benjamin M. Seaton*. Waco: Texian Press, 1965.

————. *Hood's Texas Brigade: A Compendium*. Hillsboro, Texas: Hill College Press, 1977.

————. *Hood's Texas Brigade: Lee's Grenadier Guard*. Dallas: Alcor Pub. Co., 1983.

————, ed. *Hood's Texas Brigade in Poetry and Song*. Hillsboro, Texas: Hill College Press, 1968.

Smith, C. A., ed. *Library of Southern Literature*. Vol. 14. Atlanta: Martin & Hoyt Co.

Smith, Maj. William A. *The Anson Guards: Company C, Fourteenth Regiment North Carolina Volunteers, 1861–1865*. Charlotte, N.C.: Stone Pub. Co., 1914.

Sonneck, Oscar. *Bibliography of Early Secular American Music*. 1905. Reprint, New York: Da Capo Press, 1964.

Sorrel, Gilbert Moxley. *Recollections of a Confederate Staff Officer*. Jackson, Tenn.: McCowat-Mercer Press, Inc., 1958.

Southall, Geneva Handy. *Blind Tom: The Post-Civil War Enslavement of a Black Musical Genius*. Minneapolis: Challenge Productions, 2 vols., 1979–1983.

Southern, Eileen. *The Music of Black Americans: A History*. New York: W. W. Norton, 1971.

Sowell, Thomas. *Conquests and Cultures: An International History*. New York: Basic Books, 1998.

Spaeth, Sigmund Gottfried. *A History of Popular Music in America*. New York: Random House, 1948.

Stampp, Kenneth M., ed. *The Causes of the Civil War*. New York: Touchstone Books, 1986.

Stanley, Dorothy, ed. *The Autobiography of Sir Henry Morton Stanley*. Boston: Houghton Mifflin Co., 1909.

Stern, Philip Van Doren. *An End to Valor: The Last Days of the Civil War*. Boston: Houghton Mifflin Co., 1958.

Stoutamire, Albert. *Music of the Old South*. Rutherford, N.J.: Fairleigh Dickinson University Press, 1972.

Stowe, Steven M. *Intimacy and Power in the Old South: Ritual in the Lives of the Planters*. Baltimore: Johns Hopkins University Press, 1987.

Stiles, Robert. *Four Years under Marse Robert*. New York: Neale Publishing Co., 1903.

Sullivan, Edward Robert. *Rambles and Scrambles in North and South America*. London: R. Bentley, 1852.

Sutherland, Daniel E. *The Confederate Carpetbaggers.* Baton Rouge: Louisiana State University Press, 1988.

————. *Reminiscences of a Private: William E. Bevens of the First Arkansas Infantry, C.S.A.* Fayetteville: University of Arkansas Press, 1992.

Sword, Wiley. *Shiloh: Bloody April.* New York: Morrow, 1974.

Tapert, Annette, ed. *The Brothers' War.* New York: Times Books, 1988.

Tasker, John Howard. *Stephen Foster: America's Troubadour.* New York: T.Y. Crowell, 1953.

Tawa, Nicolas. *A Music for the Millions: Antebellum Democratic Attitudes and the Birth of American Popular Music.* New York: Pendragon Press, 1984.

————. *Sweet Songs for Gentle Americans: The Parlor Song in America, 1790–1860.* Bowling Green: Bowling Green University Popular Press, 1980.

Taylor, Benjamin. *Pictures of Life in Camp and Field.* Chicago: S.C. Griggs & Co., 1888.

Taylor, F. Jay, ed. *Reluctant Rebel: The Secret Diary of Robert Patrick, 1861–1865.* Baton Rouge: Louisiana State University Press, 1959.

Taylor, William R. *Cavalier and Yankee.* New York: G. Brazilier, 1961.

Thomas, E. M. *The Confederacy as a Revolutionary Experience.* Englewood Cliffs, N.J.: Prentice Hall, Inc., 1971.

Thomas, Emory M. *The Confederate Nation, 1861–1865.* New York: Harper and Row, 1979.

Thomas, H. W. *History of the Doles-Cook Brigade, Army of Northern Virginia.* Atlanta: Franklin Print and Pub. Co., 1903.

Thompson, Edwin Porter. *History of the Orphan Brigade.* 1898. Reprint, Dayton, Ohio: Morningside Bookshop, 1995.

Thompson, S. Millet. *Thirteenth Regiment of New Hampshire Volunteer Infantry in the War of the Rebellion, 1861–1865.* Boston: Houghton, Mifflin and Co., 1888.

Tick, Judith. *American Women Composers before 1870.* Ann Arbor: UMI Research Press, 1983.

Tindall, G. "Mythology: A New Frontier in Southern History." In *The Idea of the South: Pursuit of a General Theme,* edited by E. Frank Vandiver. Chicago: University of Chicago Press, 1964.

Tobie, Edward Parsons. *History of the First Maine Cavalry, 1861–1865.* Boston: Emery and Hughes, 1887.

Toll, Robert C. *Blacking Up: The Minstrel Show in Nineteenth Century America.* New York: Oxford University Press, 1974.

Tower, R. Lockwood, ed. *A Carolinian Goes to War: The Civil War Narrative of Arthur Middleton Manigault, Brigadier General, C.S.A.* Charleston: University of South Carolina Press, 1983.

Tribe, Ivan M. *Mountaineer Jamboree: Country Music in West Virginia.* Lexington: University Press of Kentucky, 1984.

Trout, Robert J., ed. *Riding with Stuart: Reminiscences of an Aide-de-Camp by Captain Theodore Stanford Garnett.* Shippensburg, Pa.: White Mane Pub. Co., 1994.

Tunnard, William H. *Southern Record: The History of the Third Regiment, Louisiana Infantry.* Dayton, Ohio: Morningside Books, 1970.

Turnbo, Silas Claiborn. *History of the Twenty-Seventh Arkansas Confederate Infantry.* Fayetteville: University of Arkansas Press, 1989.

Turner, Charles W., ed. *Ted Barclay, Liberty Hall Volunteers: Letters from the Stonewall Brigade.* Natural Bridge Station, Va.: Rockbridge Pub. Co., 1992.

Turner, Martha Anne. *The Yellow Rose of Texas: Her Saga and Her Song: With the Santa Anna Legend.* Austin: Shoah Creek Pub., 1976.

Van der Heuvel, Gerry. *Crowns of Thorns and Glory: Mary Todd Lincoln and Varina Howell Davis: The Two First Ladies of the Civil War.* New York: Dutton, 1988.

Vaughan, A. J. *Personal Record of the Thirteenth Regiment, Tennessee Infantry.* Memphis: S. C. Toof and Co., 1897.

Wagner, John W. "Some Early Musical Moments in Augusta." In *Music in Georgia,* edited by Frank W. Hoogerwerf. New York: Da Capo Press, 1984.

Waldo, J. Curtis. *Illustrated Visitors' Guide to New Orleans.* New Orleans: Waldo, 1879.

Wallace, Lee A. *A Guide to Virginia Military Organizations, 1861–1865.* Richmond: Virginia Civil War Commission, 1964.

Walther, Eric H. *The Fire-Eaters.* Baton Rouge: Louisiana State University Press, 1992.

Watkins, Samiel R. *Co. Aytch: Maury Grays First Tennessee.* Nashville: Cumberland Presbyterian Pub. House, 1882.

Watson, William. *Life in the Confederate Army: Being the Observations and Experiences of an Alien in the South during the American Civil War.* New York: Scribner and Welford, 1888.

Whitman, Walt. *Leaves of Grass.* Reprint, Boston: Thayer and Eldridge, 1860.

White, Richard Grant. *National Hymns: How They Are Written and How They Are Not Written: A Lyric and National Study for the Times.* New York: Rudd and Carleton, 1861.

Whitney, Henry Clay. *Life on the Circuit with Lincoln.* Boston: Estes and Lauriat, 1892.

Whittall, Arnold. *Romantic Music: A Concise History from Schubert to Sibelius.* London: Thames and Hudson, 1978.

Wiley, Bell I. *The Life of Billy Yank.* 1952. Reprint, Baton Rouge: Louisiana State University Press, 1978).

———. *The life of Johnny Reb.* 1943. Reprint, Baton Rouge: Louisiana State University Press, 1984.

———, ed. *This Infernal War: The Confederate Letters of Sgt. Edwin H. Fay.* Austin: University of Texas Press, 1958.

Wilk, Max. *They're Playing Our Song.* New York: Athenaeum, 1973.

Wilerson, John. *Narrative of a Blockade Runner.* New York: Sheldon & Co., 1877.

Williams, William H. A. *'Twas Only an Irishman's Dream.* Urbana: University of Illinois Press, 1996.

Willoughby, Larry. *Texas Rhythm, Texas Rhyme.* Austin: Texas Monthly Press, 1984.

Wilson, James Grant. *General Grant.* New York: D. Appleton and Co., 1897.

Wilson, Le Grand James. *The Confederate Soldier.* Memphis: Memphis State University Press, 1973.

Winstock, Lewis S. *Songs and Music of the Redcoats: A History of the War Music of the British Army.* London: Leo Cooper, 1970.

Wintermute, H. Ogden. *Daniel Decatur Emmett.* Columbus, Ohio: Heers Printing Co., 1955.

Wise, John S. *The End of an Era.* Boston: Houghton, Mifflin and Co., 1902.

Wittke, Carl Frederick. *Tambo and Bones: A History of the American Minstrel Stage.* Westport, Conn.: Greenwood Press, 1968.

Wolfe, Richard J. *Secular Music in America, 1800–1825.* New York: New York Public Library, 1964.

Woodward, C. Vann. *Mary Chesnut's Civil War.* New Haven: Yale University Press, 1981.

Worsham, John H. *One of Jackson's Foot Cavalry: His Experience and What He Saw during the War, 1861–1865: Including a History of "F Company," Richmond, Va., 21st Regiment Virginia Infantry, Second Brigade, Jackson's*

Division, Second Corps, A.N. Va. 1912. Reprint, Wilmington, N.C.: Broadfoot Pub. Co., 1991.

Worsham, W. J. *The Old Nineteenth Tennessee Regiment, C.S.A., June 1861–April 1865.* Knoxville, Tenn.: Paragon Printing Co., 1902.

Wright, Louise Wigfall. *A Southern Girl in '61: The War-time Memories of A Confederate Senator's Daughter.* New York: Doubleday, Page & Co., 1905.

Wyatt-Brown, Bertrand. *Southern Honor.* New York: Oxford University Press, 1982.

Zelinsky, Wilbur. *Nation into State: The Shifting Symbolic Foundations of American Nationalism.* Chapel Hill: University of North Carolina Press, 1988.

INDEX